GARTH ENNIS   JACEN BURROWS

chronicles of WORMWOOD™

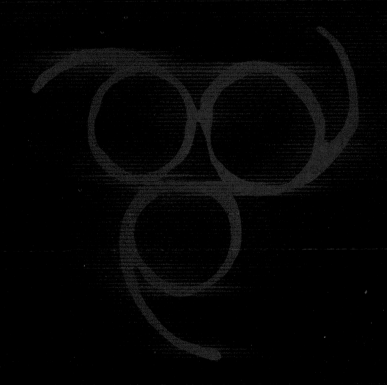

story **GARTH ENNIS**
artwork **JACEN BURROWS**
color **ANDREW DALHOUSE**

editor in chief **WILLIAM CHRISTENSEN**
creative director **MARK SEIFERT**
marketing director **DAVID MARKS**

www.avatarpress.com

 **AVATAR**™

GARTH ENNIS CHRONICLES OF WORMWOOD VOLUME 1, Sept 2007. Published by Avatar Press, Inc., 515 N. Century Blvd, Rantoul, IL 61866. ©2007 Avatar Press, Inc. Wormwood and all related properties TM & ©2007 Garth Ennis. All characters as depicted in this story are over the age of 18. The stories, characters, and incidents mentioned in this magazine are entirely fictional. Third Printing July 2014. Printed in Canada.

In memory of Massimo Belardinelli

1938-2007

Ten ten, never again

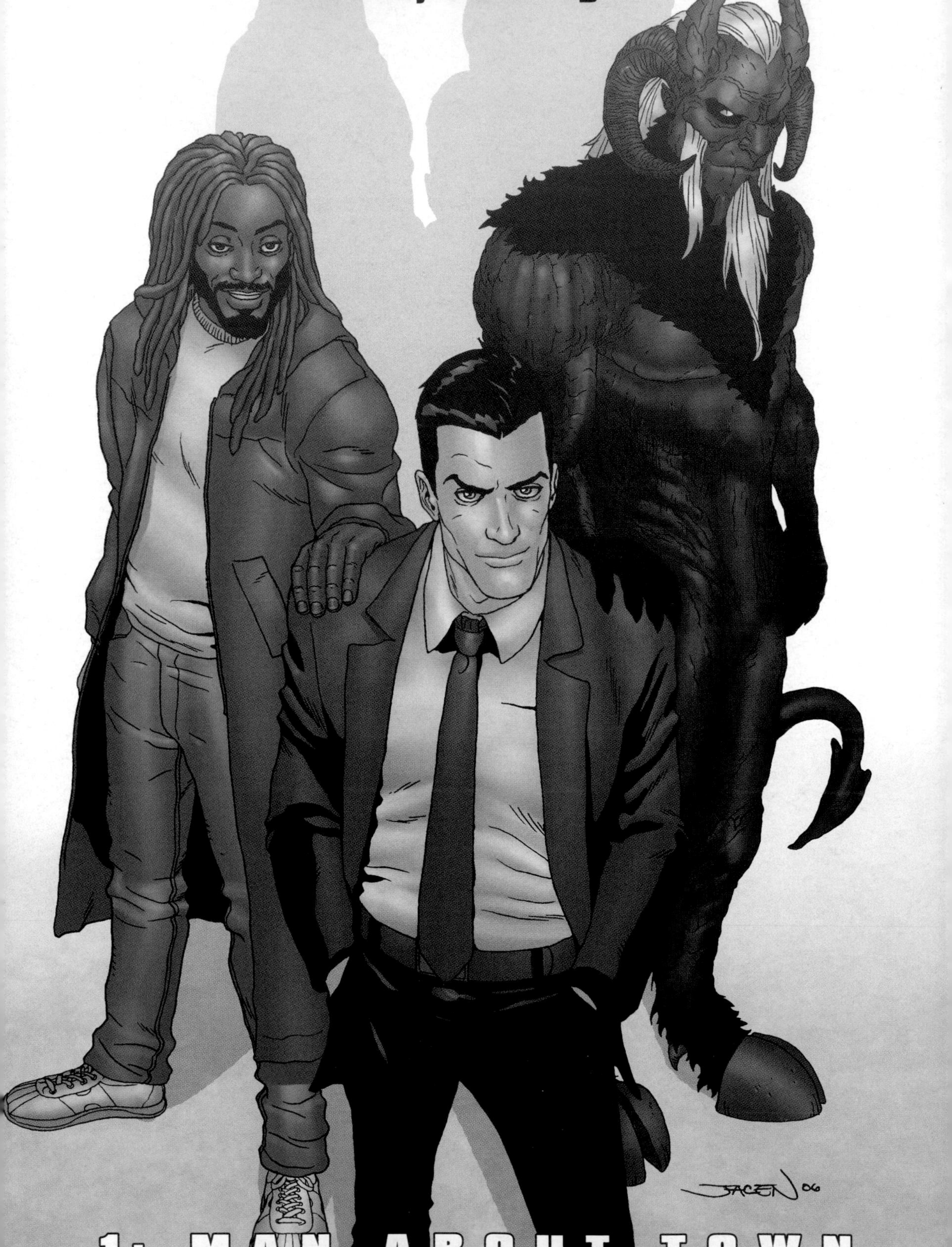
JACEN 06

1: MAN ABOUT TOWN

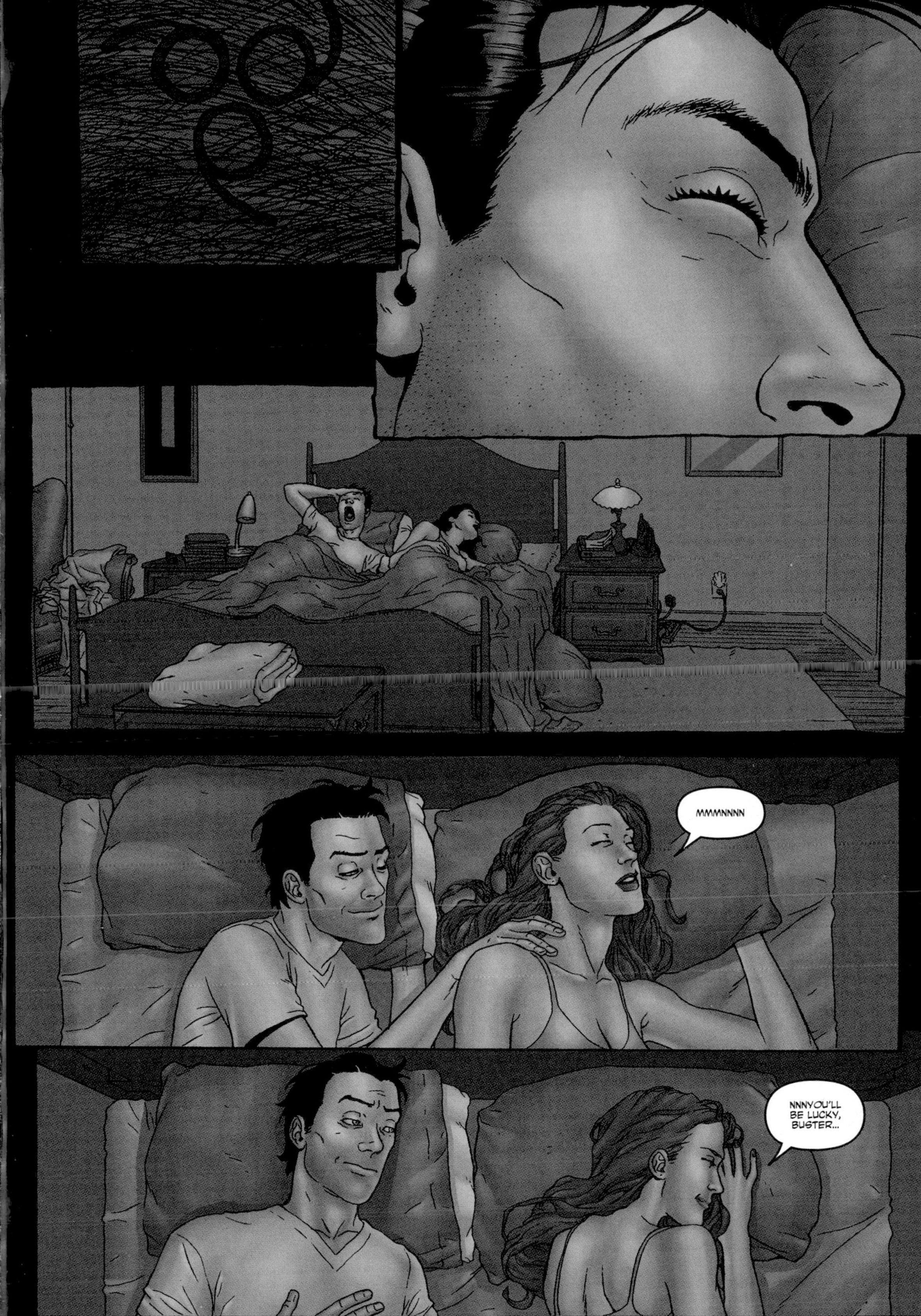
MMMNNNN
NNNYOU'LL BE LUCKY, BUSTER...

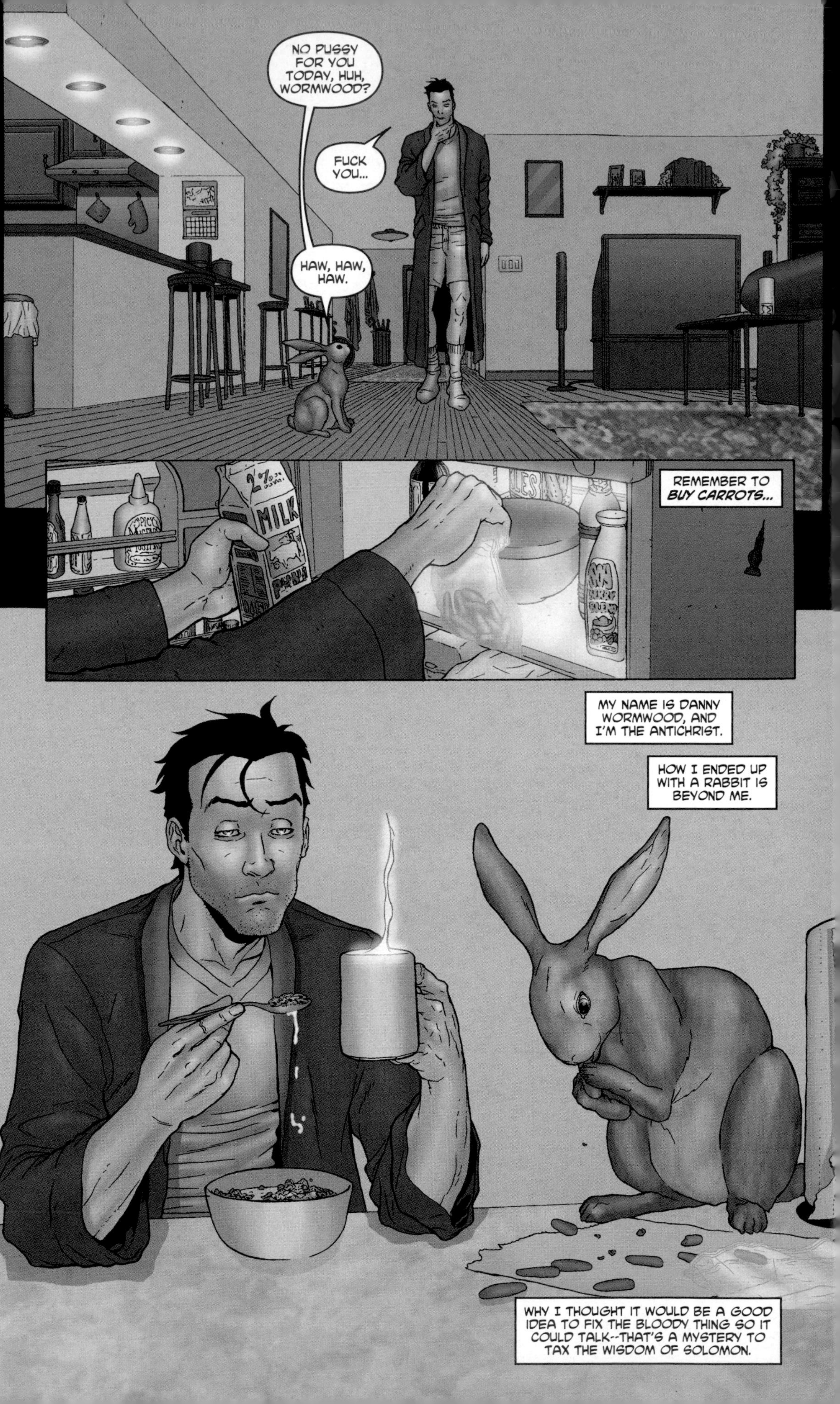
NO PUSSY FOR YOU TODAY, HUH, WORMWOOD?
FUCK YOU...
HAW, HAW, HAW.
REMEMBER TO BUY CARROTS...
MY NAME IS DANNY WORMWOOD, AND I'M THE ANTICHRIST.
HOW I ENDED UP WITH A RABBIT IS BEYOND ME.
WHY I THOUGHT IT WOULD BE A GOOD IDEA TO FIX THE BLOODY THING SO IT COULD TALK--THAT'S A MYSTERY TO TAX THE WISDOM OF SOLOMON.

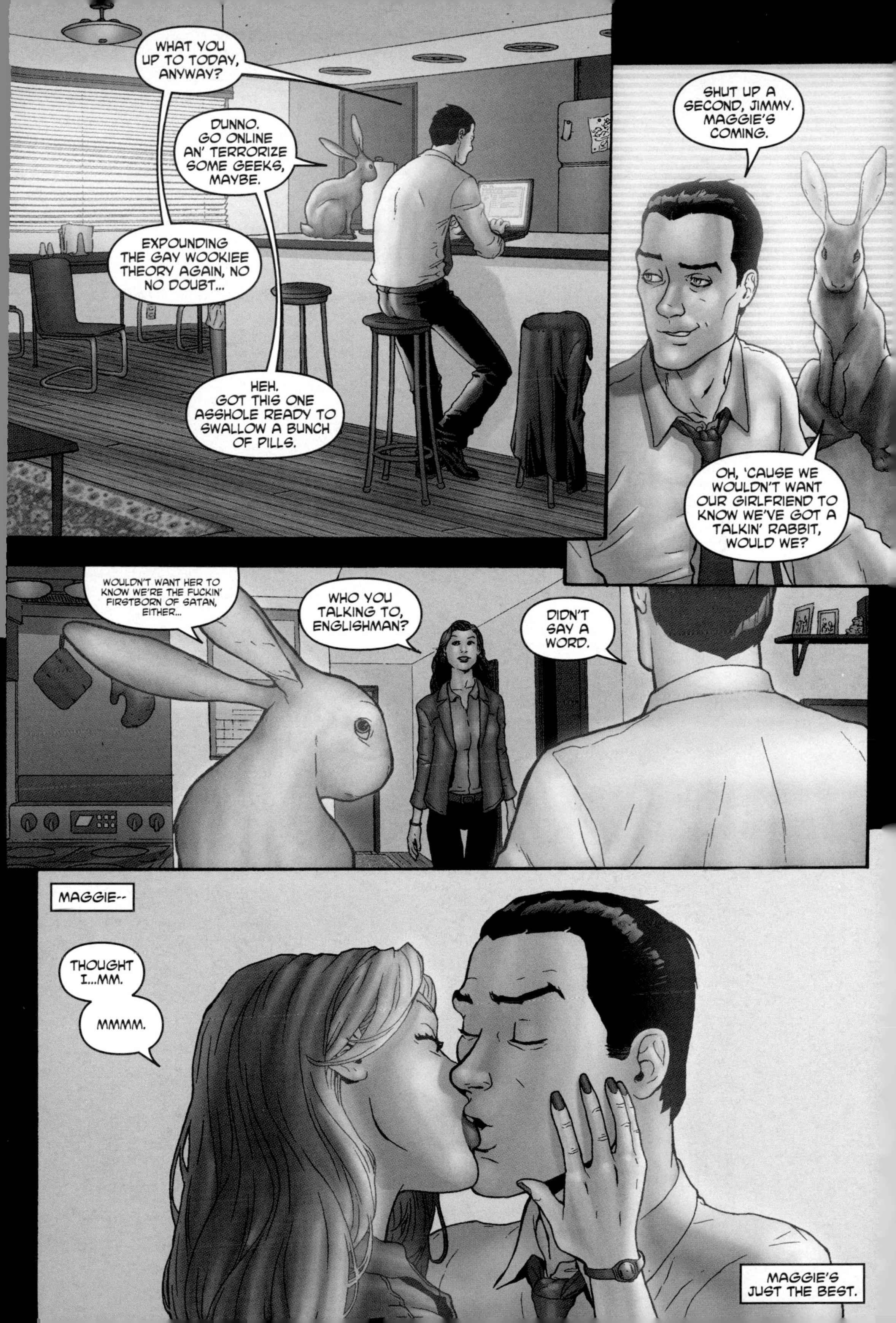
WHAT YOU UP TO TODAY, ANYWAY?
DUNNO. GO ONLINE AN' TERRORIZE SOME GEEKS, MAYBE.
EXPOUNDING THE GAY WOOKIEE THEORY AGAIN, NO NO DOUBT...
HEH. GOT THIS ONE ASSHOLE READY TO SWALLOW A BUNCH OF PILLS.
SHUT UP A SECOND, JIMMY. MAGGIE'S COMING.
OH, 'CAUSE WE WOULDN'T WANT OUR GIRLFRIEND TO KNOW WE'VE GOT A TALKIN' RABBIT, WOULD WE?
WOULDN'T WANT HER TO KNOW WE'RE THE FUCKIN' FIRSTBORN OF SATAN, EITHER...
WHO YOU TALKING TO, ENGLISHMAN?
DIDN'T SAY A WORD.
MAGGIE--
THOUGHT I...MM.
MMMM.
MAGGIE'S JUST THE BEST.

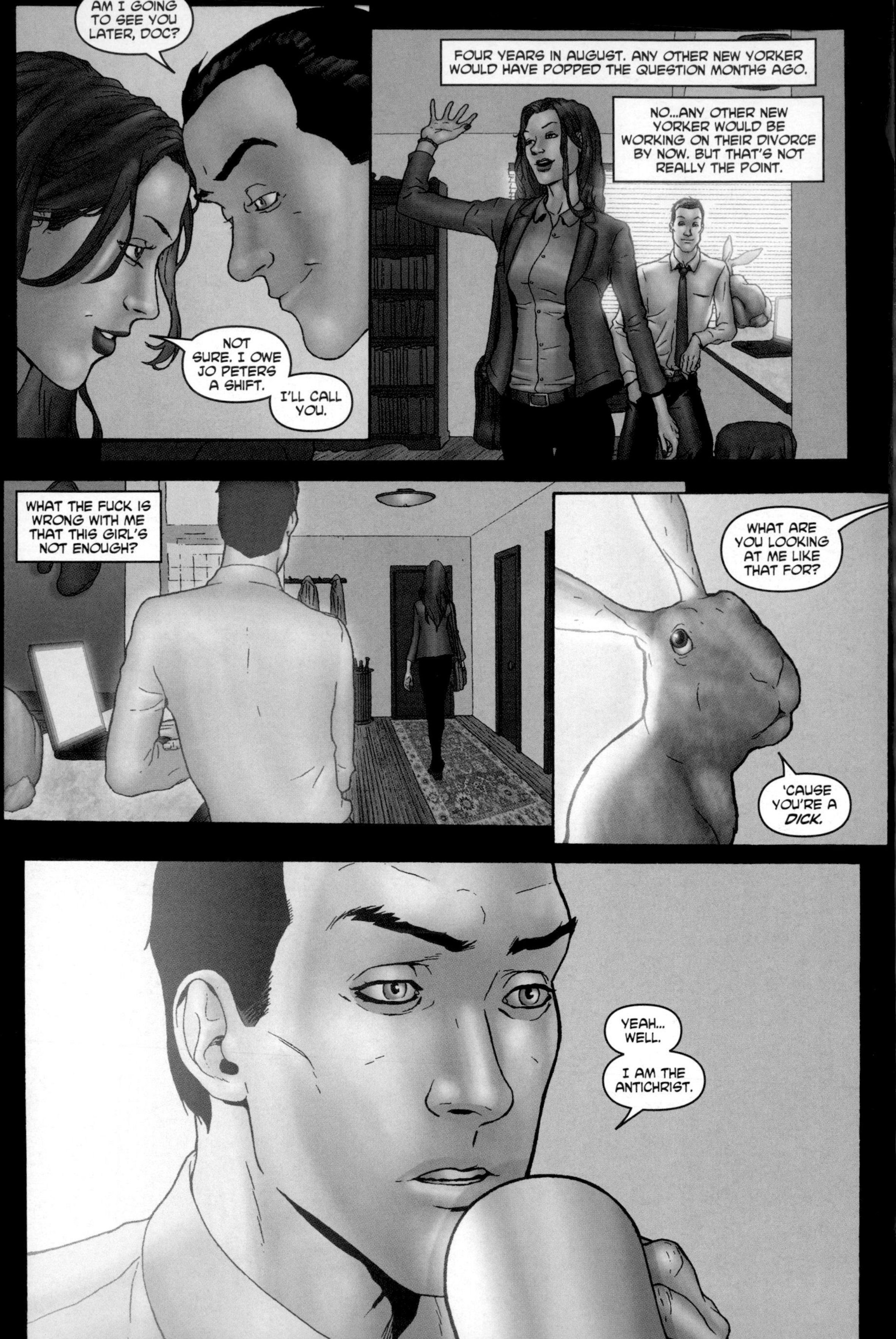
AM I GOING TO SEE YOU LATER, DOC?
NOT SURE. I OWE JO PETERS A SHIFT.
I'LL CALL YOU.
FOUR YEARS IN AUGUST. ANY OTHER NEW YORKER WOULD HAVE POPPED THE QUESTION MONTHS AGO.
NO...ANY OTHER NEW YORKER WOULD BE WORKING ON THEIR DIVORCE BY NOW. BUT THAT'S NOT REALLY THE POINT.
WHAT THE FUCK IS WRONG WITH ME THAT THIS GIRL'S NOT ENOUGH?
WHAT ARE YOU LOOKING AT ME LIKE THAT FOR?
'CAUSE YOU'RE A *DICK.*
YEAH... WELL.
I AM THE ANTICHRIST.

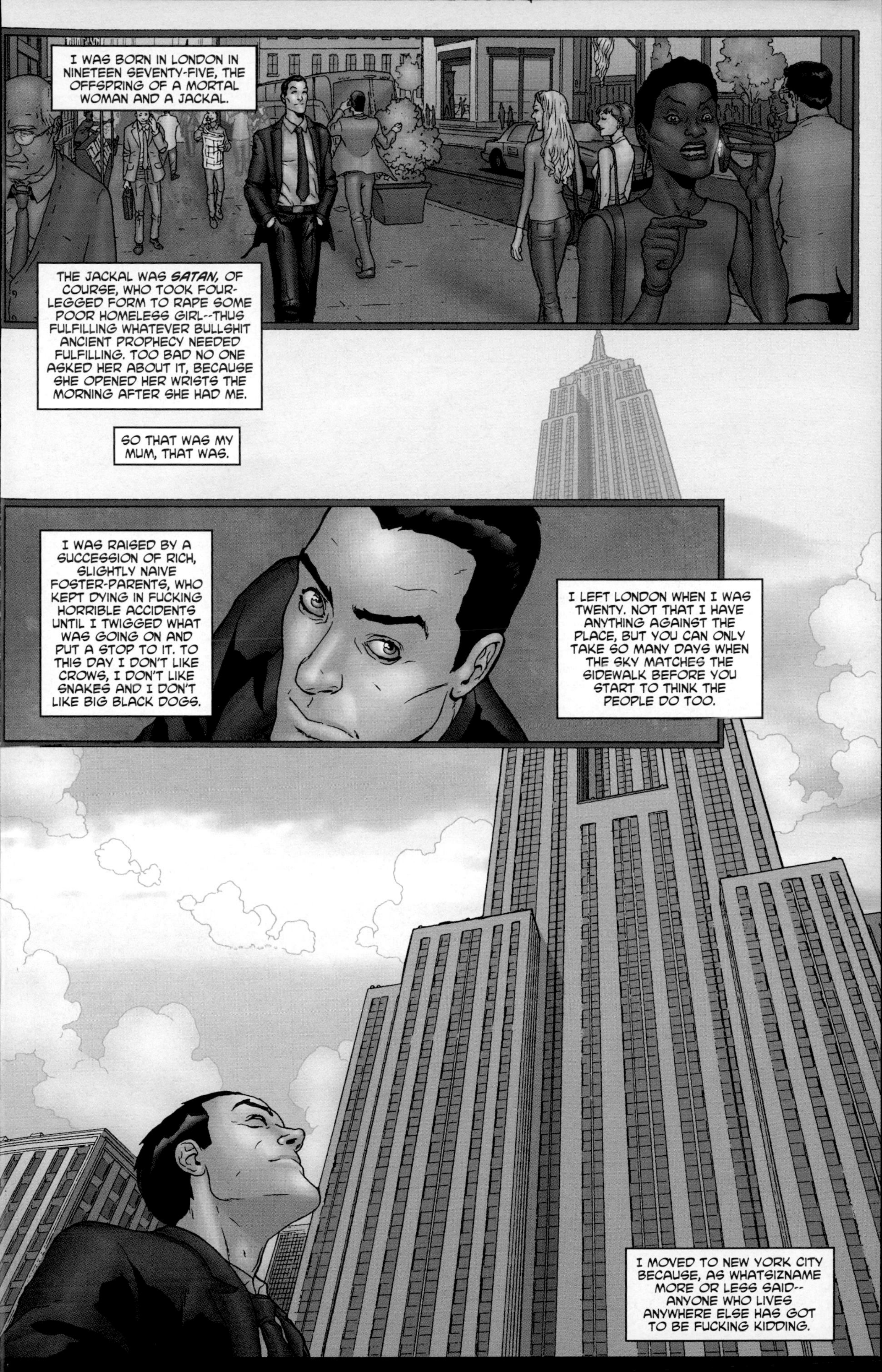
I WAS BORN IN LONDON IN NINETEEN SEVENTY-FIVE, THE OFFSPRING OF A MORTAL WOMAN AND A JACKAL.
THE JACKAL WAS SATAN, OF COURSE, WHO TOOK FOUR-LEGGED FORM TO RAPE SOME POOR HOMELESS GIRL--THUS FULFILLING WHATEVER BULLSHIT ANCIENT PROPHECY NEEDED FULFILLING. TOO BAD NO ONE ASKED HER ABOUT IT, BECAUSE SHE OPENED HER WRISTS THE MORNING AFTER SHE HAD ME.
SO THAT WAS MY MUM, THAT WAS.
I WAS RAISED BY A SUCCESSION OF RICH, SLIGHTLY NAIVE FOSTER-PARENTS, WHO KEPT DYING IN FUCKING HORRIBLE ACCIDENTS UNTIL I TWIGGED WHAT WAS GOING ON AND PUT A STOP TO IT. TO THIS DAY I DON'T LIKE CROWS, I DON'T LIKE SNAKES AND I DON'T LIKE BIG BLACK DOGS.
I LEFT LONDON WHEN I WAS TWENTY. NOT THAT I HAVE ANYTHING AGAINST THE PLACE, BUT YOU CAN ONLY TAKE SO MANY DAYS WHEN THE SKY MATCHES THE SIDEWALK BEFORE YOU START TO THINK THE PEOPLE DO TOO.
I MOVED TO NEW YORK CITY BECAUSE, AS WHATSIZNAME MORE OR LESS SAID-- ANYONE WHO LIVES ANYWHERE ELSE HAS GOT TO BE FUCKING KIDDING.

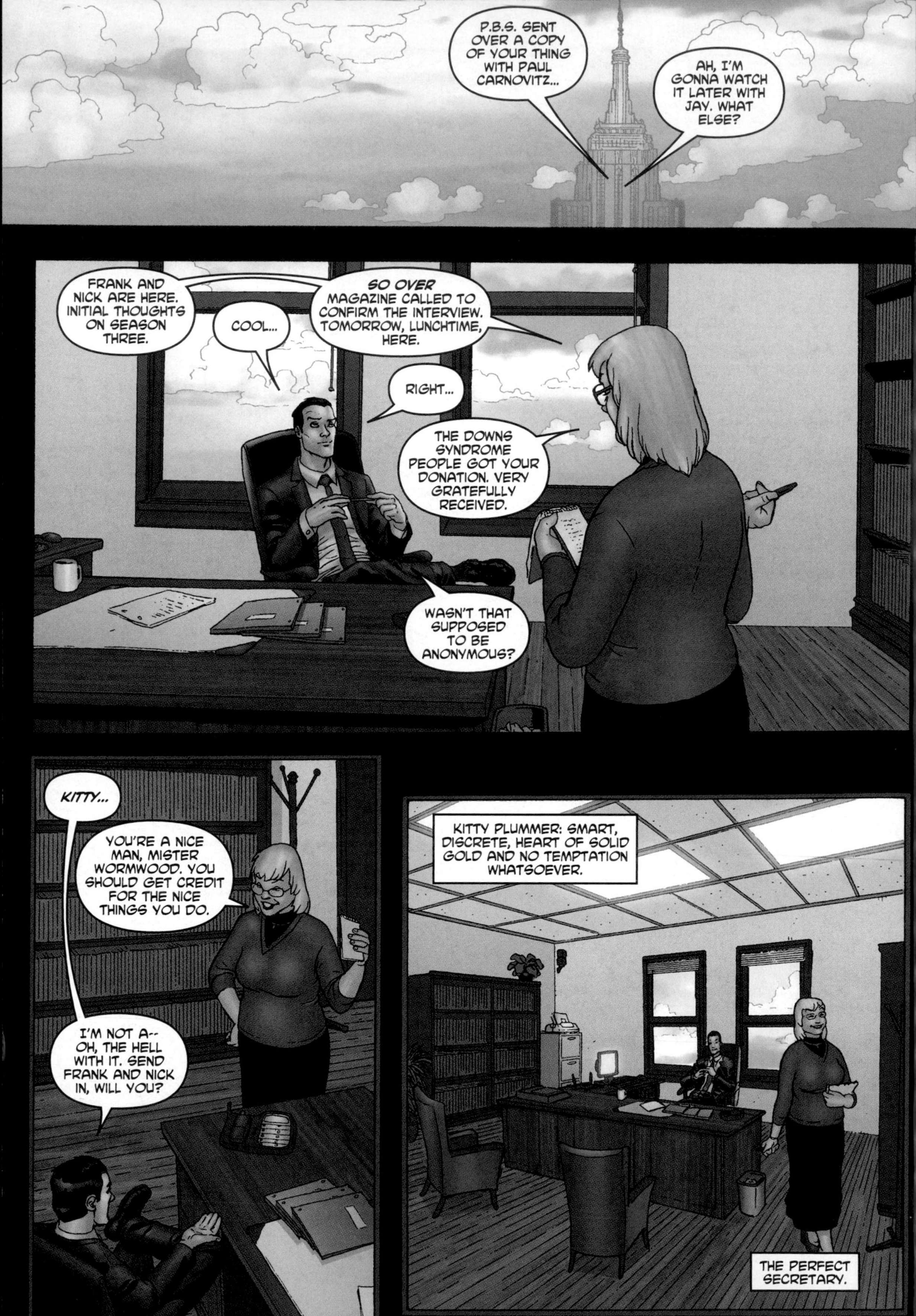
P.B.S. SENT OVER A COPY OF YOUR THING WITH PAUL CARNOVITZ...
AH, I'M GONNA WATCH IT LATER WITH JAY. WHAT ELSE?
FRANK AND NICK ARE HERE. INITIAL THOUGHTS ON SEASON THREE.
COOL...
SO OVER MAGAZINE CALLED TO CONFIRM THE INTERVIEW. TOMORROW, LUNCHTIME, HERE.
RIGHT...
THE DOWNS SYNDROME PEOPLE GOT YOUR DONATION. VERY GRATEFULLY RECEIVED.
WASN'T THAT SUPPOSED TO BE ANONYMOUS?
KITTY...
YOU'RE A NICE MAN, MISTER WORMWOOD. YOU SHOULD GET CREDIT FOR THE NICE THINGS YOU DO.
I'M NOT A-- OH, THE HELL WITH IT. SEND FRANK AND NICK IN, WILL YOU?
KITTY PLUMMER: SMART, DISCRETE, HEART OF SOLID GOLD AND NO TEMPTATION WHATSOEVER.
THE PERFECT SECRETARY.

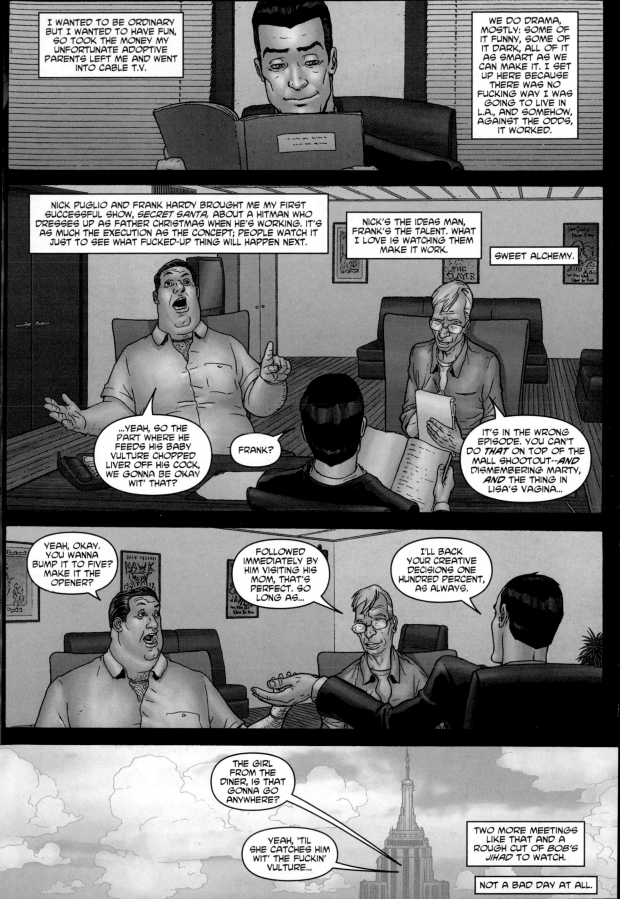

I WANTED TO BE ORDINARY BUT I WANTED TO HAVE FUN, SO TOOK THE MONEY MY UNFORTUNATE ADOPTIVE PARENTS LEFT ME AND WENT INTO CABLE T.V.

WE DO DRAMA, MOSTLY: SOME OF IT FUNNY, SOME OF IT DARK, ALL OF IT AS SMART AS WE CAN MAKE IT. I SET UP HERE BECAUSE THERE WAS NO FUCKING WAY I WAS GOING TO LIVE IN L.A., AND SOMEHOW, AGAINST THE ODDS, IT WORKED.

NICK PUGLIO AND FRANK HARDY BROUGHT ME MY FIRST SUCCESSFUL SHOW, *SECRET SANTA*, ABOUT A HITMAN WHO DRESSES UP AS FATHER CHRISTMAS WHEN HE'S WORKING. IT'S AS MUCH THE EXECUTION AS THE CONCEPT; PEOPLE WATCH IT JUST TO SEE WHAT FUCKED-UP THING WILL HAPPEN NEXT.

NICK'S THE IDEAS MAN, FRANK'S THE TALENT. WHAT I LOVE IS WATCHING THEM MAKE IT WORK.

SWEET ALCHEMY.

...YEAH, SO THE PART WHERE HE FEEDS HIS BABY VULTURE CHOPPED LIVER OFF HIS COCK, WE GONNA BE OKAY WIT' THAT?

FRANK?

IT'S IN THE WRONG EPISODE. YOU CAN'T DO *THAT* ON TOP OF THE MALL SHOOTOUT--*AND* DISMEMBERING MARTY, *AND* THE THING IN LISA'S VAGINA...

YEAH, OKAY. YOU WANNA BUMP IT TO FIVE? MAKE IT THE OPENER?

FOLLOWED IMMEDIATELY BY HIM VISITING HIS MOM, THAT'S PERFECT. SO LONG AS...

I'LL BACK YOUR CREATIVE DECISIONS ONE HUNDRED PERCENT, AS ALWAYS.

THE GIRL FROM THE DINER, IS THAT GONNA GO ANYWHERE?

YEAH, 'TIL SHE CATCHES HIM WIT' THE FUCKIN' VULTURE...

TWO MORE MEETINGS LIKE THAT AND A ROUGH CUT OF *BOB'S JIHAD* TO WATCH.

NOT A BAD DAY AT ALL.

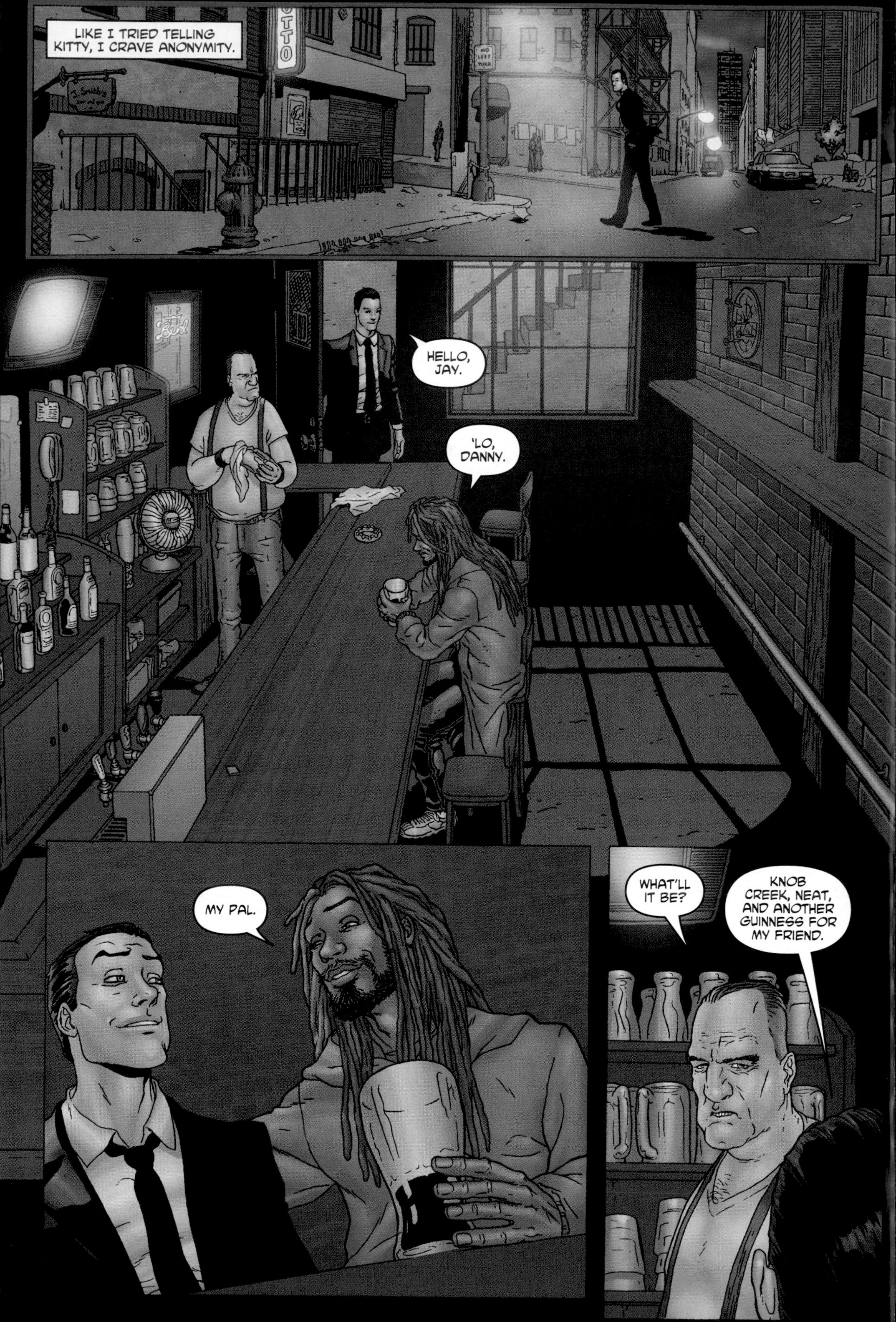
LIKE I TRIED TELLING KITTY, I CRAVE ANONYMITY.
HELLO, JAY.
'LO, DANNY.
MY PAL.
WHAT'LL IT BE?
KNOB CREEK, NEAT, AND ANOTHER GUINNESS FOR MY FRIEND.

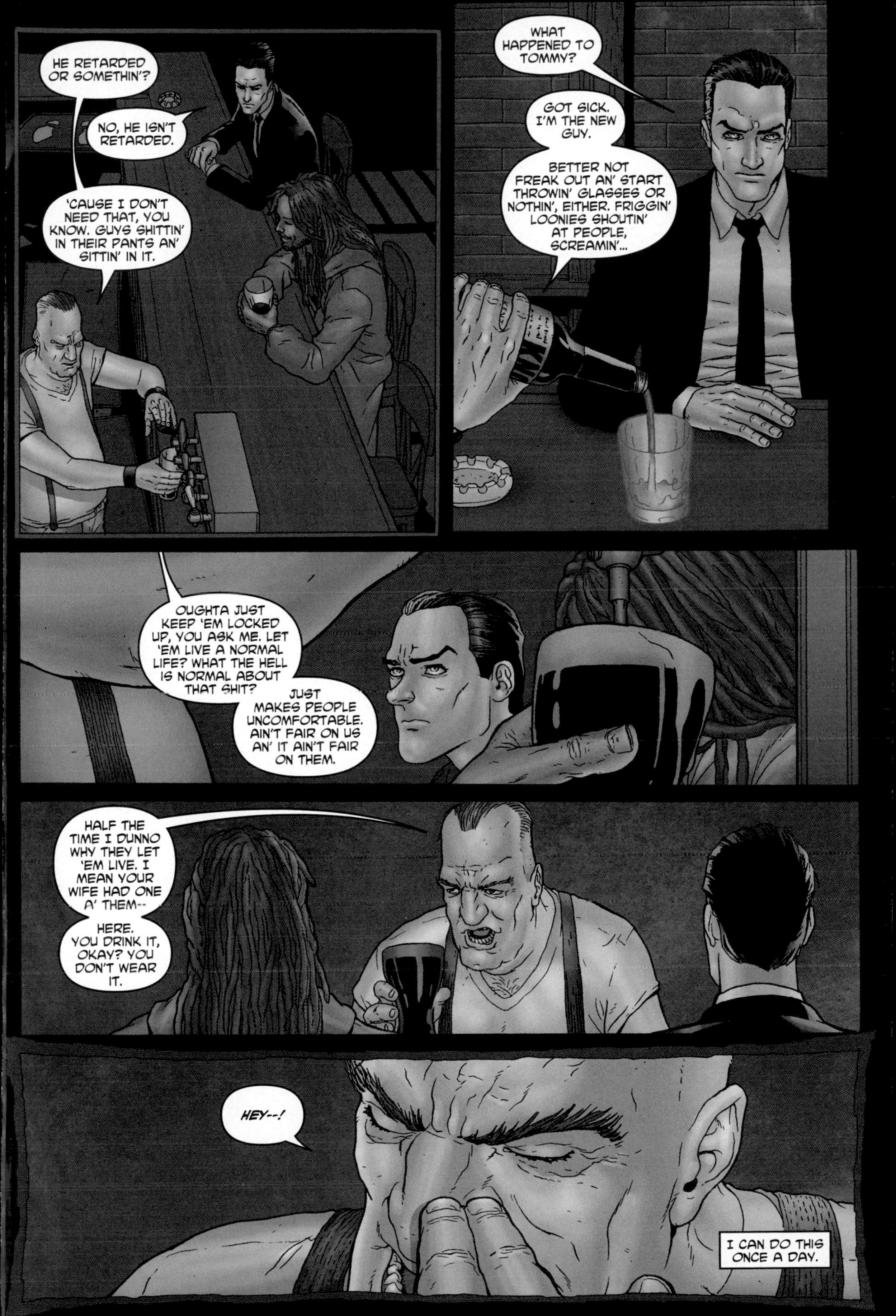
HE RETARDED OR SOMETHIN'?
NO, HE ISN'T RETARDED.
'CAUSE I DON'T NEED THAT, YOU KNOW. GUYS SHITTIN' IN THEIR PANTS AN' SITTIN' IN IT.
WHAT HAPPENED TO TOMMY?
GOT SICK. I'M THE NEW GUY.
BETTER NOT FREAK OUT AN' START THROWIN' GLASSES OR NOTHIN', EITHER. FRIGGIN' LOONIES SHOUTIN' AT PEOPLE, SCREAMIN'...
OUGHTA JUST KEEP 'EM LOCKED UP, YOU ASK ME. LET 'EM LIVE A NORMAL LIFE? WHAT THE HELL IS NORMAL ABOUT THAT SHIT?
JUST MAKES PEOPLE UNCOMFORTABLE. AIN'T FAIR ON US AN' IT AIN'T FAIR ON THEM.
HALF THE TIME I DUNNO WHY THEY LET 'EM LIVE. I MEAN YOUR WIFE HAD ONE A' THEM--
HERE. YOU DRINK IT, OKAY? YOU DON'T WEAR IT.
HEY--!
I CAN DO THIS ONCE A DAY.

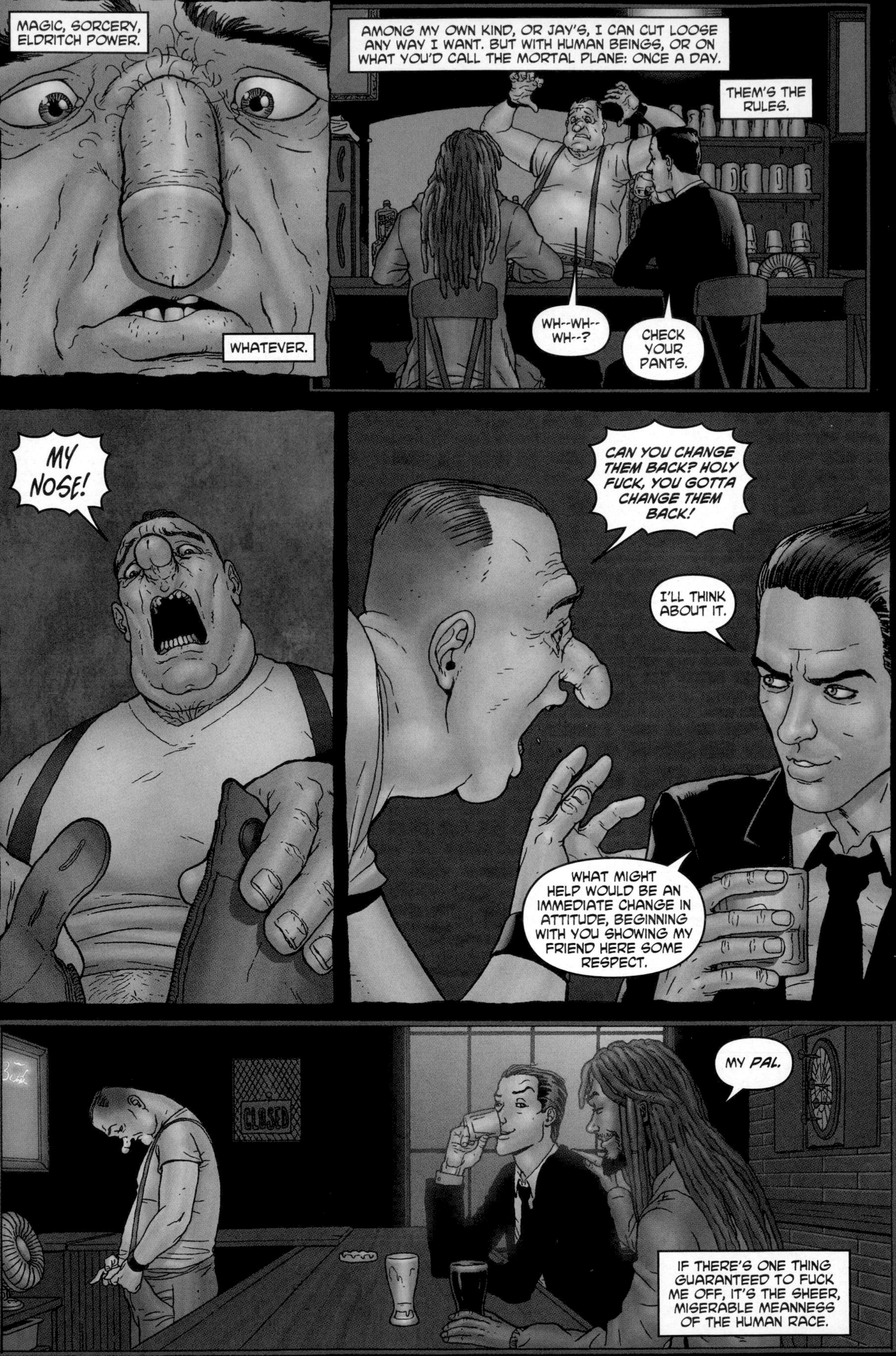
MAGIC, SORCERY, ELDRITCH POWER.
WHATEVER.
AMONG MY OWN KIND, OR JAY'S, I CAN CUT LOOSE ANY WAY I WANT. BUT WITH HUMAN BEINGS, OR ON WHAT YOU'D CALL THE MORTAL PLANE: ONCE A DAY.
THEM'S THE RULES.
WH--WH-- WH--?
CHECK YOUR PANTS.
MY NOSE!
CAN YOU CHANGE THEM BACK? HOLY FUCK, YOU GOTTA CHANGE THEM BACK!
I'LL THINK ABOUT IT.
WHAT MIGHT HELP WOULD BE AN IMMEDIATE CHANGE IN ATTITUDE, BEGINNING WITH YOU SHOWING MY FRIEND HERE SOME RESPECT.
CLOSED
MY PAL.
IF THERE'S ONE THING GUARANTEED TO FUCK ME OFF, IT'S THE SHEER, MISERABLE MEANNESS OF THE HUMAN RACE.

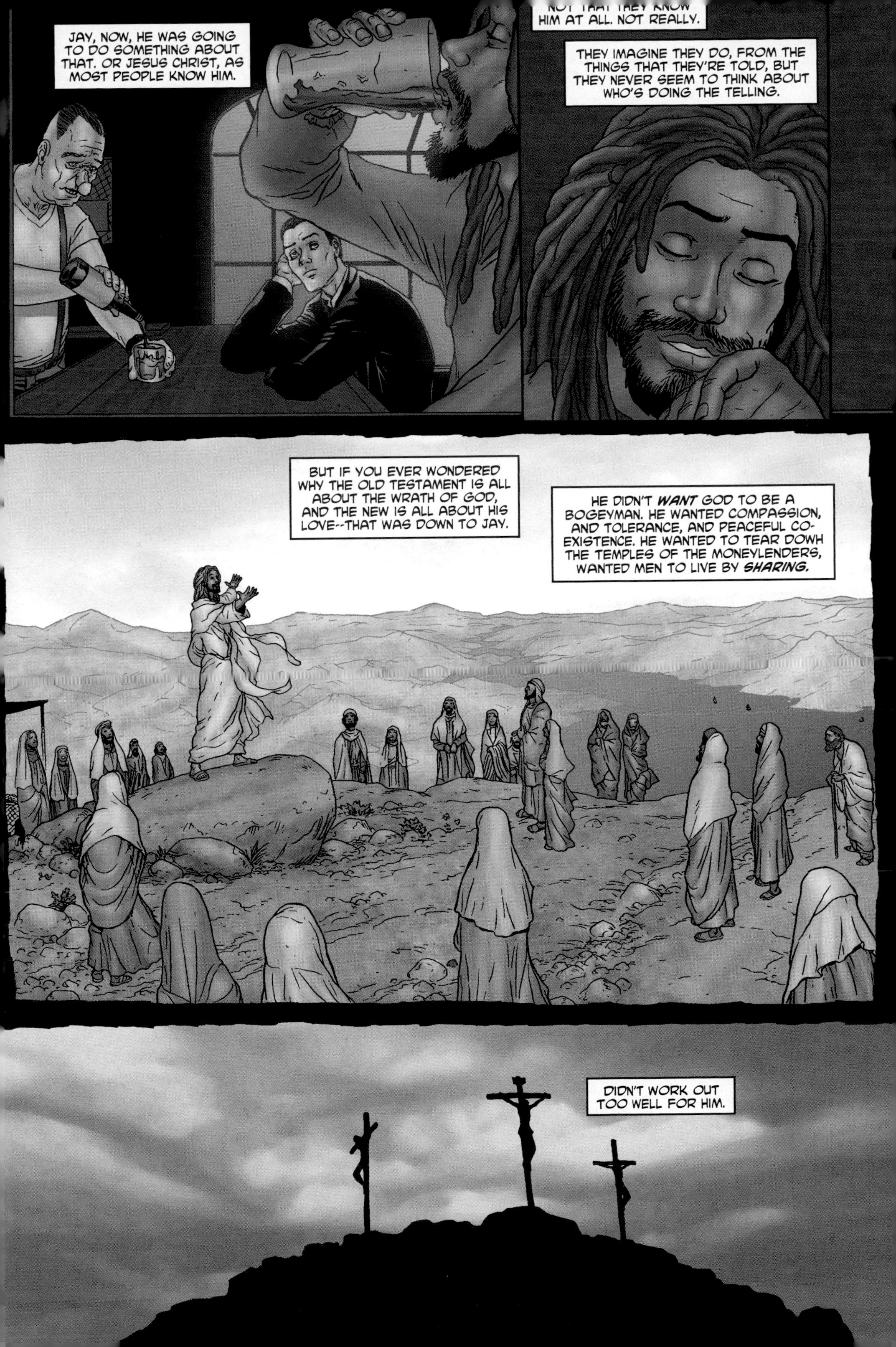
JAY, NOW, HE WAS GOING TO DO SOMETHING ABOUT THAT. OR JESUS CHRIST, AS MOST PEOPLE KNOW HIM.
NOT THAT THEY KNOW HIM AT ALL. NOT REALLY.
THEY IMAGINE THEY DO, FROM THE THINGS THAT THEY'RE TOLD, BUT THEY NEVER SEEM TO THINK ABOUT WHO'S DOING THE TELLING.
BUT IF YOU EVER WONDERED WHY THE OLD TESTAMENT IS ALL ABOUT THE WRATH OF GOD, AND THE NEW IS ALL ABOUT HIS LOVE--THAT WAS DOWN TO JAY.
HE DIDN'T WANT GOD TO BE A BOGEYMAN. HE WANTED COMPASSION, AND TOLERANCE, AND PEACEFUL CO-EXISTENCE. HE WANTED TO TEAR DOWH THE TEMPLES OF THE MONEYLENDERS, WANTED MEN TO LIVE BY SHARING.
DIDN'T WORK OUT TOO WELL FOR HIM.

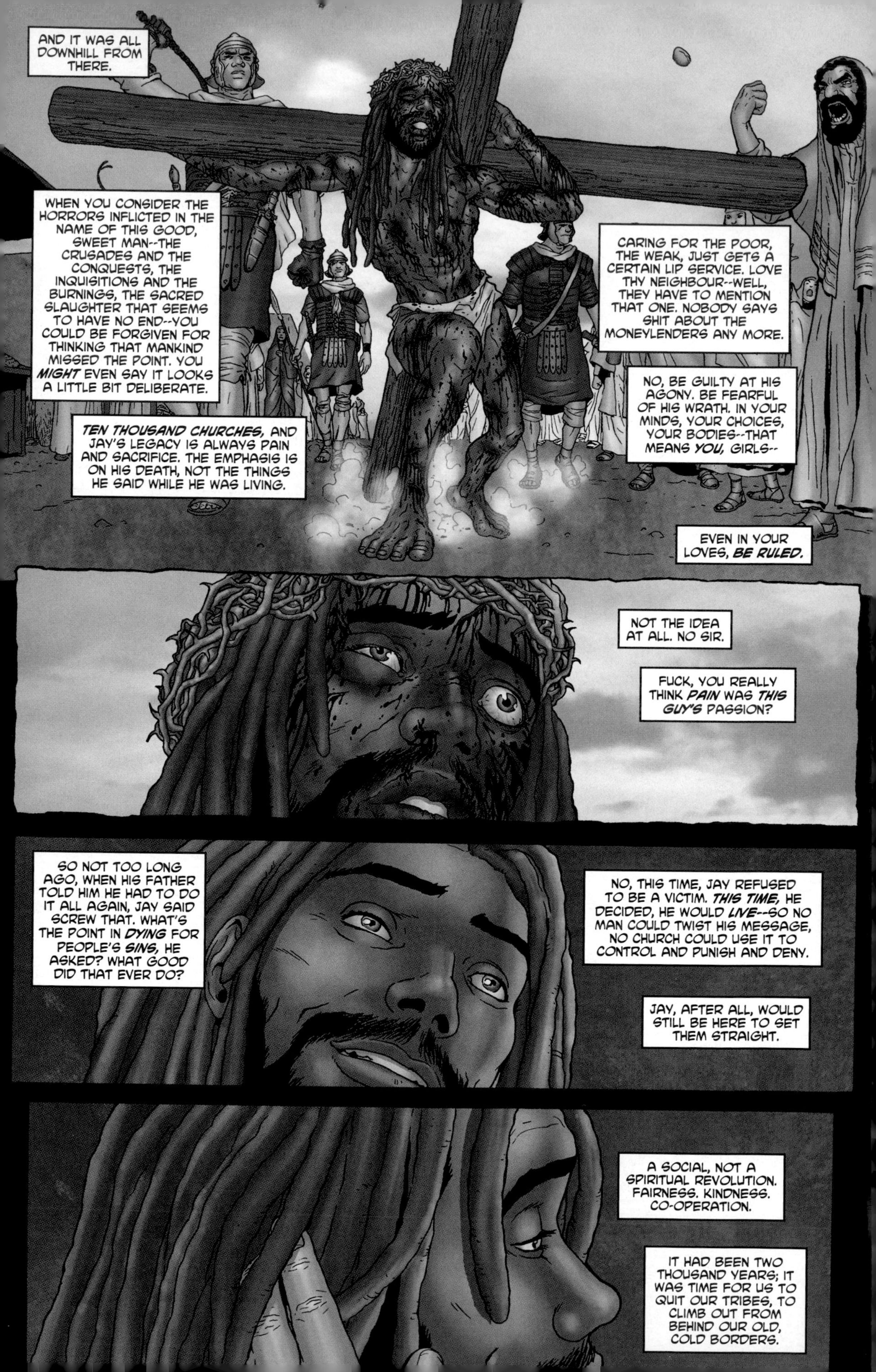
AND IT WAS ALL DOWNHILL FROM THERE.
WHEN YOU CONSIDER THE HORRORS INFLICTED IN THE NAME OF THIS GOOD, SWEET MAN--THE CRUSADES AND THE CONQUESTS, THE INQUISITIONS AND THE BURNINGS, THE SACRED SLAUGHTER THAT SEEMS TO HAVE NO END--YOU COULD BE FORGIVEN FOR THINKING THAT MANKIND MISSED THE POINT. YOU *MIGHT* EVEN SAY IT LOOKS A LITTLE BIT DELIBERATE.
TEN THOUSAND CHURCHES, AND JAY'S LEGACY IS ALWAYS PAIN AND SACRIFICE. THE EMPHASIS IS ON HIS DEATH, NOT THE THINGS HE SAID WHILE HE WAS LIVING.
CARING FOR THE POOR, THE WEAK, JUST GETS A CERTAIN LIP SERVICE. LOVE THY NEIGHBOUR--WELL, THEY HAVE TO MENTION THAT ONE. NOBODY SAYS SHIT ABOUT THE MONEYLENDERS ANY MORE.
NO, BE GUILTY AT HIS AGONY. BE FEARFUL OF HIS WRATH. IN YOUR MINDS, YOUR CHOICES, YOUR BODIES--THAT MEANS *YOU,* GIRLS--
EVEN IN YOUR LOVES, ***BE RULED.***
NOT THE IDEA AT ALL. NO SIR.
FUCK, YOU REALLY THINK *PAIN* WAS *THIS GUY'S* PASSION?
SO NOT TOO LONG AGO, WHEN HIS FATHER TOLD HIM HE HAD TO DO IT ALL AGAIN, JAY SAID SCREW THAT. WHAT'S THE POINT IN *DYING* FOR PEOPLE'S *SINS,* HE ASKED? WHAT GOOD DID THAT EVER DO?
NO, THIS TIME, JAY REFUSED TO BE A VICTIM. *THIS TIME,* HE DECIDED, HE WOULD *LIVE*--SO NO MAN COULD TWIST HIS MESSAGE, NO CHURCH COULD USE IT TO CONTROL AND PUNISH AND DENY.
JAY, AFTER ALL, WOULD STILL BE HERE TO SET THEM STRAIGHT.
A SOCIAL, NOT A SPIRITUAL REVOLUTION. FAIRNESS. KINDNESS. CO-OPERATION.
IT HAD BEEN TWO THOUSAND YEARS; IT WAS TIME FOR US TO QUIT OUR TRIBES, TO CLIMB OUT FROM BEHIND OUR OLD, COLD BORDERS.

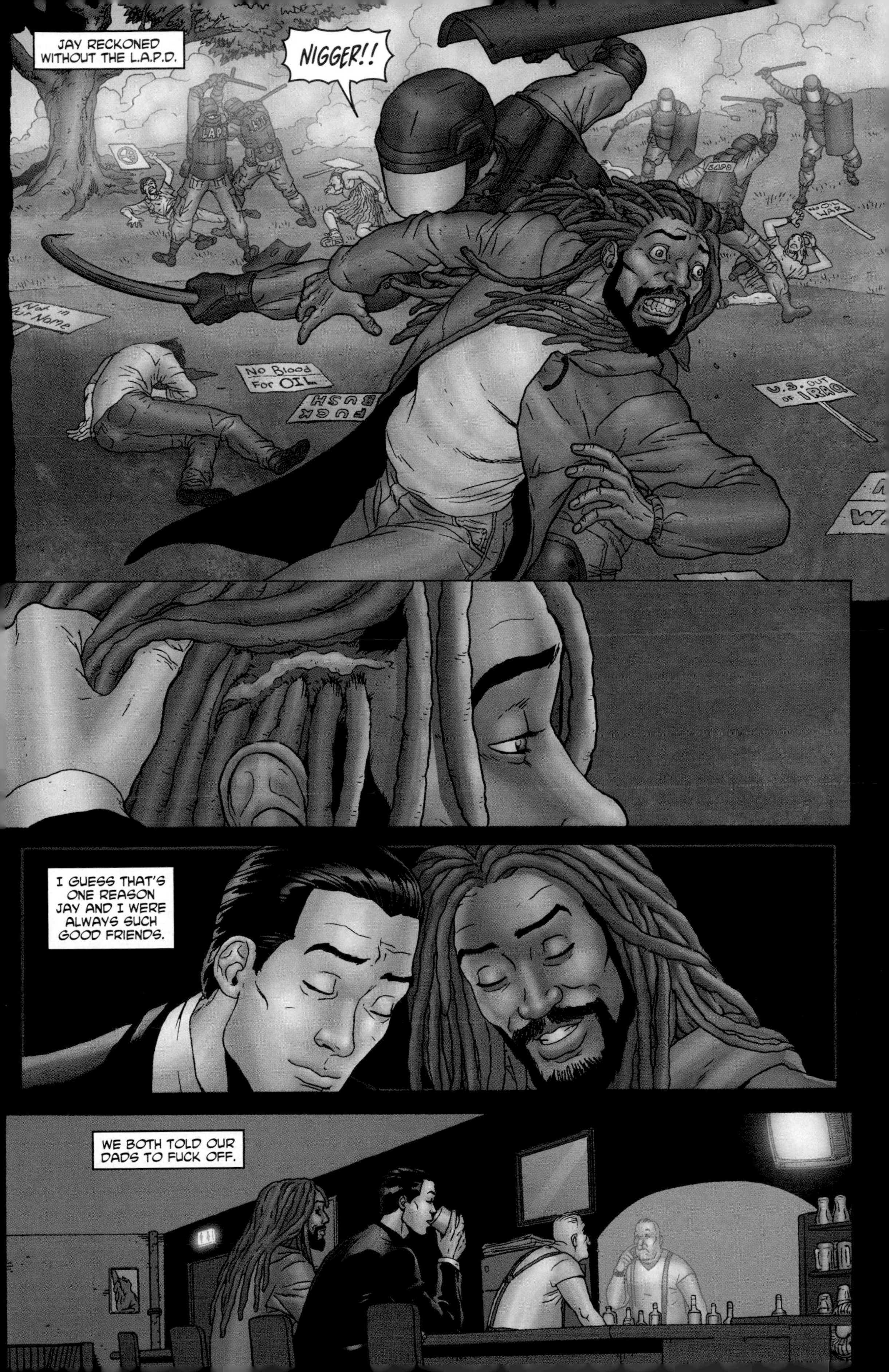
JAY RECKONED WITHOUT THE L.A.P.D.
NIGGER!!
No Blood For OIL
FUCK BUSH
U.S. OUT OF IRAQ
NO OIL WAR
I GUESS THAT'S ONE REASON JAY AND I WERE ALWAYS SUCH GOOD FRIENDS.
WE BOTH TOLD OUR DADS TO FUCK OFF.

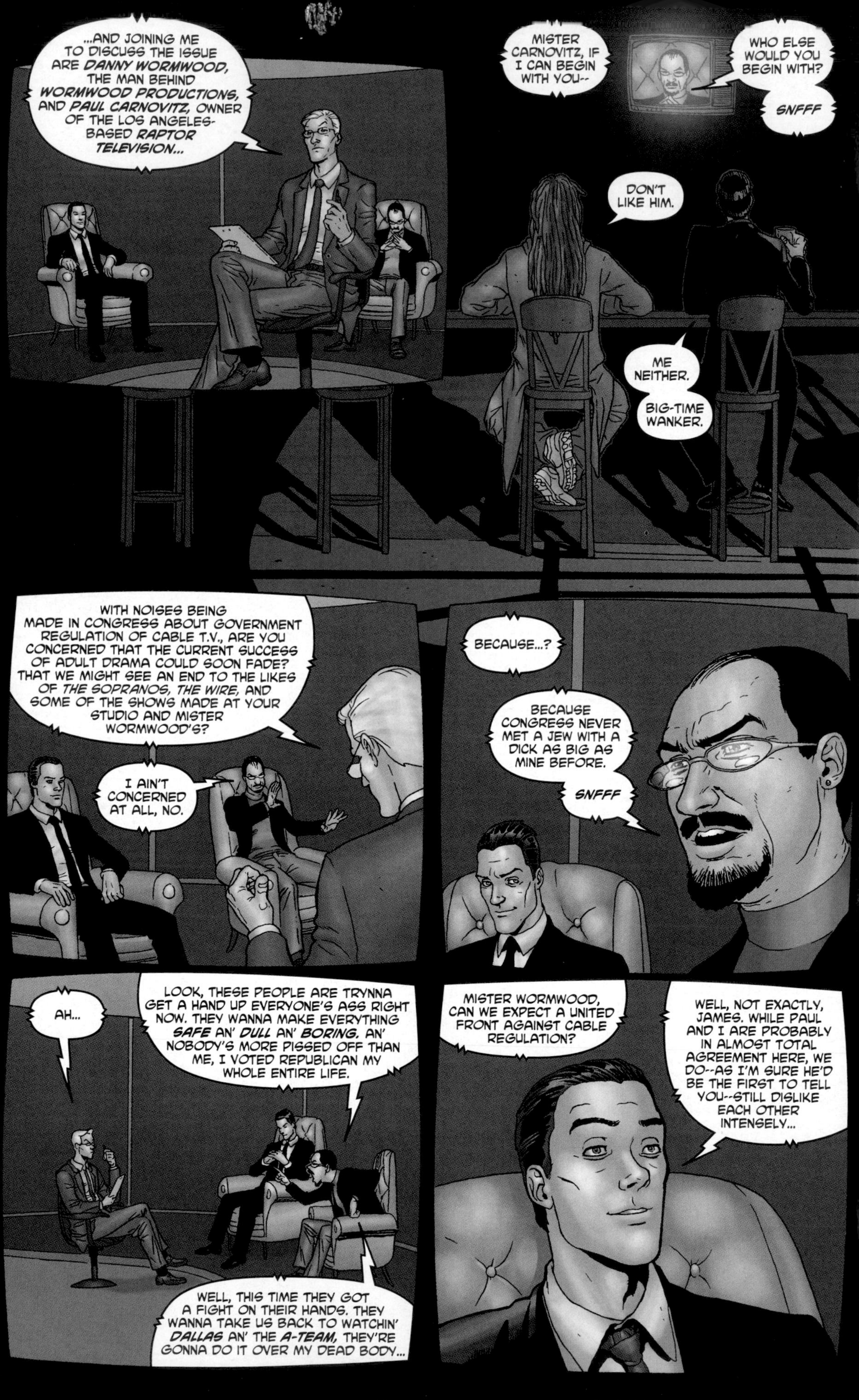
...AND JOINING ME TO DISCUSS THE ISSUE ARE DANNY WORMWOOD, THE MAN BEHIND WORMWOOD PRODUCTIONS, AND PAUL CARNOVITZ, OWNER OF THE LOS ANGELES-BASED RAPTOR TELEVISION...
MISTER CARNOVITZ, IF I CAN BEGIN WITH YOU--
WHO ELSE WOULD YOU BEGIN WITH?
SNFFF
DON'T LIKE HIM.
ME NEITHER.
BIG-TIME WANKER.
WITH NOISES BEING MADE IN CONGRESS ABOUT GOVERNMENT REGULATION OF CABLE T.V., ARE YOU CONCERNED THAT THE CURRENT SUCCESS OF ADULT DRAMA COULD SOON FADE? THAT WE MIGHT SEE AN END TO THE LIKES OF THE SOPRANOS, THE WIRE, AND SOME OF THE SHOWS MADE AT YOUR STUDIO AND MISTER WORMWOOD'S?
I AIN'T CONCERNED AT ALL, NO.
BECAUSE...?
BECAUSE CONGRESS NEVER MET A JEW WITH A DICK AS BIG AS MINE BEFORE.
SNFFF
AH...
LOOK, THESE PEOPLE ARE TRYNNA GET A HAND UP EVERYONE'S ASS RIGHT NOW. THEY WANNA MAKE EVERYTHING SAFE AN' DULL AN' BORING. AN' NOBODY'S MORE PISSED OFF THAN ME, I VOTED REPUBLICAN MY WHOLE ENTIRE LIFE.
WELL, THIS TIME THEY GOT A FIGHT ON THEIR HANDS. THEY WANNA TAKE US BACK TO WATCHIN' DALLAS AN' THE A-TEAM, THEY'RE GONNA DO IT OVER MY DEAD BODY...
MISTER WORMWOOD, CAN WE EXPECT A UNITED FRONT AGAINST CABLE REGULATION?
WELL, NOT EXACTLY, JAMES. WHILE PAUL AND I ARE PROBABLY IN ALMOST TOTAL AGREEMENT HERE, WE DO--AS I'M SURE HE'D BE THE FIRST TO TELL YOU--STILL DISLIKE EACH OTHER INTENSELY...

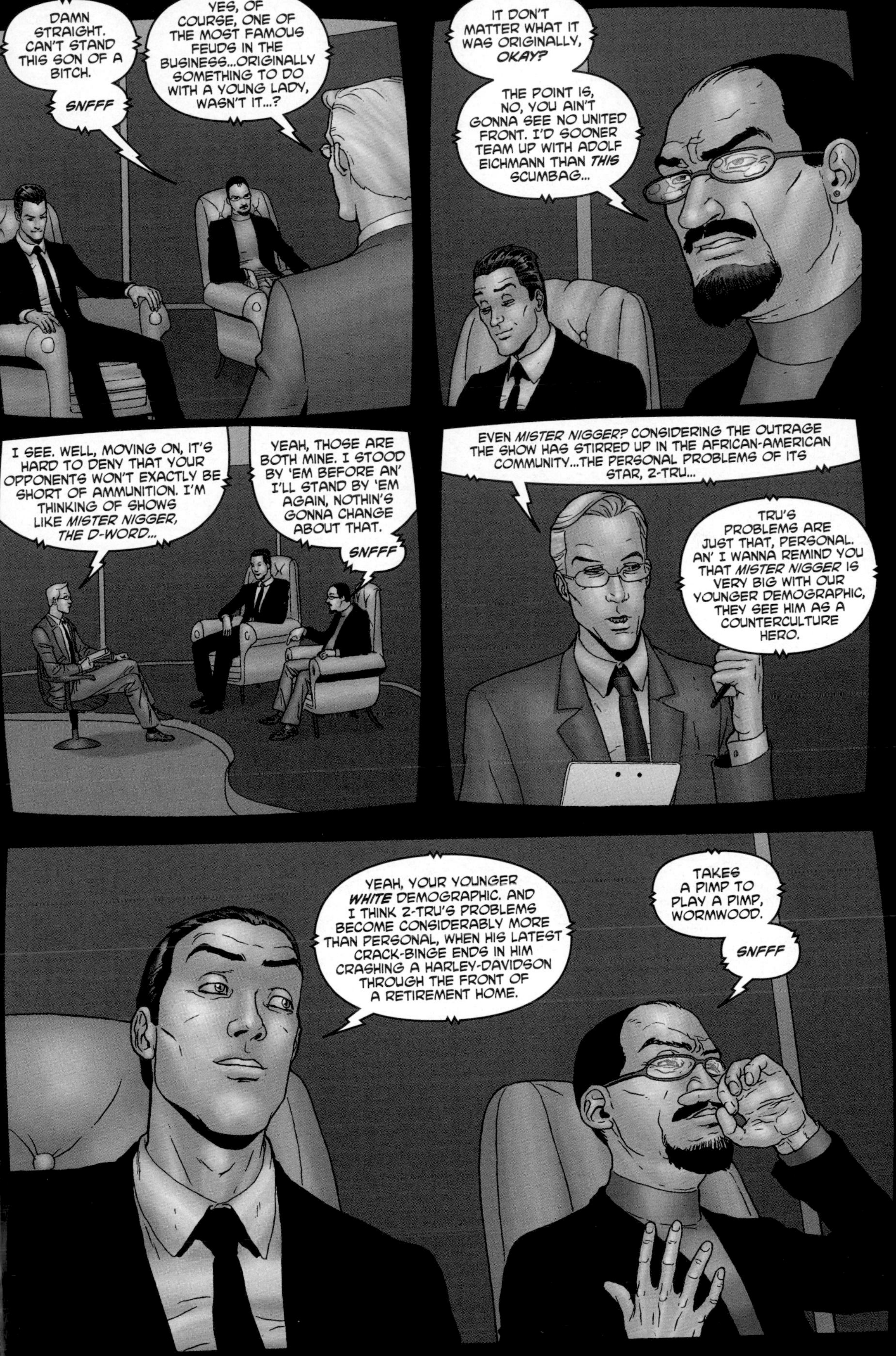
DAMN STRAIGHT. CAN'T STAND THIS SON OF A BITCH.
SNFFF
YES, OF COURSE, ONE OF THE MOST FAMOUS FEUDS IN THE BUSINESS...ORIGINALLY SOMETHING TO DO WITH A YOUNG LADY, WASN'T IT...?
IT DON'T MATTER WHAT IT WAS ORIGINALLY, OKAY?
THE POINT IS, NO, YOU AIN'T GONNA SEE NO UNITED FRONT. I'D SOONER TEAM UP WITH ADOLF EICHMANN THAN THIS SCUMBAG...
I SEE. WELL, MOVING ON, IT'S HARD TO DENY THAT YOUR OPPONENTS WON'T EXACTLY BE SHORT OF AMMUNITION. I'M THINKING OF SHOWS LIKE MISTER NIGGER, THE D-WORD...
YEAH, THOSE ARE BOTH MINE. I STOOD BY 'EM BEFORE AN' I'LL STAND BY 'EM AGAIN, NOTHIN'S GONNA CHANGE ABOUT THAT.
SNFFF
EVEN MISTER NIGGER? CONSIDERING THE OUTRAGE THE SHOW HAS STIRRED UP IN THE AFRICAN-AMERICAN COMMUNITY...THE PERSONAL PROBLEMS OF ITS STAR, 2-TRU...
TRU'S PROBLEMS ARE JUST THAT, PERSONAL. AN' I WANNA REMIND YOU THAT MISTER NIGGER IS VERY BIG WITH OUR YOUNGER DEMOGRAPHIC, THEY SEE HIM AS A COUNTERCULTURE HERO.
YEAH, YOUR YOUNGER WHITE DEMOGRAPHIC. AND I THINK 2-TRU'S PROBLEMS BECOME CONSIDERABLY MORE THAN PERSONAL, WHEN HIS LATEST CRACK-BINGE ENDS IN HIM CRASHING A HARLEY-DAVIDSON THROUGH THE FRONT OF A RETIREMENT HOME.
TAKES A PIMP TO PLAY A PIMP, WORMWOOD.
SNFFF

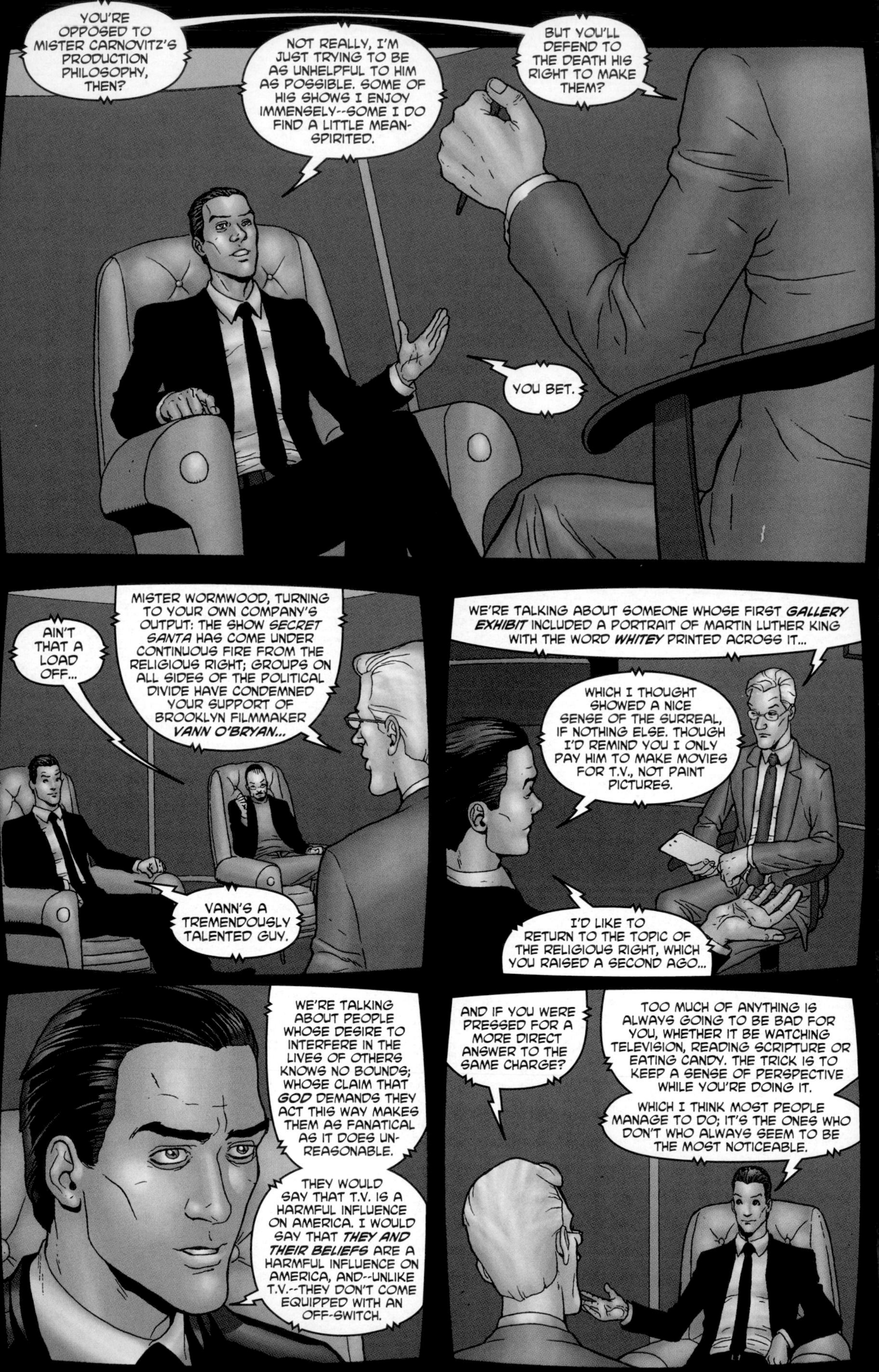
YOU'RE OPPOSED TO MISTER CARNOVITZ'S PRODUCTION PHILOSOPHY, THEN?
NOT REALLY, I'M JUST TRYING TO BE AS UNHELPFUL TO HIM AS POSSIBLE. SOME OF HIS SHOWS I ENJOY IMMENSELY--SOME I DO FIND A LITTLE MEAN-SPIRITED.
BUT YOU'LL DEFEND TO THE DEATH HIS RIGHT TO MAKE THEM?
YOU BET.
MISTER WORMWOOD, TURNING TO YOUR OWN COMPANY'S OUTPUT: THE SHOW *SECRET SANTA* HAS COME UNDER CONTINUOUS FIRE FROM THE RELIGIOUS RIGHT; GROUPS ON ALL SIDES OF THE POLITICAL DIVIDE HAVE CONDEMNED YOUR SUPPORT OF BROOKLYN FILMMAKER ***VANN O'BRYAN...***
AIN'T THAT A LOAD OFF...
VANN'S A TREMENDOUSLY TALENTED GUY.
WE'RE TALKING ABOUT SOMEONE WHOSE FIRST ***GALLERY EXHIBIT*** INCLUDED A PORTRAIT OF MARTIN LUTHER KING WITH THE WORD ***WHITEY*** PRINTED ACROSS IT...
WHICH I THOUGHT SHOWED A NICE SENSE OF THE SURREAL, IF NOTHING ELSE. THOUGH I'D REMIND YOU I ONLY PAY HIM TO MAKE MOVIES FOR T.V., NOT PAINT PICTURES.
I'D LIKE TO RETURN TO THE TOPIC OF THE RELIGIOUS RIGHT, WHICH YOU RAISED A SECOND AGO...
WE'RE TALKING ABOUT PEOPLE WHOSE DESIRE TO INTERFERE IN THE LIVES OF OTHERS KNOWS NO BOUNDS; WHOSE CLAIM THAT ***GOD*** DEMANDS THEY ACT THIS WAY MAKES THEM AS FANATICAL AS IT DOES UN-REASONABLE.
THEY WOULD SAY THAT T.V. IS A HARMFUL INFLUENCE ON AMERICA. I WOULD SAY THAT ***THEY AND THEIR BELIEFS*** ARE A HARMFUL INFLUENCE ON AMERICA, AND--UNLIKE T.V.--THEY DON'T COME EQUIPPED WITH AN OFF-SWITCH.
AND IF YOU WERE PRESSED FOR A MORE DIRECT ANSWER TO THE SAME CHARGE?
TOO MUCH OF ANYTHING IS ALWAYS GOING TO BE BAD FOR YOU, WHETHER IT BE WATCHING TELEVISION, READING SCRIPTURE OR EATING CANDY. THE TRICK IS TO KEEP A SENSE OF PERSPECTIVE WHILE YOU'RE DOING IT.
WHICH I THINK MOST PEOPLE MANAGE TO DO; IT'S THE ONES WHO DON'T WHO ALWAYS SEEM TO BE THE MOST NOTICEABLE.

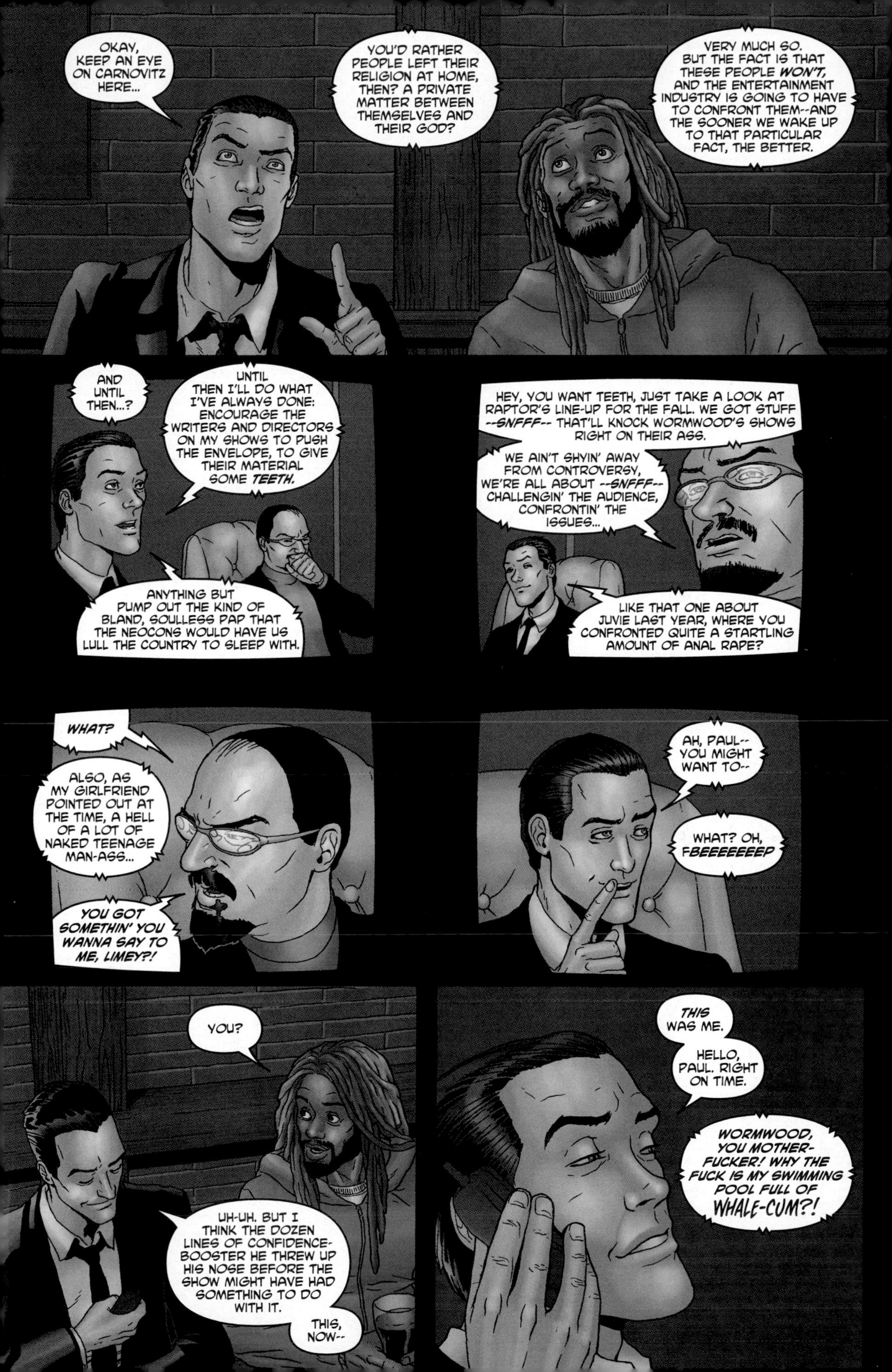
OKAY, KEEP AN EYE ON CARNOVITZ HERE...
YOU'D RATHER PEOPLE LEFT THEIR RELIGION AT HOME, THEN? A PRIVATE MATTER BETWEEN THEMSELVES AND THEIR GOD?
VERY MUCH SO. BUT THE FACT IS THAT THESE PEOPLE WON'T, AND THE ENTERTAINMENT INDUSTRY IS GOING TO HAVE TO CONFRONT THEM--AND THE SOONER WE WAKE UP TO THAT PARTICULAR FACT, THE BETTER.
AND UNTIL THEN...?
UNTIL THEN I'LL DO WHAT I'VE ALWAYS DONE: ENCOURAGE THE WRITERS AND DIRECTORS ON MY SHOWS TO PUSH THE ENVELOPE, TO GIVE THEIR MATERIAL SOME TEETH.
ANYTHING BUT PUMP OUT THE KIND OF BLAND, SOULLESS PAP THAT THE NEOCONS WOULD HAVE US LULL THE COUNTRY TO SLEEP WITH.
HEY, YOU WANT TEETH, JUST TAKE A LOOK AT RAPTOR'S LINE-UP FOR THE FALL. WE GOT STUFF --SNFFF-- THAT'LL KNOCK WORMWOOD'S SHOWS RIGHT ON THEIR ASS.
WE AIN'T SHYIN' AWAY FROM CONTROVERSY, WE'RE ALL ABOUT --SNFFF-- CHALLENGIN' THE AUDIENCE, CONFRONTIN' THE ISSUES...
LIKE THAT ONE ABOUT JUVIE LAST YEAR, WHERE YOU CONFRONTED QUITE A STARTLING AMOUNT OF ANAL RAPE?
WHAT?
ALSO, AS MY GIRLFRIEND POINTED OUT AT THE TIME, A HELL OF A LOT OF NAKED TEENAGE MAN-ASS...
YOU GOT SOMETHIN' YOU WANNA SAY TO ME, LIMEY?!
AH, PAUL-- YOU MIGHT WANT TO--
WHAT? OH, FBEEEEEEEP
YOU?
UH-UH. BUT I THINK THE DOZEN LINES OF CONFIDENCE-BOOSTER HE THREW UP HIS NOSE BEFORE THE SHOW MIGHT HAVE HAD SOMETHING TO DO WITH IT.
THIS, NOW--
THIS WAS ME.
HELLO, PAUL. RIGHT ON TIME.
WORMWOOD, YOU MOTHER-FUCKER! WHY THE FUCK IS MY SWIMMING POOL FULL OF WHALE-CUM?!

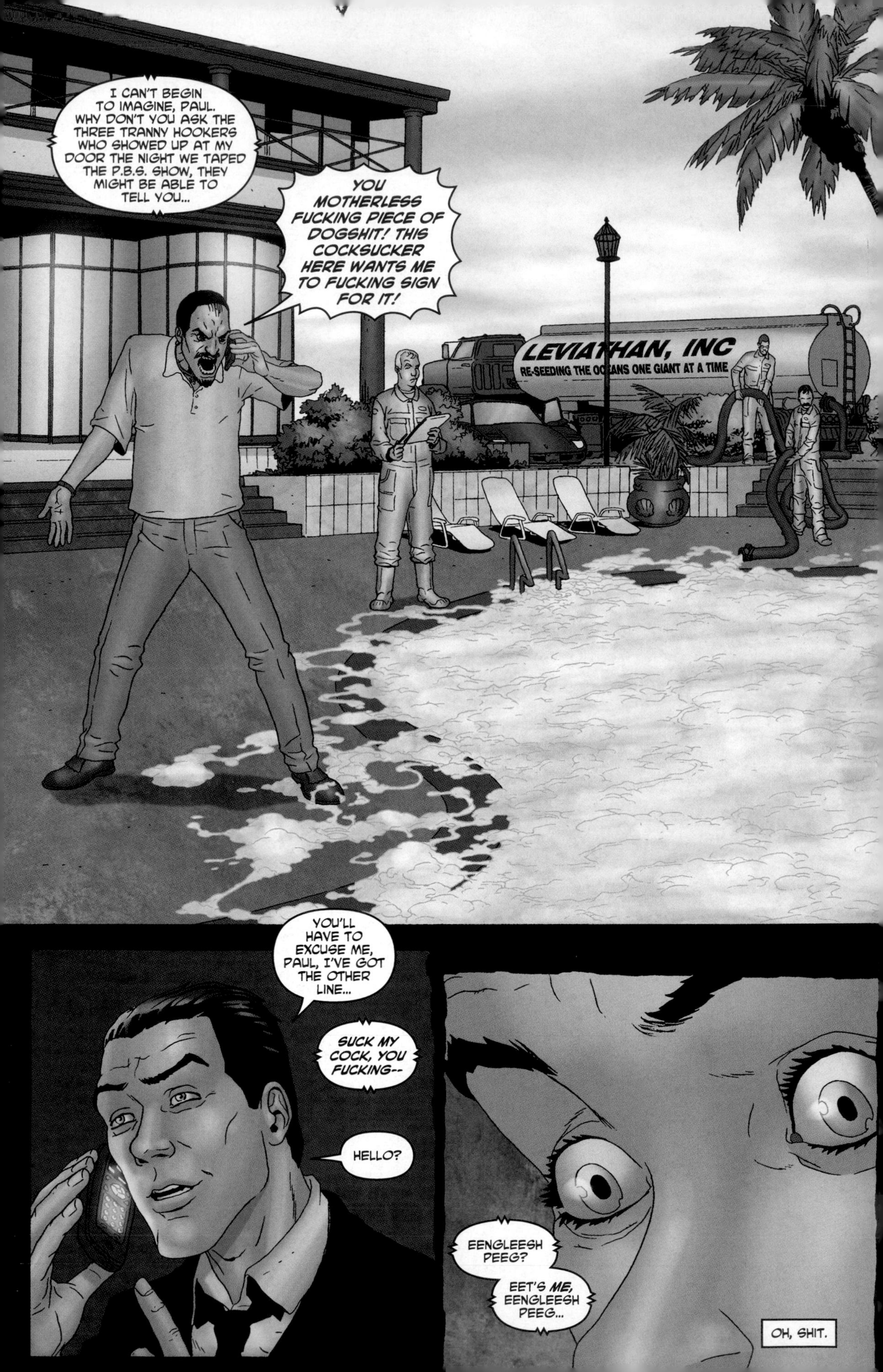
I CAN'T BEGIN TO IMAGINE, PAUL. WHY DON'T YOU ASK THE THREE TRANNY HOOKERS WHO SHOWED UP AT MY DOOR THE NIGHT WE TAPED THE P.B.S. SHOW, THEY MIGHT BE ABLE TO TELL YOU...
YOU MOTHERLESS FUCKING PIECE OF DOGSHIT! THIS COCKSUCKER HERE WANTS ME TO FUCKING SIGN FOR IT!
LEVIATHAN, INC
RE-SEEDING THE OCEANS ONE GIANT AT A TIME
YOU'LL HAVE TO EXCUSE ME, PAUL, I'VE GOT THE OTHER LINE...
SUCK MY COCK, YOU FUCKING--
HELLO?
EENGLEESH PEEG?
EET'S *ME*, EENGLEESH PEEG...
OH, SHIT.

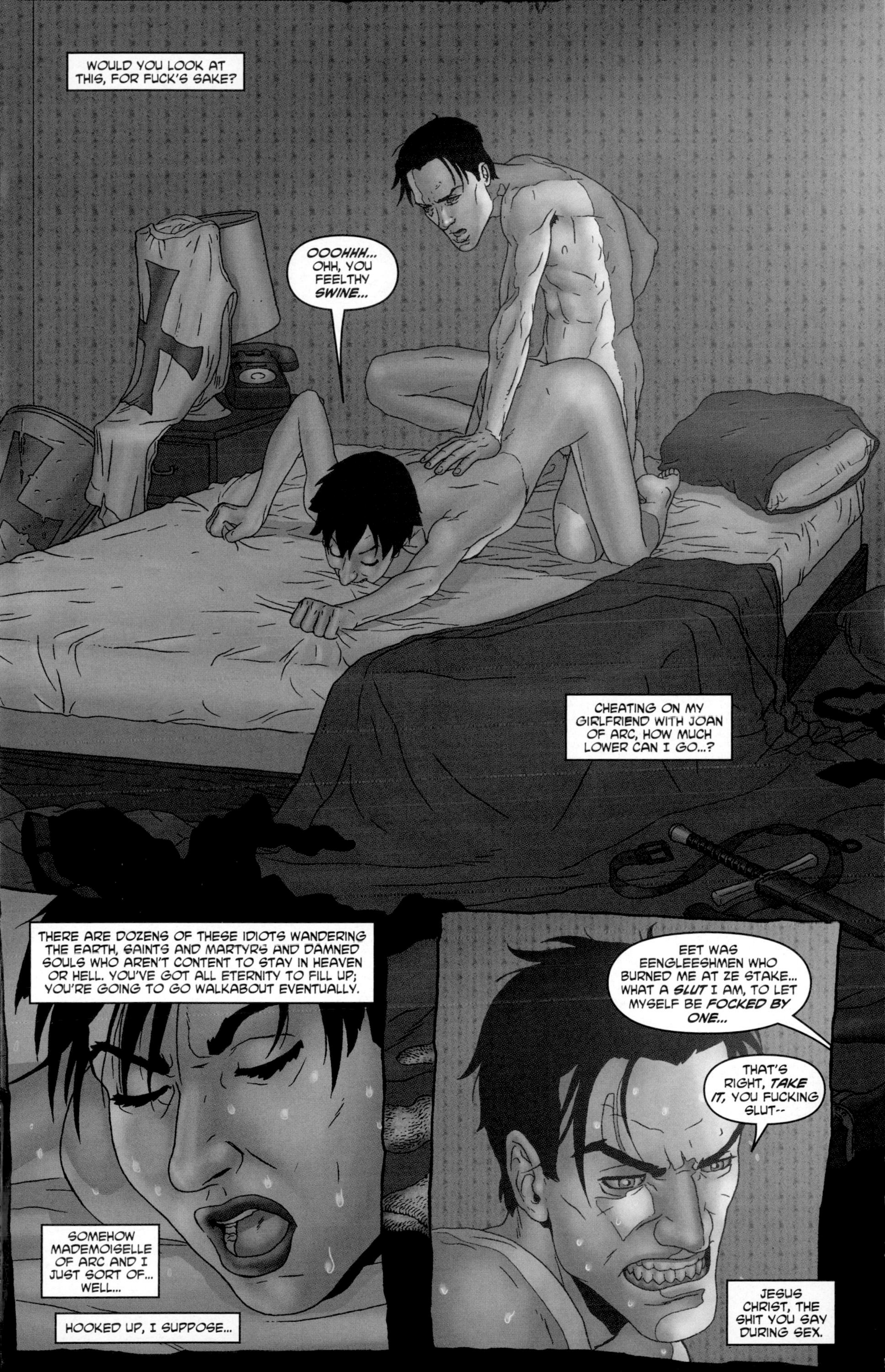
WOULD YOU LOOK AT THIS, FOR FUCK'S SAKE?
OOOHHH... OHH, YOU FEELTHY SWINE...
CHEATING ON MY GIRLFRIEND WITH JOAN OF ARC, HOW MUCH LOWER CAN I GO...?
THERE ARE DOZENS OF THESE IDIOTS WANDERING THE EARTH, SAINTS AND MARTYRS AND DAMNED SOULS WHO AREN'T CONTENT TO STAY IN HEAVEN OR HELL. YOU'VE GOT ALL ETERNITY TO FILL UP; YOU'RE GOING TO GO WALKABOUT EVENTUALLY.
SOMEHOW MADEMOISELLE OF ARC AND I JUST SORT OF... WELL...
HOOKED UP, I SUPPOSE...
EET WAS EENGLEESHMEN WHO BURNED ME AT ZE STAKE... WHAT A SLUT I AM, TO LET MYSELF BE FOCKED BY ONE...
THAT'S RIGHT, TAKE IT, YOU FUCKING SLUT--
JESUS CHRIST, THE SHIT YOU SAY DURING SEX.

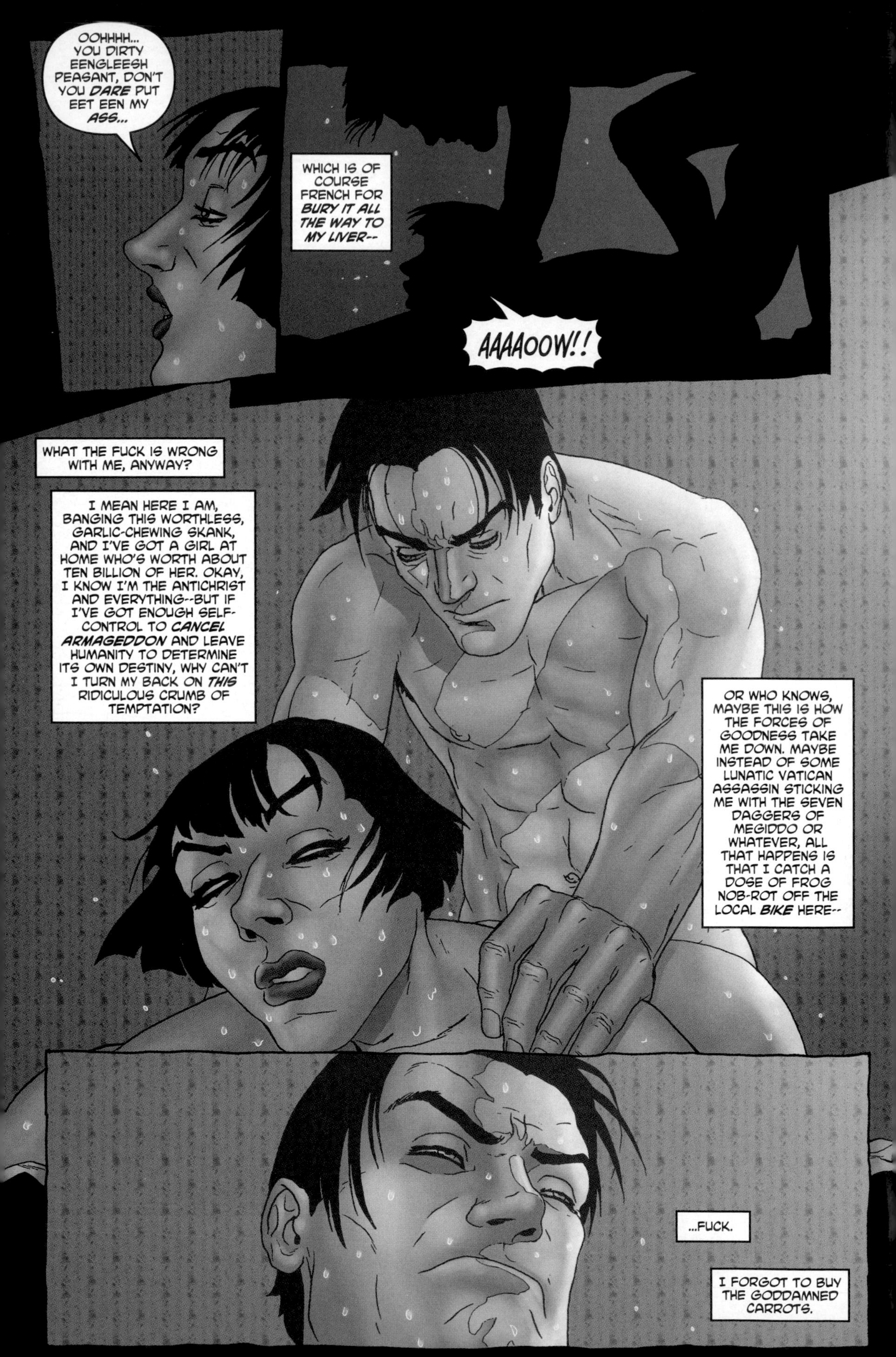
OOHHHH... YOU DIRTY EENGLEESH PEASANT, DON'T YOU DARE PUT EET EEN MY ASS...
WHICH IS OF COURSE FRENCH FOR BURY IT ALL THE WAY TO MY LIVER--
AAAAOOW!!
WHAT THE FUCK IS WRONG WITH ME, ANYWAY?
I MEAN HERE I AM, BANGING THIS WORTHLESS, GARLIC-CHEWING SKANK, AND I'VE GOT A GIRL AT HOME WHO'S WORTH ABOUT TEN BILLION OF HER. OKAY, I KNOW I'M THE ANTICHRIST AND EVERYTHING--BUT IF I'VE GOT ENOUGH SELF-CONTROL TO CANCEL ARMAGEDDON AND LEAVE HUMANITY TO DETERMINE ITS OWN DESTINY, WHY CAN'T I TURN MY BACK ON THIS RIDICULOUS CRUMB OF TEMPTATION?
OR WHO KNOWS, MAYBE THIS IS HOW THE FORCES OF GOODNESS TAKE ME DOWN. MAYBE INSTEAD OF SOME LUNATIC VATICAN ASSASSIN STICKING ME WITH THE SEVEN DAGGERS OF MEGIDDO OR WHATEVER, ALL THAT HAPPENS IS THAT I CATCH A DOSE OF FROG NOB-ROT OFF THE LOCAL BIKE HERE--
...FUCK.
I FORGOT TO BUY THE GODDAMNED CARROTS.

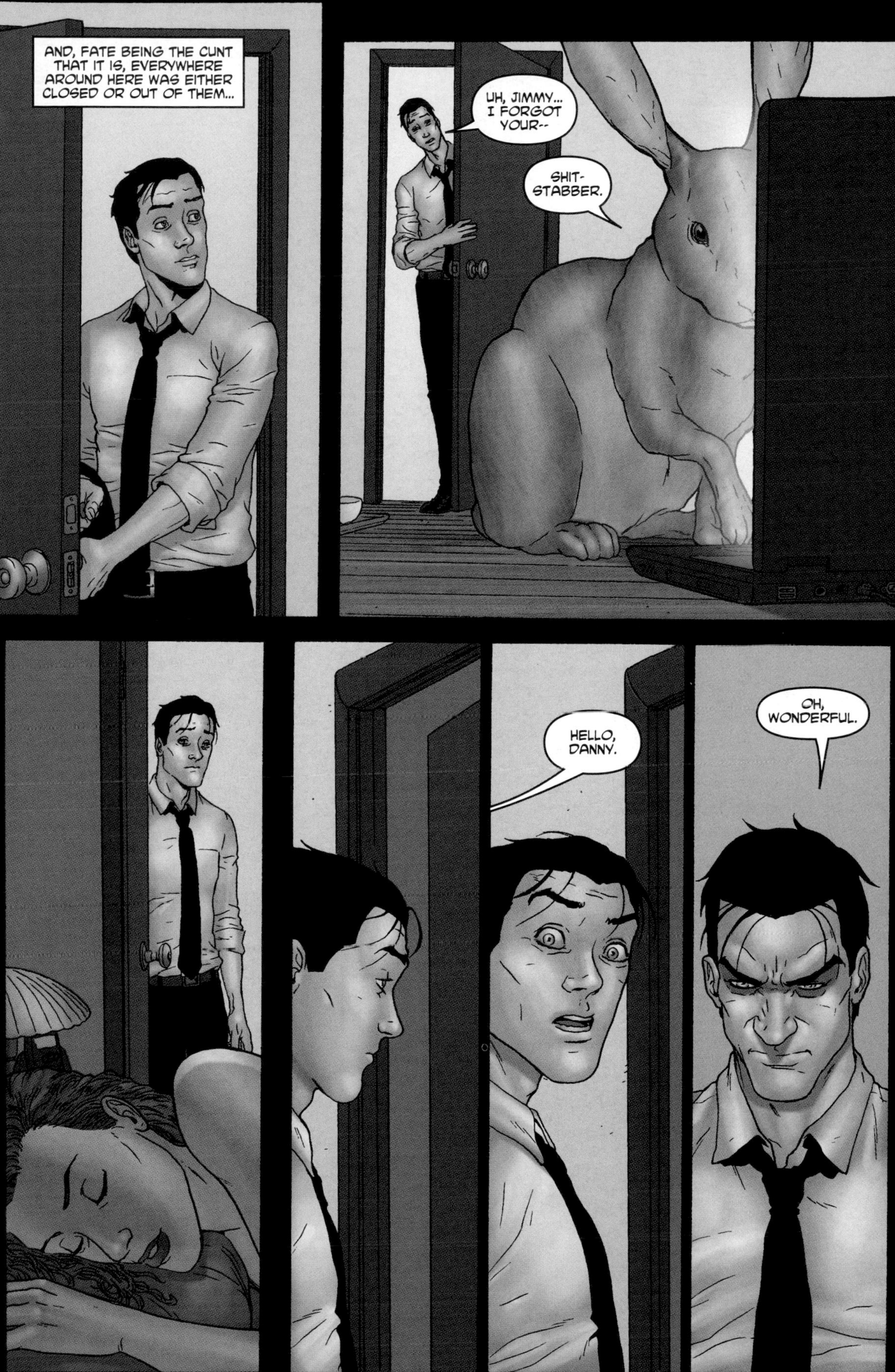
AND, FATE BEING THE CUNT THAT IT IS, EVERYWHERE AROUND HERE WAS EITHER CLOSED OR OUT OF THEM...
UH, JIMMY... I FORGOT YOUR--
SHIT-STABBER.
HELLO, DANNY.
OH, WONDERFUL.

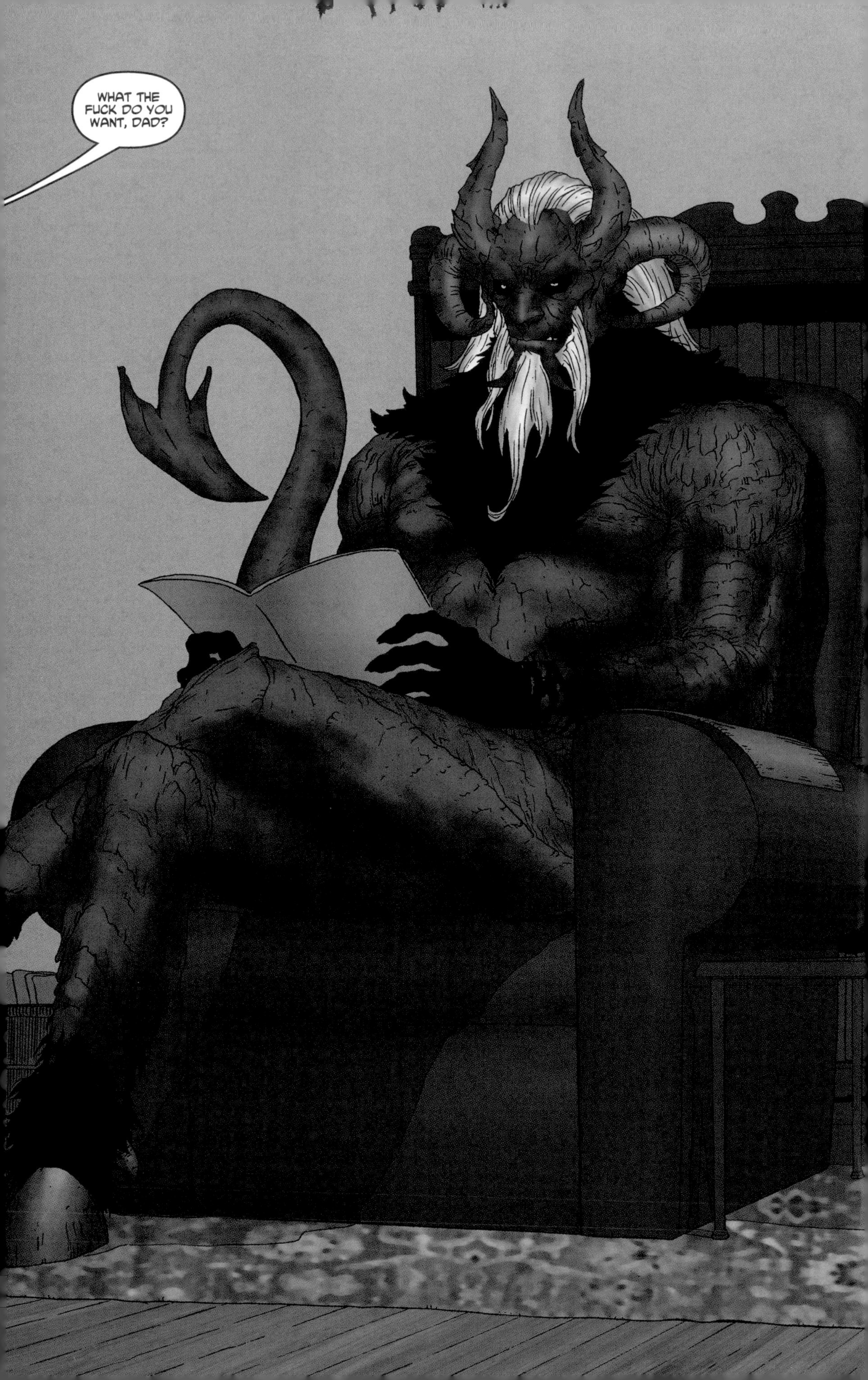
WHAT THE FUCK DO YOU WANT, DAD?

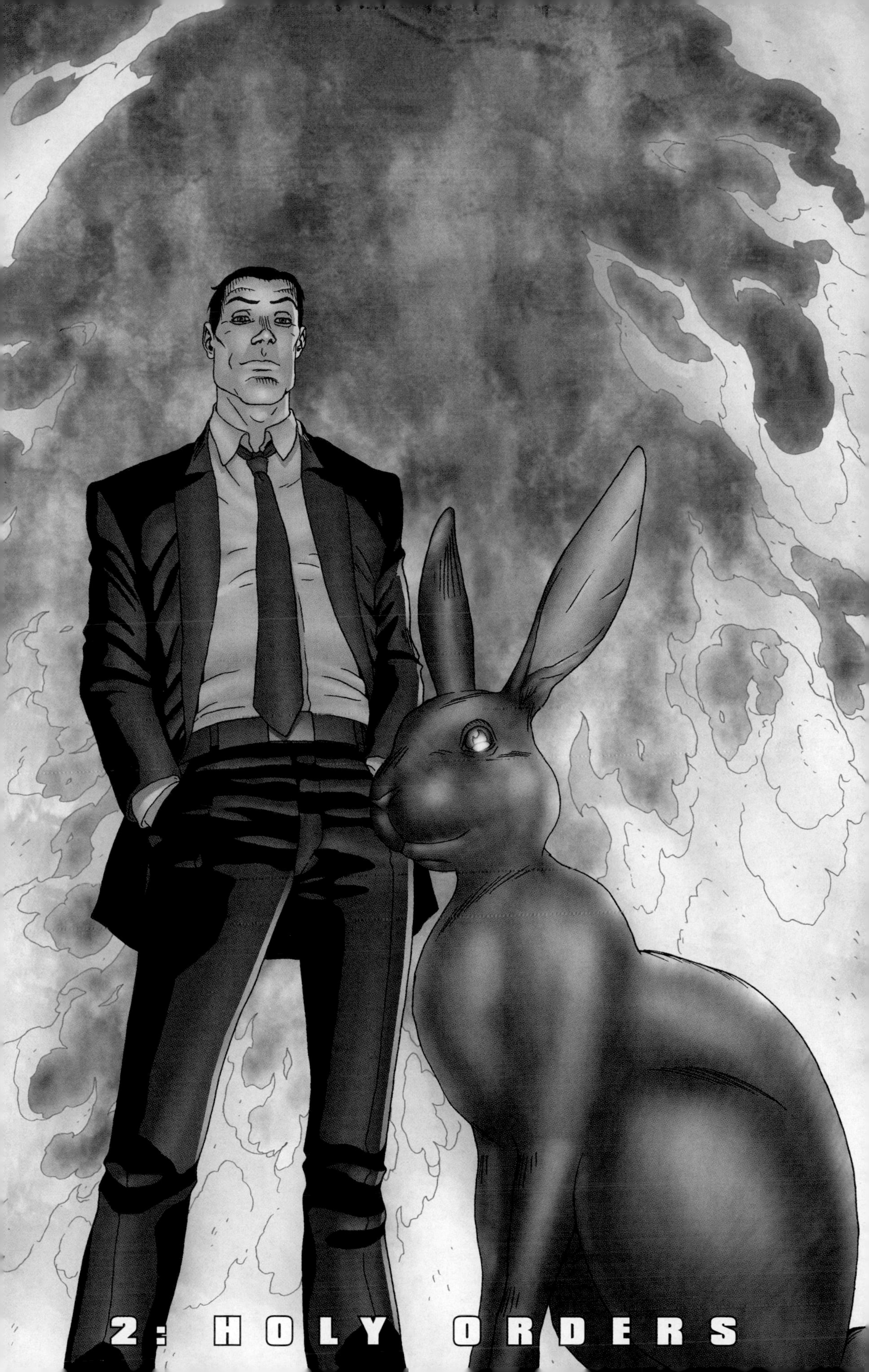
2: HOLY ORDERS

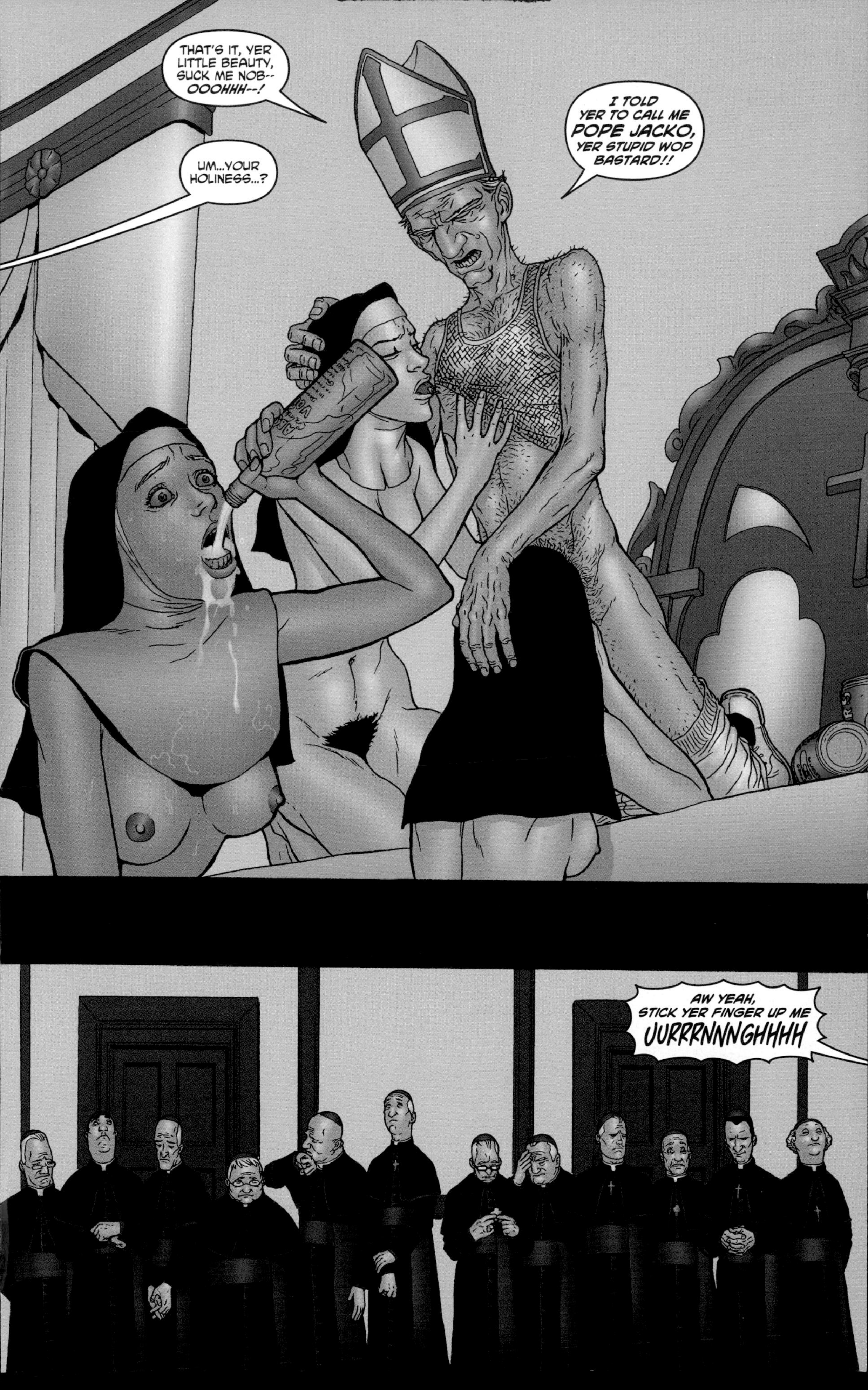
THAT'S IT, YER LITTLE BEAUTY, SUCK ME NOB-- OOOHHH--!
UM...YOUR HOLINESS...?
I TOLD YER TO CALL ME POPE JACKO, YER STUPID WOP BASTARD!!
AW YEAH, STICK YER FINGER UP ME UURRRNNNGHHHH

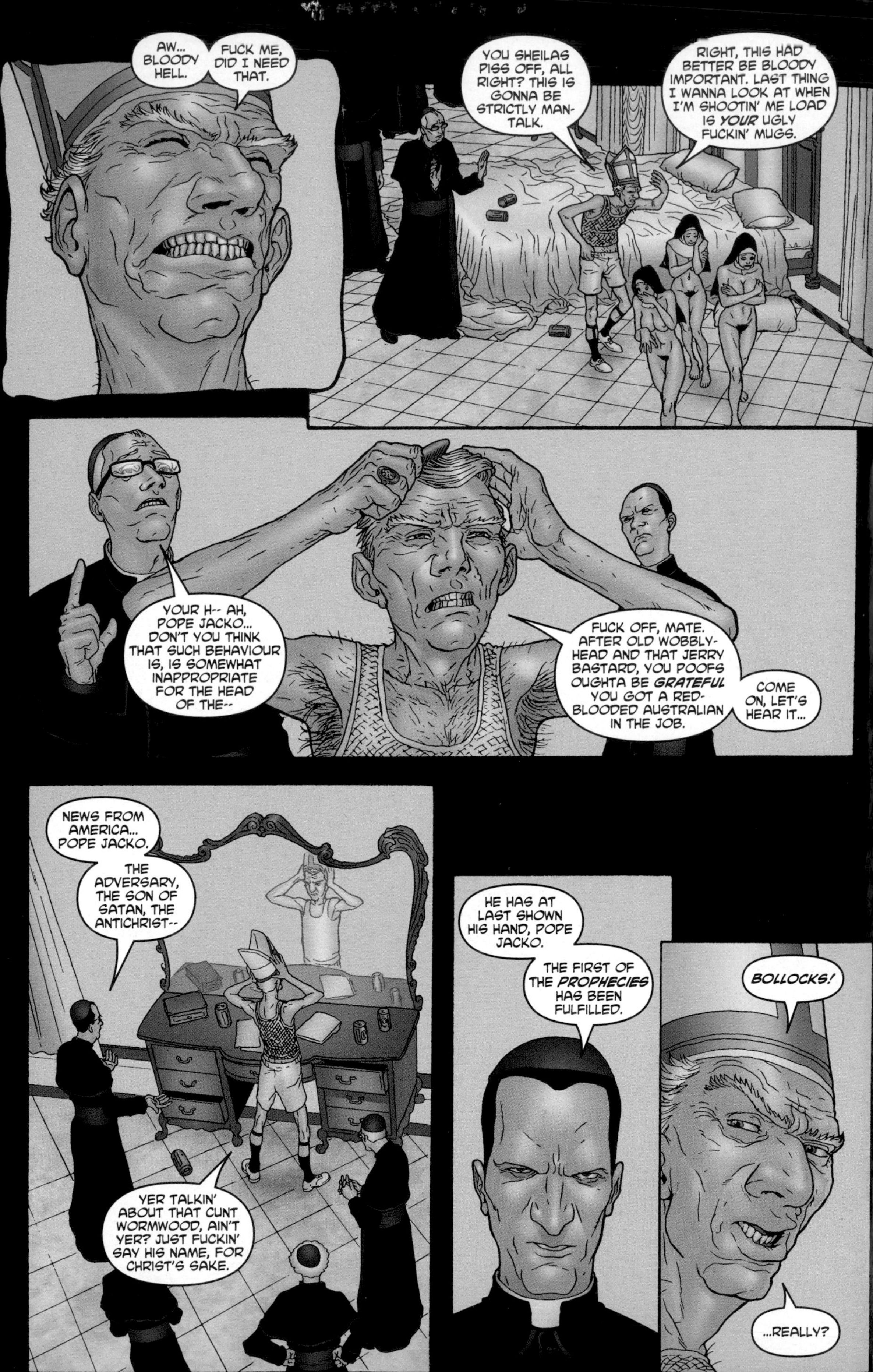
AW... BLOODY HELL.
FUCK ME, DID I NEED THAT.
YOU SHEILAS PISS OFF, ALL RIGHT? THIS IS GONNA BE STRICTLY MAN-TALK.
RIGHT, THIS HAD BETTER BE BLOODY IMPORTANT. LAST THING I WANNA LOOK AT WHEN I'M SHOOTIN' ME LOAD IS *YOUR* UGLY FUCKIN' MUGS.
YOUR H-- AH, POPE JACKO... DON'T YOU THINK THAT SUCH BEHAVIOUR IS, IS SOMEWHAT INAPPROPRIATE FOR THE HEAD OF THE--
FUCK OFF, MATE. AFTER OLD WOBBLY-HEAD AND THAT JERRY BASTARD, YOU POOFS OUGHTA BE *GRATEFUL* YOU GOT A RED-BLOODED AUSTRALIAN IN THE JOB.
COME ON, LET'S HEAR IT...
NEWS FROM AMERICA... POPE JACKO.
THE ADVERSARY, THE SON OF SATAN, THE ANTICHRIST--
YER TALKIN' ABOUT THAT CUNT WORMWOOD, AIN'T YER? JUST FUCKIN' SAY HIS NAME, FOR CHRIST'S SAKE.
HE HAS AT LAST SHOWN HIS HAND, POPE JACKO.
THE FIRST OF THE *PROPHECIES* HAS BEEN FULFILLED.
BOLLOCKS!
...REALLY?

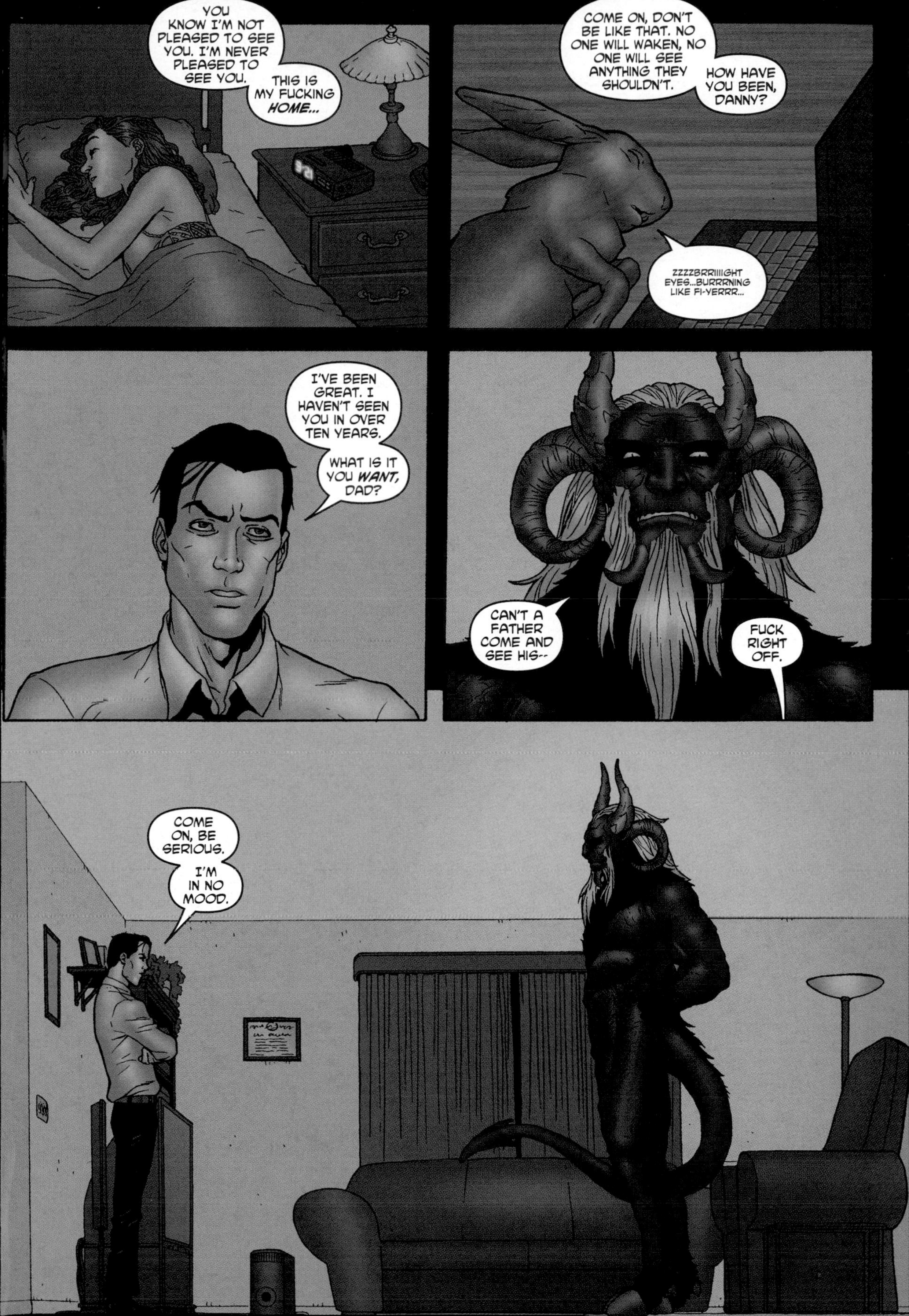
YOU KNOW I'M NOT PLEASED TO SEE YOU. I'M NEVER PLEASED TO SEE YOU.
THIS IS MY FUCKING *HOME*...
COME ON, DON'T BE LIKE THAT. NO ONE WILL WAKEN, NO ONE WILL SEE ANYTHING THEY SHOULDN'T.
HOW HAVE YOU BEEN, DANNY?
ZZZZBRRIIIIGHT EYES...BURRRNING LIKE FI-YERRR...
I'VE BEEN GREAT. I HAVEN'T SEEN YOU IN OVER TEN YEARS.
WHAT IS IT YOU *WANT,* DAD?
CAN'T A FATHER COME AND SEE HIS--
FUCK RIGHT OFF.
COME ON, BE SERIOUS.
I'M IN NO MOOD.

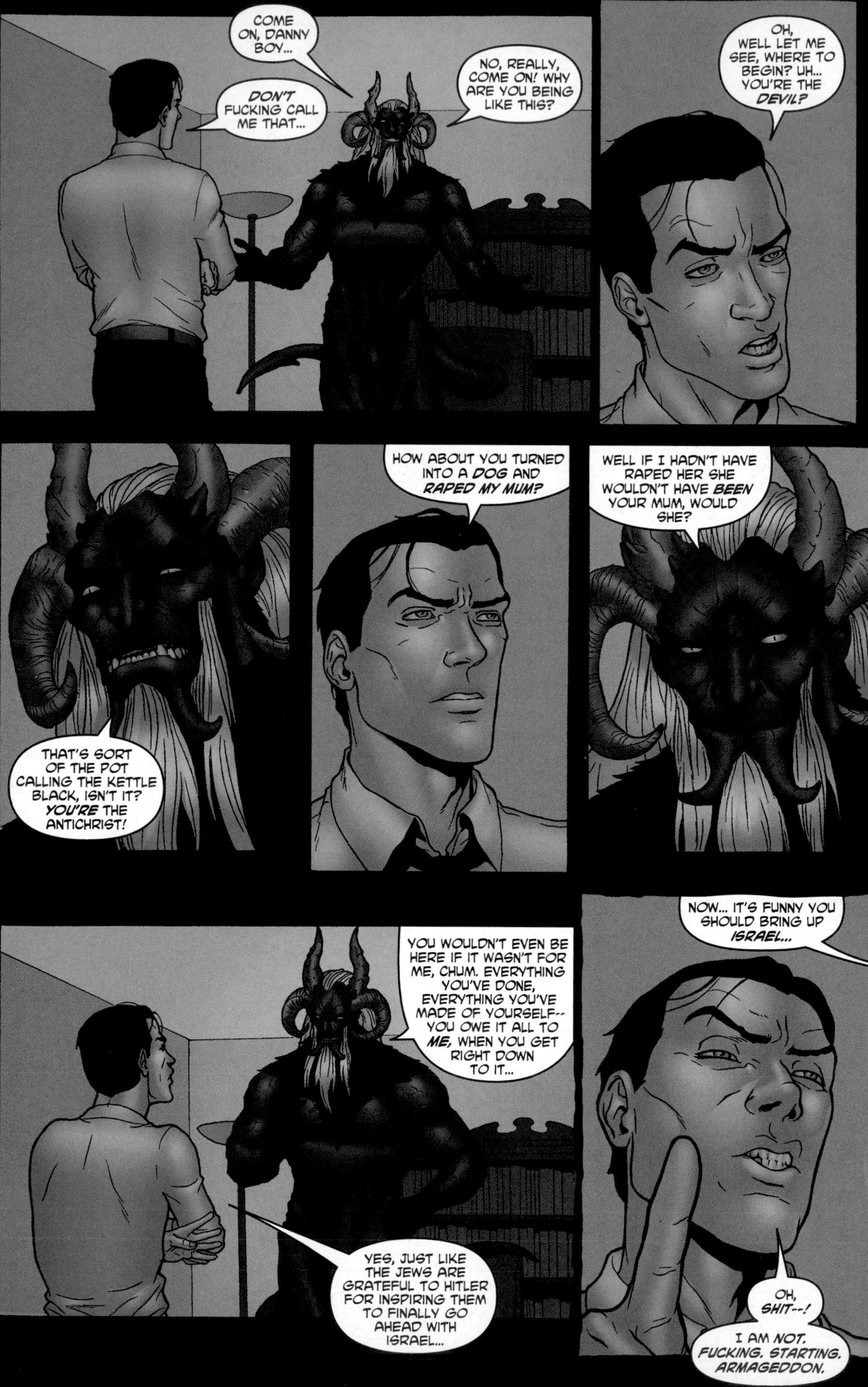
COME ON, DANNY BOY...
DON'T FUCKING CALL ME THAT...
NO, REALLY, COME ON! WHY ARE YOU BEING LIKE THIS?
OH, WELL LET ME SEE, WHERE TO BEGIN? UH... YOU'RE THE DEVIL?
THAT'S SORT OF THE POT CALLING THE KETTLE BLACK, ISN'T IT? YOU'RE THE ANTICHRIST!
HOW ABOUT YOU TURNED INTO A DOG AND RAPED MY MUM?
WELL IF I HADN'T HAVE RAPED HER SHE WOULDN'T HAVE BEEN YOUR MUM, WOULD SHE?
YOU WOULDN'T EVEN BE HERE IF IT WASN'T FOR ME, CHUM. EVERYTHING YOU'VE DONE, EVERYTHING YOU'VE MADE OF YOURSELF-- YOU OWE IT ALL TO ME, WHEN YOU GET RIGHT DOWN TO IT...
YES, JUST LIKE THE JEWS ARE GRATEFUL TO HITLER FOR INSPIRING THEM TO FINALLY GO AHEAD WITH ISRAEL...
NOW... IT'S FUNNY YOU SHOULD BRING UP ISRAEL...
OH, SHIT--!
I AM NOT. FUCKING. STARTING. ARMAGEDDON.

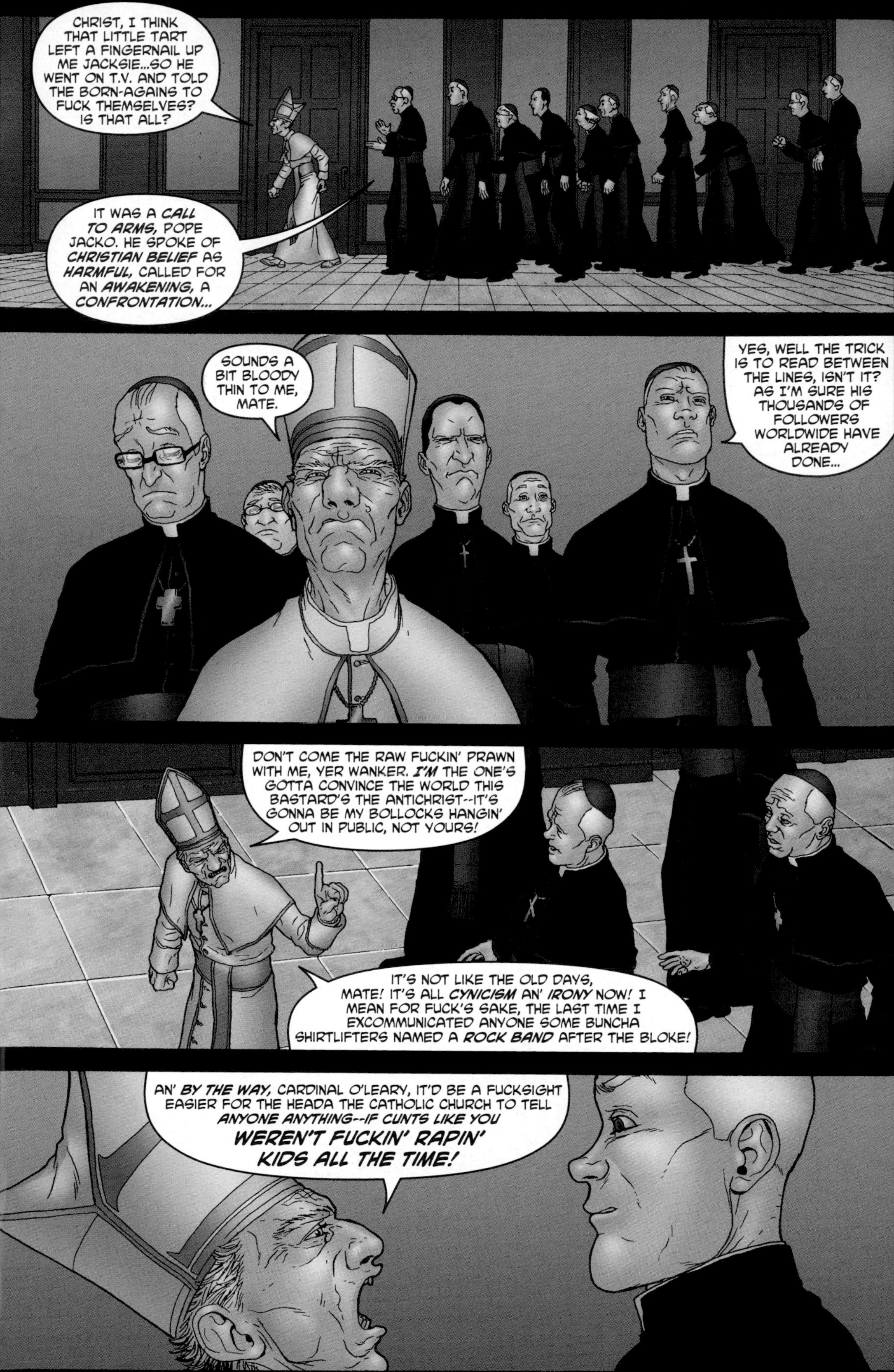
CHRIST, I THINK THAT LITTLE TART LEFT A FINGERNAIL UP ME JACKSIE...SO HE WENT ON T.V. AND TOLD THE BORN-AGAINS TO FUCK THEMSELVES? IS THAT ALL?
IT WAS A CALL TO ARMS, POPE JACKO. HE SPOKE OF CHRISTIAN BELIEF AS HARMFUL, CALLED FOR AN AWAKENING, A CONFRONTATION...
SOUNDS A BIT BLOODY THIN TO ME, MATE.
YES, WELL THE TRICK IS TO READ BETWEEN THE LINES, ISN'T IT? AS I'M SURE HIS THOUSANDS OF FOLLOWERS WORLDWIDE HAVE ALREADY DONE...
DON'T COME THE RAW FUCKIN' PRAWN WITH ME, YER WANKER. I'M THE ONE'S GOTTA CONVINCE THE WORLD THIS BASTARD'S THE ANTICHRIST--IT'S GONNA BE MY BOLLOCKS HANGIN' OUT IN PUBLIC, NOT YOURS!
IT'S NOT LIKE THE OLD DAYS, MATE! IT'S ALL CYNICISM AN' IRONY NOW! I MEAN FOR FUCK'S SAKE, THE LAST TIME I EXCOMMUNICATED ANYONE SOME BUNCHA SHIRTLIFTERS NAMED A ROCK BAND AFTER THE BLOKE!
AN' BY THE WAY, CARDINAL O'LEARY, IT'D BE A FUCKSIGHT EASIER FOR THE HEADA THE CATHOLIC CHURCH TO TELL ANYONE ANYTHING--IF CUNTS LIKE YOU WEREN'T FUCKIN' RAPIN' KIDS ALL THE TIME!

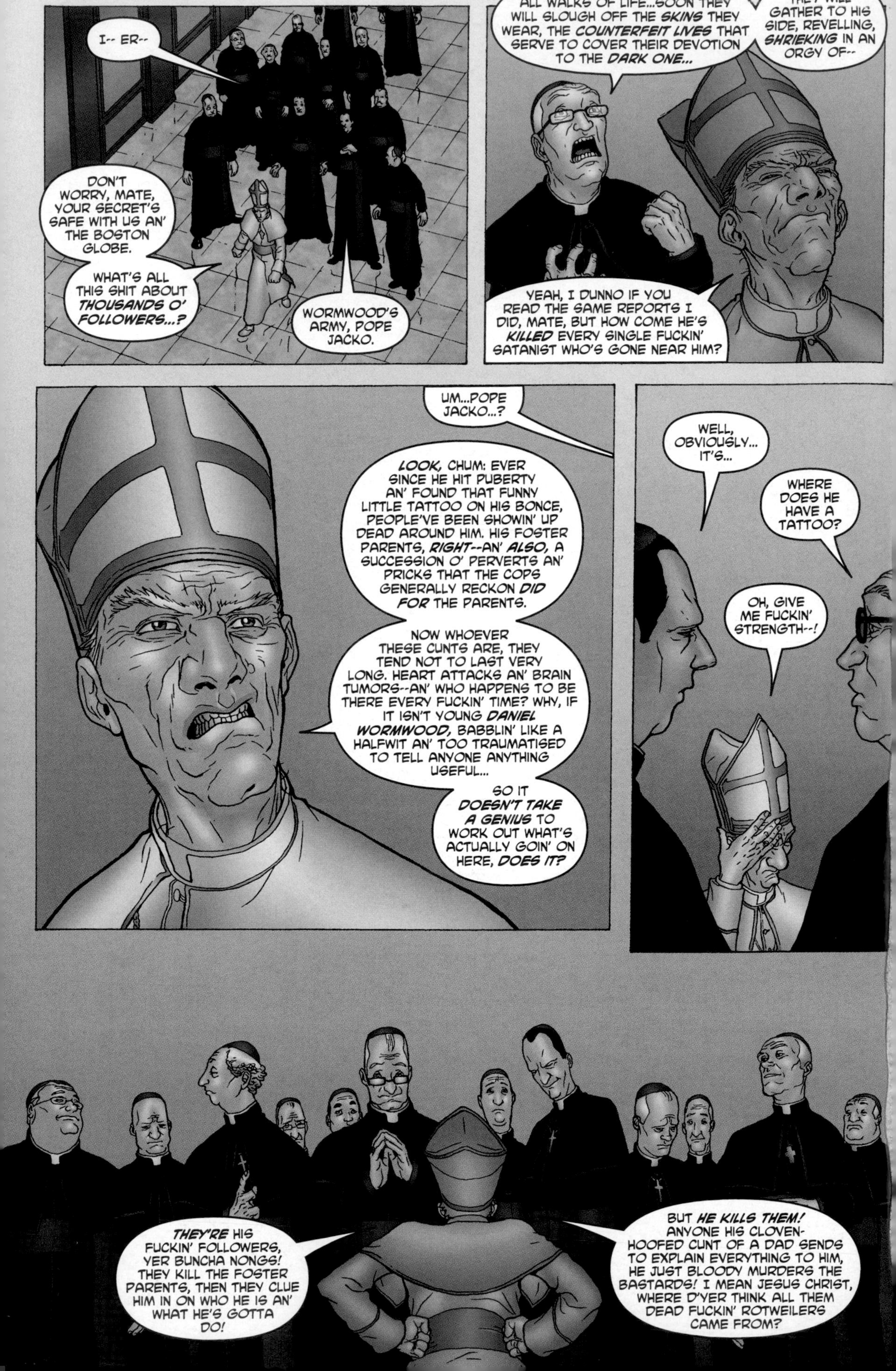
I-- ER--
DON'T WORRY, MATE, YOUR SECRET'S SAFE WITH US AN' THE BOSTON GLOBE.
WHAT'S ALL THIS SHIT ABOUT *THOUSANDS O' FOLLOWERS...?*
WORMWOOD'S ARMY, POPE JACKO.
ALL OVER THE WORLD, IN ALL WALKS OF LIFE...SOON THEY WILL SLOUGH OFF THE *SKINS* THEY WEAR, THE *COUNTERFEIT LIVES* THAT SERVE TO COVER THEIR DEVOTION TO THE *DARK ONE...*
THEY WILL GATHER TO HIS SIDE, REVELLING, *SHRIEKING* IN AN ORGY OF--
YEAH, I DUNNO IF YOU READ THE SAME REPORTS I DID, MATE, BUT HOW COME HE'S *KILLED* EVERY SINGLE FUCKIN' SATANIST WHO'S GONE NEAR HIM?
UM...POPE JACKO...?
LOOK, CHUM: EVER SINCE HE HIT PUBERTY AN' FOUND THAT FUNNY LITTLE TATTOO ON HIS BONCE, PEOPLE'VE BEEN SHOWIN' UP DEAD AROUND HIM. HIS FOSTER PARENTS, *RIGHT*--AN' *ALSO,* A SUCCESSION O' PERVERTS AN' PRICKS THAT THE COPS GENERALLY RECKON *DID FOR* THE PARENTS.
NOW WHOEVER THESE CUNTS ARE, THEY TEND NOT TO LAST VERY LONG. HEART ATTACKS AN' BRAIN TUMORS--AN' WHO HAPPENS TO BE THERE EVERY FUCKIN' TIME? WHY, IF IT ISN'T YOUNG *DANIEL WORMWOOD,* BABBLIN' LIKE A HALFWIT AN' TOO TRAUMATISED TO TELL ANYONE ANYTHING USEFUL...
SO IT *DOESN'T TAKE A GENIUS* TO WORK OUT WHAT'S ACTUALLY GOIN' ON HERE, *DOES IT?*
WELL, OBVIOUSLY... IT'S...
WHERE DOES HE HAVE A TATTOO?
OH, GIVE ME FUCKIN' STRENGTH--!
THEY'RE HIS FUCKIN' FOLLOWERS, YER BUNCHA NONGS! THEY KILL THE FOSTER PARENTS, THEN THEY CLUE HIM IN ON WHO HE IS AN' WHAT HE'S GOTTA DO!
BUT *HE KILLS THEM!* ANYONE HIS CLOVEN-HOOFED CUNT OF A DAD SENDS TO EXPLAIN EVERYTHING TO HIM, HE JUST BLOODY MURDERS THE BASTARDS! I MEAN JESUS CHRIST, WHERE D'YER THINK ALL THEM DEAD FUCKIN' ROTWEILERS CAME FROM?

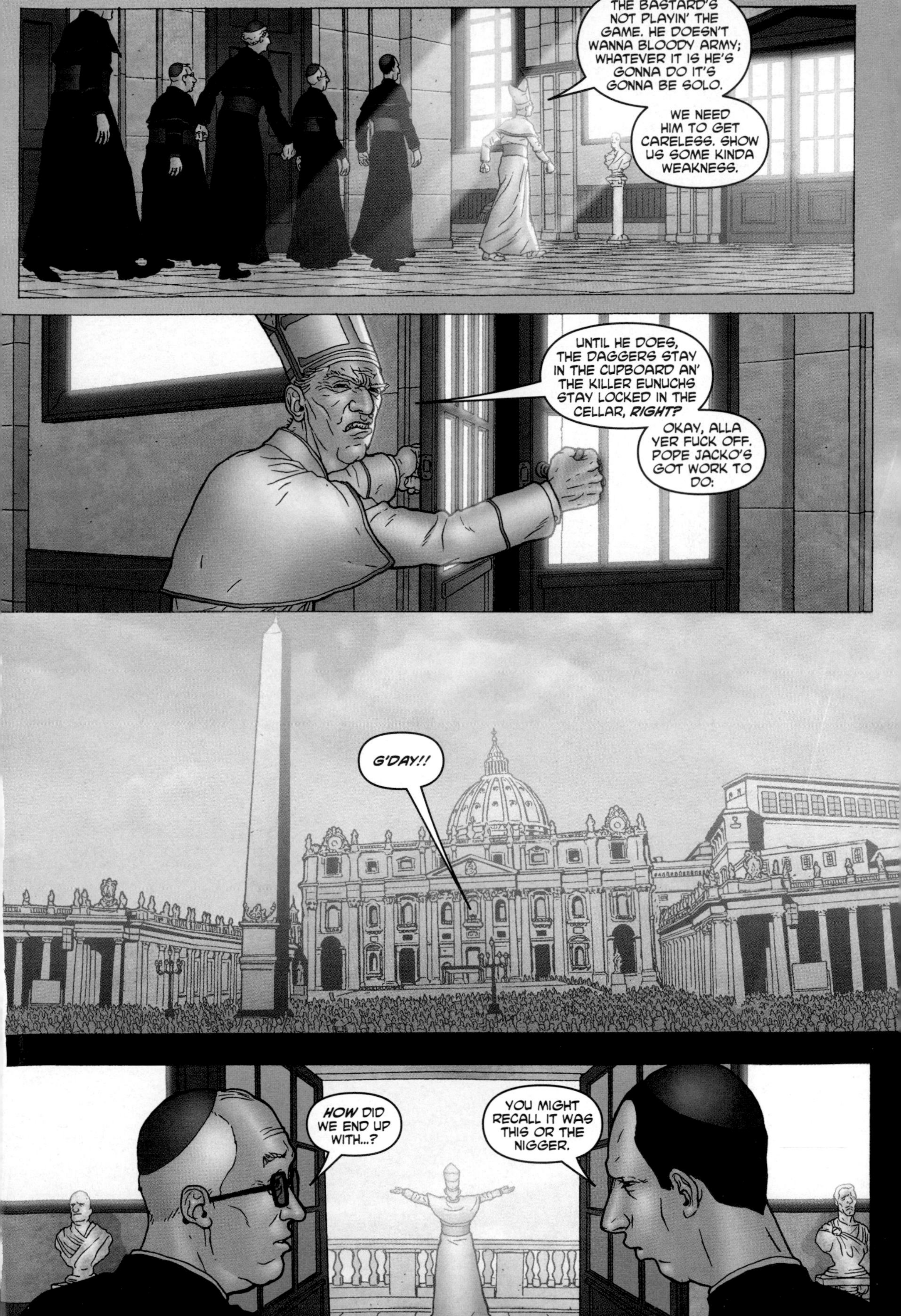
THE BASTARD'S NOT PLAYIN' THE GAME. HE DOESN'T WANNA BLOODY ARMY; WHATEVER IT IS HE'S GONNA DO IT'S GONNA BE SOLO.
WE NEED HIM TO GET CARELESS. SHOW US SOME KINDA WEAKNESS.
UNTIL HE DOES, THE DAGGERS STAY IN THE CUPBOARD AN' THE KILLER EUNUCHS STAY LOCKED IN THE CELLAR, *RIGHT?*
OKAY, ALLA YER FUCK OFF. POPE JACKO'S GOT WORK TO DO:
G'DAY!!
HOW DID WE END UP WITH...?
YOU MIGHT RECALL IT WAS THIS OR THE NIGGER.

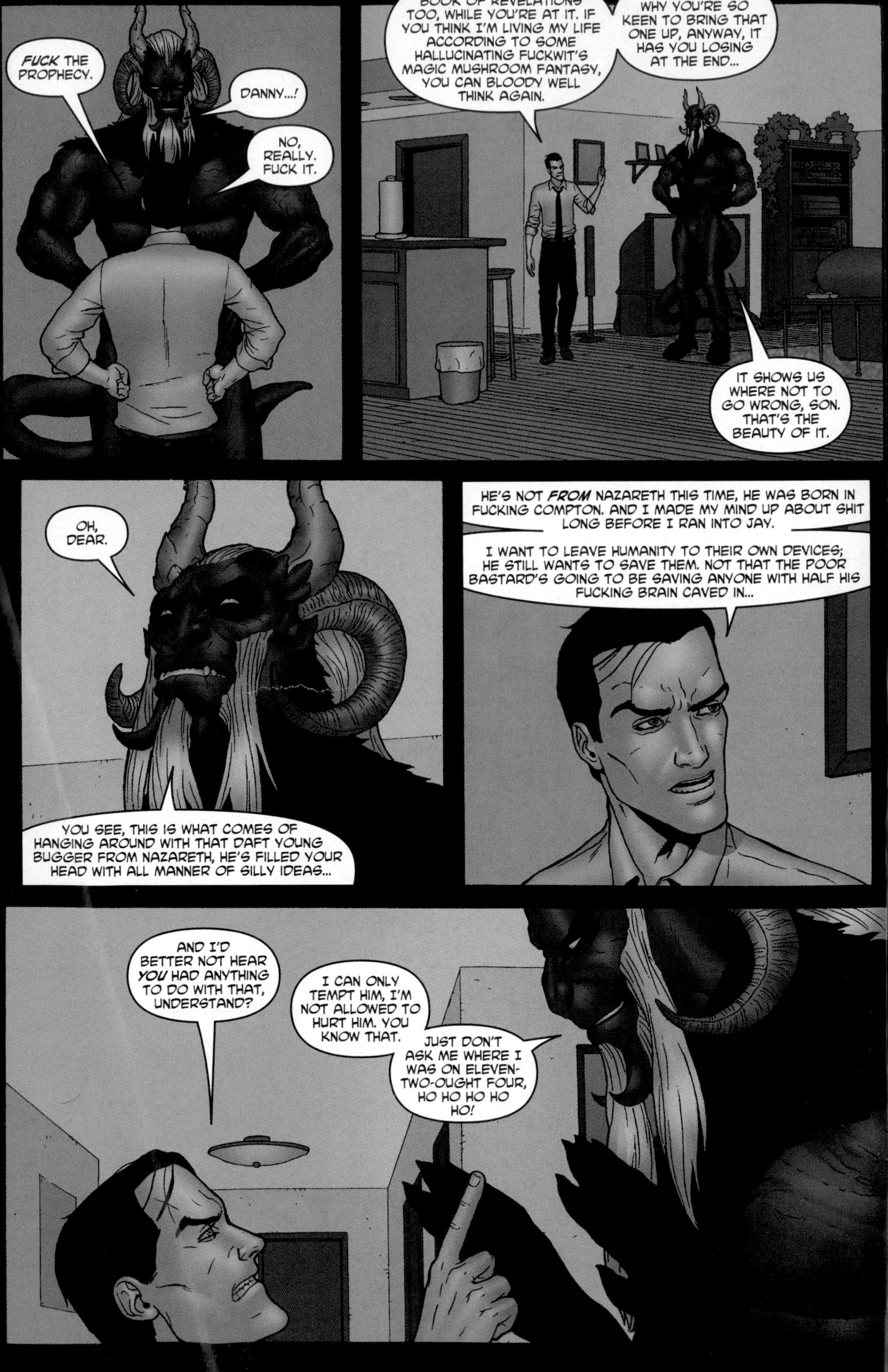
FUCK THE PROPHECY.
DANNY...!
NO, REALLY. FUCK IT.
AND FUCK THE BOOK OF REVELATIONS TOO, WHILE YOU'RE AT IT. IF YOU THINK I'M LIVING MY LIFE ACCORDING TO SOME HALLUCINATING FUCKWIT'S MAGIC MUSHROOM FANTASY, YOU CAN BLOODY WELL THINK AGAIN.
I DON'T KNOW WHY YOU'RE SO KEEN TO BRING THAT ONE UP, ANYWAY, IT HAS YOU LOSING AT THE END...
IT SHOWS US WHERE NOT TO GO WRONG, SON. THAT'S THE BEAUTY OF IT.
OH, DEAR.
YOU SEE, THIS IS WHAT COMES OF HANGING AROUND WITH THAT DAFT YOUNG BUGGER FROM NAZARETH, HE'S FILLED YOUR HEAD WITH ALL MANNER OF SILLY IDEAS...
HE'S NOT *FROM* NAZARETH THIS TIME, HE WAS BORN IN FUCKING COMPTON. AND I MADE MY MIND UP ABOUT SHIT LONG BEFORE I RAN INTO JAY.
I WANT TO LEAVE HUMANITY TO THEIR OWN DEVICES; HE STILL WANTS TO SAVE THEM. NOT THAT THE POOR BASTARD'S GOING TO BE SAVING ANYONE WITH HALF HIS FUCKING BRAIN CAVED IN...
AND I'D BETTER NOT HEAR *YOU* HAD ANYTHING TO DO WITH THAT, UNDERSTAND?
I CAN ONLY TEMPT HIM, I'M NOT ALLOWED TO HURT HIM. YOU KNOW THAT.
JUST DON'T ASK ME WHERE I WAS ON ELEVEN-TWO-OUGHT FOUR, HO HO HO HO HO!

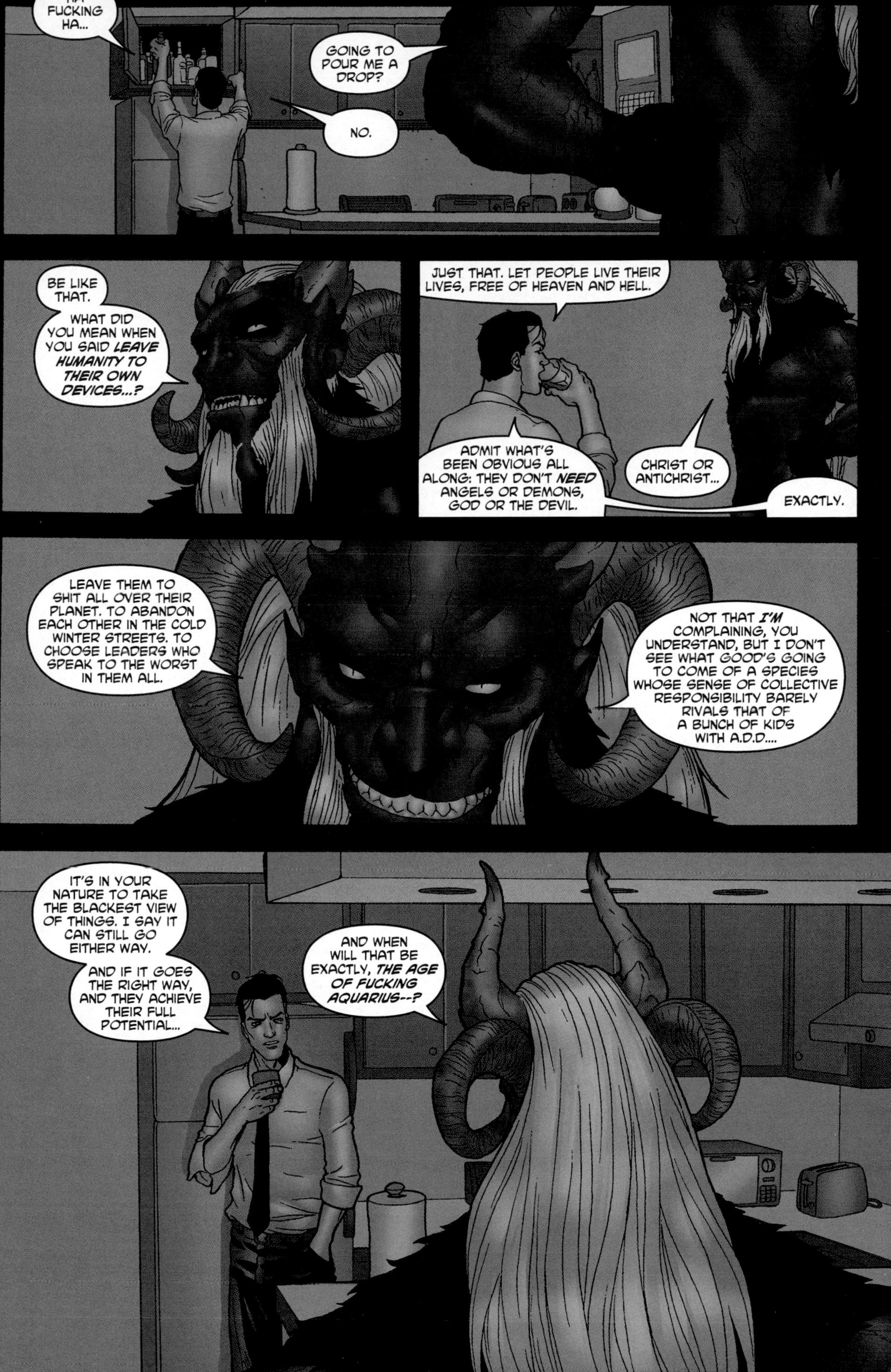
HA FUCKING HA...
GOING TO POUR ME A DROP?
NO.
BE LIKE THAT.
WHAT DID YOU MEAN WHEN YOU SAID *LEAVE HUMANITY TO THEIR OWN DEVICES...?*
JUST THAT. LET PEOPLE LIVE THEIR LIVES, FREE OF HEAVEN AND HELL.
ADMIT WHAT'S BEEN OBVIOUS ALL ALONG: THEY DON'T *NEED* ANGELS OR DEMONS, GOD OR THE DEVIL.
CHRIST OR ANTICHRIST...
EXACTLY.
LEAVE THEM TO SHIT ALL OVER THEIR PLANET. TO ABANDON EACH OTHER IN THE COLD WINTER STREETS. TO CHOOSE LEADERS WHO SPEAK TO THE WORST IN THEM ALL.
NOT THAT *I'M* COMPLAINING, YOU UNDERSTAND, BUT I DON'T SEE WHAT GOOD'S GOING TO COME OF A SPECIES WHOSE SENSE OF COLLECTIVE RESPONSIBILITY BARELY RIVALS THAT OF A BUNCH OF KIDS WITH A.D.D....
IT'S IN YOUR NATURE TO TAKE THE BLACKEST VIEW OF THINGS. I SAY IT CAN STILL GO EITHER WAY.
AND IF IT GOES THE RIGHT WAY, AND THEY ACHIEVE THEIR FULL POTENTIAL...
AND WHEN WILL THAT BE EXACTLY, *THE AGE OF FUCKING AQUARIUS--?*

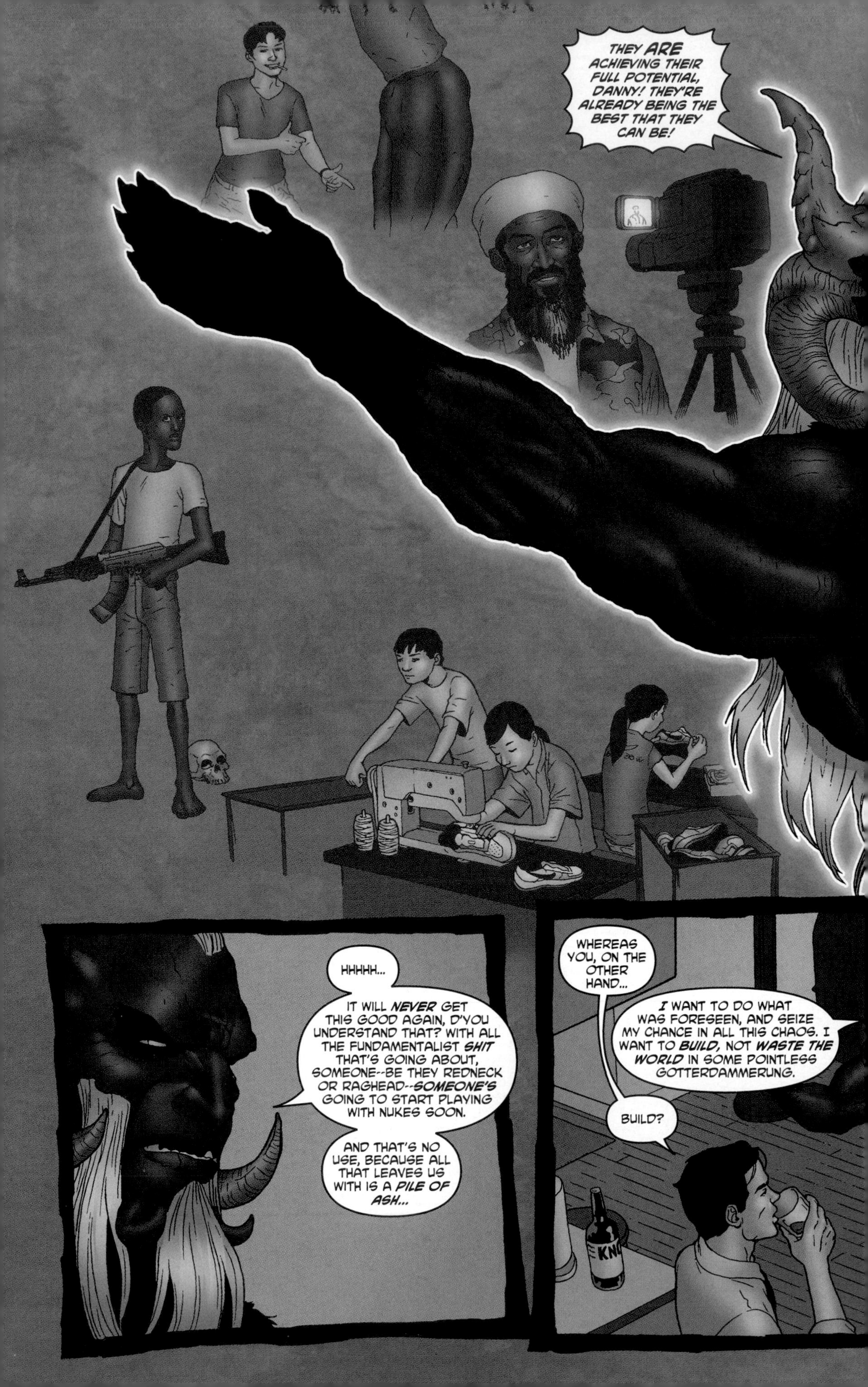
THEY ARE ACHIEVING THEIR FULL POTENTIAL, DANNY! THEY'RE ALREADY BEING THE BEST THAT THEY CAN BE!
HHHHH...
IT WILL NEVER GET THIS GOOD AGAIN, D'YOU UNDERSTAND THAT? WITH ALL THE FUNDAMENTALIST SHIT THAT'S GOING ABOUT, SOMEONE--BE THEY REDNECK OR RAGHEAD--SOMEONE'S GOING TO START PLAYING WITH NUKES SOON.
AND THAT'S NO USE, BECAUSE ALL THAT LEAVES US WITH IS A PILE OF ASH...
WHEREAS YOU, ON THE OTHER HAND...
I WANT TO DO WHAT WAS FORESEEN, AND SEIZE MY CHANCE IN ALL THIS CHAOS. I WANT TO BUILD, NOT WASTE THE WORLD IN SOME POINTLESS GOTTERDAMMERUNG.
BUILD?

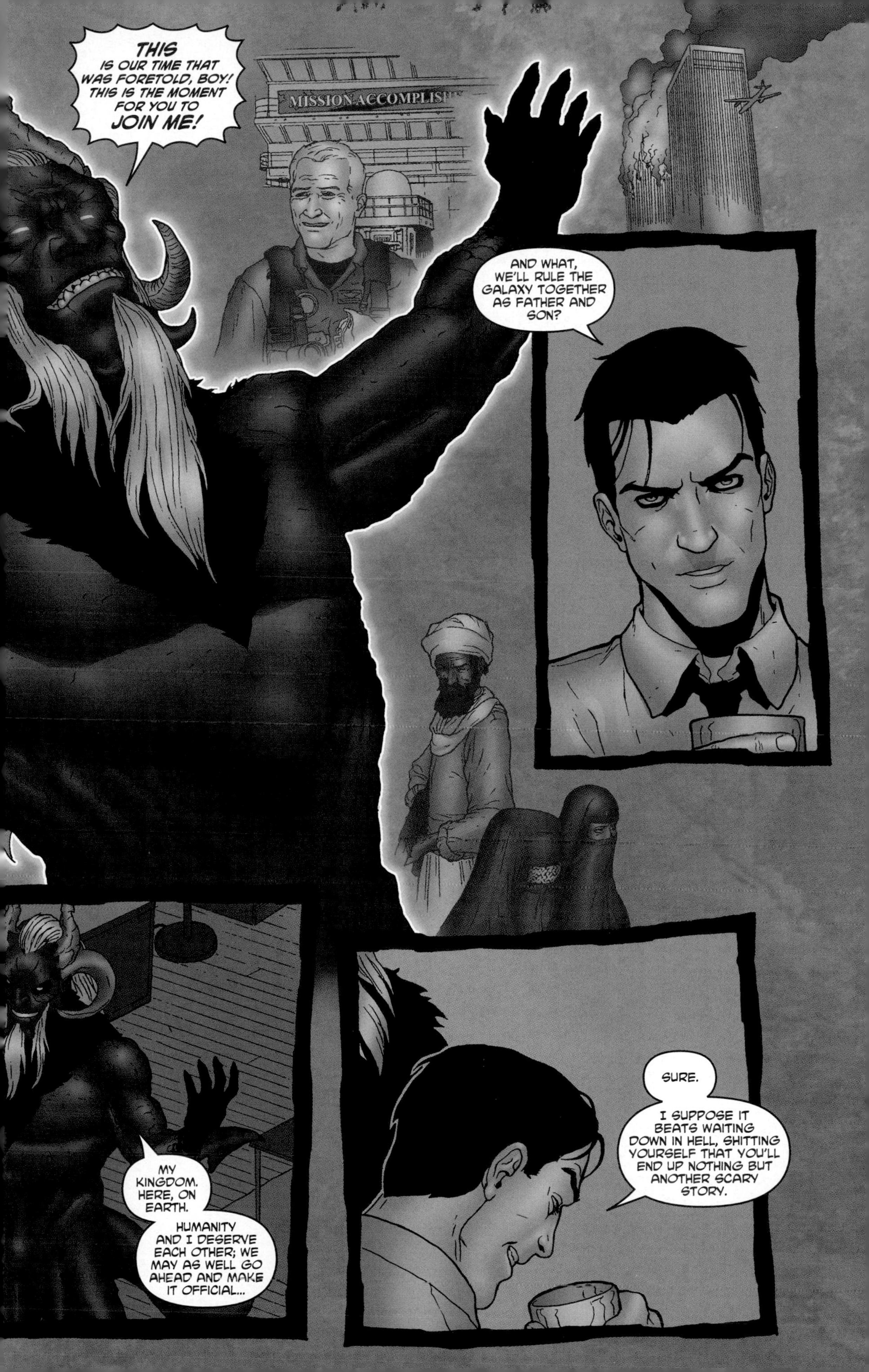
THIS IS OUR TIME THAT WAS FORETOLD, BOY! THIS IS THE MOMENT FOR YOU TO JOIN ME!
MISSION ACCOMPLISH
AND WHAT, WE'LL RULE THE GALAXY TOGETHER AS FATHER AND SON?
MY KINGDOM. HERE, ON EARTH.
HUMANITY AND I DESERVE EACH OTHER; WE MAY AS WELL GO AHEAD AND MAKE IT OFFICIAL...
SURE.
I SUPPOSE IT BEATS WAITING DOWN IN HELL, SHITTING YOURSELF THAT YOU'LL END UP NOTHING BUT ANOTHER SCARY STORY.

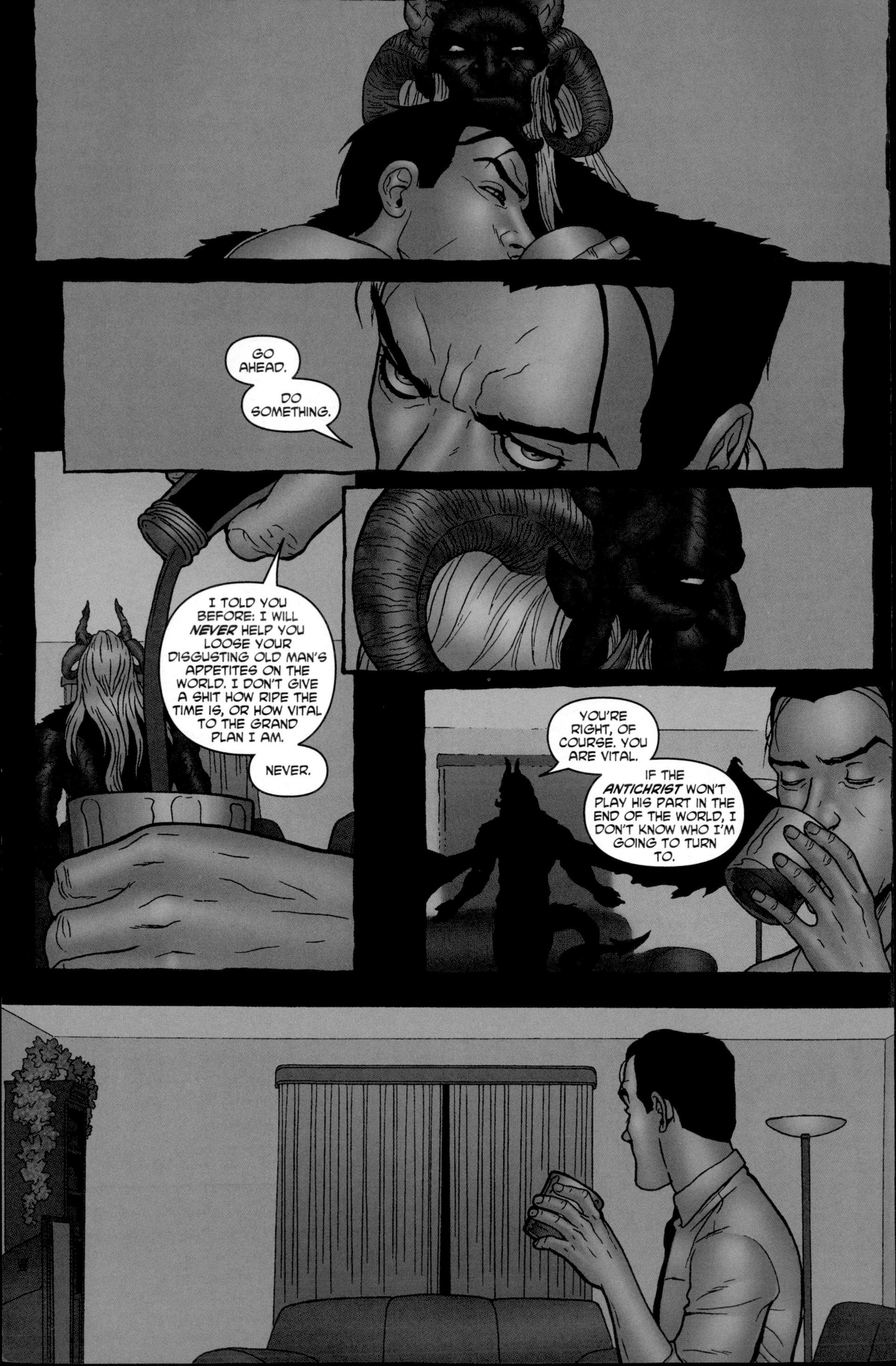
GO AHEAD.
DO SOMETHING.
I TOLD YOU BEFORE: I WILL NEVER HELP YOU LOOSE YOUR DISGUSTING OLD MAN'S APPETITES ON THE WORLD. I DON'T GIVE A SHIT HOW RIPE THE TIME IS, OR HOW VITAL TO THE GRAND PLAN I AM.
NEVER.
YOU'RE RIGHT, OF COURSE. YOU ARE VITAL.
IF THE ANTICHRIST WON'T PLAY HIS PART IN THE END OF THE WORLD, I DON'T KNOW WHO I'M GOING TO TURN TO.

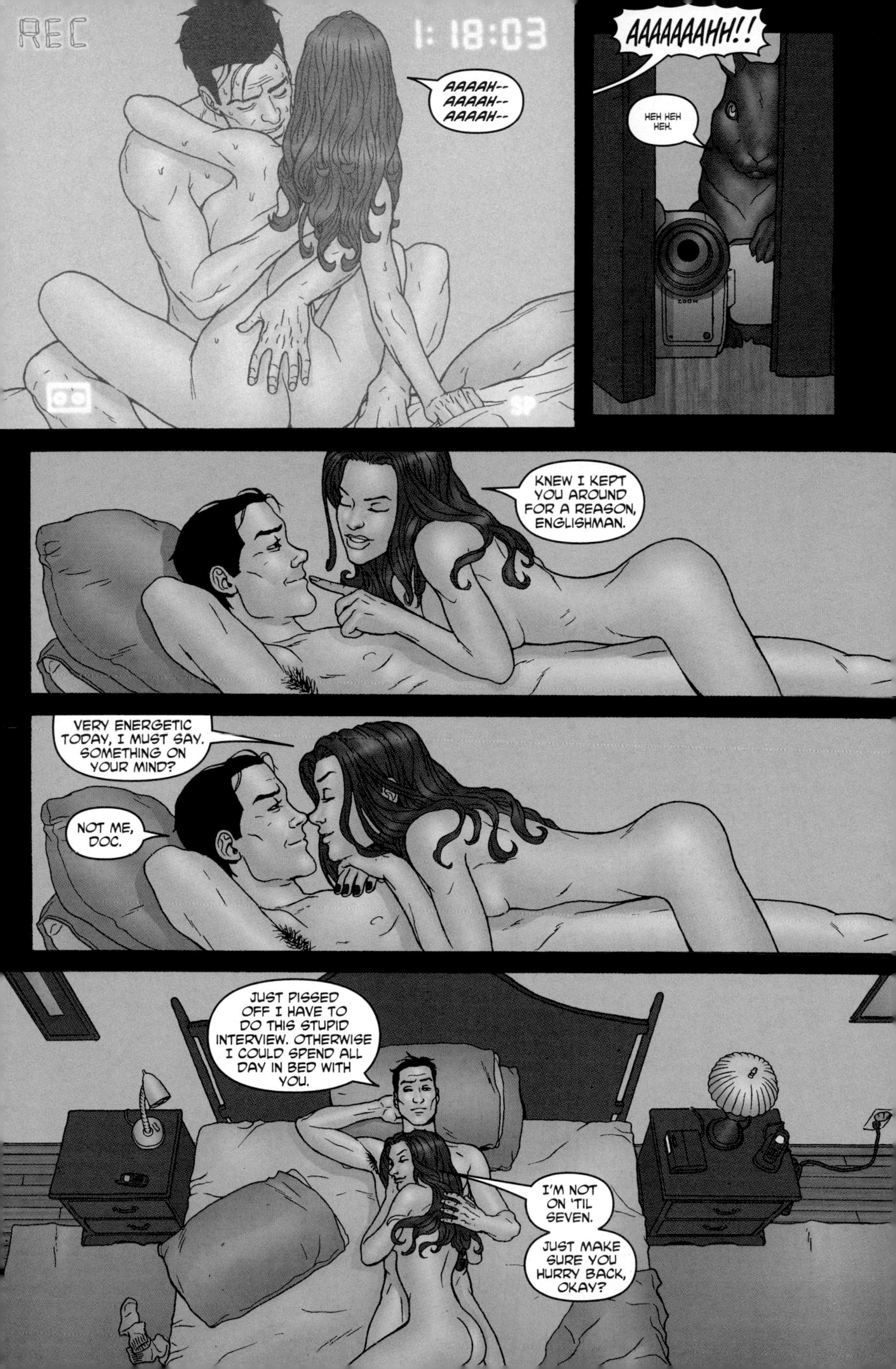
REC
1:18:03
AAAAH--
AAAAH--
AAAAH--
SP
AAAAAAAHH!!
HEH HEH HEH.
ZOOM
KNEW I KEPT YOU AROUND FOR A REASON, ENGLISHMAN.
VERY ENERGETIC TODAY, I MUST SAY. SOMETHING ON YOUR MIND?
NOT ME, DOC.
JUST PISSED OFF I HAVE TO DO THIS STUPID INTERVIEW. OTHERWISE I COULD SPEND ALL DAY IN BED WITH YOU.
I'M NOT ON 'TIL SEVEN.
JUST MAKE SURE YOU HURRY BACK, OKAY?

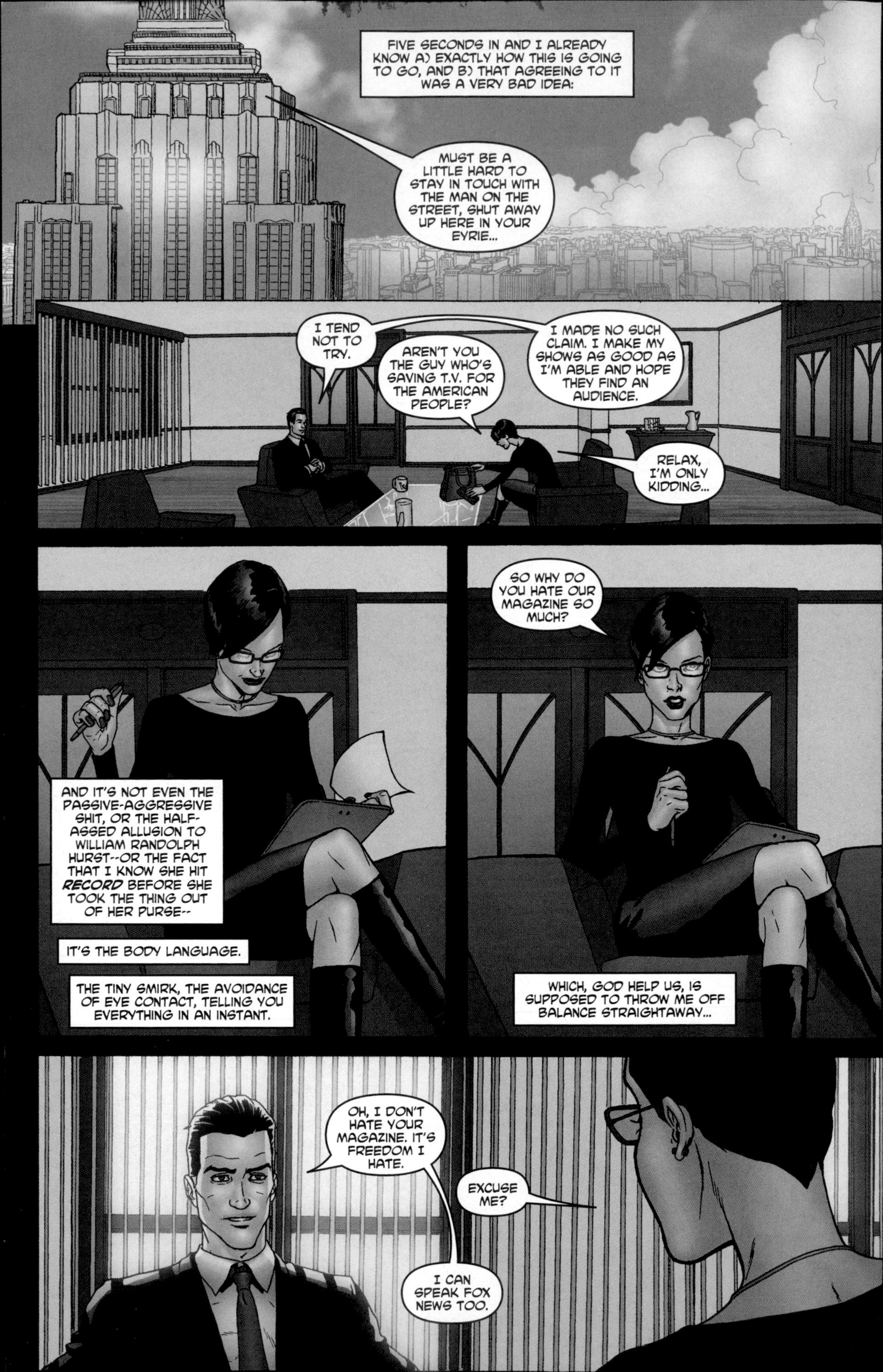

FIVE SECONDS IN AND I ALREADY KNOW A) EXACTLY HOW THIS IS GOING TO GO, AND B) THAT AGREEING TO IT WAS A VERY BAD IDEA:
MUST BE A LITTLE HARD TO STAY IN TOUCH WITH THE MAN ON THE STREET, SHUT AWAY UP HERE IN YOUR EYRIE...
I TEND NOT TO TRY.
AREN'T YOU THE GUY WHO'S SAVING T.V. FOR THE AMERICAN PEOPLE?
I MADE NO SUCH CLAIM. I MAKE MY SHOWS AS GOOD AS I'M ABLE AND HOPE THEY FIND AN AUDIENCE.
RELAX, I'M ONLY KIDDING...
AND IT'S NOT EVEN THE PASSIVE-AGGRESSIVE SHIT, OR THE HALF-ASSED ALLUSION TO WILLIAM RANDOLPH HURST--OR THE FACT THAT I KNOW SHE HIT *RECORD* BEFORE SHE TOOK THE THING OUT OF HER PURSE--
IT'S THE BODY LANGUAGE.
THE TINY SMIRK, THE AVOIDANCE OF EYE CONTACT, TELLING YOU EVERYTHING IN AN INSTANT.
SO WHY DO YOU HATE OUR MAGAZINE SO MUCH?
WHICH, GOD HELP US, IS SUPPOSED TO THROW ME OFF BALANCE STRAIGHTAWAY...
OH, I DON'T HATE YOUR MAGAZINE. IT'S FREEDOM I HATE.
EXCUSE ME?
I CAN SPEAK FOX NEWS TOO.

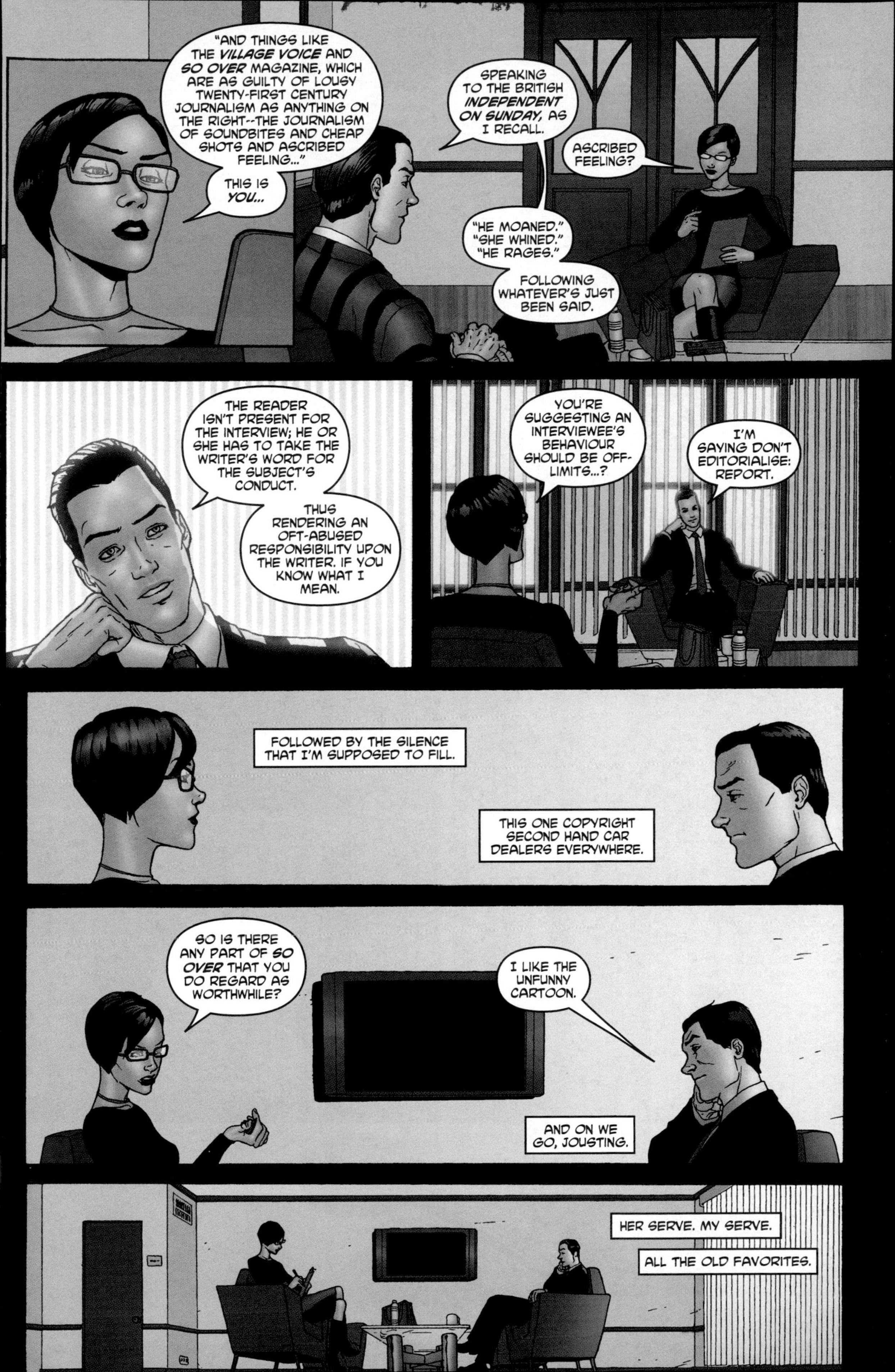
"AND THINGS LIKE THE VILLAGE VOICE AND SO OVER MAGAZINE, WHICH ARE AS GUILTY OF LOUSY TWENTY-FIRST CENTURY JOURNALISM AS ANYTHING ON THE RIGHT--THE JOURNALISM OF SOUNDBITES AND CHEAP SHOTS AND ASCRIBED FEELING..."
THIS IS YOU...
SPEAKING TO THE BRITISH INDEPENDENT ON SUNDAY, AS I RECALL.
ASCRIBED FEELING?
"HE MOANED." "SHE WHINED." "HE RAGES."
FOLLOWING WHATEVER'S JUST BEEN SAID.
THE READER ISN'T PRESENT FOR THE INTERVIEW; HE OR SHE HAS TO TAKE THE WRITER'S WORD FOR THE SUBJECT'S CONDUCT.
THUS RENDERING AN OFT-ABUSED RESPONSIBILITY UPON THE WRITER. IF YOU KNOW WHAT I MEAN.
YOU'RE SUGGESTING AN INTERVIEWEE'S BEHAVIOUR SHOULD BE OFF-LIMITS...?
I'M SAYING DON'T EDITORIALISE: REPORT.
FOLLOWED BY THE SILENCE THAT I'M SUPPOSED TO FILL.
THIS ONE COPYRIGHT SECOND HAND CAR DEALERS EVERYWHERE.
SO IS THERE ANY PART OF SO OVER THAT YOU DO REGARD AS WORTHWHILE?
I LIKE THE UNFUNNY CARTOON.
AND ON WE GO, JOUSTING.
HER SERVE. MY SERVE.
ALL THE OLD FAVORITES.

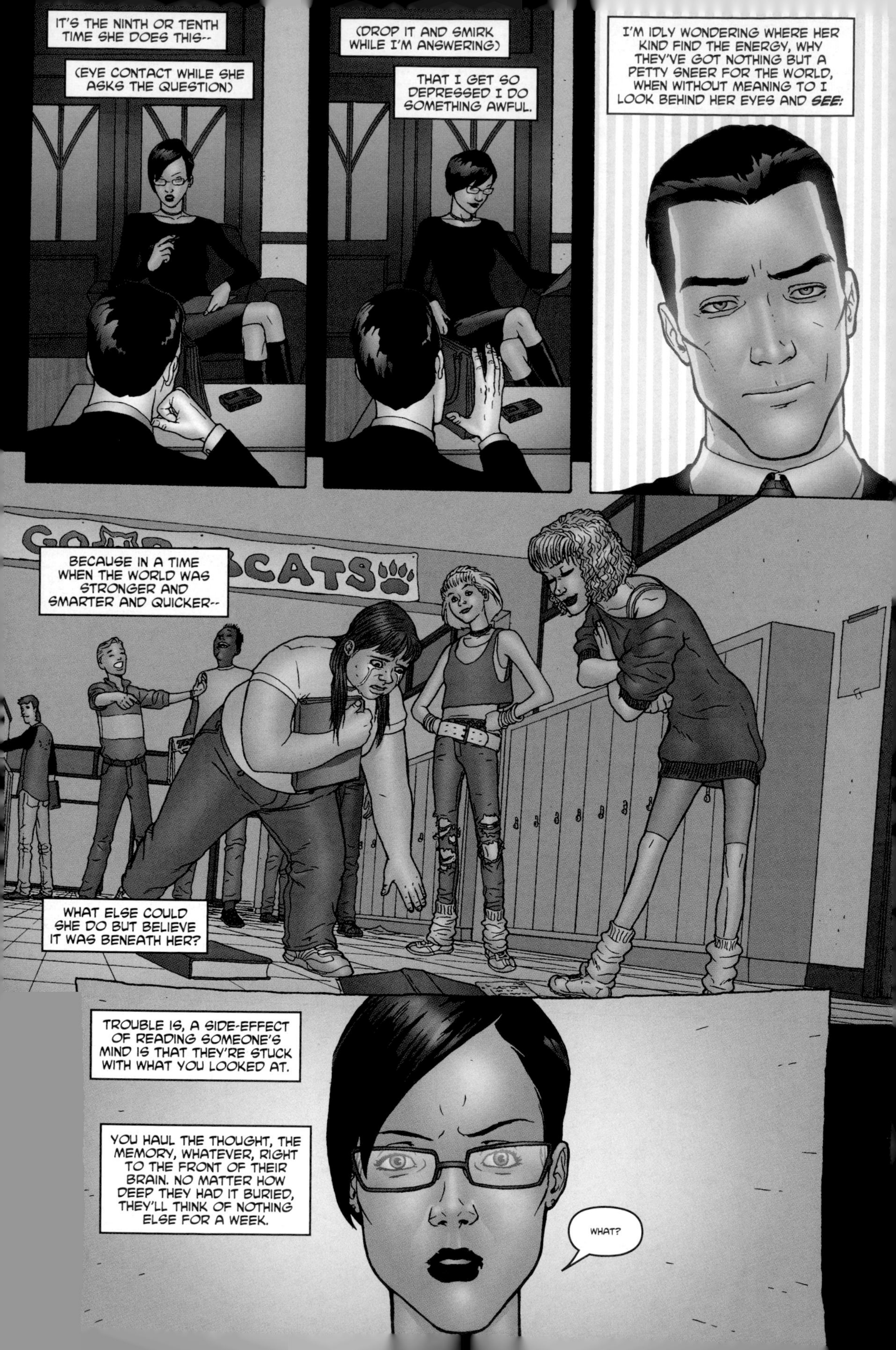
IT'S THE NINTH OR TENTH TIME SHE DOES THIS--
(EYE CONTACT WHILE SHE ASKS THE QUESTION)
(DROP IT AND SMIRK WHILE I'M ANSWERING)
THAT I GET SO DEPRESSED I DO SOMETHING AWFUL.
I'M IDLY WONDERING WHERE HER KIND FIND THE ENERGY, WHY THEY'VE GOT NOTHING BUT A PETTY SNEER FOR THE WORLD, WHEN WITHOUT MEANING TO I LOOK BEHIND HER EYES AND ***SEE:***
BECAUSE IN A TIME WHEN THE WORLD WAS STRONGER AND SMARTER AND QUICKER--
CATS
WHAT ELSE COULD SHE DO BUT BELIEVE IT WAS BENEATH HER?
TROUBLE IS, A SIDE-EFFECT OF READING SOMEONE'S MIND IS THAT THEY'RE STUCK WITH WHAT YOU LOOKED AT.
YOU HAUL THE THOUGHT, THE MEMORY, WHATEVER, RIGHT TO THE FRONT OF THEIR BRAIN. NO MATTER HOW DEEP THEY HAD IT BURIED, THEY'LL THINK OF NOTHING ELSE FOR A WEEK.
WHAT?

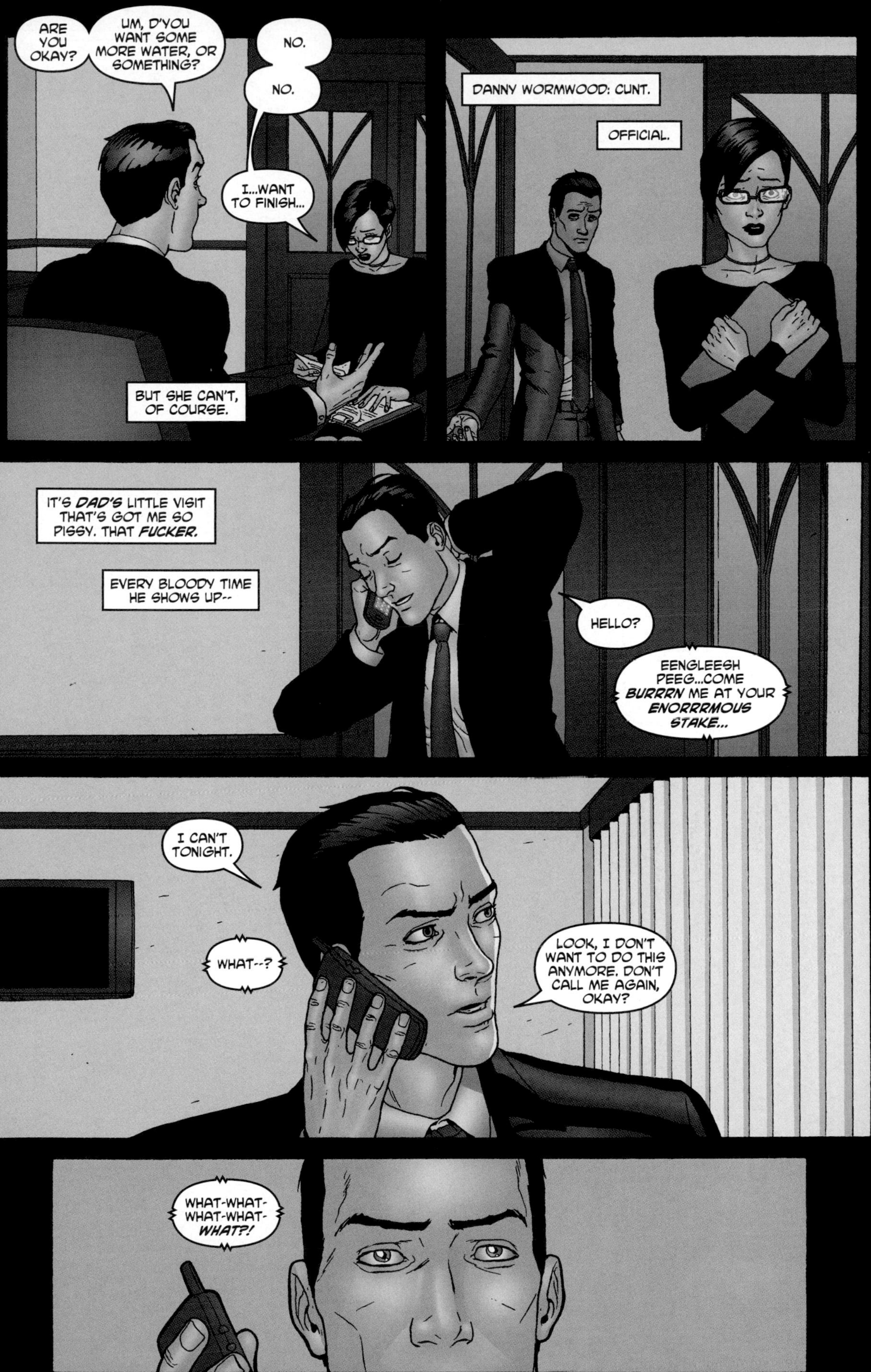
ARE YOU OKAY?
UM, D'YOU WANT SOME MORE WATER, OR SOMETHING?
NO.
NO.
I...WANT TO FINISH...
BUT SHE CAN'T, OF COURSE.
DANNY WORMWOOD: CUNT.
OFFICIAL.
IT'S DAD'S LITTLE VISIT THAT'S GOT ME SO PISSY. THAT FUCKER.
EVERY BLOODY TIME HE SHOWS UP--
HELLO?
EENGLEESH PEEG...COME BURRRN ME AT YOUR ENORRRMOUS STAKE...
I CAN'T TONIGHT.
WHAT--?
LOOK, I DON'T WANT TO DO THIS ANYMORE. DON'T CALL ME AGAIN, OKAY?
WHAT-WHAT-WHAT-WHAT-WHAT?!

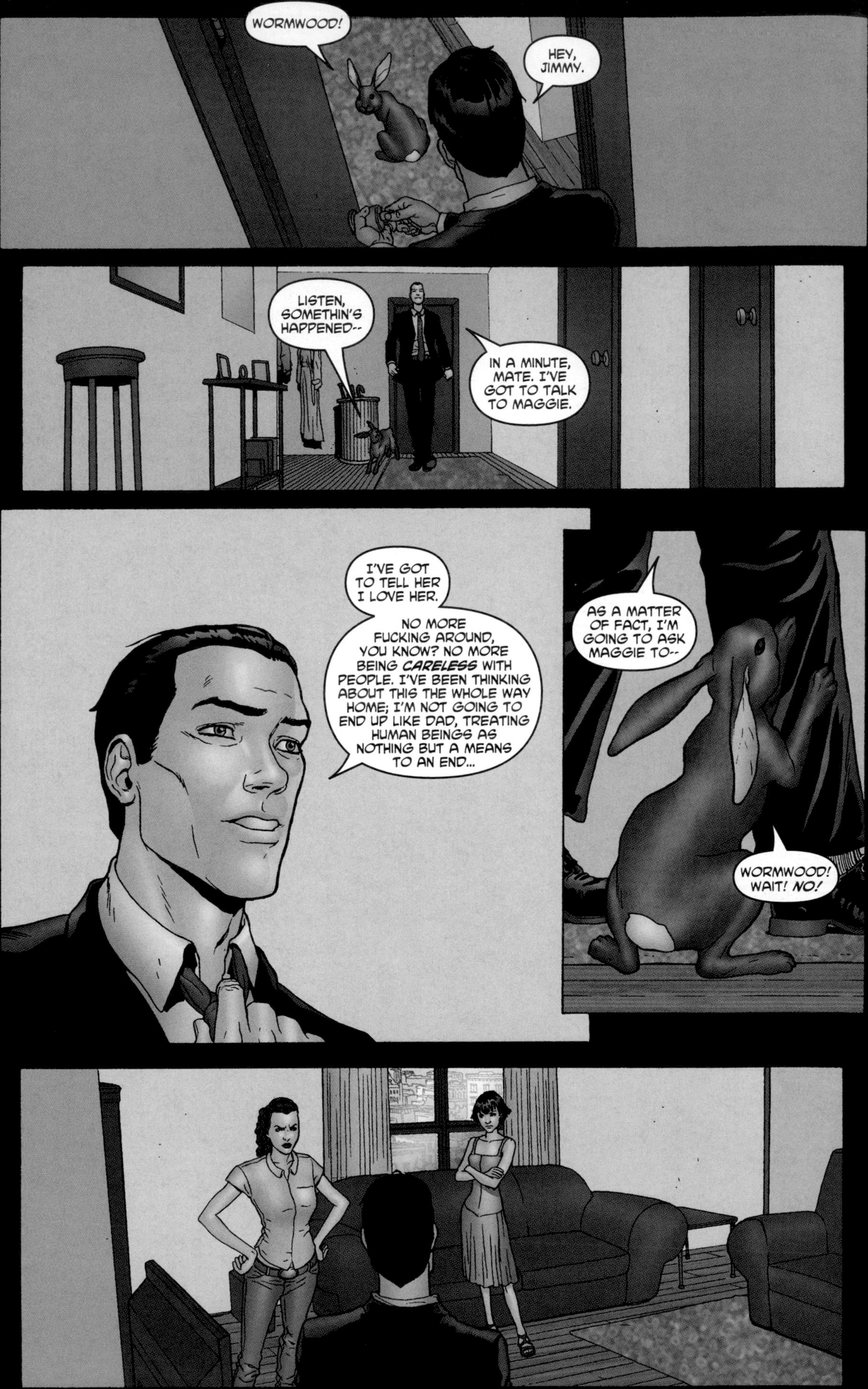
WORMWOOD!
HEY, JIMMY.
LISTEN, SOMETHIN'S HAPPENED--
IN A MINUTE, MATE. I'VE GOT TO TALK TO MAGGIE.
I'VE GOT TO TELL HER I LOVE HER.
NO MORE FUCKING AROUND, YOU KNOW? NO MORE BEING *CARELESS* WITH PEOPLE. I'VE BEEN THINKING ABOUT THIS THE WHOLE WAY HOME; I'M NOT GOING TO END UP LIKE DAD, TREATING HUMAN BEINGS AS NOTHING BUT A MEANS TO AN END...
AS A MATTER OF FACT, I'M GOING TO ASK MAGGIE TO--
WORMWOOD! WAIT! *NO!*

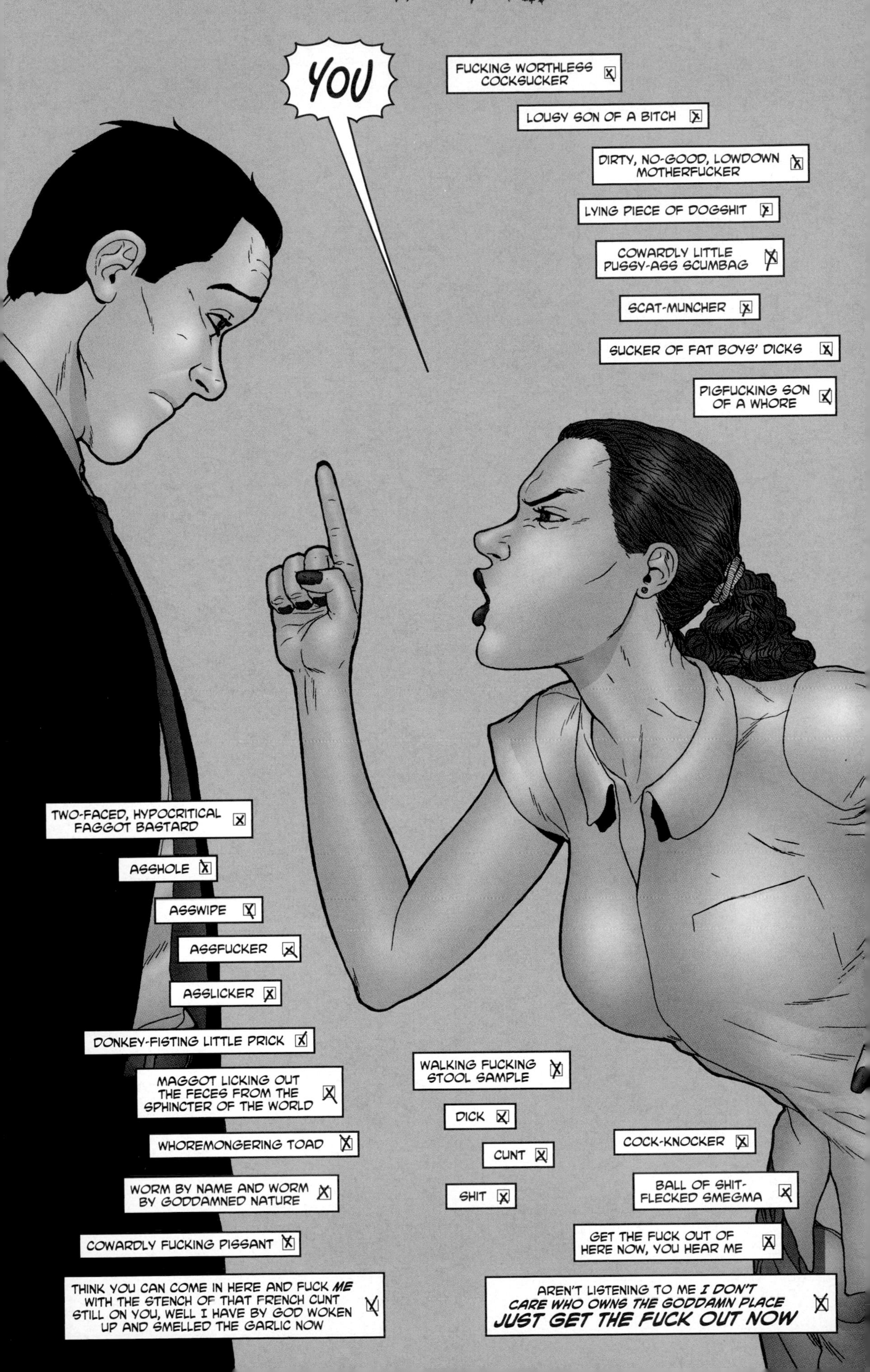
YOU
FUCKING WORTHLESS COCKSUCKER
LOUSY SON OF A BITCH
DIRTY, NO-GOOD, LOWDOWN MOTHERFUCKER
LYING PIECE OF DOGSHIT
COWARDLY LITTLE PUSSY-ASS SCUMBAG
SCAT-MUNCHER
SUCKER OF FAT BOYS' DICKS
PIGFUCKING SON OF A WHORE
TWO-FACED, HYPOCRITICAL FAGGOT BASTARD
ASSHOLE
ASSWIPE
ASSFUCKER
ASSLICKER
DONKEY-FISTING LITTLE PRICK
MAGGOT LICKING OUT THE FECES FROM THE SPHINCTER OF THE WORLD
WHOREMONGERING TOAD
WORM BY NAME AND WORM BY GODDAMNED NATURE
COWARDLY FUCKING PISSANT
THINK YOU CAN COME IN HERE AND FUCK *ME* WITH THE STENCH OF THAT FRENCH CUNT STILL ON YOU, WELL I HAVE BY GOD WOKEN UP AND SMELLED THE GARLIC NOW
WALKING FUCKING STOOL SAMPLE
DICK
CUNT
SHIT
COCK-KNOCKER
BALL OF SHIT-FLECKED SMEGMA
GET THE FUCK OUT OF HERE NOW, YOU HEAR ME
AREN'T LISTENING TO ME *I DON'T CARE WHO OWNS THE GODDAMN PLACE* ***JUST GET THE FUCK OUT NOW***

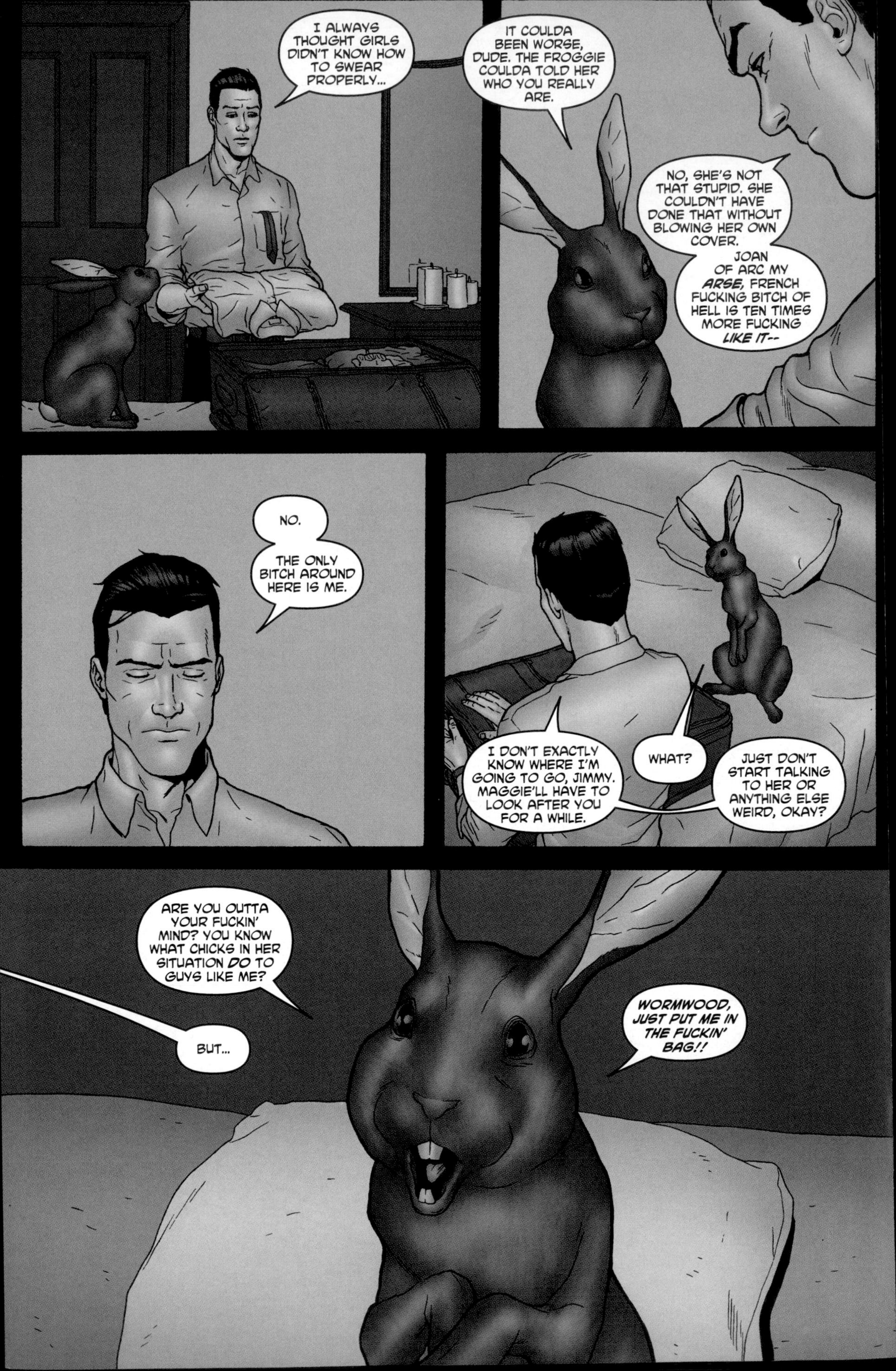
I ALWAYS THOUGHT GIRLS DIDN'T KNOW HOW TO SWEAR PROPERLY...
IT COULDA BEEN WORSE, DUDE. THE FROGGIE COULDA TOLD HER WHO YOU REALLY ARE.
NO, SHE'S NOT THAT STUPID. SHE COULDN'T HAVE DONE THAT WITHOUT BLOWING HER OWN COVER.
JOAN OF ARC MY ***ARSE***, FRENCH FUCKING BITCH OF HELL IS TEN TIMES MORE FUCKING ***LIKE IT--***
NO.
THE ONLY BITCH AROUND HERE IS ME.
I DON'T EXACTLY KNOW WHERE I'M GOING TO GO, JIMMY. MAGGIE'LL HAVE TO LOOK AFTER YOU FOR A WHILE.
WHAT?
JUST DON'T START TALKING TO HER OR ANYTHING ELSE WEIRD, OKAY?
ARE YOU OUTTA YOUR FUCKIN' MIND? YOU KNOW WHAT CHICKS IN HER SITUATION ***DO*** TO GUYS LIKE ME?
BUT...
WORMWOOD, JUST PUT ME IN THE FUCKIN' BAG!!

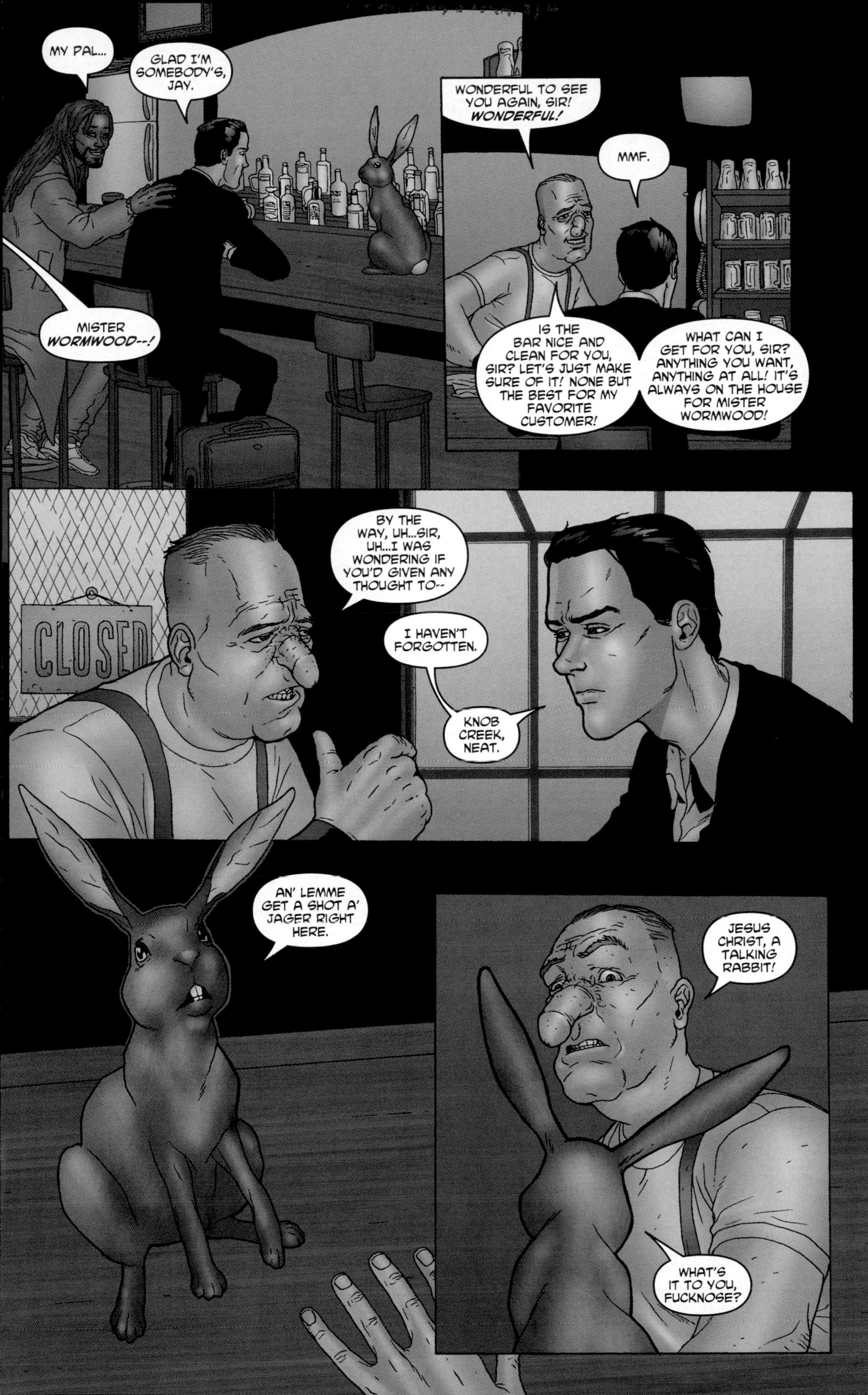
MY PAL...
GLAD I'M SOMEBODY'S, JAY.
MISTER WORMWOOD--!
WONDERFUL TO SEE YOU AGAIN, SIR! WONDERFUL!
MMF.
IS THE BAR NICE AND CLEAN FOR YOU, SIR? LET'S JUST MAKE SURE OF IT! NONE BUT THE BEST FOR MY FAVORITE CUSTOMER!
WHAT CAN I GET FOR YOU, SIR? ANYTHING YOU WANT, ANYTHING AT ALL! IT'S ALWAYS ON THE HOUSE FOR MISTER WORMWOOD!
CLOSED
BY THE WAY, UH...SIR, UH...I WAS WONDERING IF YOU'D GIVEN ANY THOUGHT TO--
I HAVEN'T FORGOTTEN.
KNOB CREEK, NEAT.
AN' LEMME GET A SHOT A' JAGER RIGHT HERE.
JESUS CHRIST, A TALKING RABBIT!
WHAT'S IT TO YOU, FUCKNOSE?

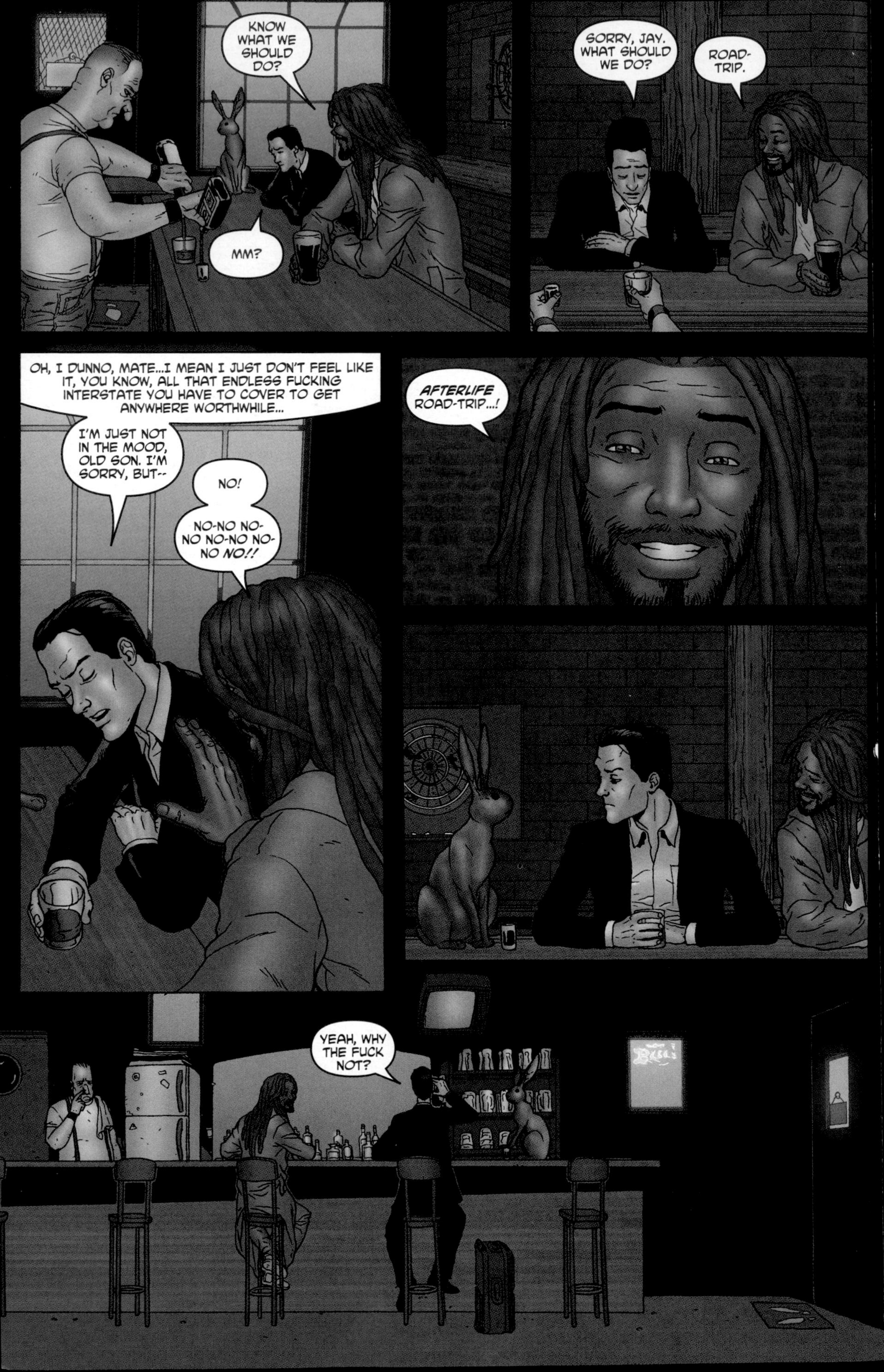
KNOW WHAT WE SHOULD DO?
MM?
SORRY, JAY. WHAT SHOULD WE DO?
ROAD-TRIP.
OH, I DUNNO, MATE...I MEAN I JUST DON'T FEEL LIKE IT, YOU KNOW, ALL THAT ENDLESS FUCKING INTERSTATE YOU HAVE TO COVER TO GET ANYWHERE WORTHWHILE...
I'M JUST NOT IN THE MOOD, OLD SON. I'M SORRY, BUT--
NO!
NO-NO NO-NO NO-NO NO-NO *NO!!*
AFTERLIFE ROAD-TRIP...!
YEAH, WHY THE FUCK NOT?

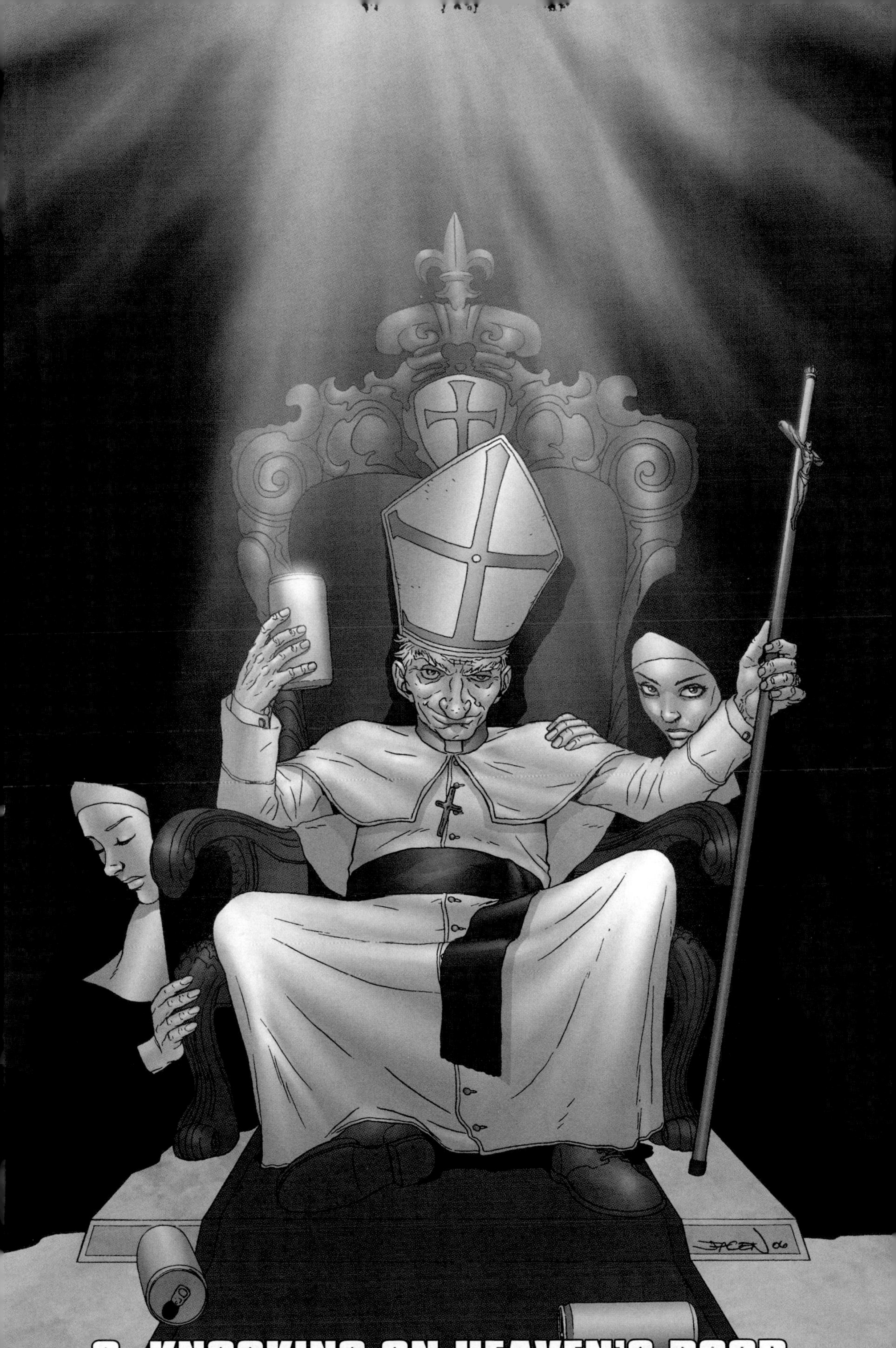

3: KNOCKING ON HEAVEN'S DOOR

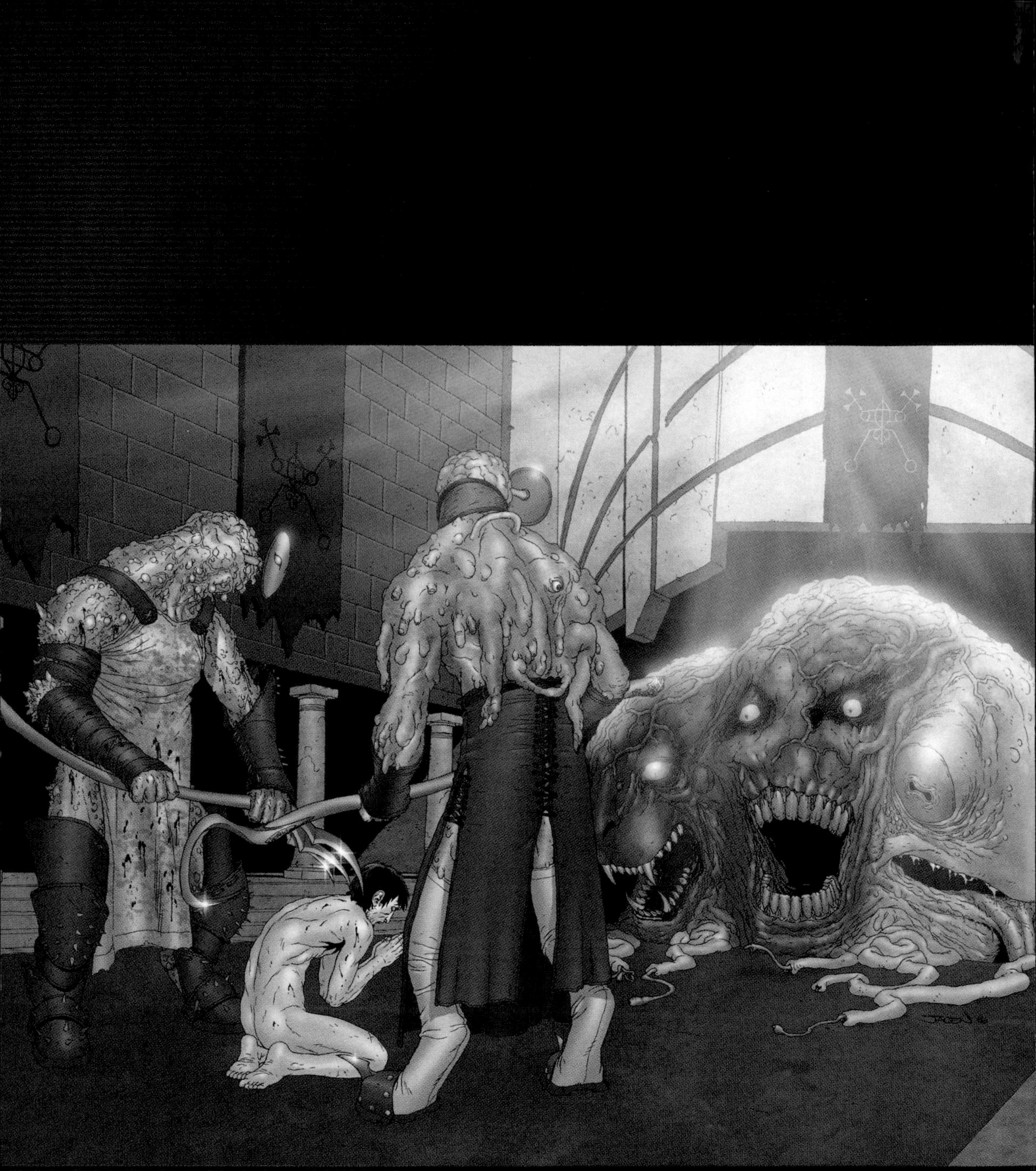

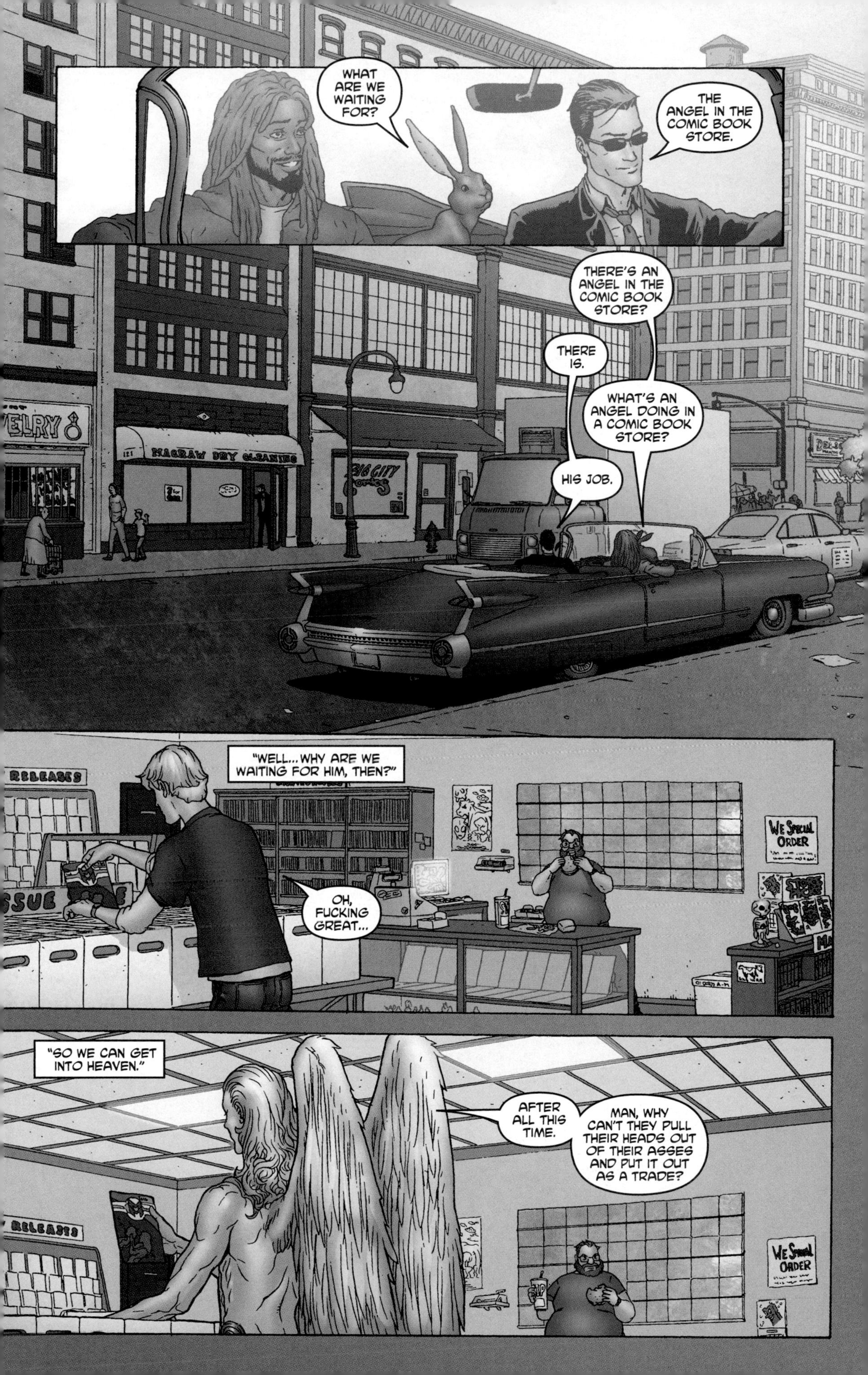
WHAT ARE WE WAITING FOR?
THE ANGEL IN THE COMIC BOOK STORE.
THERE'S AN ANGEL IN THE COMIC BOOK STORE?
THERE IS.
WHAT'S AN ANGEL DOING IN A COMIC BOOK STORE?
HIS JOB.
MAGRAW DRY CLEANING
BIG CITY Comics
"WELL...WHY ARE WE WAITING FOR HIM, THEN?"
OH, FUCKING GREAT...
WE SPECIAL ORDER
"SO WE CAN GET INTO HEAVEN."
AFTER ALL THIS TIME.
MAN, WHY CAN'T THEY PULL THEIR HEADS OUT OF THEIR ASSES AND PUT IT OUT AS A TRADE?
RELEASES
WE SPECIAL ORDER

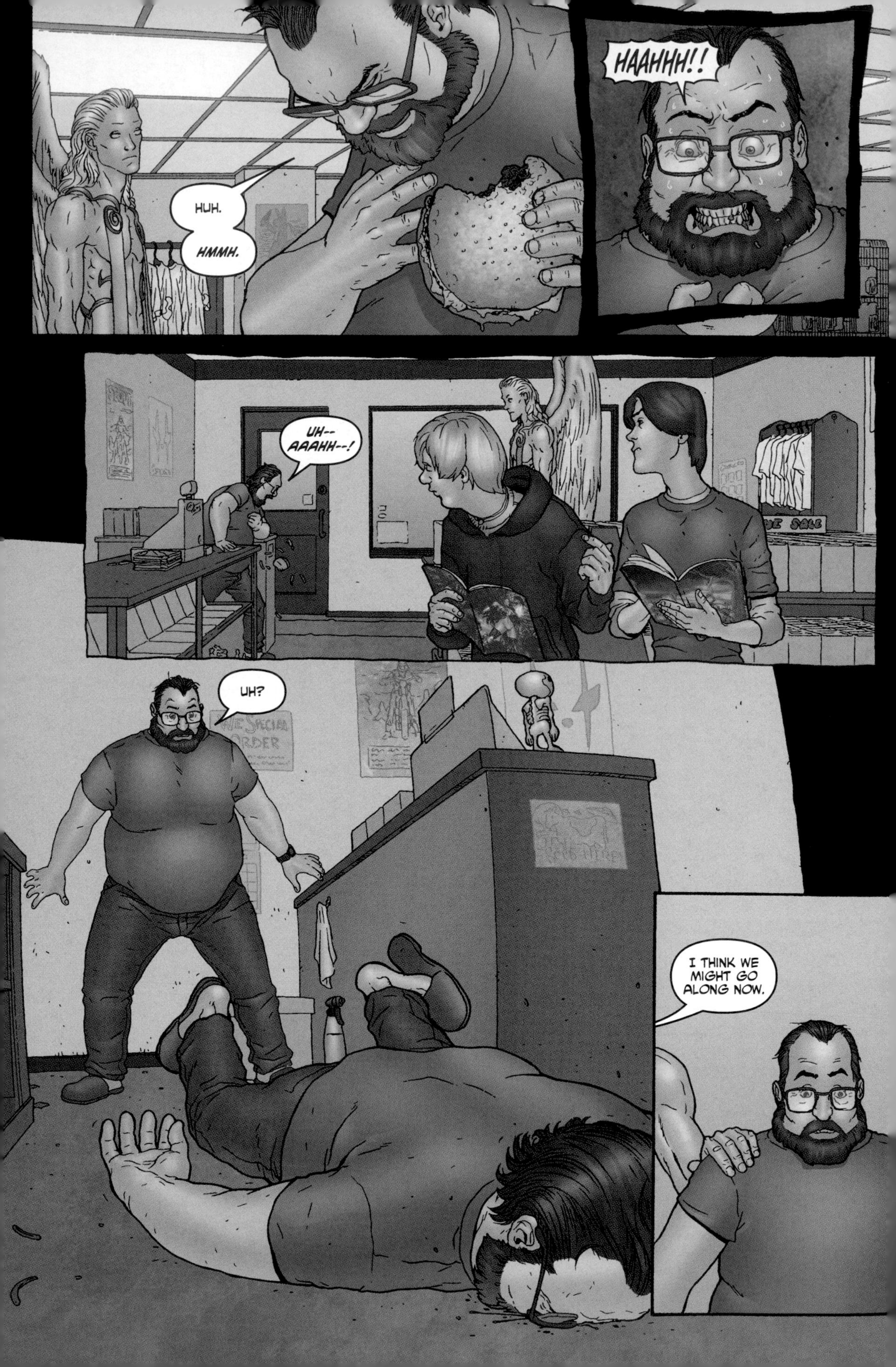

HUH.
HMMH.
HAAHHH!!
UH--
AAAHH--!
UH?
I THINK WE MIGHT GO ALONG NOW.

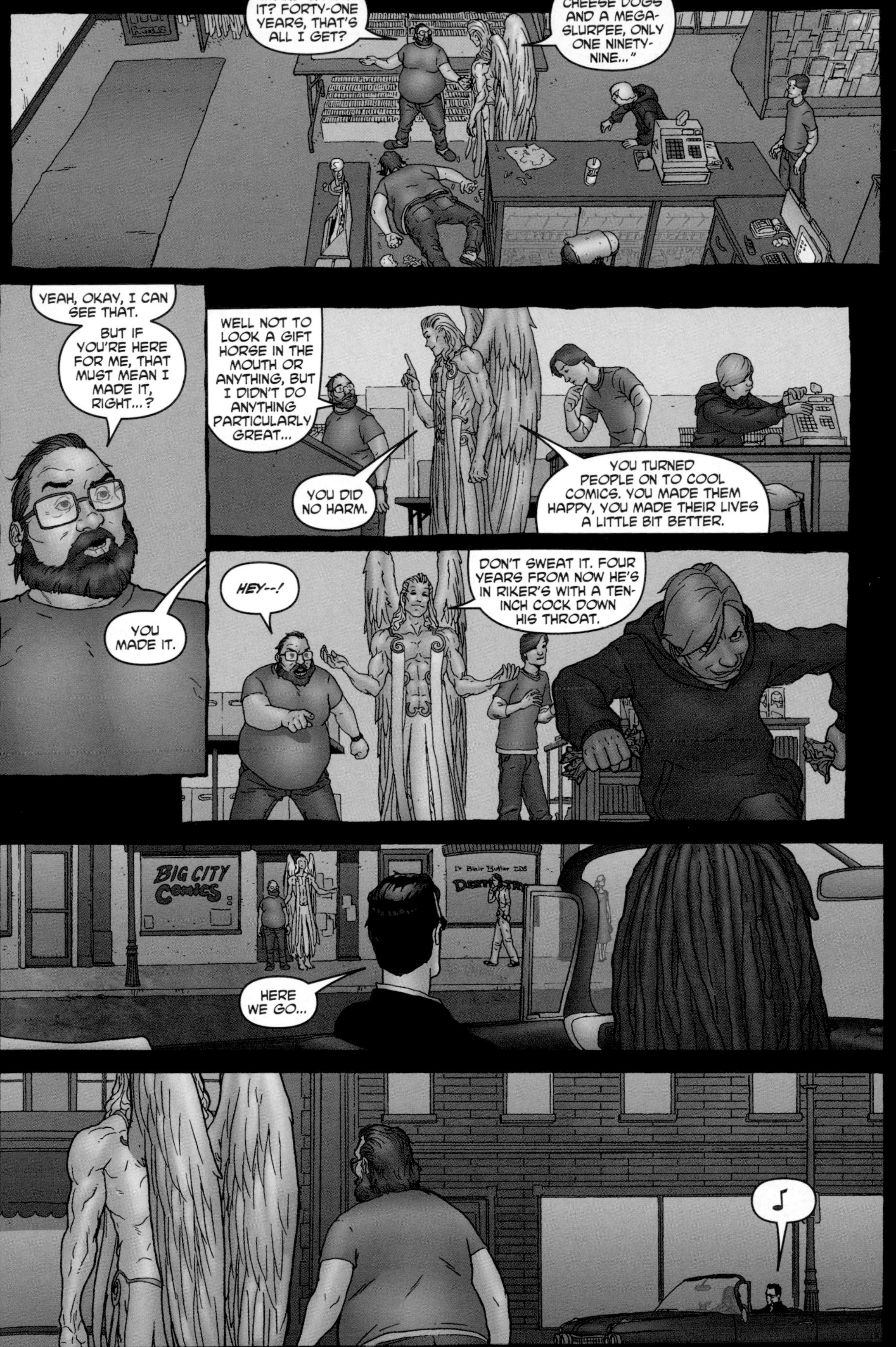
...AND THAT'S IT? FORTY-ONE YEARS, THAT'S ALL I GET?
"TWO CHILI-CHEESE DOGS AND A MEGA-SLURPEE, ONLY ONE NINETY-NINE..."
YEAH, OKAY, I CAN SEE THAT.
BUT IF YOU'RE HERE FOR ME, THAT MUST MEAN I MADE IT, RIGHT...?
YOU MADE IT.
WELL NOT TO LOOK A GIFT HORSE IN THE MOUTH OR ANYTHING, BUT I DIDN'T DO ANYTHING PARTICULARLY GREAT...
YOU DID NO HARM.
YOU TURNED PEOPLE ON TO COOL COMICS. YOU MADE THEM HAPPY, YOU MADE THEIR LIVES A LITTLE BIT BETTER.
HEY--!
DON'T SWEAT IT. FOUR YEARS FROM NOW HE'S IN RIKER'S WITH A TEN-INCH COCK DOWN HIS THROAT.
BIG CITY COMICS
Dr Blair Butler DDS
HERE WE GO...

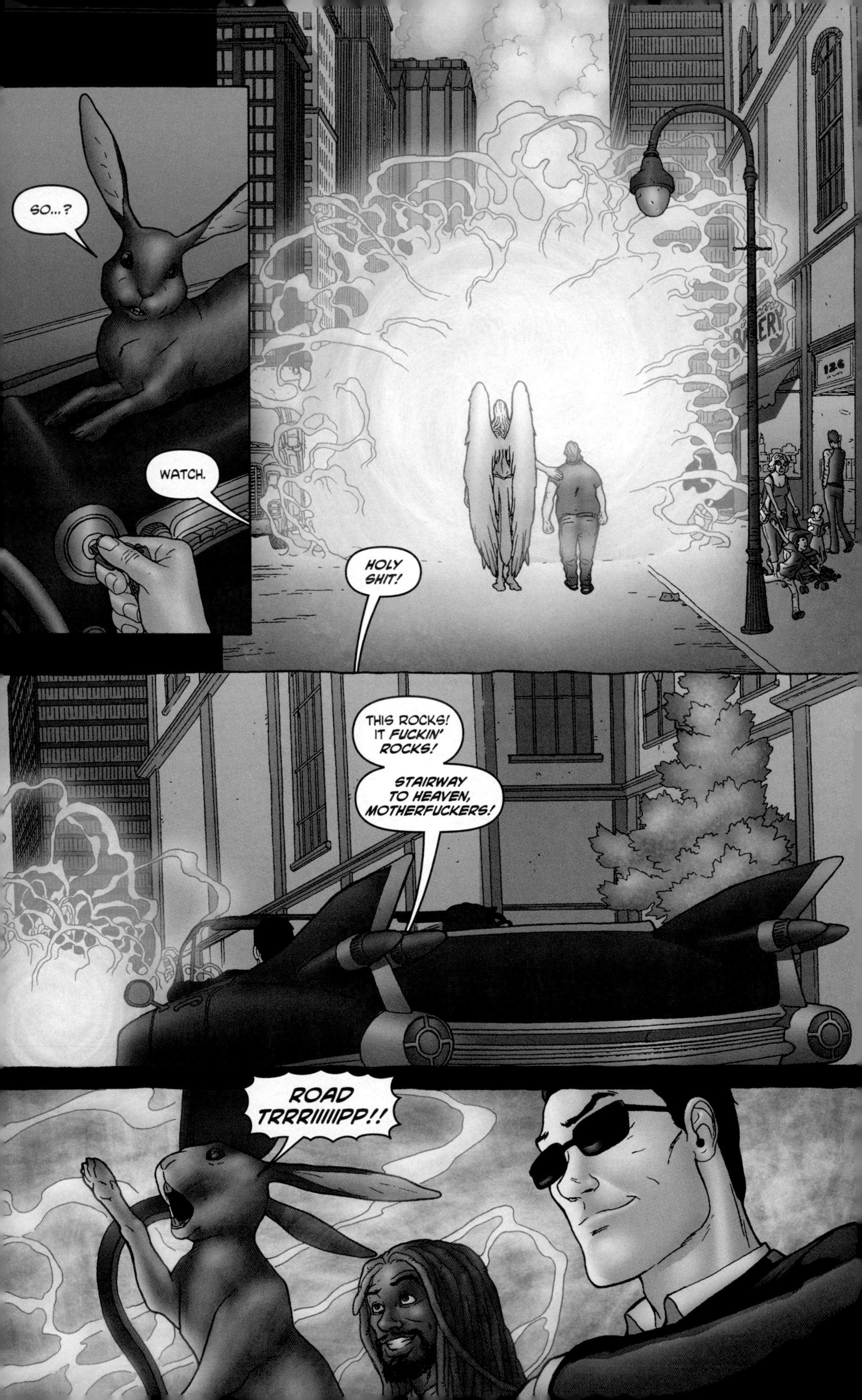
SO...?
WATCH.
HOLY SHIT!
THIS ROCKS! IT FUCKIN' ROCKS!
STAIRWAY TO HEAVEN, MOTHERFUCKERS!
ROAD TRRRIIIIIIPP!!

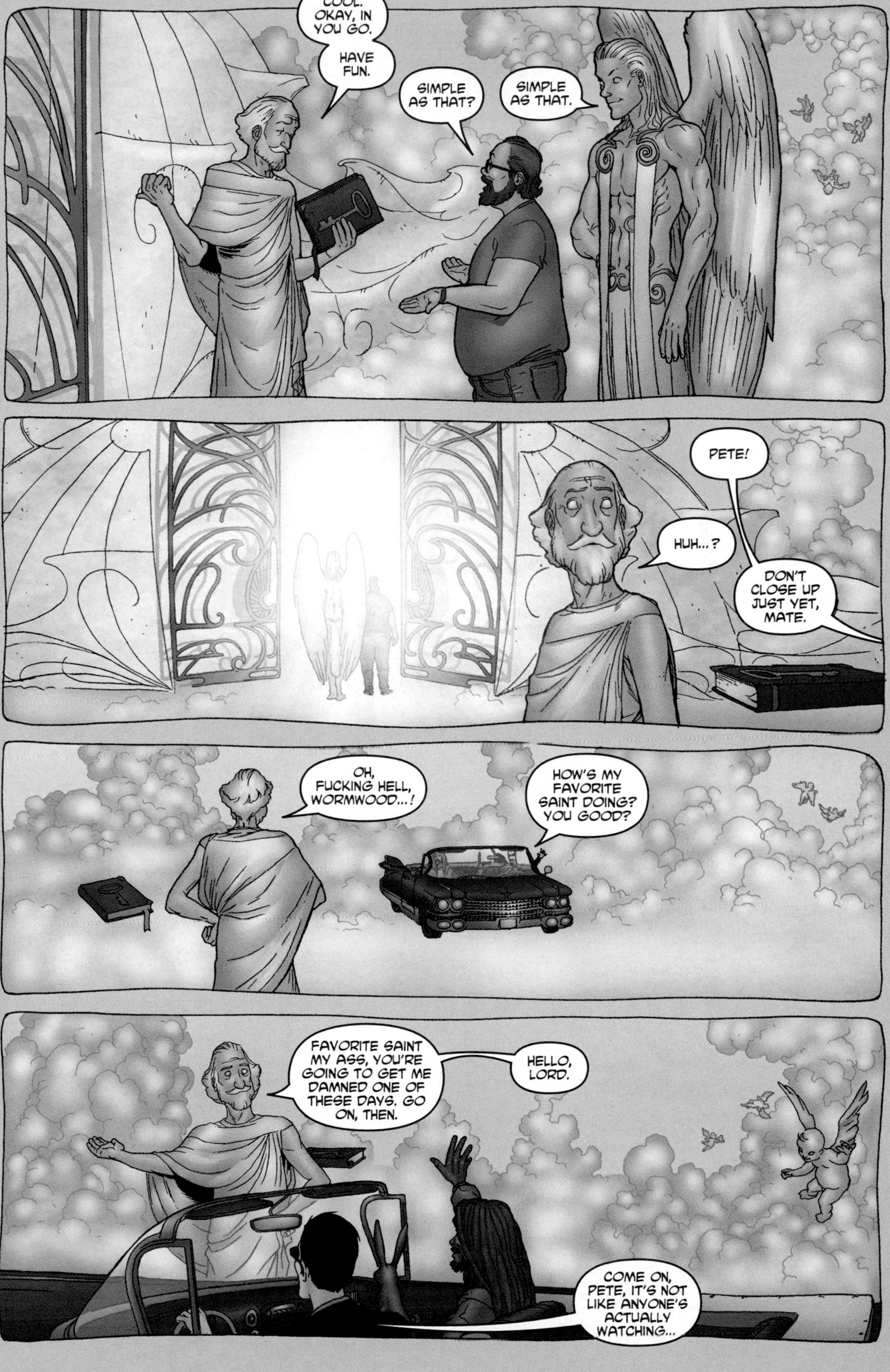
COOL. OKAY, IN YOU GO.
HAVE FUN.
SIMPLE AS THAT?
SIMPLE AS THAT.
PETE!
HUH...?
DON'T CLOSE UP JUST YET, MATE.
OH, FUCKING HELL, WORMWOOD...!
HOW'S MY FAVORITE SAINT DOING? YOU GOOD?
FAVORITE SAINT MY ASS, YOU'RE GOING TO GET ME DAMNED ONE OF THESE DAYS. GO ON, THEN.
HELLO, LORD.
COME ON, PETE, IT'S NOT LIKE ANYONE'S ACTUALLY WATCHING...

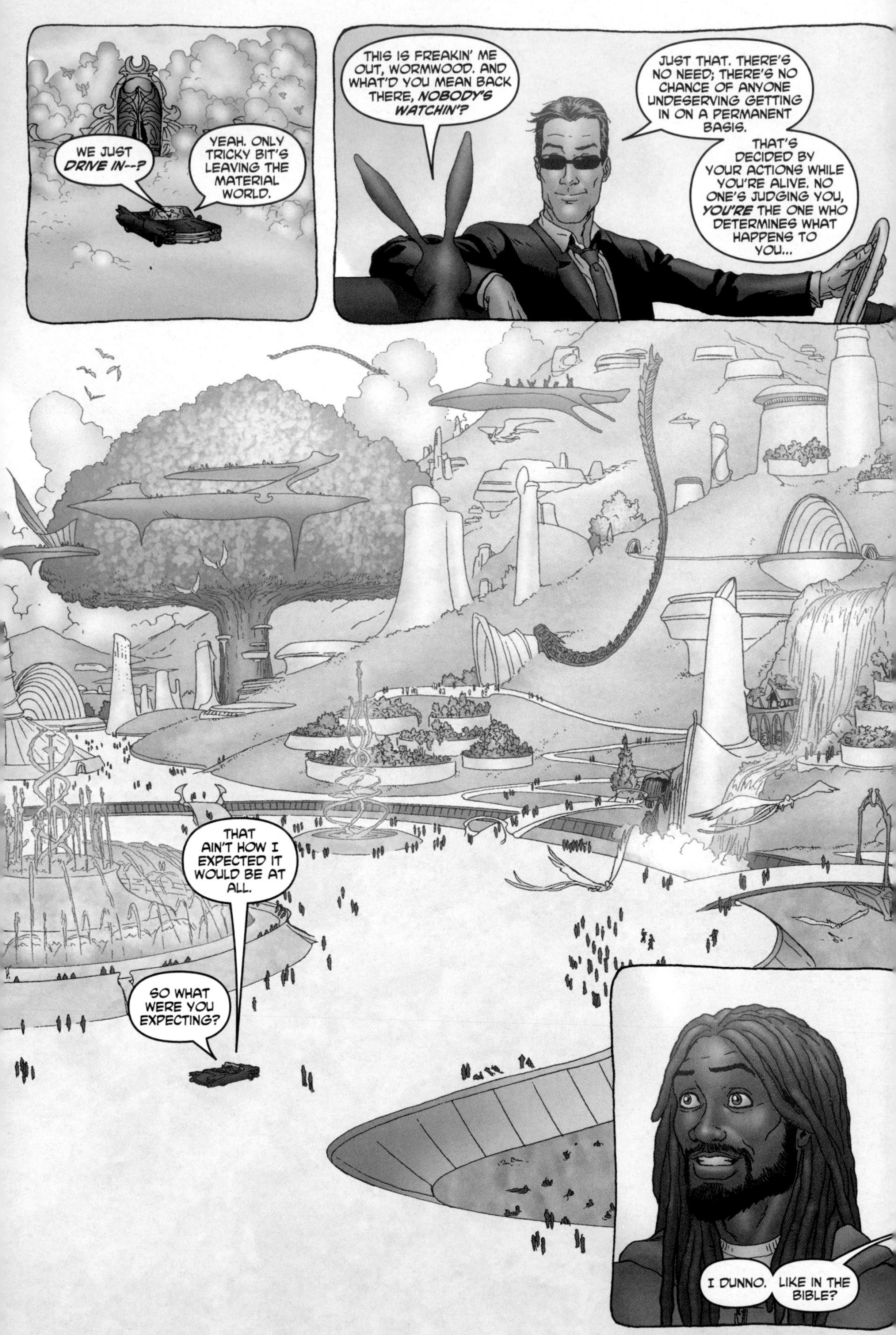
WE JUST *DRIVE IN--?*
YEAH. ONLY TRICKY BIT'S LEAVING THE MATERIAL WORLD.
THIS IS FREAKIN' ME OUT, WORMWOOD. AND WHAT'D YOU MEAN BACK THERE, *NOBODY'S WATCHIN'?*
JUST THAT. THERE'S NO NEED; THERE'S NO CHANCE OF ANYONE UNDESERVING GETTING IN ON A PERMANENT BASIS.
THAT'S DECIDED BY YOUR ACTIONS WHILE YOU'RE ALIVE. NO ONE'S JUDGING YOU, *YOU'RE* THE ONE WHO DETERMINES WHAT HAPPENS TO YOU...
THAT AIN'T HOW I EXPECTED IT WOULD BE AT ALL.
SO WHAT WERE YOU EXPECTING?
I DUNNO.
LIKE IN THE BIBLE?

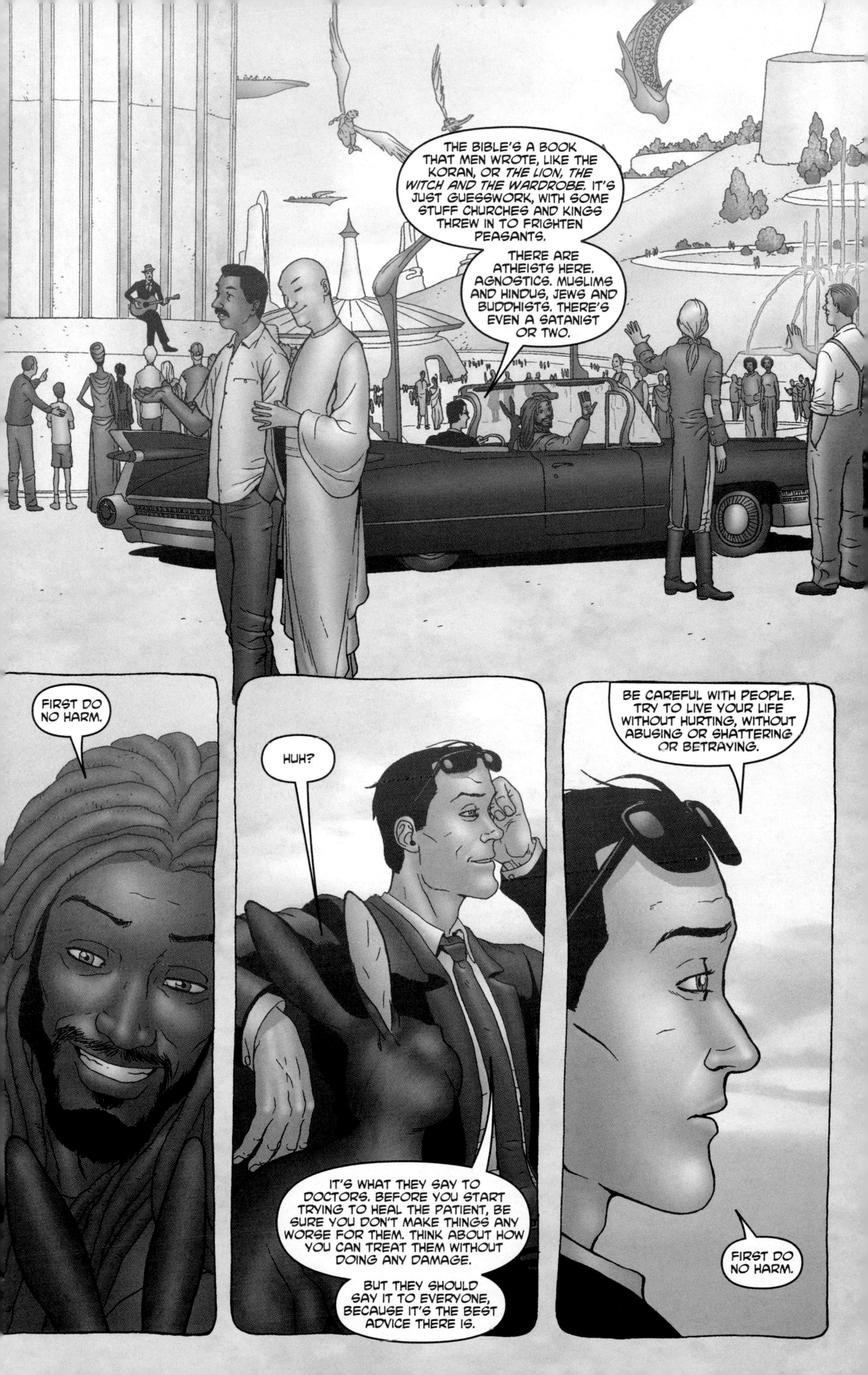
THE BIBLE'S A BOOK THAT MEN WROTE, LIKE THE KORAN, OR *THE LION, THE WITCH AND THE WARDROBE.* IT'S JUST GUESSWORK, WITH SOME STUFF CHURCHES AND KINGS THREW IN TO FRIGHTEN PEASANTS.
THERE ARE ATHEISTS HERE. AGNOSTICS. MUSLIMS AND HINDUS, JEWS AND BUDDHISTS. THERE'S EVEN A SATANIST OR TWO.
FIRST DO NO HARM.
HUH?
IT'S WHAT THEY SAY TO DOCTORS. BEFORE YOU START TRYING TO HEAL THE PATIENT, BE SURE YOU DON'T MAKE THINGS ANY WORSE FOR THEM. THINK ABOUT HOW YOU CAN TREAT THEM WITHOUT DOING ANY DAMAGE.
BUT THEY SHOULD SAY IT TO EVERYONE, BECAUSE IT'S THE BEST ADVICE THERE IS.
BE CAREFUL WITH PEOPLE. TRY TO LIVE YOUR LIFE WITHOUT HURTING, WITHOUT ABUSING OR SHATTERING OR BETRAYING.
FIRST DO NO HARM.

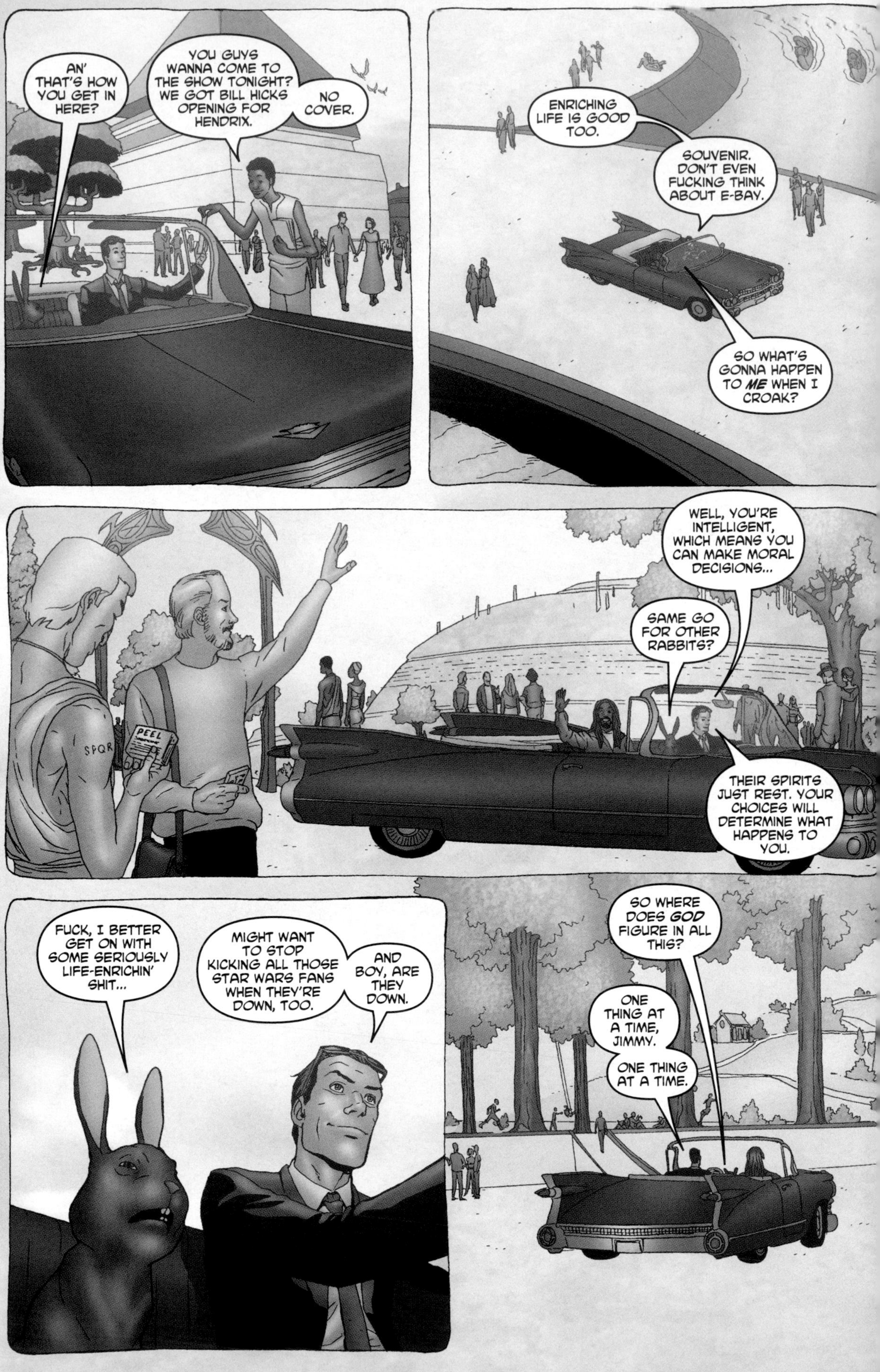
AN' THAT'S HOW YOU GET IN HERE?
YOU GUYS WANNA COME TO THE SHOW TONIGHT? WE GOT BILL HICKS OPENING FOR HENDRIX.
NO COVER.
ENRICHING LIFE IS GOOD TOO.
SOUVENIR. DON'T EVEN FUCKING THINK ABOUT E-BAY.
SO WHAT'S GONNA HAPPEN TO *ME* WHEN I CROAK?
PEEL
SPQR
WELL, YOU'RE INTELLIGENT, WHICH MEANS YOU CAN MAKE MORAL DECISIONS...
SAME GO FOR OTHER RABBITS?
THEIR SPIRITS JUST REST. YOUR CHOICES WILL DETERMINE WHAT HAPPENS TO YOU.
FUCK, I BETTER GET ON WITH SOME SERIOUSLY LIFE-ENRICHIN' SHIT...
MIGHT WANT TO STOP KICKING ALL THOSE STAR WARS FANS WHEN THEY'RE DOWN, TOO.
AND BOY, ARE THEY DOWN.
SO WHERE DOES *GOD* FIGURE IN ALL THIS?
ONE THING AT A TIME, JIMMY.
ONE THING AT A TIME.

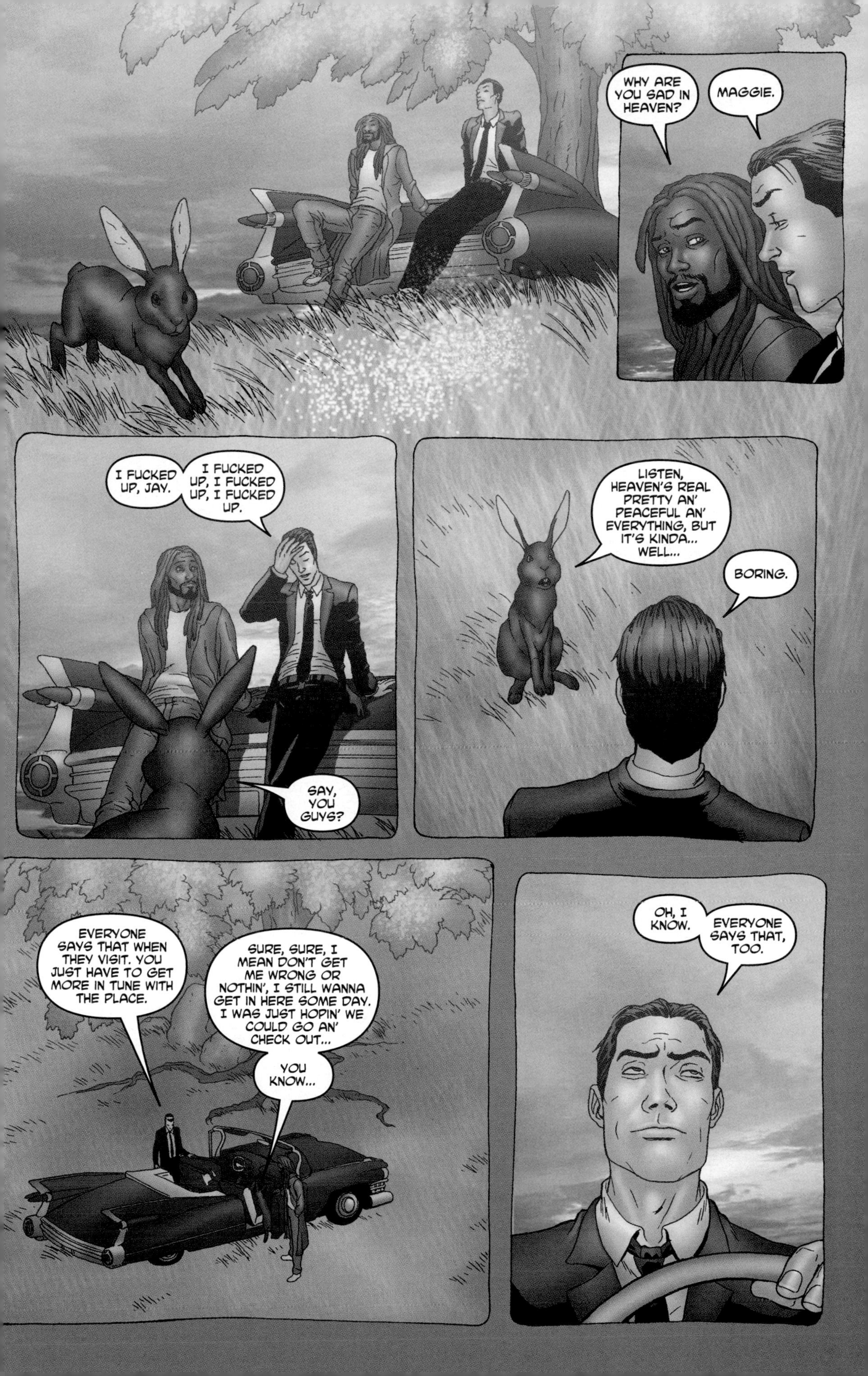
WHY ARE YOU SAD IN HEAVEN?
MAGGIE.
I FUCKED UP, JAY.
I FUCKED UP, I FUCKED UP, I FUCKED UP.
SAY, YOU GUYS?
LISTEN, HEAVEN'S REAL PRETTY AN' PEACEFUL AN' EVERYTHING, BUT IT'S KINDA... WELL...
BORING.
EVERYONE SAYS THAT WHEN THEY VISIT. YOU JUST HAVE TO GET MORE IN TUNE WITH THE PLACE.
SURE, SURE, I MEAN DON'T GET ME WRONG OR NOTHIN', I STILL WANNA GET IN HERE SOME DAY. I WAS JUST HOPIN' WE COULD GO AN' CHECK OUT...
YOU KNOW...
OH, I KNOW.
EVERYONE SAYS THAT, TOO.

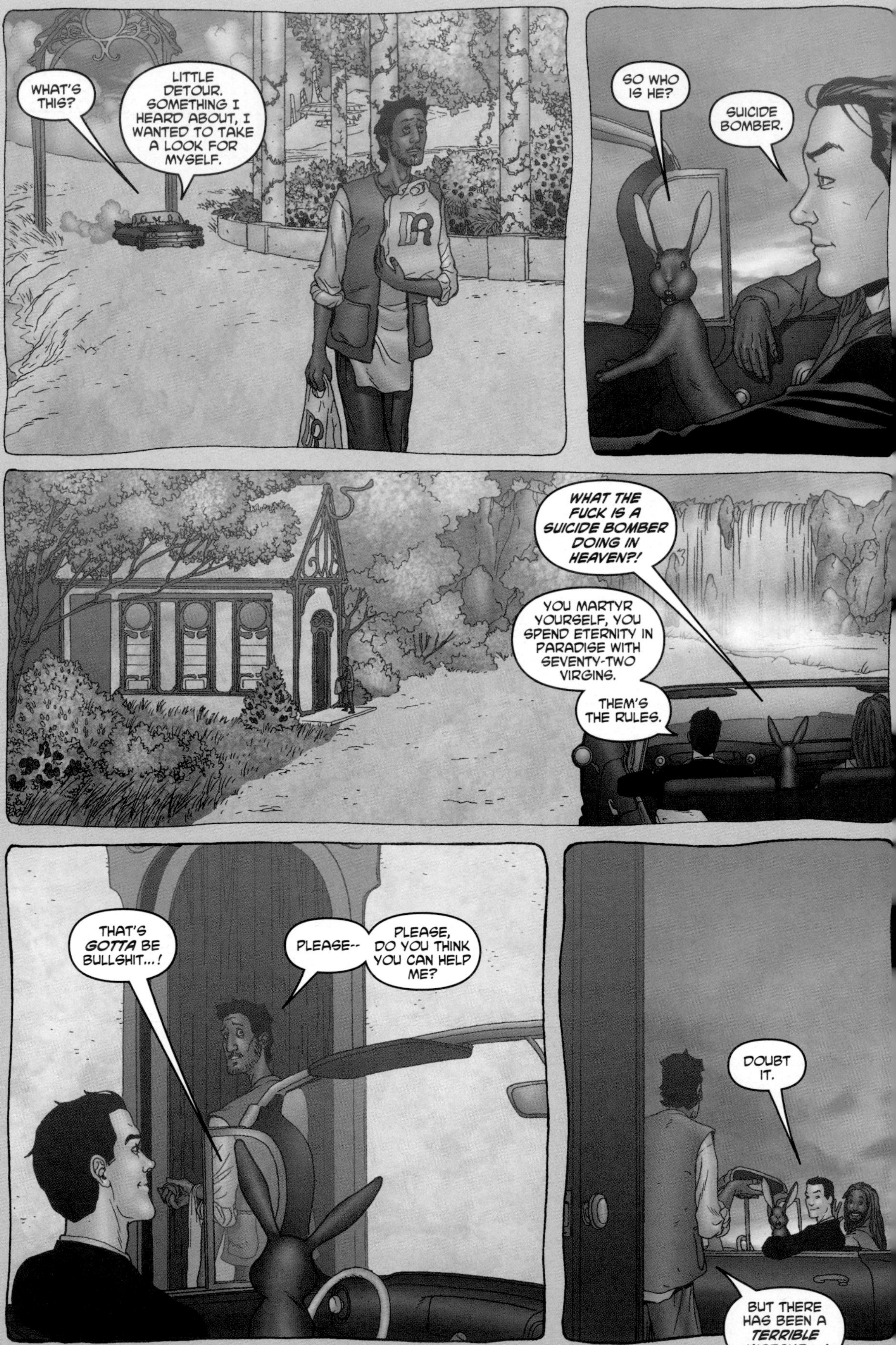

WHAT'S THIS?
LITTLE DETOUR. SOMETHING I HEARD ABOUT, I WANTED TO TAKE A LOOK FOR MYSELF.
SO WHO IS HE?
SUICIDE BOMBER.
WHAT THE FUCK IS A SUICIDE BOMBER DOING IN HEAVEN?!
YOU MARTYR YOURSELF, YOU SPEND ETERNITY IN PARADISE WITH SEVENTY-TWO VIRGINS.
THEM'S THE RULES.
THAT'S GOTTA BE BULLSHIT...!
PLEASE--
PLEASE, DO YOU THINK YOU CAN HELP ME?
DOUBT IT.
BUT THERE HAS BEEN A TERRIBLE MISTAKE...!

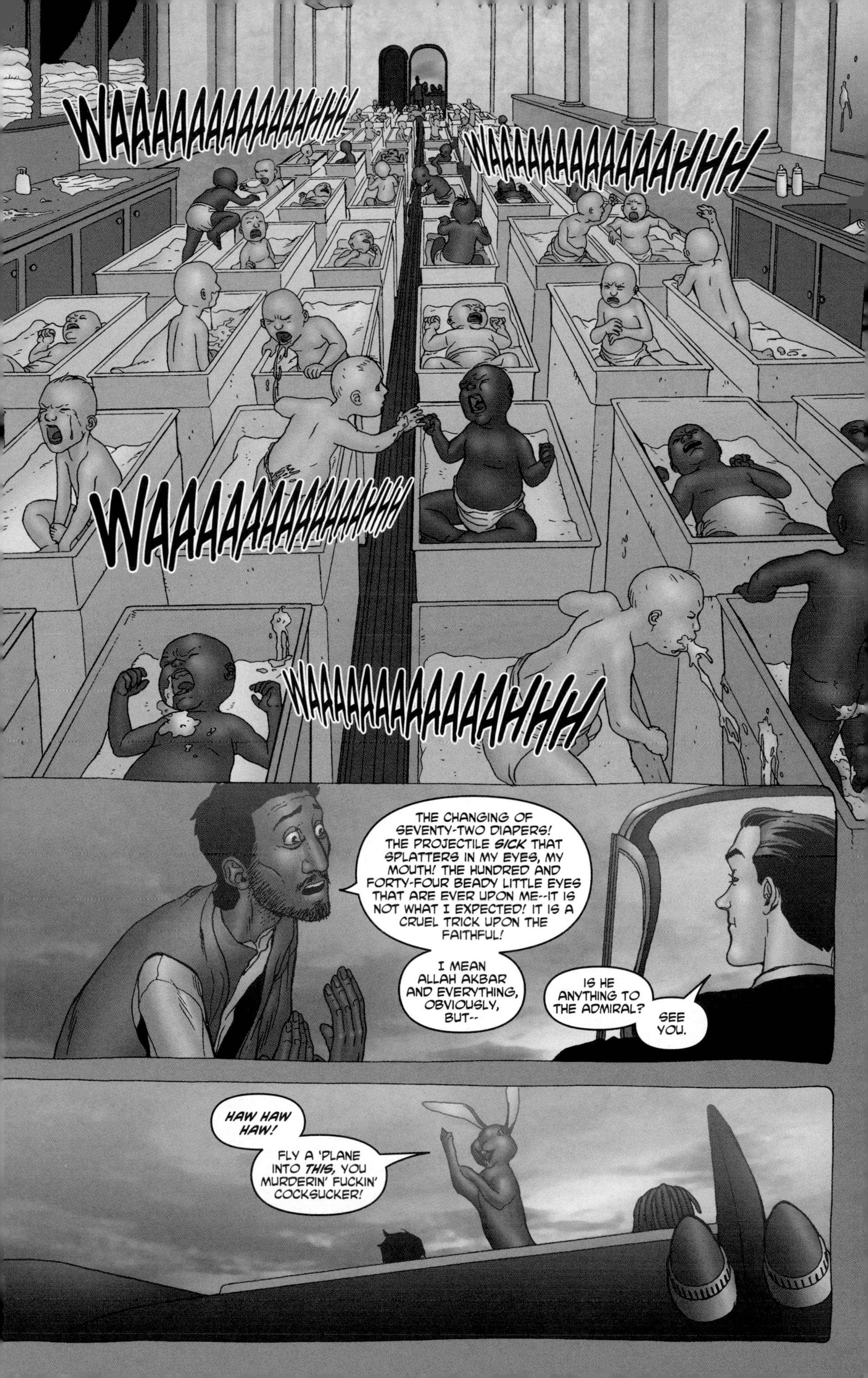
WAAAAAAAAAAAAHH
WAAAAAAAAAAAAAAHHH
WAAAAAAAAAAAAAAHH
WAAAAAAAAAAAAAAHHH
THE CHANGING OF SEVENTY-TWO DIAPERS! THE PROJECTILE SICK THAT SPLATTERS IN MY EYES, MY MOUTH! THE HUNDRED AND FORTY-FOUR BEADY LITTLE EYES THAT ARE EVER UPON ME--IT IS NOT WHAT I EXPECTED! IT IS A CRUEL TRICK UPON THE FAITHFUL!
I MEAN ALLAH AKBAR AND EVERYTHING, OBVIOUSLY, BUT--
IS HE ANYTHING TO THE ADMIRAL?
SEE YOU.
HAW HAW HAW!
FLY A 'PLANE INTO THIS, YOU MURDERIN' FUCKIN' COCKSUCKER!

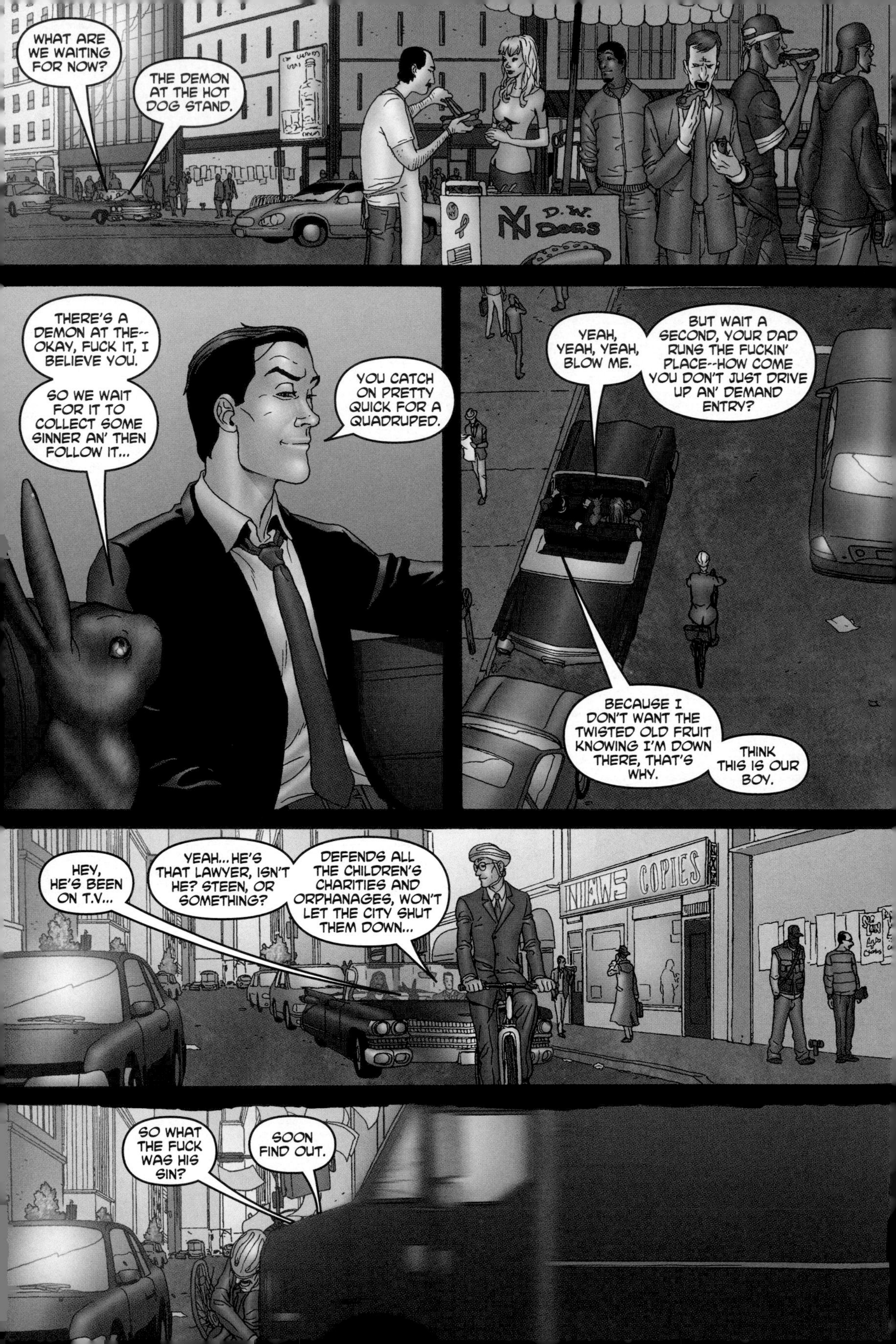

WHAT ARE WE WAITING FOR NOW?
THE DEMON AT THE HOT DOG STAND.
D.W. DOGS
THERE'S A DEMON AT THE--OKAY, FUCK IT, I BELIEVE YOU.
SO WE WAIT FOR IT TO COLLECT SOME SINNER AN' THEN FOLLOW IT...
YOU CATCH ON PRETTY QUICK FOR A QUADRUPED.
YEAH, YEAH, YEAH, BLOW ME.
BUT WAIT A SECOND, YOUR DAD RUNS THE FUCKIN' PLACE--HOW COME YOU DON'T JUST DRIVE UP AN' DEMAND ENTRY?
BECAUSE I DON'T WANT THE TWISTED OLD FRUIT KNOWING I'M DOWN THERE, THAT'S WHY.
THINK THIS IS OUR BOY.
HEY, HE'S BEEN ON T.V...
YEAH... HE'S THAT LAWYER, ISN'T HE? STEEN, OR SOMETHING?
DEFENDS ALL THE CHILDREN'S CHARITIES AND ORPHANAGES, WON'T LET THE CITY SHUT THEM DOWN...
COPIES
SO WHAT THE FUCK WAS HIS SIN?
SOON FIND OUT.

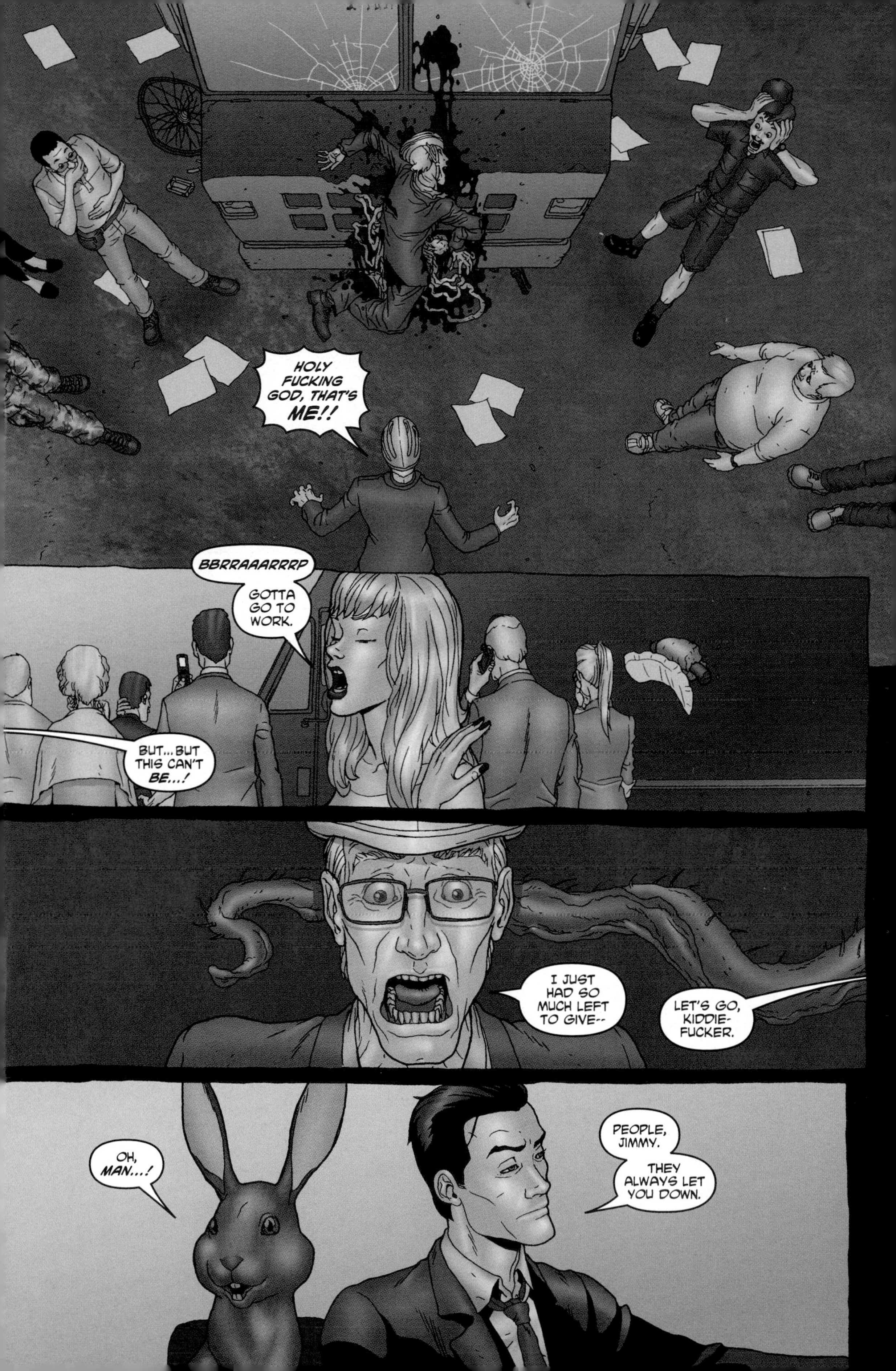

HOLY FUCKING GOD, THAT'S ME!!
BBRRAAARRRP
GOTTA GO TO WORK.
BUT...BUT THIS CAN'T BE...!
I JUST HAD SO MUCH LEFT TO GIVE--
LET'S GO, KIDDIE-FUCKER.
OH, MAN...!
PEOPLE, JIMMY.
THEY ALWAYS LET YOU DOWN.

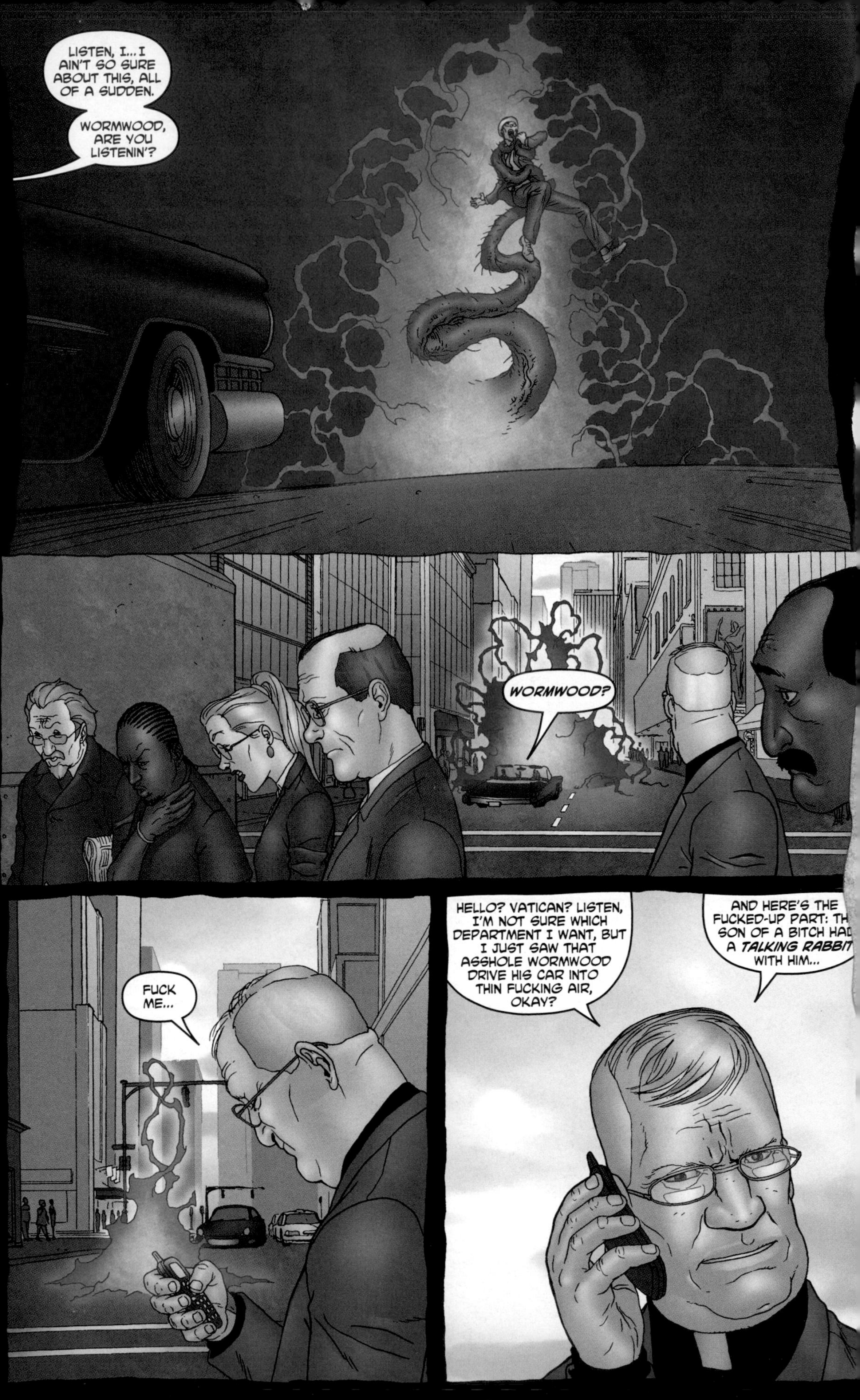
LISTEN, I... I AIN'T SO SURE ABOUT THIS, ALL OF A SUDDEN.
WORMWOOD, ARE YOU LISTENIN'?
WORMWOOD?
FUCK ME...
HELLO? VATICAN? LISTEN, I'M NOT SURE WHICH DEPARTMENT I WANT, BUT I JUST SAW THAT ASSHOLE WORMWOOD DRIVE HIS CAR INTO THIN FUCKING AIR, OKAY?
AND HERE'S THE FUCKED-UP PART: TH SON OF A BITCH HAD A *TALKING RABBIT* WITH HIM...

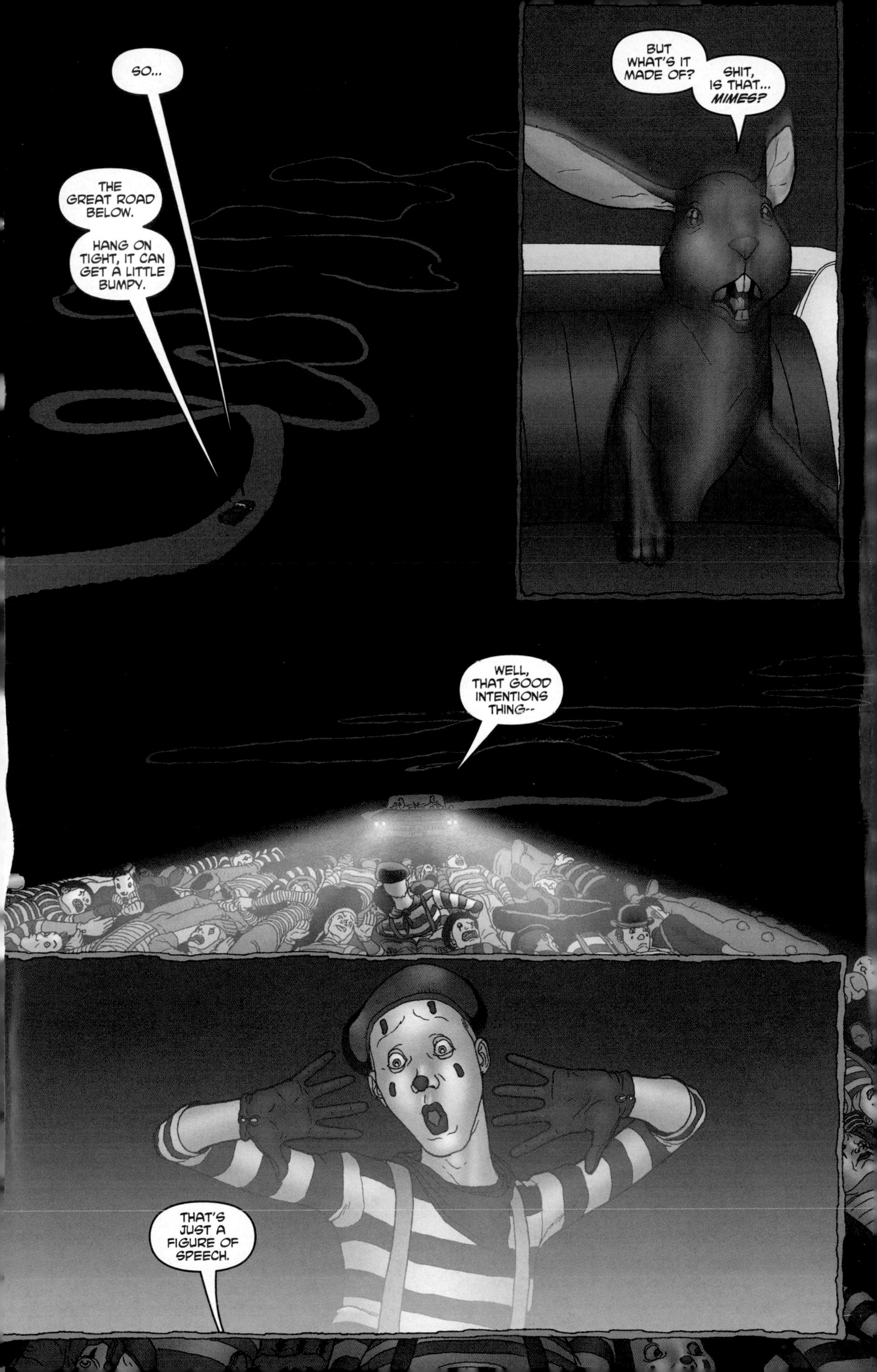
SO...
THE GREAT ROAD BELOW.
HANG ON TIGHT, IT CAN GET A LITTLE BUMPY.
BUT WHAT'S IT MADE OF?
SHIT, IS THAT... *MIMES?*
WELL, THAT GOOD INTENTIONS THING--
THAT'S JUST A FIGURE OF SPEECH.

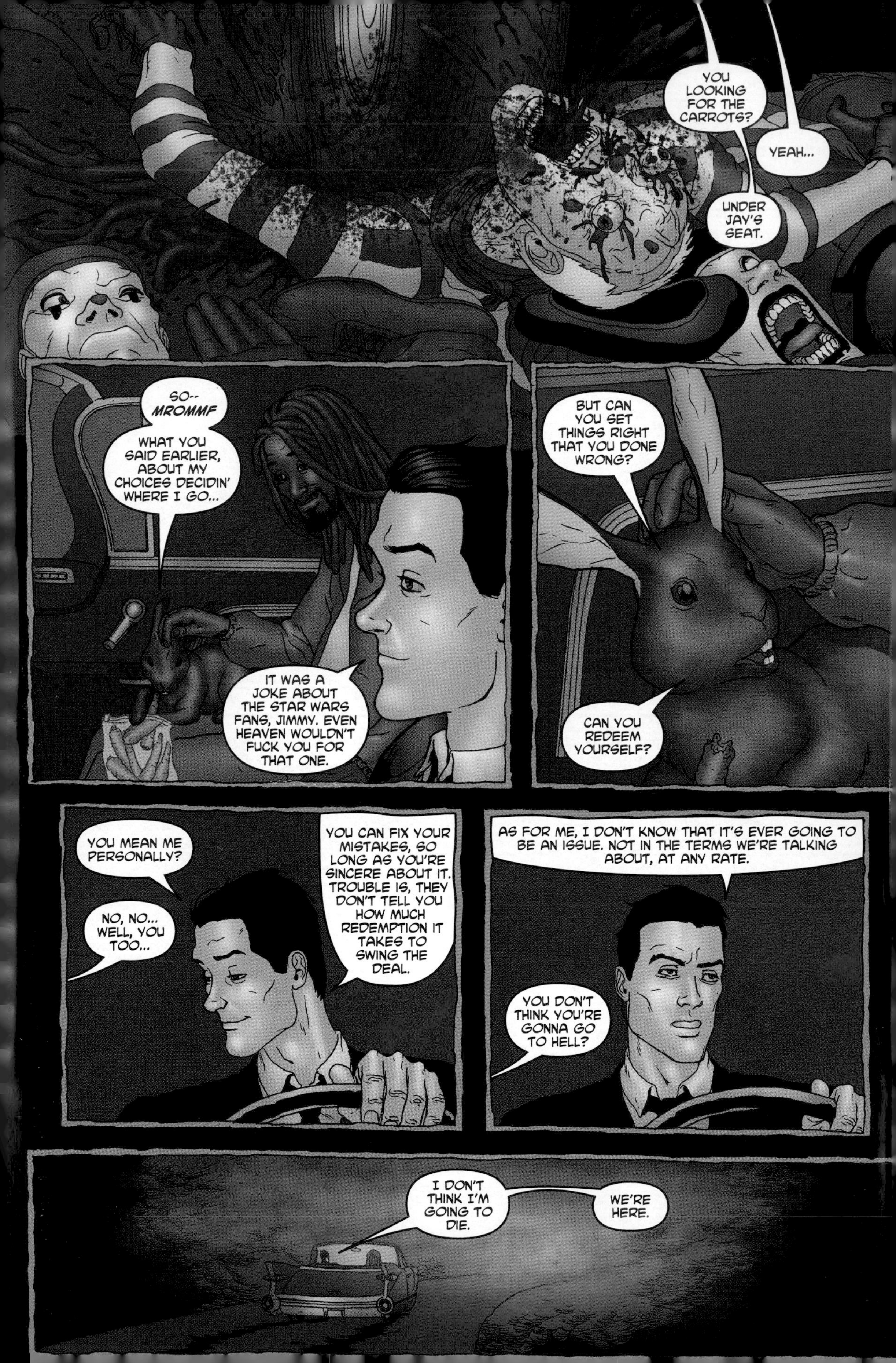
YOU LOOKING FOR THE CARROTS?
YEAH...
UNDER JAY'S SEAT.
SO-- MROMMF
WHAT YOU SAID EARLIER, ABOUT MY CHOICES DECIDIN' WHERE I GO...
IT WAS A JOKE ABOUT THE STAR WARS FANS, JIMMY. EVEN HEAVEN WOULDN'T FUCK YOU FOR THAT ONE.
BUT CAN YOU SET THINGS RIGHT THAT YOU DONE WRONG?
CAN YOU REDEEM YOURSELF?
YOU MEAN ME PERSONALLY?
NO, NO... WELL, YOU TOO...
YOU CAN FIX YOUR MISTAKES, SO LONG AS YOU'RE SINCERE ABOUT IT. TROUBLE IS, THEY DON'T TELL YOU HOW MUCH REDEMPTION IT TAKES TO SWING THE DEAL.
AS FOR ME, I DON'T KNOW THAT IT'S EVER GOING TO BE AN ISSUE. NOT IN THE TERMS WE'RE TALKING ABOUT, AT ANY RATE.
YOU DON'T THINK YOU'RE GONNA GO TO HELL?
I DON'T THINK I'M GOING TO DIE.
WE'RE HERE.

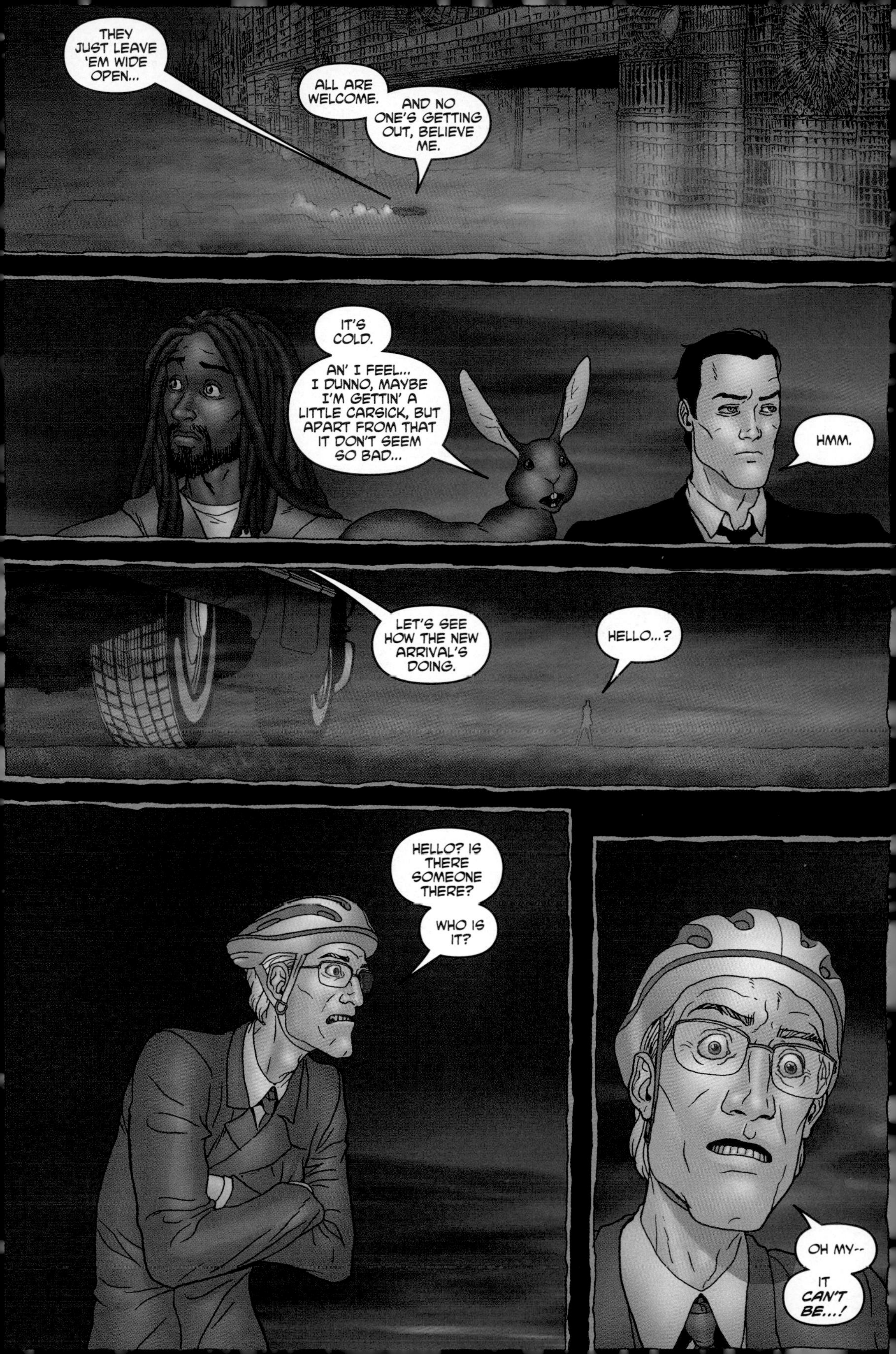
THEY JUST LEAVE 'EM WIDE OPEN...
ALL ARE WELCOME.
AND NO ONE'S GETTING OUT, BELIEVE ME.
IT'S COLD.
AN' I FEEL... I DUNNO, MAYBE I'M GETTIN' A LITTLE CARSICK, BUT APART FROM THAT IT DON'T SEEM SO BAD...
HMM.
LET'S SEE HOW THE NEW ARRIVAL'S DOING.
HELLO...?
HELLO? IS THERE SOMEONE THERE?
WHO IS IT?
OH MY--
IT *CAN'T BE...!*

BEAUTIFUL. YOU'RE ALL SO BEAUTIFUL.

MY LOVES.

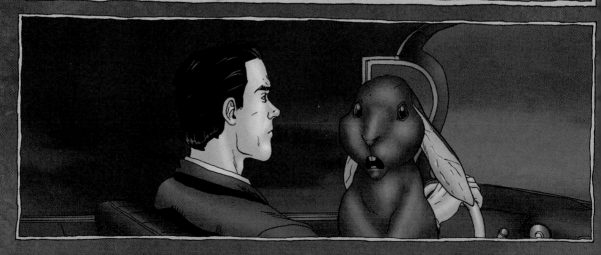

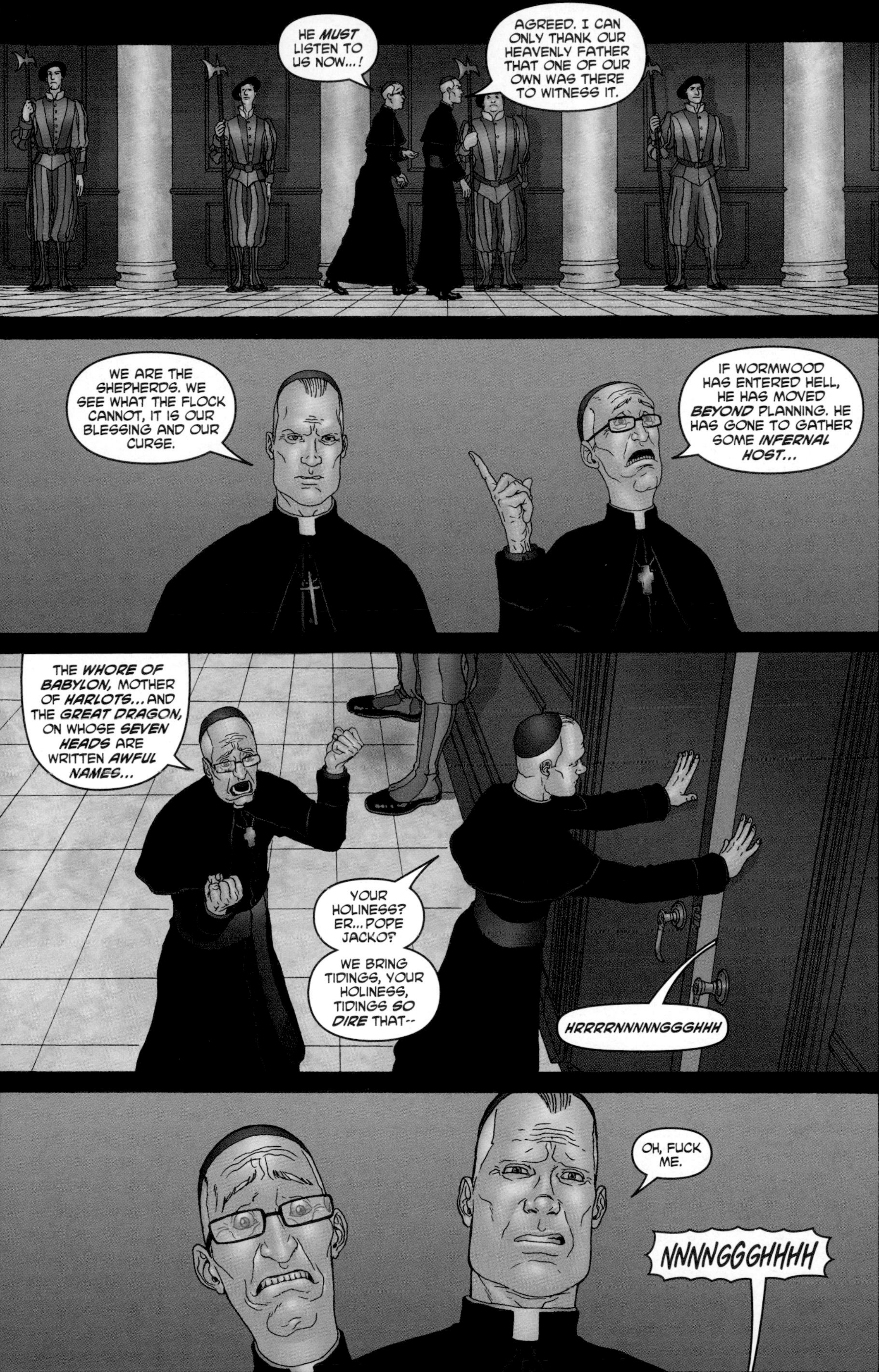
HE MUST LISTEN TO US NOW...!
AGREED. I CAN ONLY THANK OUR HEAVENLY FATHER THAT ONE OF OUR OWN WAS THERE TO WITNESS IT.
WE ARE THE SHEPHERDS. WE SEE WHAT THE FLOCK CANNOT, IT IS OUR BLESSING AND OUR CURSE.
IF WORMWOOD HAS ENTERED HELL, HE HAS MOVED BEYOND PLANNING. HE HAS GONE TO GATHER SOME INFERNAL HOST...
THE WHORE OF BABYLON, MOTHER OF HARLOTS... AND THE GREAT DRAGON, ON WHOSE SEVEN HEADS ARE WRITTEN AWFUL NAMES...
YOUR HOLINESS? ER... POPE JACKO?
WE BRING TIDINGS, YOUR HOLINESS, TIDINGS SO DIRE THAT--
HRRRRNNNNNGGGHHH
OH, FUCK ME.
NNNNGGGHHHH

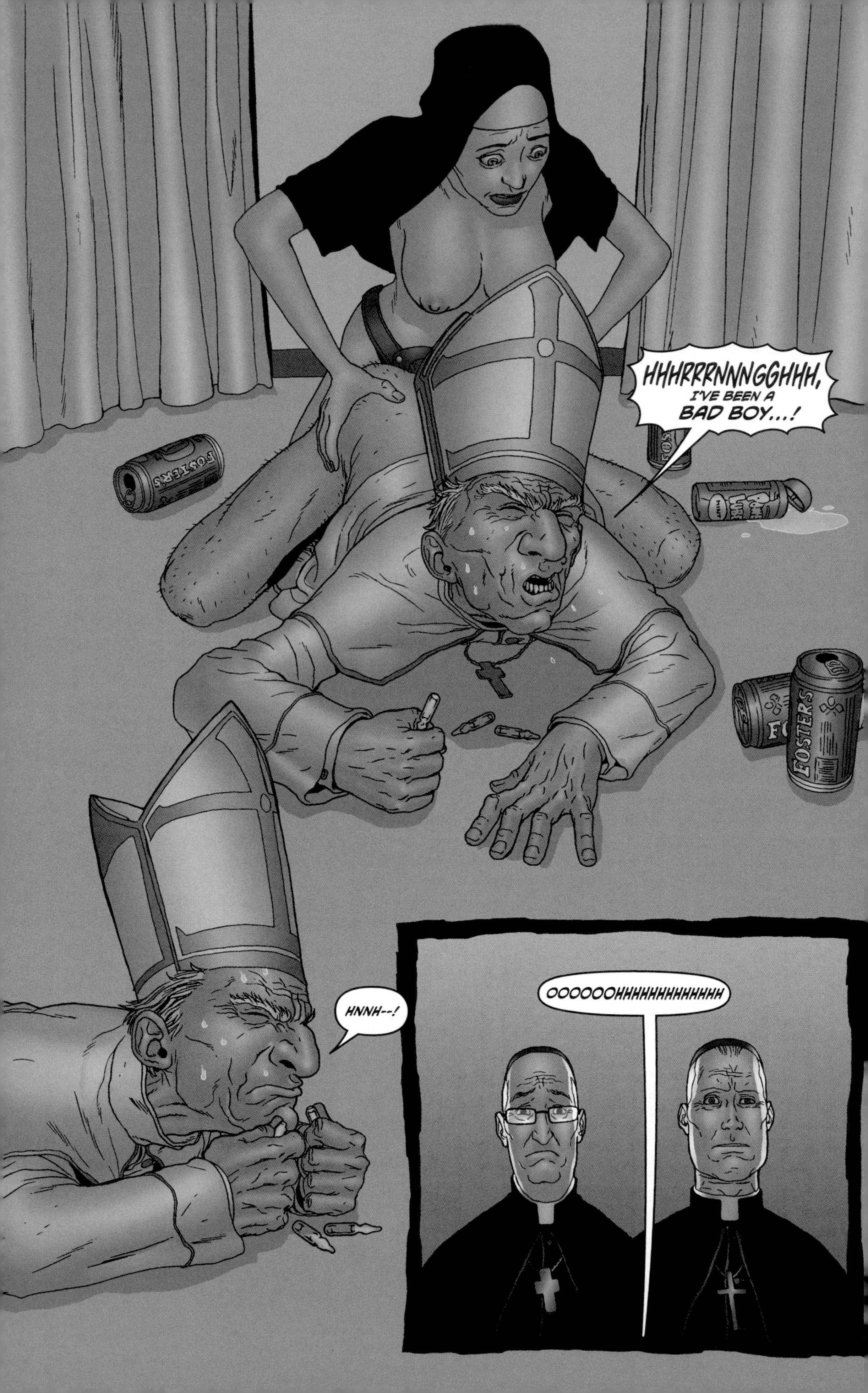
HHHRRRNNNGGHHH, I'VE BEEN A BAD BOY...!
FOSTER'S
HNNH--!
OOOOOOHHHHHHHHHHHHH

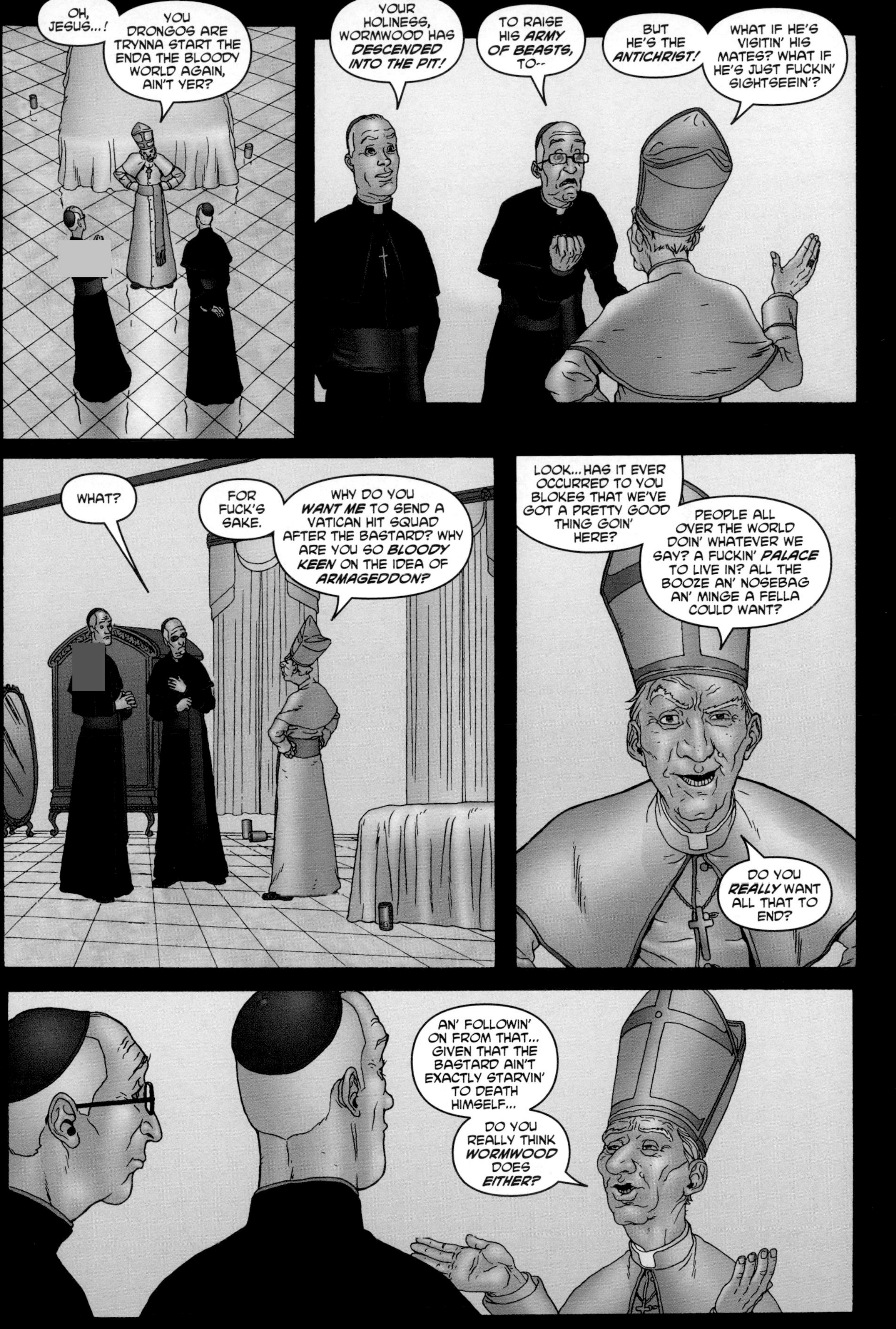
OH, JESUS...!
YOU DRONGOS ARE TRYNNA START THE ENDA THE BLOODY WORLD AGAIN, AIN'T YER?
YOUR HOLINESS, WORMWOOD HAS DESCENDED INTO THE PIT!
TO RAISE HIS ARMY OF BEASTS, TO--
BUT HE'S THE ANTICHRIST!
WHAT IF HE'S VISITIN' HIS MATES? WHAT IF HE'S JUST FUCKIN' SIGHTSEEIN'?
WHAT?
FOR FUCK'S SAKE.
WHY DO YOU WANT ME TO SEND A VATICAN HIT SQUAD AFTER THE BASTARD? WHY ARE YOU SO BLOODY KEEN ON THE IDEA OF ARMAGEDDON?
LOOK... HAS IT EVER OCCURRED TO YOU BLOKES THAT WE'VE GOT A PRETTY GOOD THING GOIN' HERE?
PEOPLE ALL OVER THE WORLD DOIN' WHATEVER WE SAY? A FUCKIN' PALACE TO LIVE IN? ALL THE BOOZE AN' NOSEBAG AN' MINGE A FELLA COULD WANT?
DO YOU REALLY WANT ALL THAT TO END?
AN' FOLLOWIN' ON FROM THAT... GIVEN THAT THE BASTARD AIN'T EXACTLY STARVIN' TO DEATH HIMSELF...
DO YOU REALLY THINK WORMWOOD DOES EITHER?

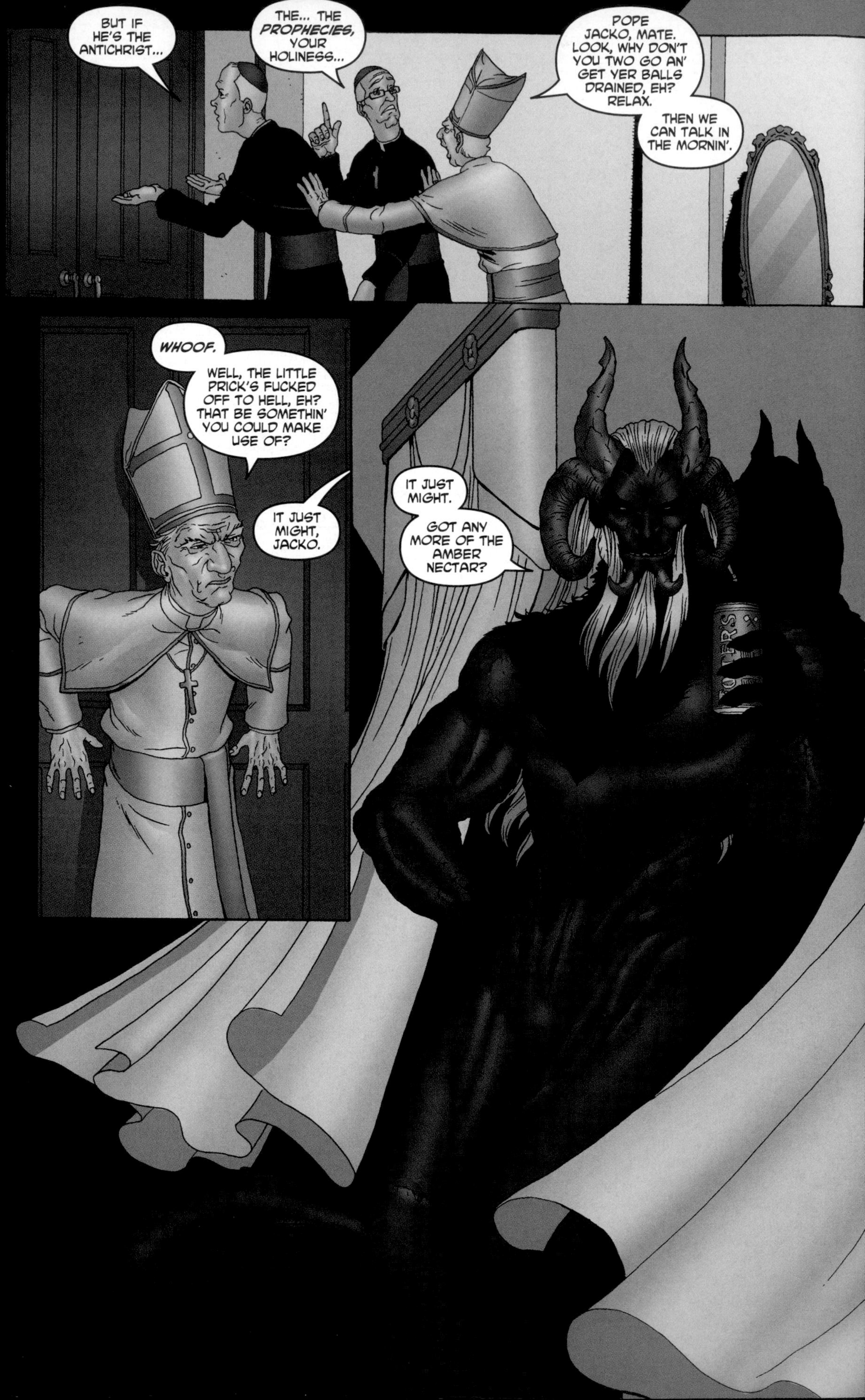
BUT IF HE'S THE ANTICHRIST...
THE... THE *PROPHECIES,* YOUR HOLINESS...
POPE JACKO, MATE. LOOK, WHY DON'T YOU TWO GO AN' GET YER BALLS DRAINED, EH? RELAX.
THEN WE CAN TALK IN THE MORNIN'.
WHOOF.
WELL, THE LITTLE PRICK'S FUCKED OFF TO HELL, EH? THAT BE SOMETHIN' YOU COULD MAKE USE OF?
IT JUST MIGHT, JACKO.
IT JUST MIGHT.
GOT ANY MORE OF THE AMBER NECTAR?

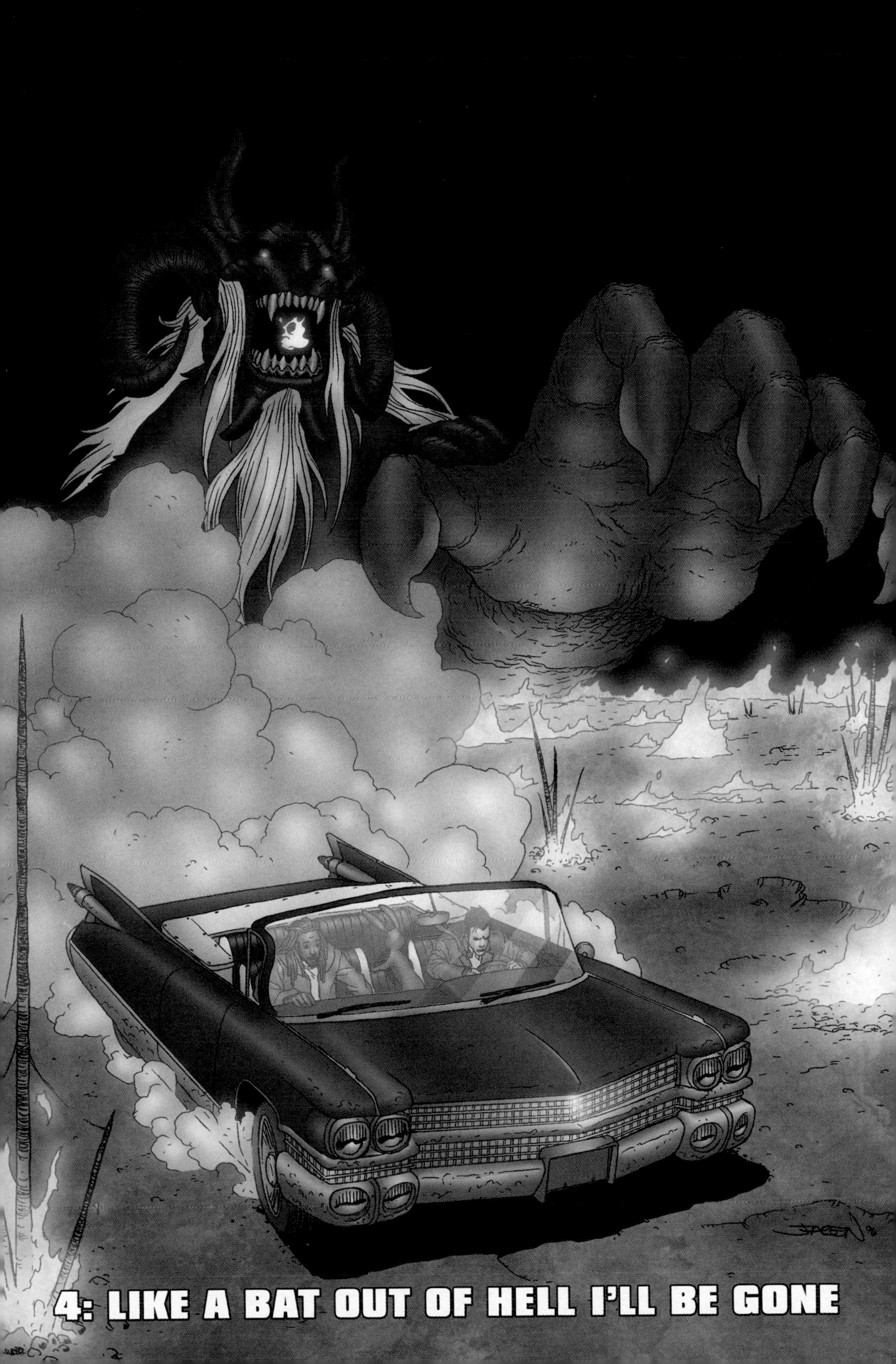

4: LIKE A BAT OUT OF HELL I'LL BE GONE

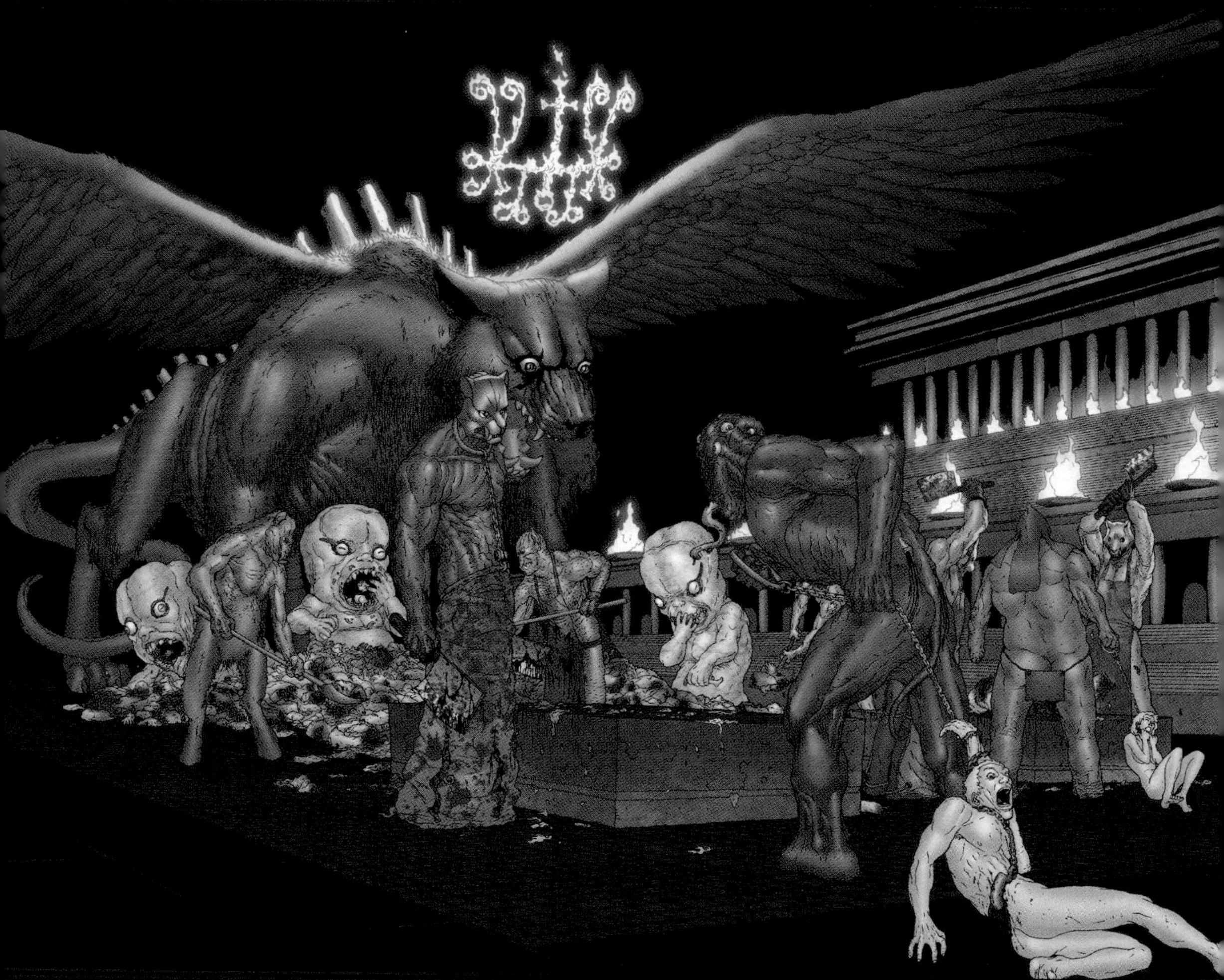

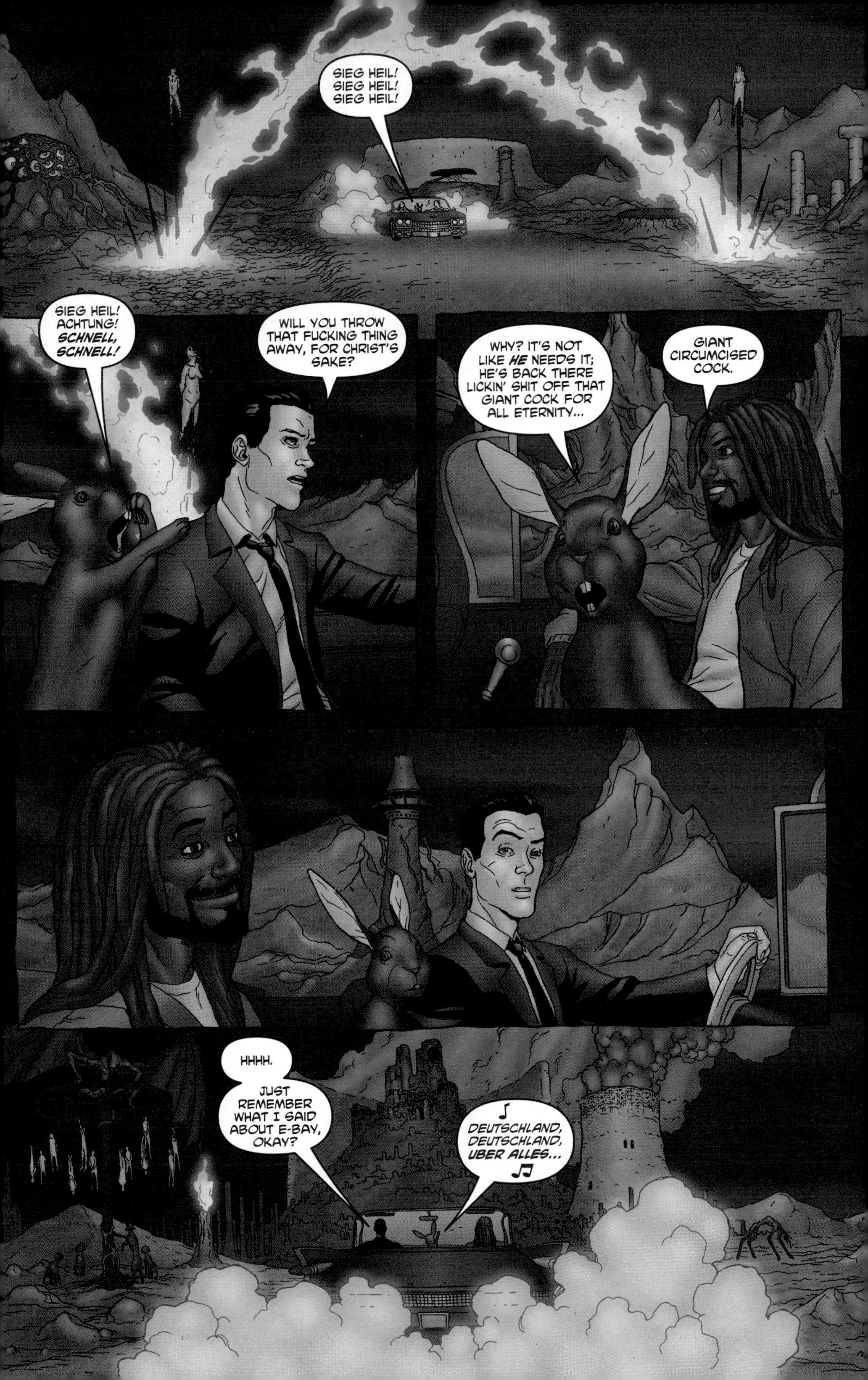
SIEG HEIL! SIEG HEIL! SIEG HEIL!
SIEG HEIL! ACHTUNG! SCHNELL, SCHNELL!
WILL YOU THROW THAT FUCKING THING AWAY, FOR CHRIST'S SAKE?
WHY? IT'S NOT LIKE HE NEEDS IT; HE'S BACK THERE LICKIN' SHIT OFF THAT GIANT COCK FOR ALL ETERNITY...
GIANT CIRCUMCISED COCK.
HHHH.
JUST REMEMBER WHAT I SAID ABOUT E-BAY, OKAY?
♪ DEUTSCHLAND, DEUTSCHLAND, UBER ALLES... ♫

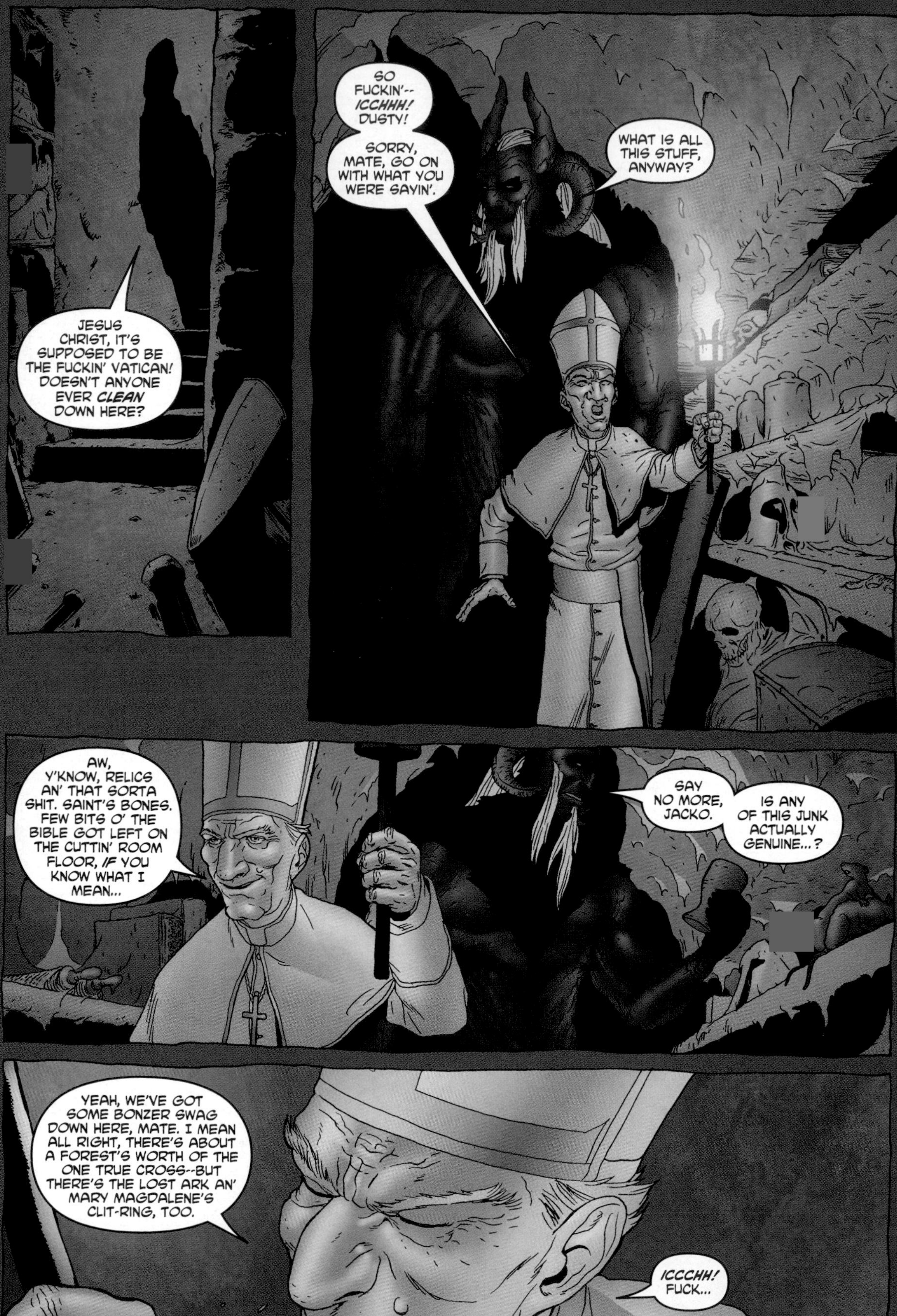
JESUS CHRIST, IT'S SUPPOSED TO BE THE FUCKIN' VATICAN! DOESN'T ANYONE EVER *CLEAN* DOWN HERE?
SO FUCKIN'-- *ICCHHH!* DUSTY!
SORRY, MATE, GO ON WITH WHAT YOU WERE SAYIN'.
WHAT IS ALL THIS STUFF, ANYWAY?
AW, Y'KNOW, RELICS AN' THAT SORTA SHIT. SAINT'S BONES. FEW BITS O' THE BIBLE GOT LEFT ON THE CUTTIN' ROOM FLOOR, *IF* YOU KNOW WHAT I MEAN...
SAY NO MORE, JACKO.
IS ANY OF THIS JUNK ACTUALLY GENUINE...?
YEAH, WE'VE GOT SOME BONZER SWAG DOWN HERE, MATE. I MEAN ALL RIGHT, THERE'S ABOUT A FOREST'S WORTH OF THE ONE TRUE CROSS--BUT THERE'S THE LOST ARK AN' MARY MAGDALENE'S CLIT-RING, TOO.
ICCCHH! FUCK...

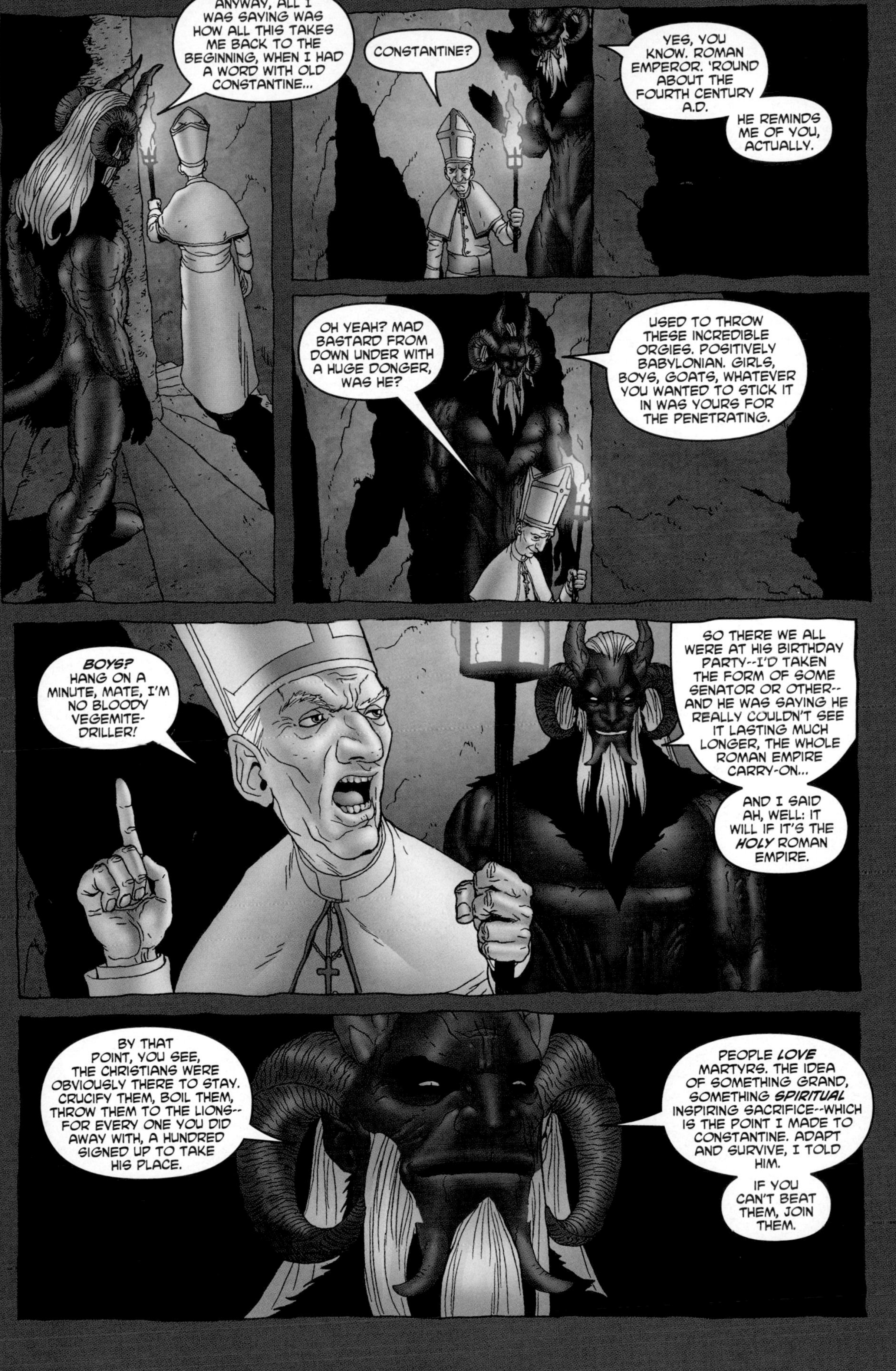
ANYWAY, ALL I WAS SAYING WAS HOW ALL THIS TAKES ME BACK TO THE BEGINNING, WHEN I HAD A WORD WITH OLD CONSTANTINE...
CONSTANTINE?
YES, YOU KNOW. ROMAN EMPEROR. 'ROUND ABOUT THE FOURTH CENTURY A.D.
HE REMINDS ME OF YOU, ACTUALLY.
OH YEAH? MAD BASTARD FROM DOWN UNDER WITH A HUGE DONGER, WAS HE?
USED TO THROW THESE INCREDIBLE ORGIES. POSITIVELY BABYLONIAN. GIRLS, BOYS, GOATS, WHATEVER YOU WANTED TO STICK IT IN WAS YOURS FOR THE PENETRATING.
BOYS? HANG ON A MINUTE, MATE, I'M NO BLOODY VEGEMITE-DRILLER!
SO THERE WE ALL WERE AT HIS BIRTHDAY PARTY--I'D TAKEN THE FORM OF SOME SENATOR OR OTHER--AND HE WAS SAYING HE REALLY COULDN'T SEE IT LASTING MUCH LONGER, THE WHOLE ROMAN EMPIRE CARRY-ON...
AND I SAID AH, WELL: IT WILL IF IT'S THE *HOLY* ROMAN EMPIRE.
BY THAT POINT, YOU SEE, THE CHRISTIANS WERE OBVIOUSLY THERE TO STAY. CRUCIFY THEM, BOIL THEM, THROW THEM TO THE LIONS--FOR EVERY ONE YOU DID AWAY WITH, A HUNDRED SIGNED UP TO TAKE HIS PLACE.
PEOPLE *LOVE* MARTYRS. THE IDEA OF SOMETHING GRAND, SOMETHING *SPIRITUAL* INSPIRING SACRIFICE--WHICH IS THE POINT I MADE TO CONSTANTINE. ADAPT AND SURVIVE, I TOLD HIM.
IF YOU CAN'T BEAT THEM, JOIN THEM.

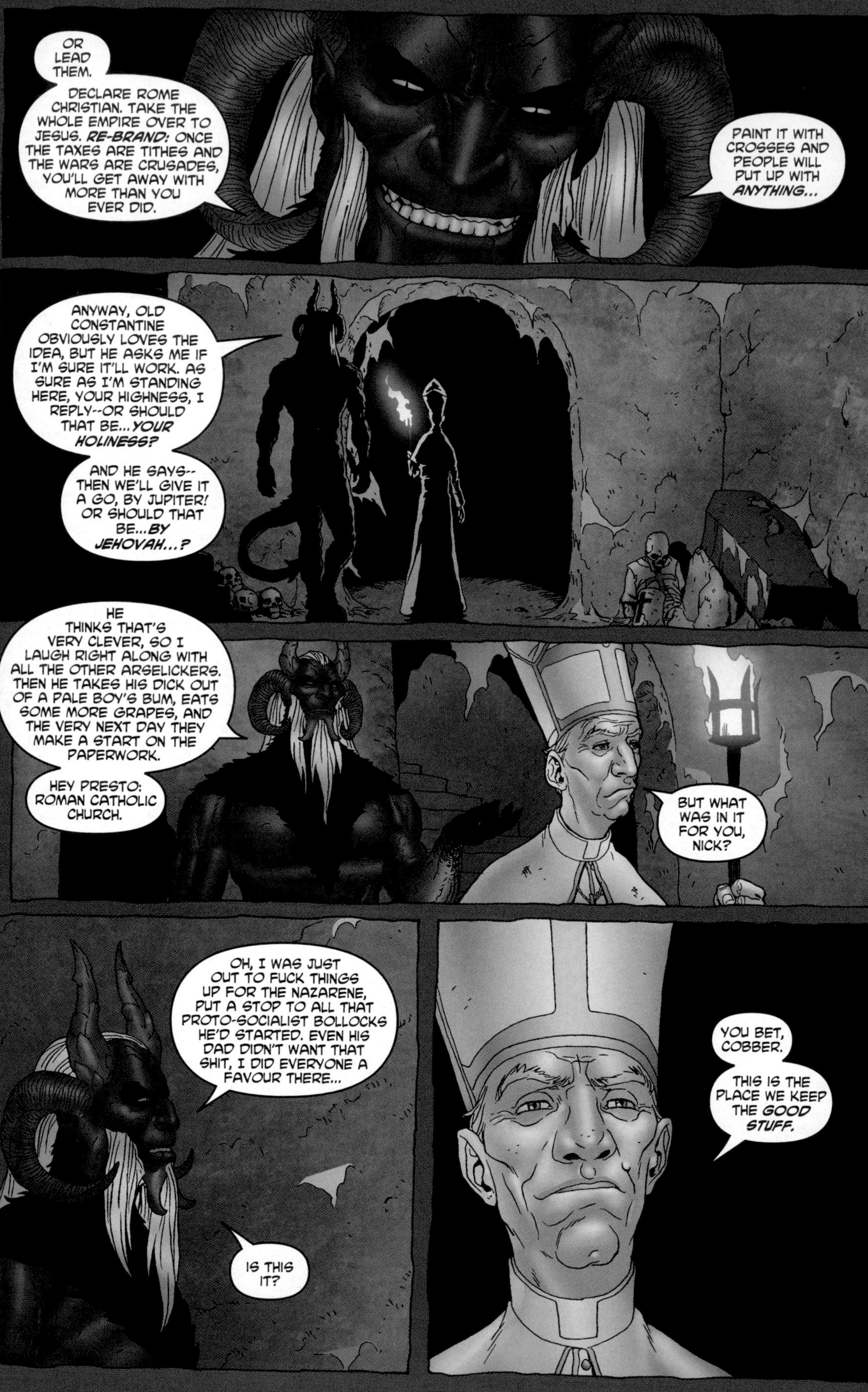
OR LEAD THEM.
DECLARE ROME CHRISTIAN. TAKE THE WHOLE EMPIRE OVER TO JESUS. RE-BRAND: ONCE THE TAXES ARE TITHES AND THE WARS ARE CRUSADES, YOU'LL GET AWAY WITH MORE THAN YOU EVER DID.
PAINT IT WITH CROSSES AND PEOPLE WILL PUT UP WITH ANYTHING...
ANYWAY, OLD CONSTANTINE OBVIOUSLY LOVES THE IDEA, BUT HE ASKS ME IF I'M SURE IT'LL WORK. AS SURE AS I'M STANDING HERE, YOUR HIGHNESS, I REPLY--OR SHOULD THAT BE...YOUR HOLINESS?
AND HE SAYS-- THEN WE'LL GIVE IT A GO, BY JUPITER! OR SHOULD THAT BE...BY JEHOVAH...?
HE THINKS THAT'S VERY CLEVER, SO I LAUGH RIGHT ALONG WITH ALL THE OTHER ARSELICKERS. THEN HE TAKES HIS DICK OUT OF A PALE BOY'S BUM, EATS SOME MORE GRAPES, AND THE VERY NEXT DAY THEY MAKE A START ON THE PAPERWORK.
HEY PRESTO: ROMAN CATHOLIC CHURCH.
BUT WHAT WAS IN IT FOR YOU, NICK?
OH, I WAS JUST OUT TO FUCK THINGS UP FOR THE NAZARENE, PUT A STOP TO ALL THAT PROTO-SOCIALIST BOLLOCKS HE'D STARTED. EVEN HIS DAD DIDN'T WANT THAT SHIT, I DID EVERYONE A FAVOUR THERE...
IS THIS IT?
YOU BET, COBBER.
THIS IS THE PLACE WE KEEP THE GOOD STUFF.

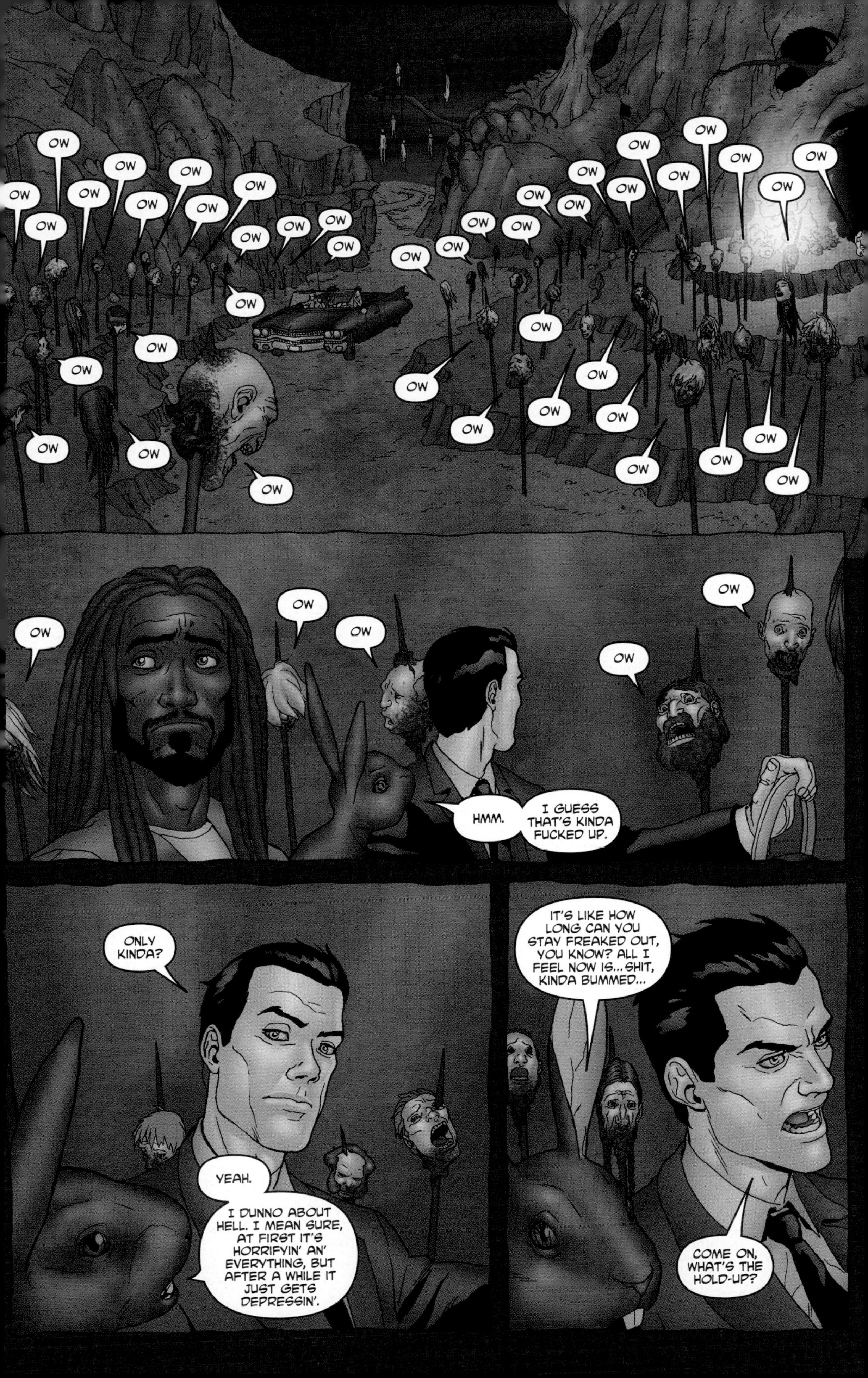
OW
OW
OW
OW
OW
OW
OW
OW
OW
OW
OW
OW
OW
OW
OW
OW
OW
OW
OW
OW
OW
OW
OW
OW
OW
OW
OW
OW
OW
OW
OW
OW
OW
OW
OW
OW
OW
OW
OW
OW
OW
OW
OW
OW
OW
OW
OW
OW
OW
HMM.
I GUESS THAT'S KINDA FUCKED UP.
ONLY KINDA?
YEAH.
I DUNNO ABOUT HELL. I MEAN SURE, AT FIRST IT'S HORRIFYIN' AN' EVERYTHING, BUT AFTER A WHILE IT JUST GETS DEPRESSIN'.
IT'S LIKE HOW LONG CAN YOU STAY FREAKED OUT, YOU KNOW? ALL I FEEL NOW IS... SHIT, KINDA BUMMED...
COME ON, WHAT'S THE HOLD-UP?

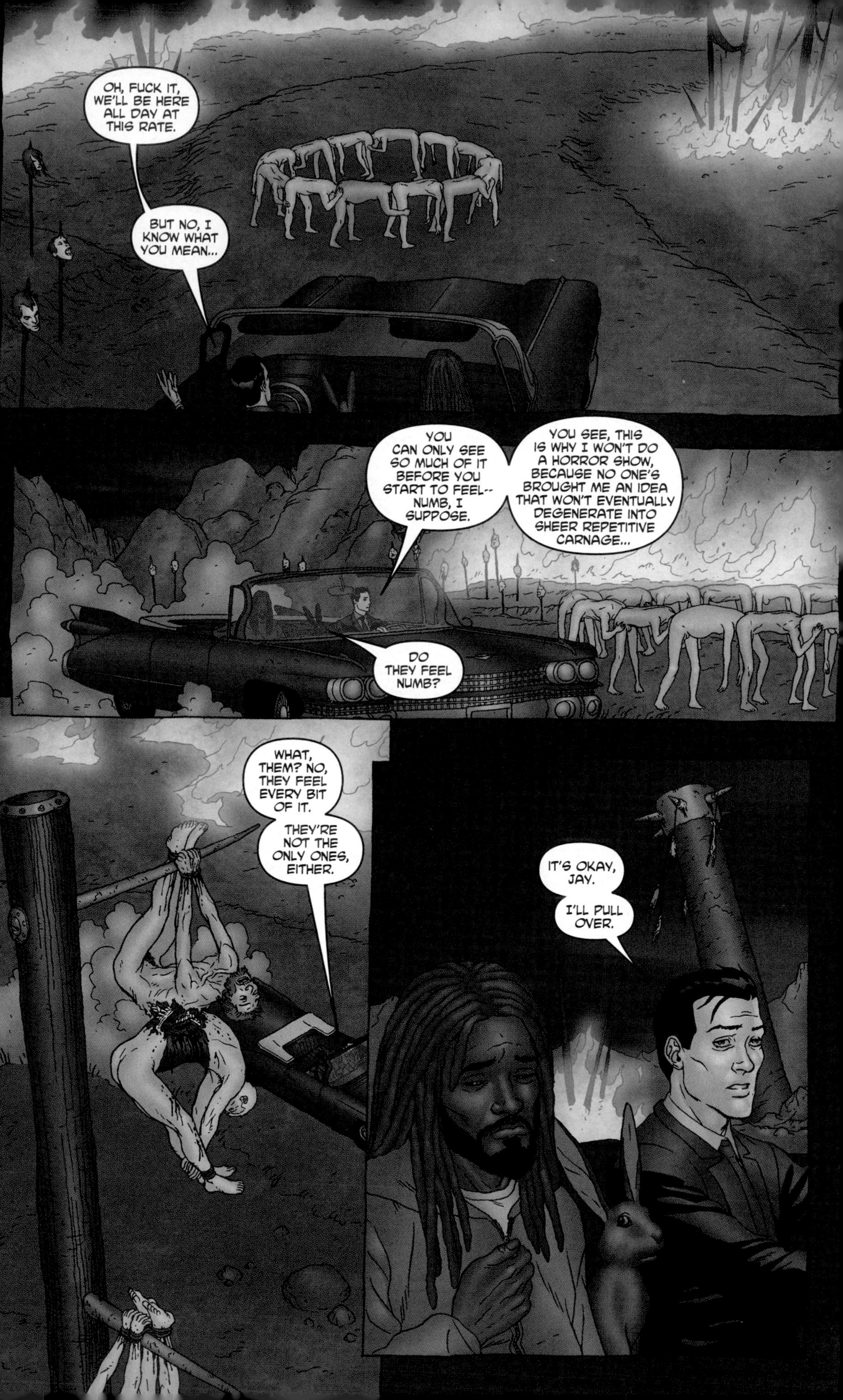
OH, FUCK IT, WE'LL BE HERE ALL DAY AT THIS RATE.
BUT NO, I KNOW WHAT YOU MEAN...
YOU CAN ONLY SEE SO MUCH OF IT BEFORE YOU START TO FEEL-- NUMB, I SUPPOSE.
YOU SEE, THIS IS WHY I WON'T DO A HORROR SHOW, BECAUSE NO ONE'S BROUGHT ME AN IDEA THAT WON'T EVENTUALLY DEGENERATE INTO SHEER REPETITIVE CARNAGE...
DO THEY FEEL NUMB?
WHAT, THEM? NO, THEY FEEL EVERY BIT OF IT.
THEY'RE NOT THE ONLY ONES, EITHER.
IT'S OKAY, JAY.
I'LL PULL OVER.

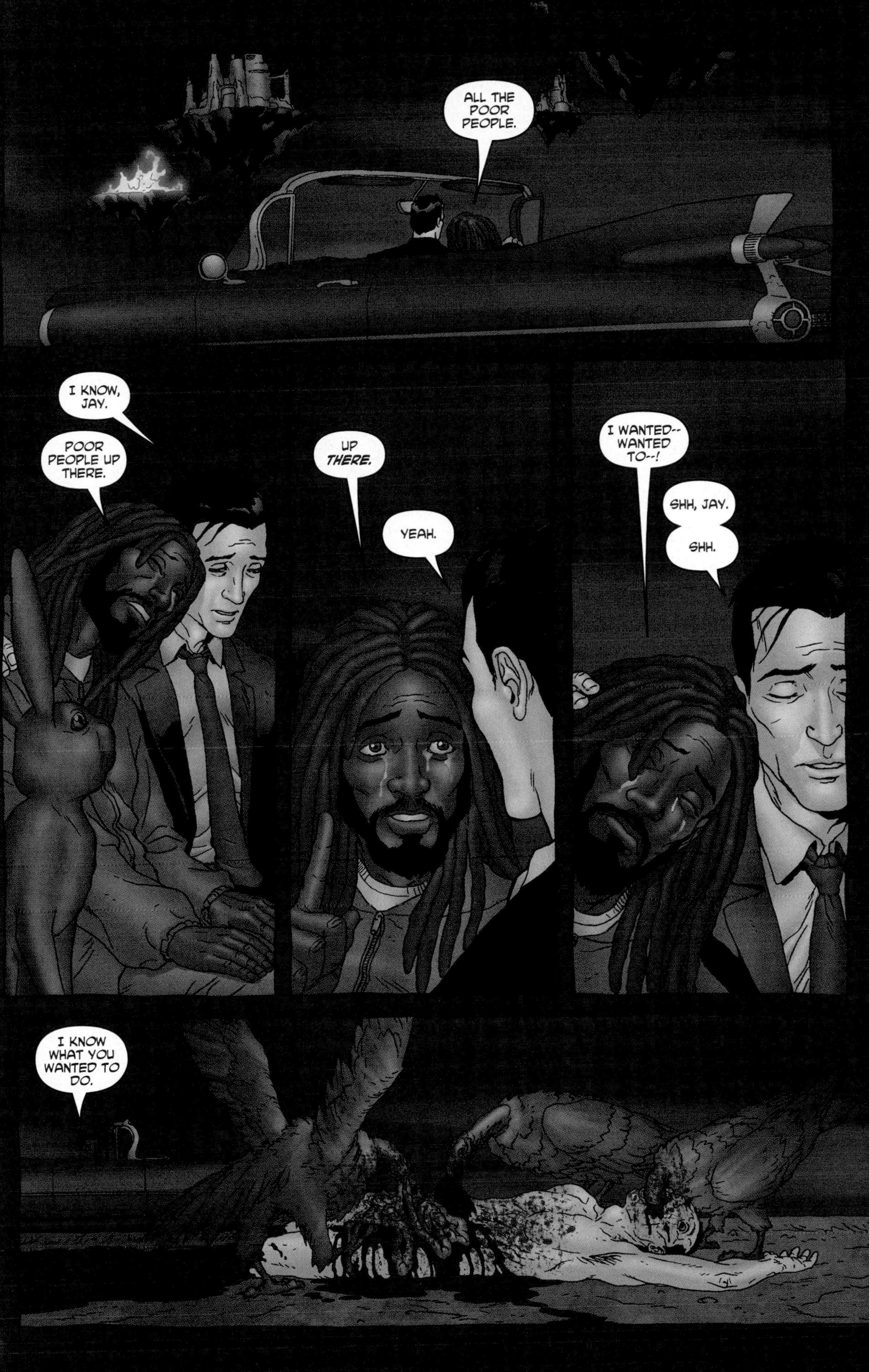
ALL THE POOR PEOPLE.
I KNOW, JAY.
POOR PEOPLE UP THERE.
UP *THERE.*
YEAH.
I WANTED-- WANTED TO--!
SHH, JAY.
SHH.
I KNOW WHAT YOU WANTED TO DO.

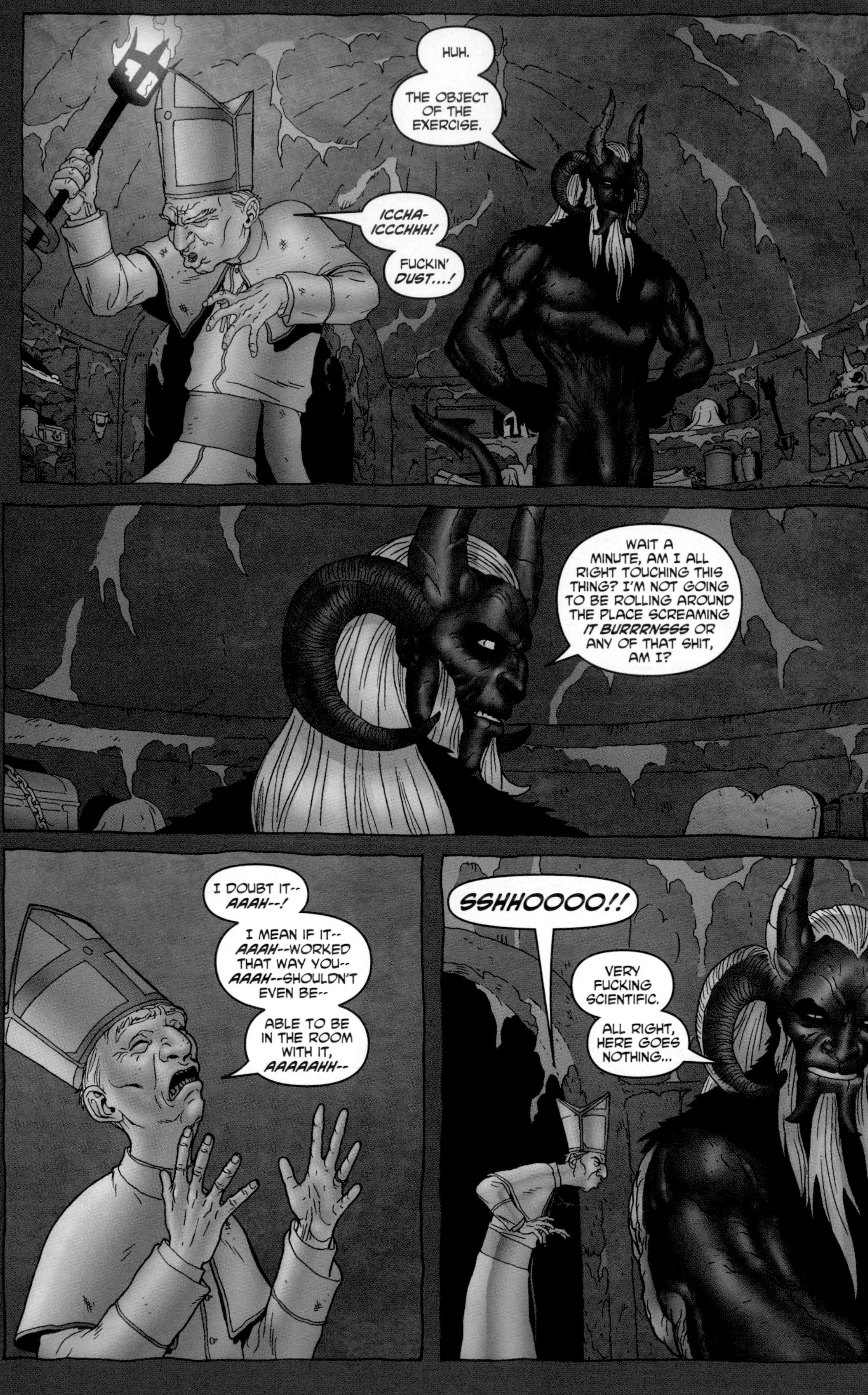
HUH.
THE OBJECT OF THE EXERCISE.
ICCHA-ICCCHHH!
FUCKIN' DUST...!
WAIT A MINUTE, AM I ALL RIGHT TOUCHING THIS THING? I'M NOT GOING TO BE ROLLING AROUND THE PLACE SCREAMING IT BURRRNSSS OR ANY OF THAT SHIT, AM I?
I DOUBT IT-- AAAH--!
I MEAN IF IT-- AAAH--WORKED THAT WAY YOU-- AAAH--SHOULDN'T EVEN BE--
ABLE TO BE IN THE ROOM WITH IT, AAAAAHH--
SSHHOOOO!!
VERY FUCKING SCIENTIFIC.
ALL RIGHT, HERE GOES NOTHING...

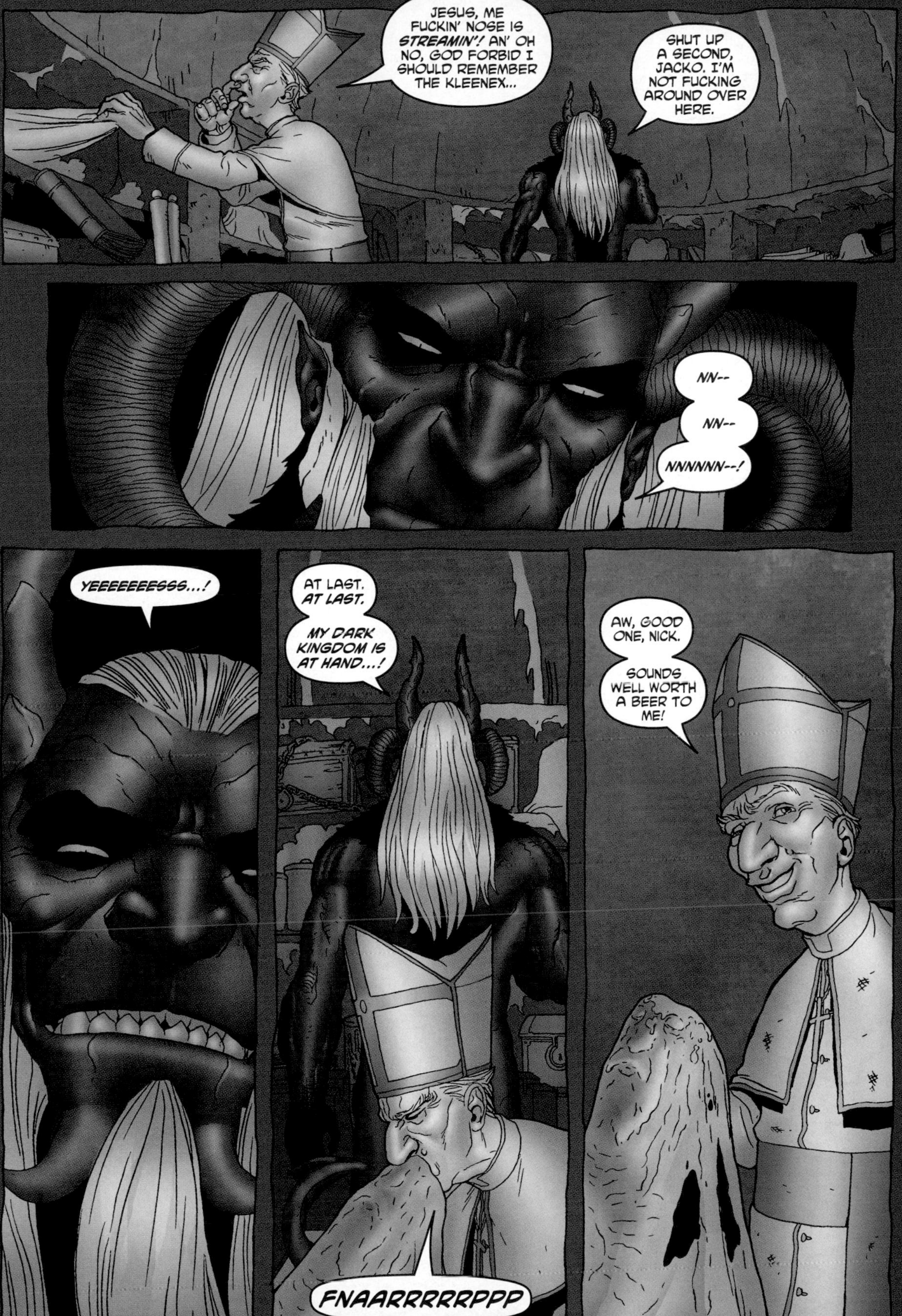
JESUS, ME FUCKIN' NOSE IS STREAMIN'! AN' OH NO, GOD FORBID I SHOULD REMEMBER THE KLEENEX...
SHUT UP A SECOND, JACKO. I'M NOT FUCKING AROUND OVER HERE.
NN--
NN--
NNNNNN--!
YEEEEEEEESSS...!
AT LAST. AT LAST.
MY DARK KINGDOM IS AT HAND...!
FNAARRRRRPPP
AW, GOOD ONE, NICK.
SOUNDS WELL WORTH A BEER TO ME!

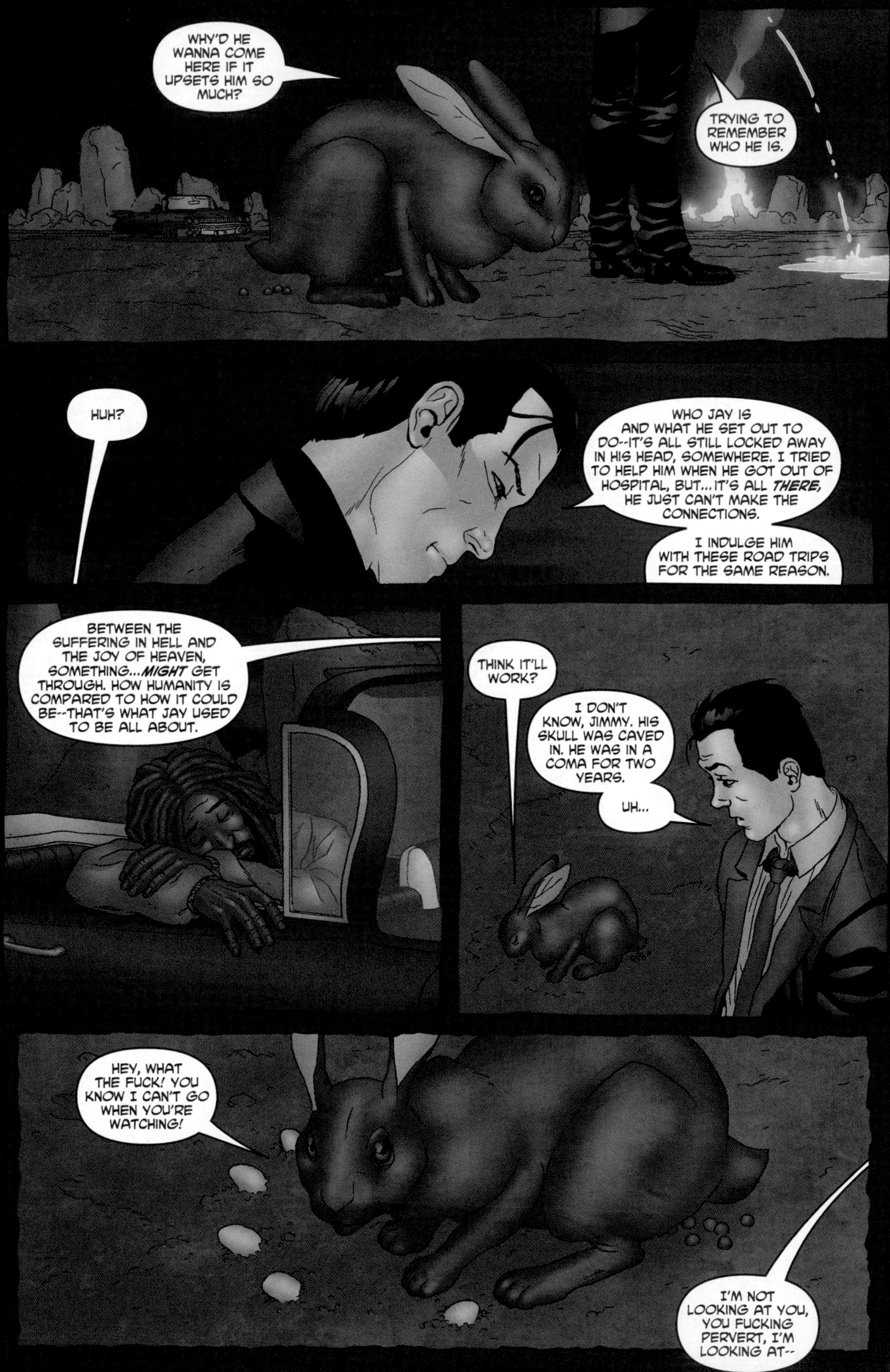
WHY'D HE WANNA COME HERE IF IT UPSETS HIM SO MUCH?
TRYING TO REMEMBER WHO HE IS.
HUH?
WHO JAY IS AND WHAT HE SET OUT TO DO--IT'S ALL STILL LOCKED AWAY IN HIS HEAD, SOMEWHERE. I TRIED TO HELP HIM WHEN HE GOT OUT OF HOSPITAL, BUT... IT'S ALL *THERE,* HE JUST CAN'T MAKE THE CONNECTIONS.
I INDULGE HIM WITH THESE ROAD TRIPS FOR THE SAME REASON.
BETWEEN THE SUFFERING IN HELL AND THE JOY OF HEAVEN, SOMETHING... ***MIGHT*** GET THROUGH. HOW HUMANITY IS COMPARED TO HOW IT COULD BE--THAT'S WHAT JAY USED TO BE ALL ABOUT.
THINK IT'LL WORK?
I DON'T KNOW, JIMMY. HIS SKULL WAS CAVED IN. HE WAS IN A COMA FOR TWO YEARS.
UH...
HEY, WHAT THE FUCK! YOU KNOW I CAN'T GO WHEN YOU'RE WATCHING!
I'M NOT LOOKING AT YOU, YOU FUCKING PERVERT, I'M LOOKING AT--

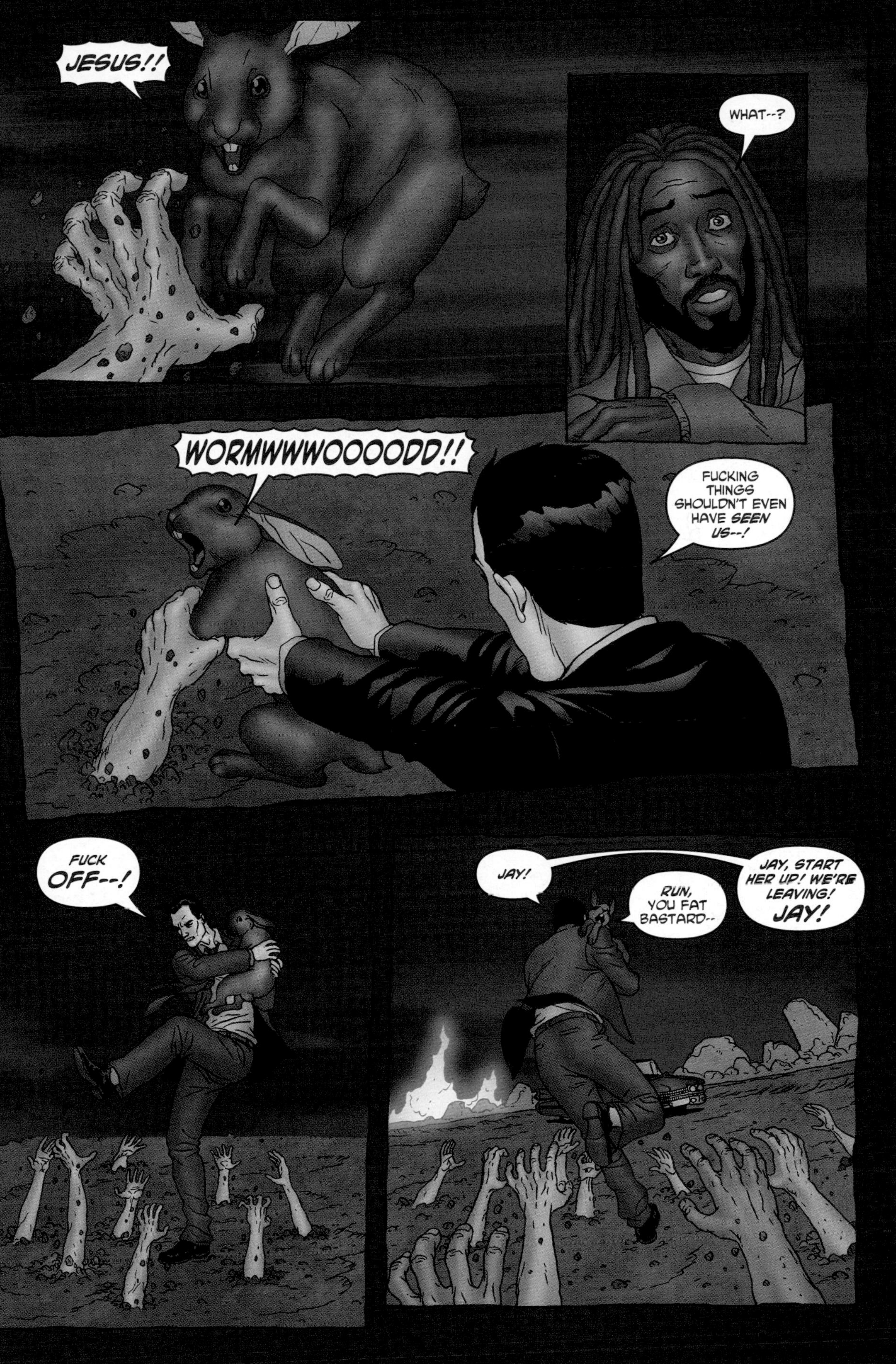
JESUS!!
WHAT--?
WORMWWWOOOODD!!
FUCKING THINGS SHOULDN'T EVEN HAVE SEEN US--!
FUCK OFF--!
JAY!
JAY, START HER UP! WE'RE LEAVING! JAY!
RUN, YOU FAT BASTARD--

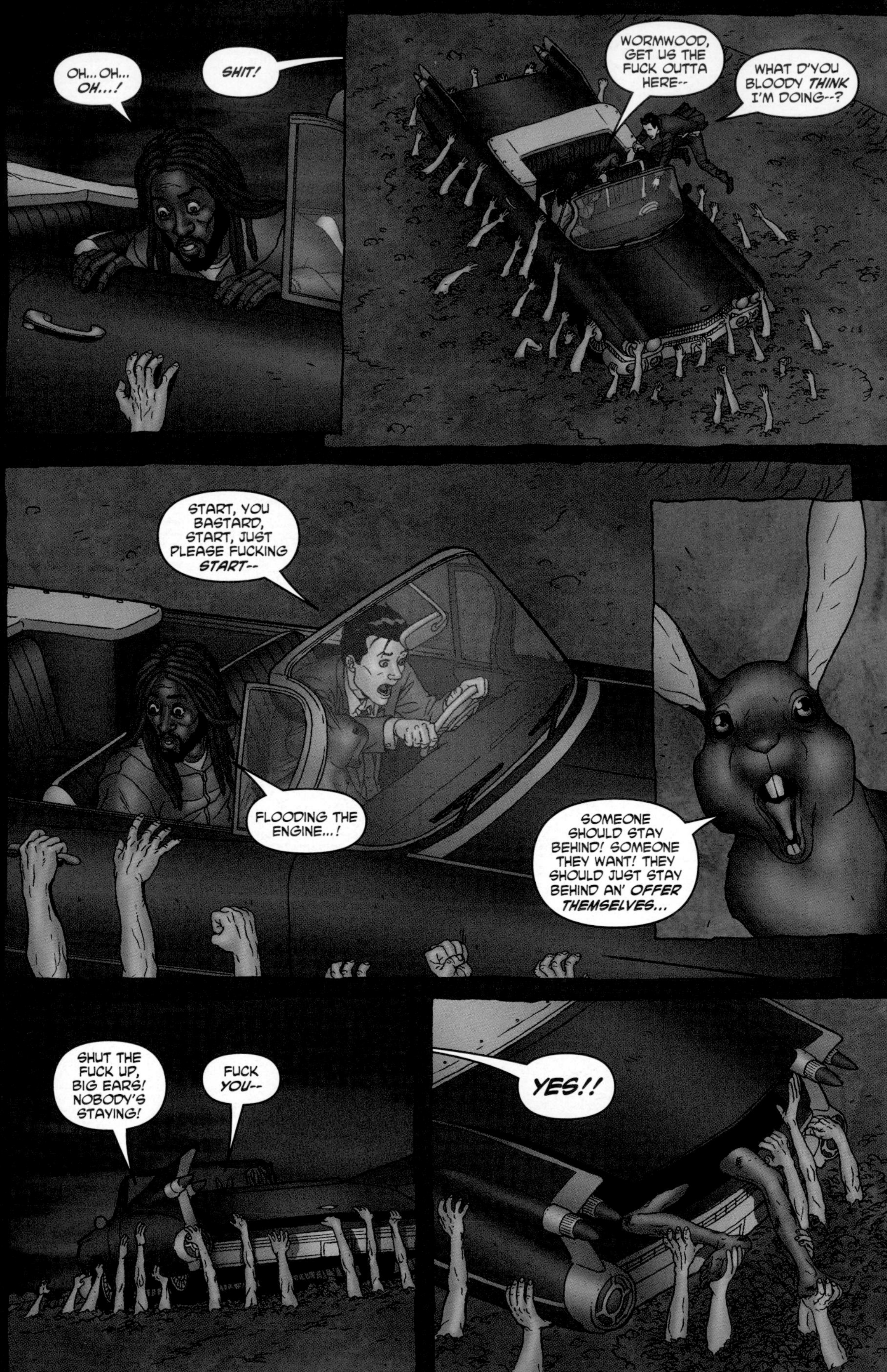
OH... OH...
OH...!
SHIT!
WORMWOOD, GET US THE FUCK OUTTA HERE--
WHAT D'YOU BLOODY THINK I'M DOING--?
START, YOU BASTARD, START, JUST PLEASE FUCKING START--
FLOODING THE ENGINE...!
SOMEONE SHOULD STAY BEHIND! SOMEONE THEY WANT! THEY SHOULD JUST STAY BEHIND AN' OFFER THEMSELVES...
SHUT THE FUCK UP, BIG EARS! NOBODY'S STAYING!
FUCK YOU--
YES!!

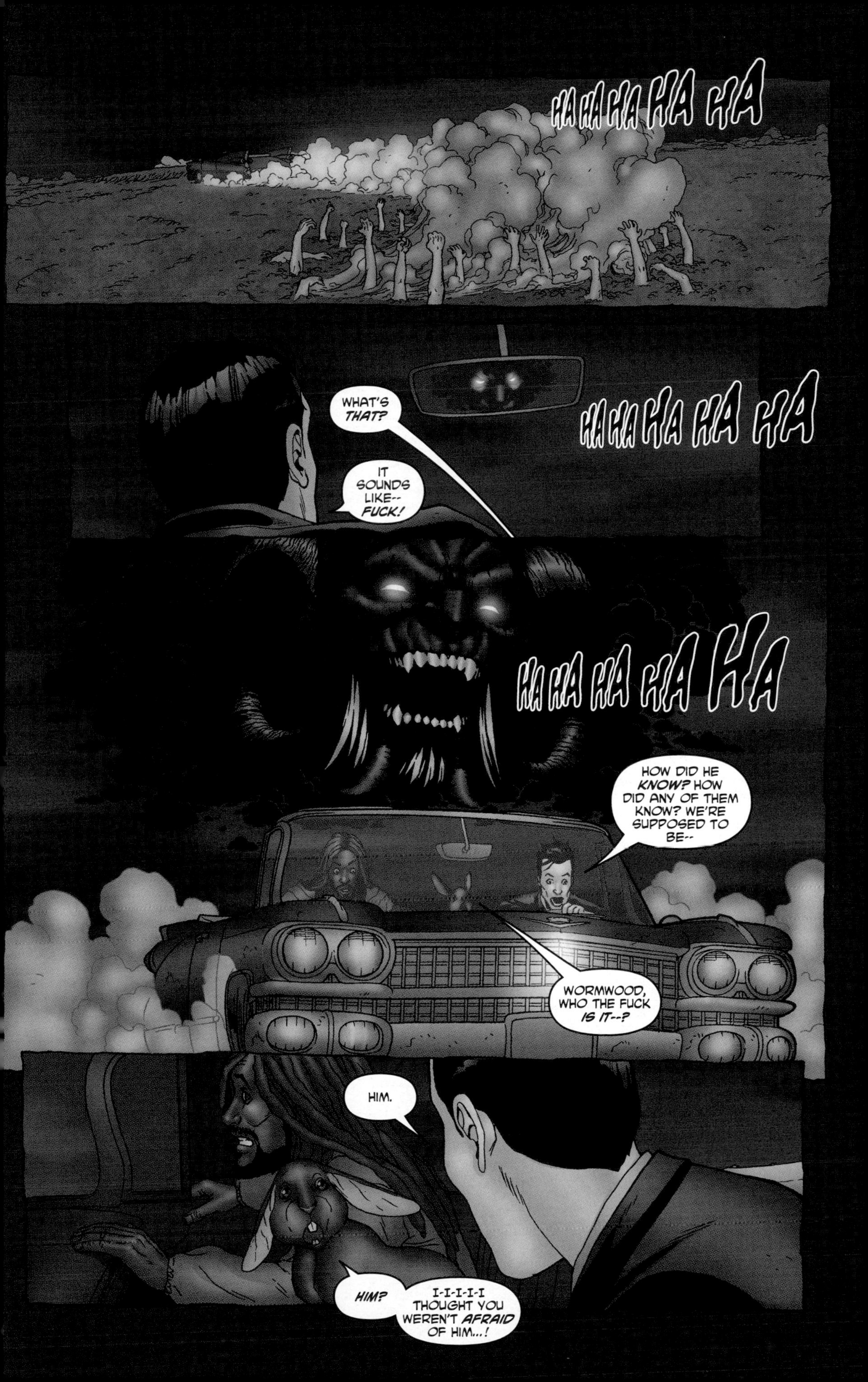
HA HA HA HA HA
WHAT'S THAT?
HA HA HA HA HA
IT SOUNDS LIKE-- FUCK!
HA HA HA HA HA
HOW DID HE KNOW? HOW DID ANY OF THEM KNOW? WE'RE SUPPOSED TO BE--
WORMWOOD, WHO THE FUCK IS IT--?
HIM.
HIM?
I-I-I-I-I THOUGHT YOU WEREN'T AFRAID OF HIM...!

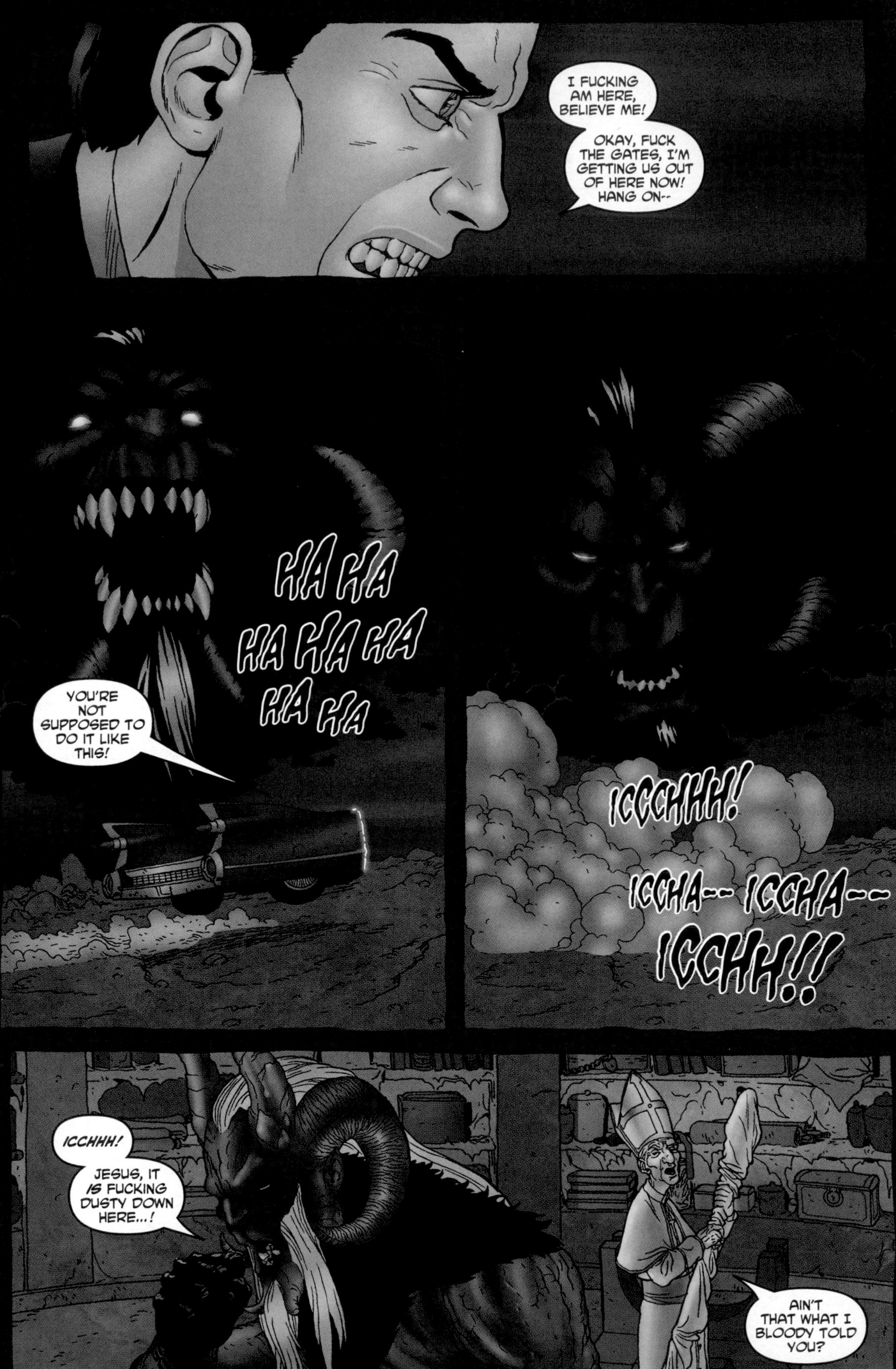
I FUCKING AM HERE, BELIEVE ME!
OKAY, FUCK THE GATES, I'M GETTING US OUT OF HERE NOW! HANG ON--
HA HA HA HA HA HA HA
YOU'RE NOT SUPPOSED TO DO IT LIKE THIS!
ICCCHHH!
ICCHA-- ICCHA-- ICCHH!!
ICCHHH!
JESUS, IT *IS* FUCKING DUSTY DOWN HERE...!
AIN'T THAT WHAT I BLOODY TOLD YOU?

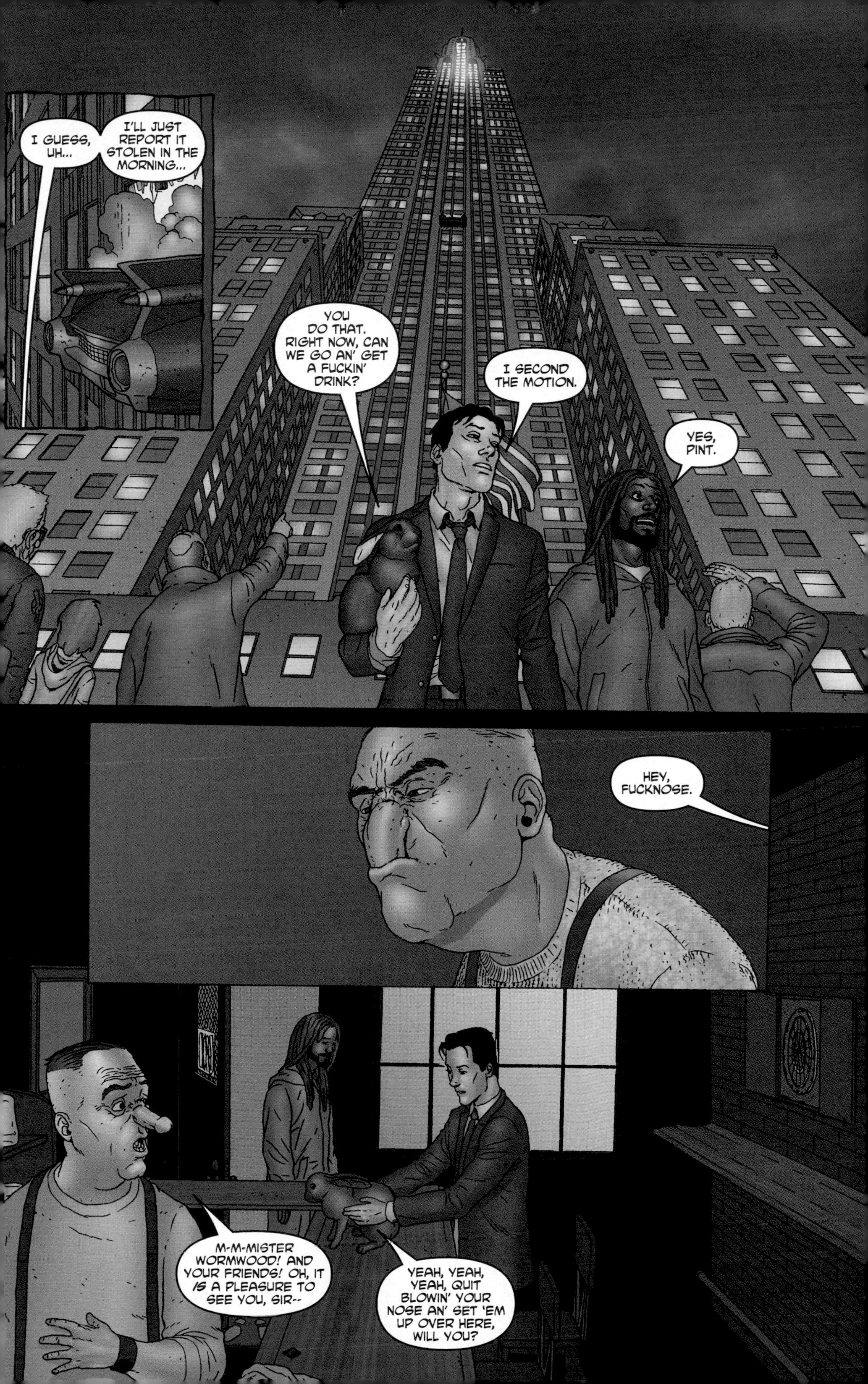
I GUESS, UH...
I'LL JUST REPORT IT STOLEN IN THE MORNING...
YOU DO THAT. RIGHT NOW, CAN WE GO AN' GET A FUCKIN' DRINK?
I SECOND THE MOTION.
YES, PINT.
HEY, FUCKNOSE.
M-M-MISTER WORMWOOD! AND YOUR FRIENDS! OH, IT *IS* A PLEASURE TO SEE YOU, SIR--
YEAH, YEAH, YEAH, QUIT BLOWIN' YOUR NOSE AN' SET 'EM UP OVER HERE, WILL YOU?

THEY WERE TIPPED OFF.

HOW YOU FIGURE THAT?

WE SHOULD HAVE BEEN INVISIBLE DOWN THERE. NOT EVEN MY CUNT OF A DAD SHOULD HAVE BEEN ABLE TO SENSE US.

BUT THEY KNEW...

SO WHO TOLD 'EM WE WERE COMIN'?

FUCK KNOWS.

YESSIR?

NOT YOU, IDIOT.

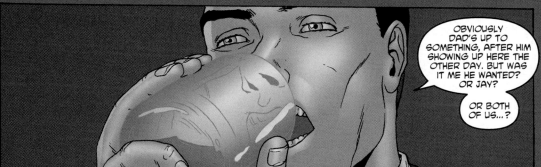

OBVIOUSLY DAD'S UP TO SOMETHING, AFTER HIM SHOWING UP HERE THE OTHER DAY. BUT WAS IT ME HE WANTED? OR JAY?

OR BOTH OF US...?

HELLO, BOYS.

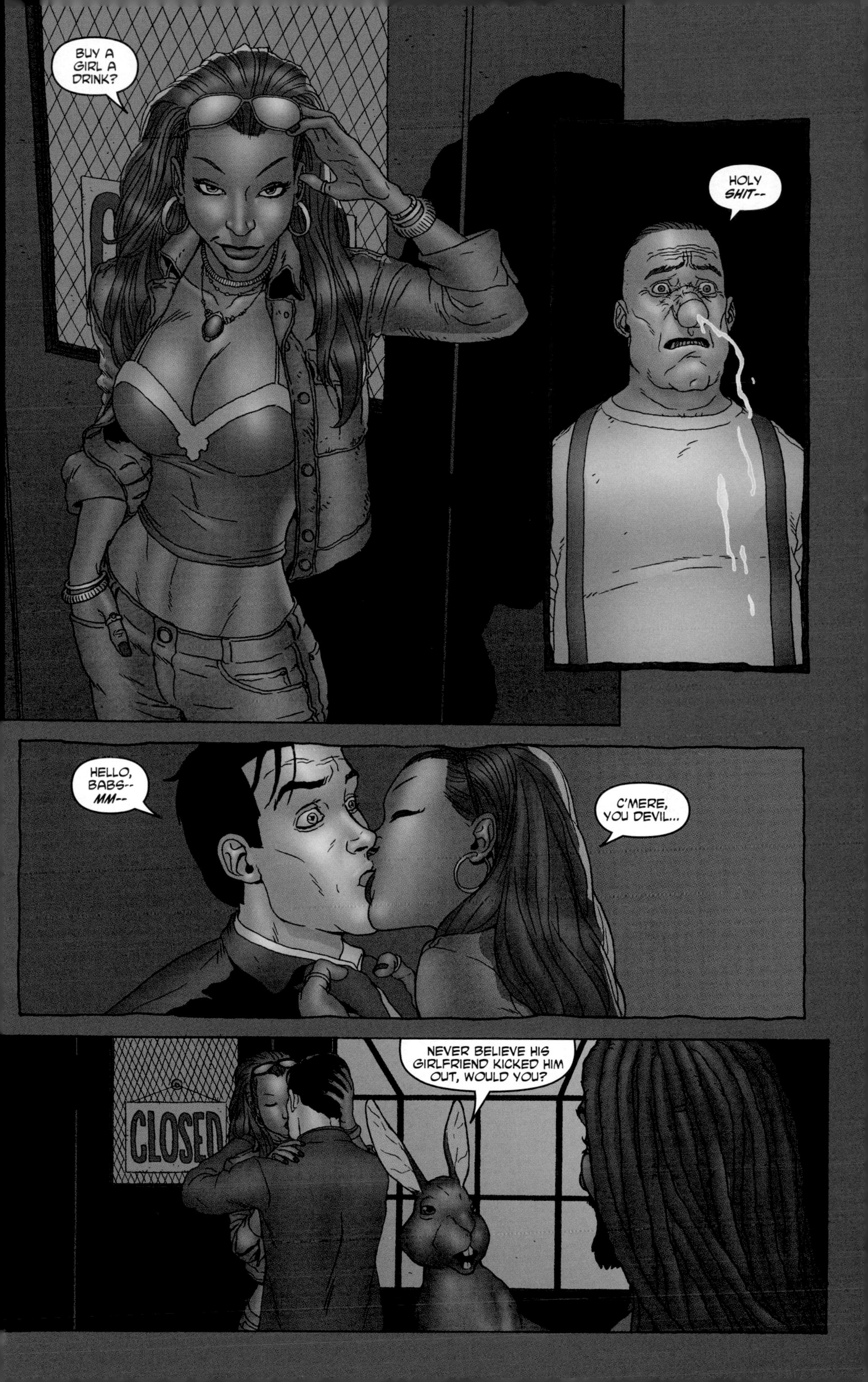
BUY A GIRL A DRINK?
HOLY SHIT--
HELLO, BABS-- MM--
C'MERE, YOU DEVIL...
CLOSED
NEVER BELIEVE HIS GIRLFRIEND KICKED HIM OUT, WOULD YOU?

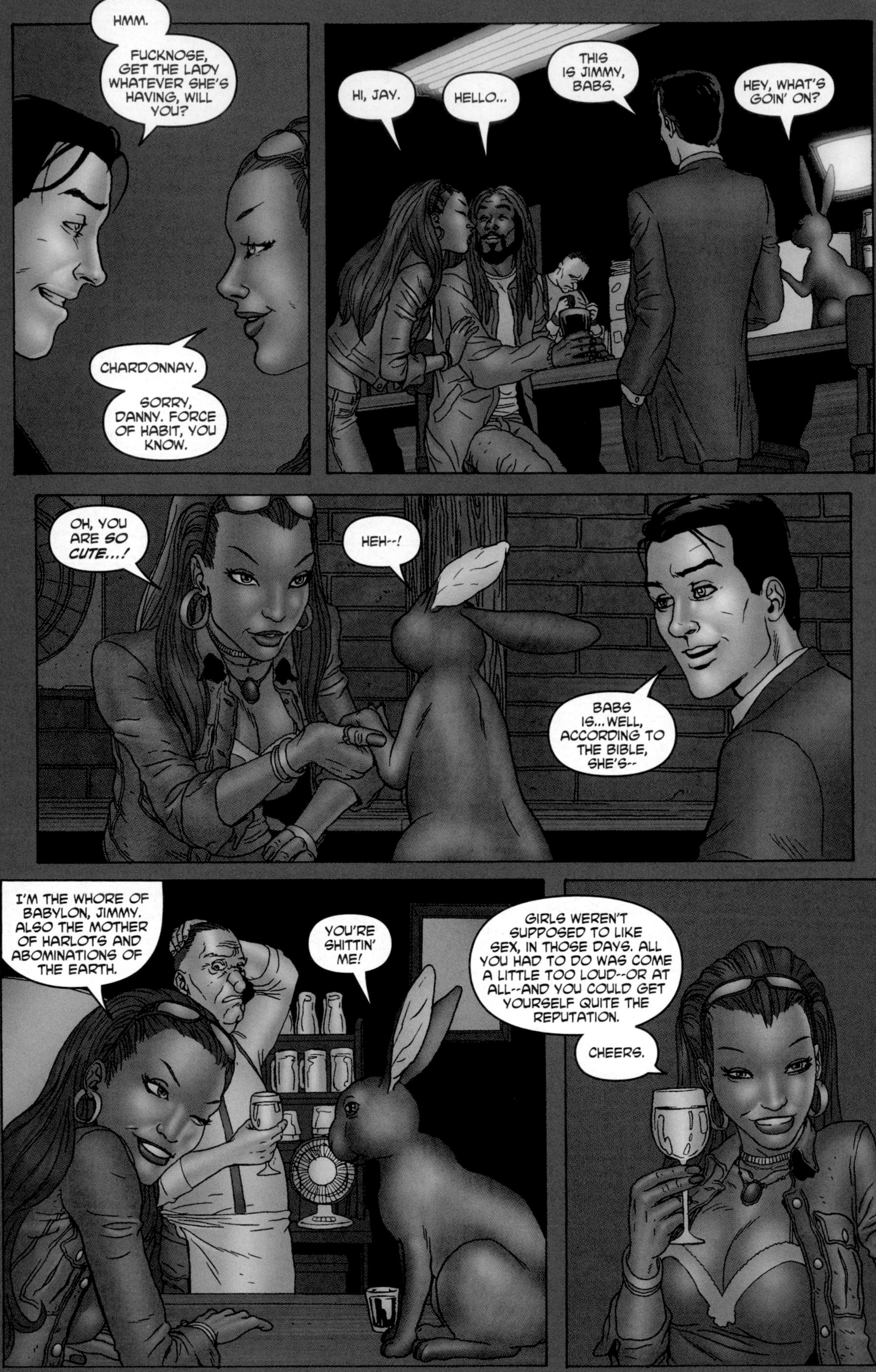
HMM.
FUCKNOSE, GET THE LADY WHATEVER SHE'S HAVING, WILL YOU?
CHARDONNAY.
SORRY, DANNY. FORCE OF HABIT, YOU KNOW.
HI, JAY.
HELLO...
THIS IS JIMMY, BABS.
HEY, WHAT'S GOIN' ON?
OH, YOU ARE SO *CUTE...!*
HEH--!
BABS IS...WELL, ACCORDING TO THE BIBLE, SHE'S--
I'M THE WHORE OF BABYLON, JIMMY. ALSO THE MOTHER OF HARLOTS AND ABOMINATIONS OF THE EARTH.
YOU'RE SHITTIN' ME!
GIRLS WEREN'T SUPPOSED TO LIKE SEX, IN THOSE DAYS. ALL YOU HAD TO DO WAS COME A LITTLE TOO LOUD--OR AT ALL--AND YOU COULD GET YOURSELF QUITE THE REPUTATION.
CHEERS.

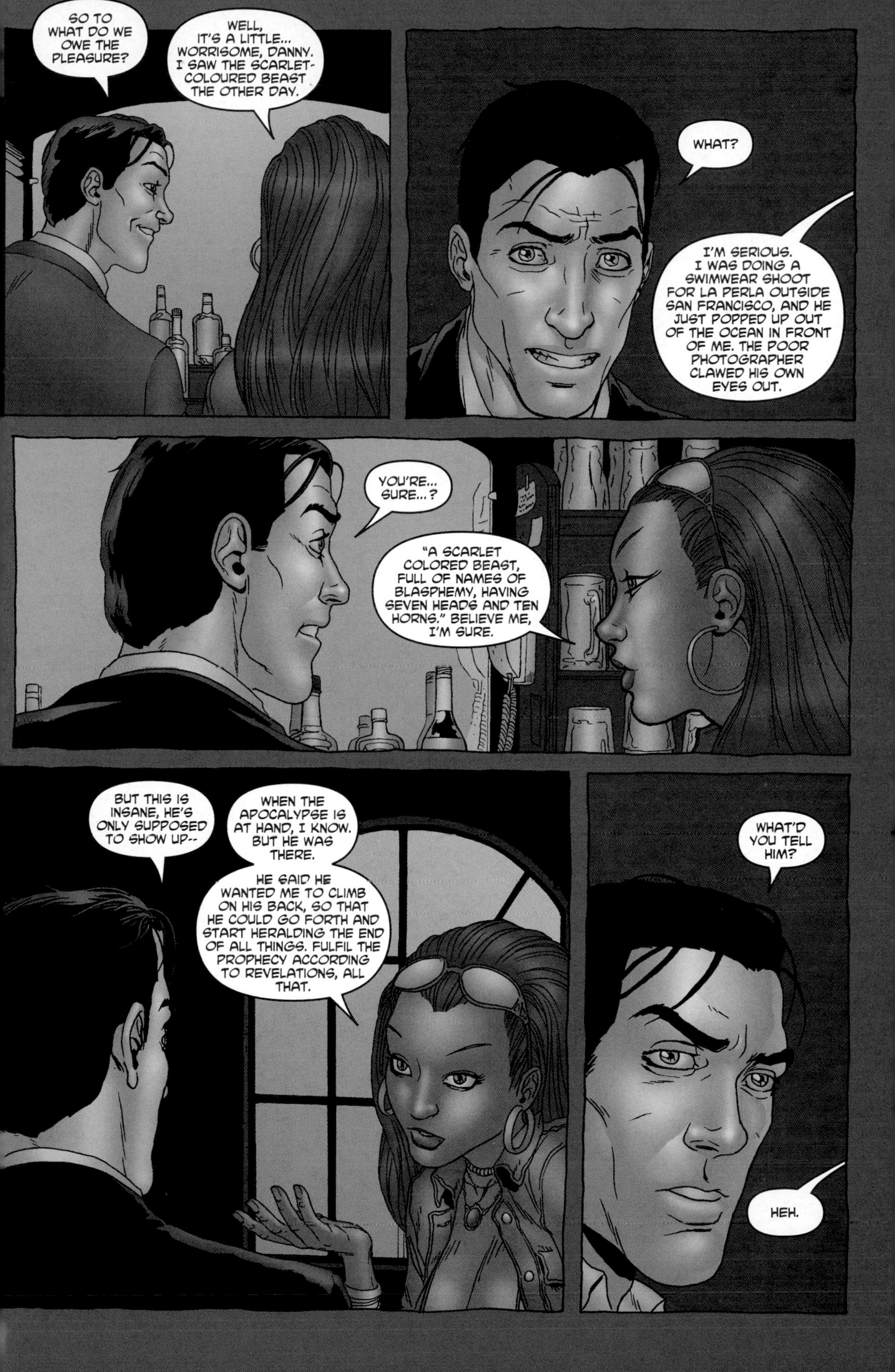
SO TO WHAT DO WE OWE THE PLEASURE?
WELL, IT'S A LITTLE... WORRISOME, DANNY. I SAW THE SCARLET-COLOURED BEAST THE OTHER DAY.
WHAT?
I'M SERIOUS. I WAS DOING A SWIMWEAR SHOOT FOR LA PERLA OUTSIDE SAN FRANCISCO, AND HE JUST POPPED UP OUT OF THE OCEAN IN FRONT OF ME. THE POOR PHOTOGRAPHER CLAWED HIS OWN EYES OUT.
YOU'RE... SURE...?
"A SCARLET COLORED BEAST, FULL OF NAMES OF BLASPHEMY, HAVING SEVEN HEADS AND TEN HORNS." BELIEVE ME, I'M SURE.
BUT THIS IS INSANE, HE'S ONLY SUPPOSED TO SHOW UP--
WHEN THE APOCALYPSE IS AT HAND, I KNOW. BUT HE WAS THERE.
HE SAID HE WANTED ME TO CLIMB ON HIS BACK, SO THAT HE COULD GO FORTH AND START HERALDING THE END OF ALL THINGS. FULFIL THE PROPHECY ACCORDING TO REVELATIONS, ALL THAT.
WHAT'D YOU TELL HIM?
HEH.

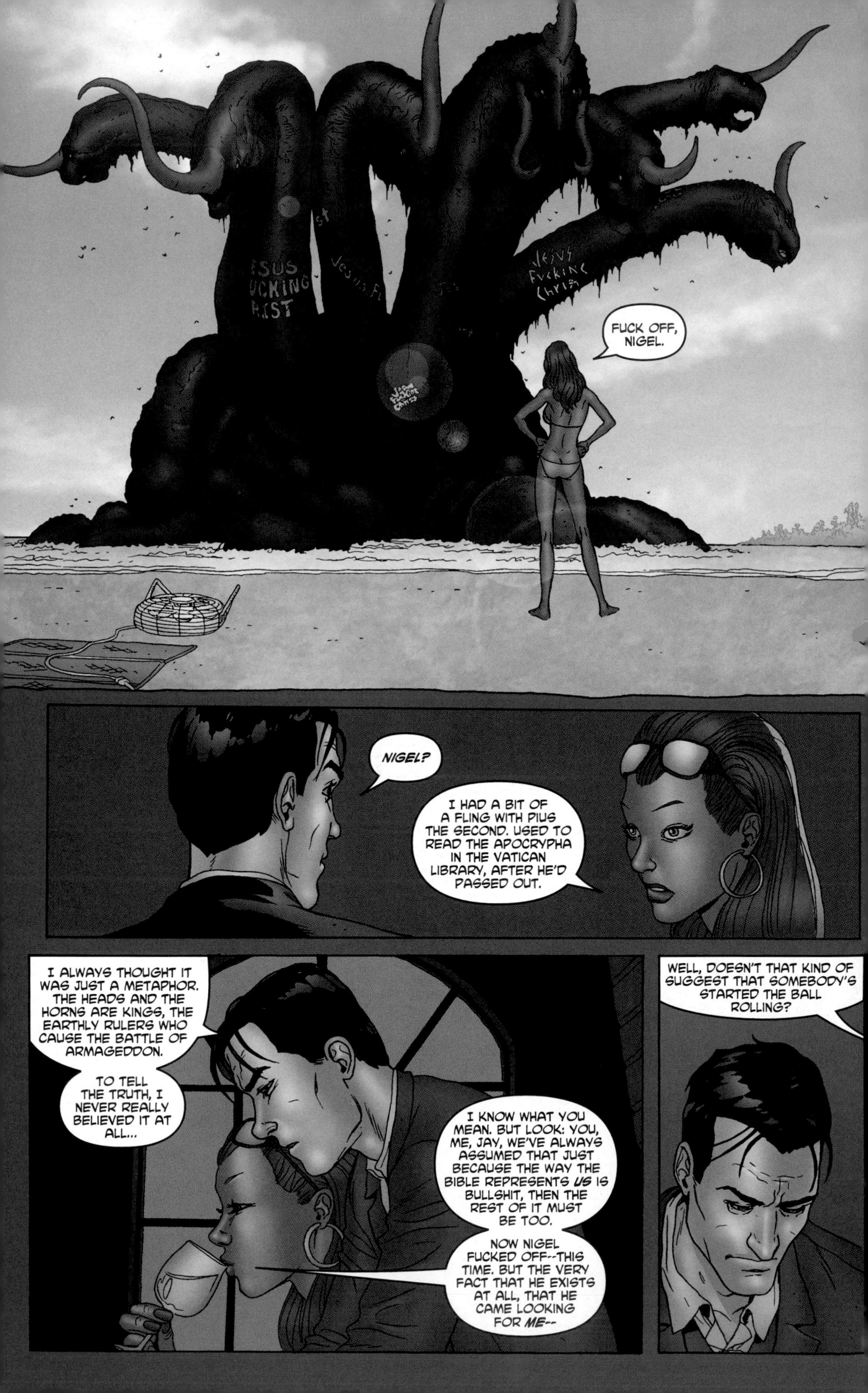

ESUS
FUCKING
RIST
Jesus
Fucking
Christ
FUCK OFF, NIGEL.
NIGEL?
I HAD A BIT OF A FLING WITH PIUS THE SECOND. USED TO READ THE APOCRYPHA IN THE VATICAN LIBRARY, AFTER HE'D PASSED OUT.
I ALWAYS THOUGHT IT WAS JUST A METAPHOR. THE HEADS AND THE HORNS ARE KINGS, THE EARTHLY RULERS WHO CAUSE THE BATTLE OF ARMAGEDDON.
TO TELL THE TRUTH, I NEVER REALLY BELIEVED IT AT ALL...
I KNOW WHAT YOU MEAN. BUT LOOK: YOU, ME, JAY, WE'VE ALWAYS ASSUMED THAT JUST BECAUSE THE WAY THE BIBLE REPRESENTS *US* IS BULLSHIT, THEN THE REST OF IT MUST BE TOO.
NOW NIGEL FUCKED OFF--THIS TIME. BUT THE VERY FACT THAT HE EXISTS AT ALL, THAT HE CAME LOOKING FOR *ME*--
WELL, DOESN'T THAT KIND OF SUGGEST THAT SOMEBODY'S STARTED THE BALL ROLLING?

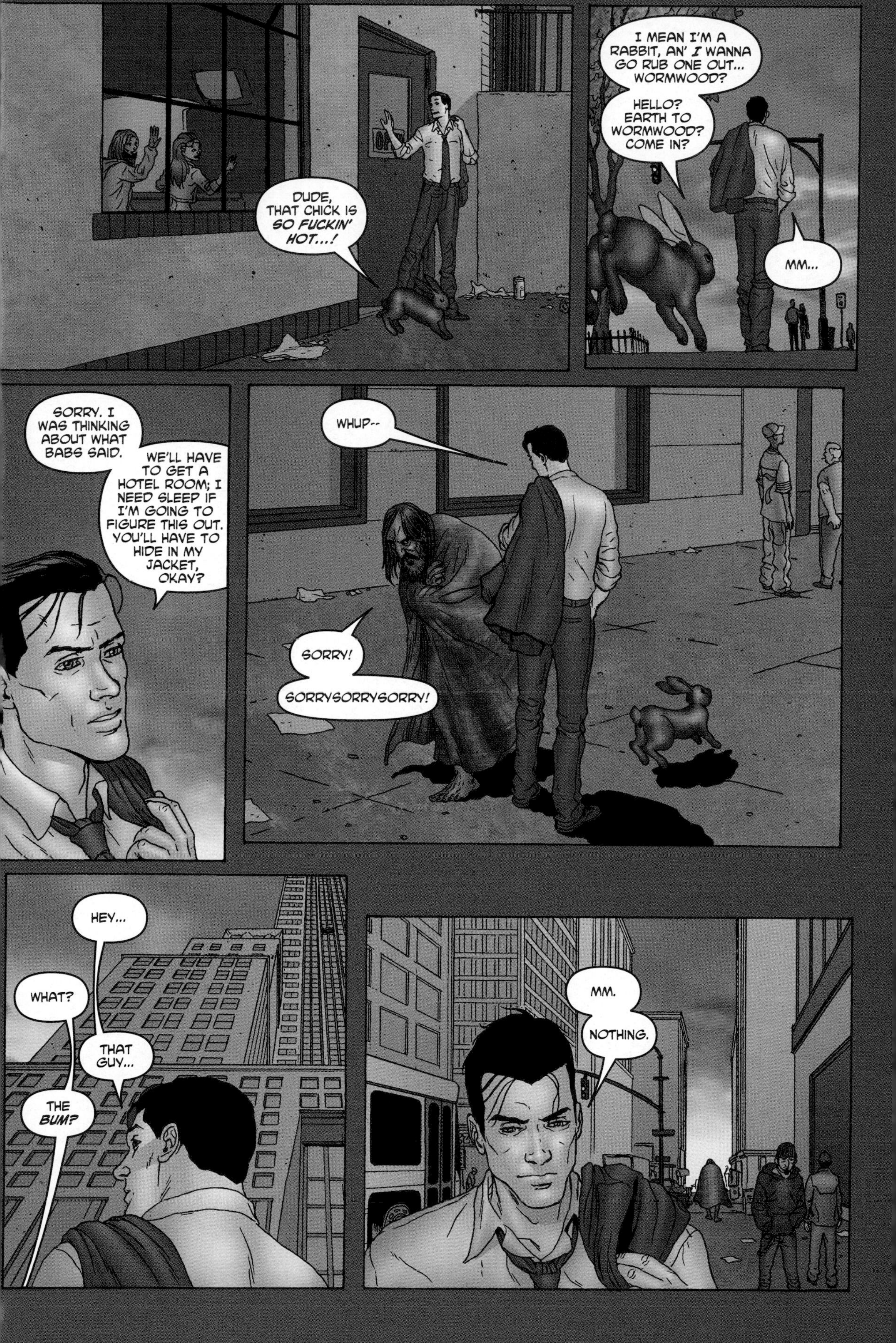
DUDE, THAT CHICK IS SO FUCKIN' HOT...!
I MEAN I'M A RABBIT, AN' I WANNA GO RUB ONE OUT... WORMWOOD?
HELLO? EARTH TO WORMWOOD? COME IN?
MM...
SORRY. I WAS THINKING ABOUT WHAT BABS SAID.
WE'LL HAVE TO GET A HOTEL ROOM; I NEED SLEEP IF I'M GOING TO FIGURE THIS OUT. YOU'LL HAVE TO HIDE IN MY JACKET, OKAY?
WHUP--
SORRY!
SORRYSORRYSORRY!
HEY...
WHAT?
THAT GUY...
THE BUM?
MM.
NOTHING.

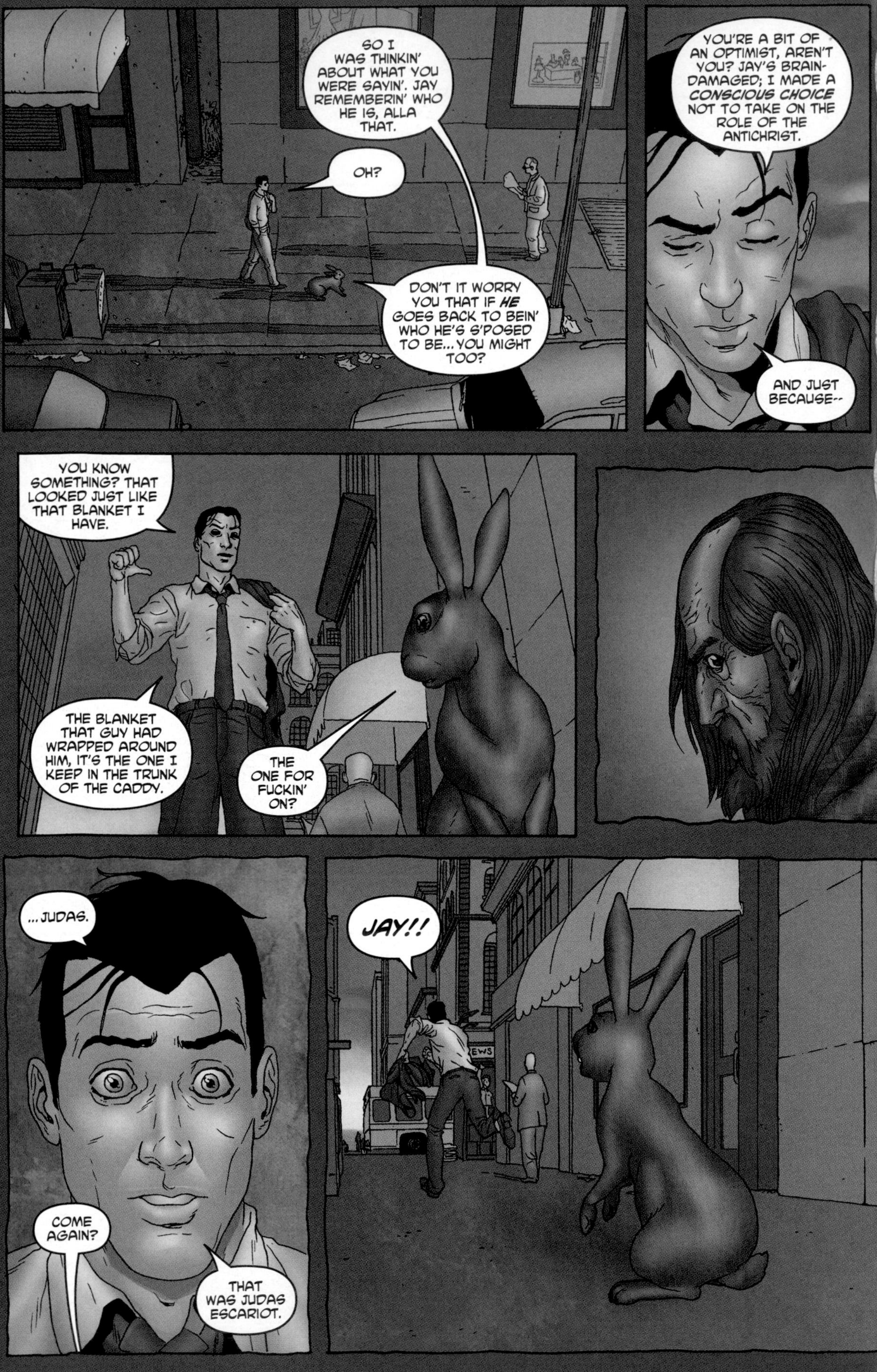
SO I WAS THINKIN' ABOUT WHAT YOU WERE SAYIN'. JAY REMEMBERIN' WHO HE IS, ALLA THAT.
OH?
DON'T IT WORRY YOU THAT IF HE GOES BACK TO BEIN' WHO HE'S S'POSED TO BE... YOU MIGHT TOO?
YOU'RE A BIT OF AN OPTIMIST, AREN'T YOU? JAY'S BRAIN-DAMAGED; I MADE A CONSCIOUS CHOICE NOT TO TAKE ON THE ROLE OF THE ANTICHRIST.
AND JUST BECAUSE--
YOU KNOW SOMETHING? THAT LOOKED JUST LIKE THAT BLANKET I HAVE.
THE BLANKET THAT GUY HAD WRAPPED AROUND HIM, IT'S THE ONE I KEEP IN THE TRUNK OF THE CADDY.
THE ONE FOR FUCKIN' ON?
...JUDAS.
COME AGAIN?
THAT WAS JUDAS ESCARIOT.
JAY!!
EWS

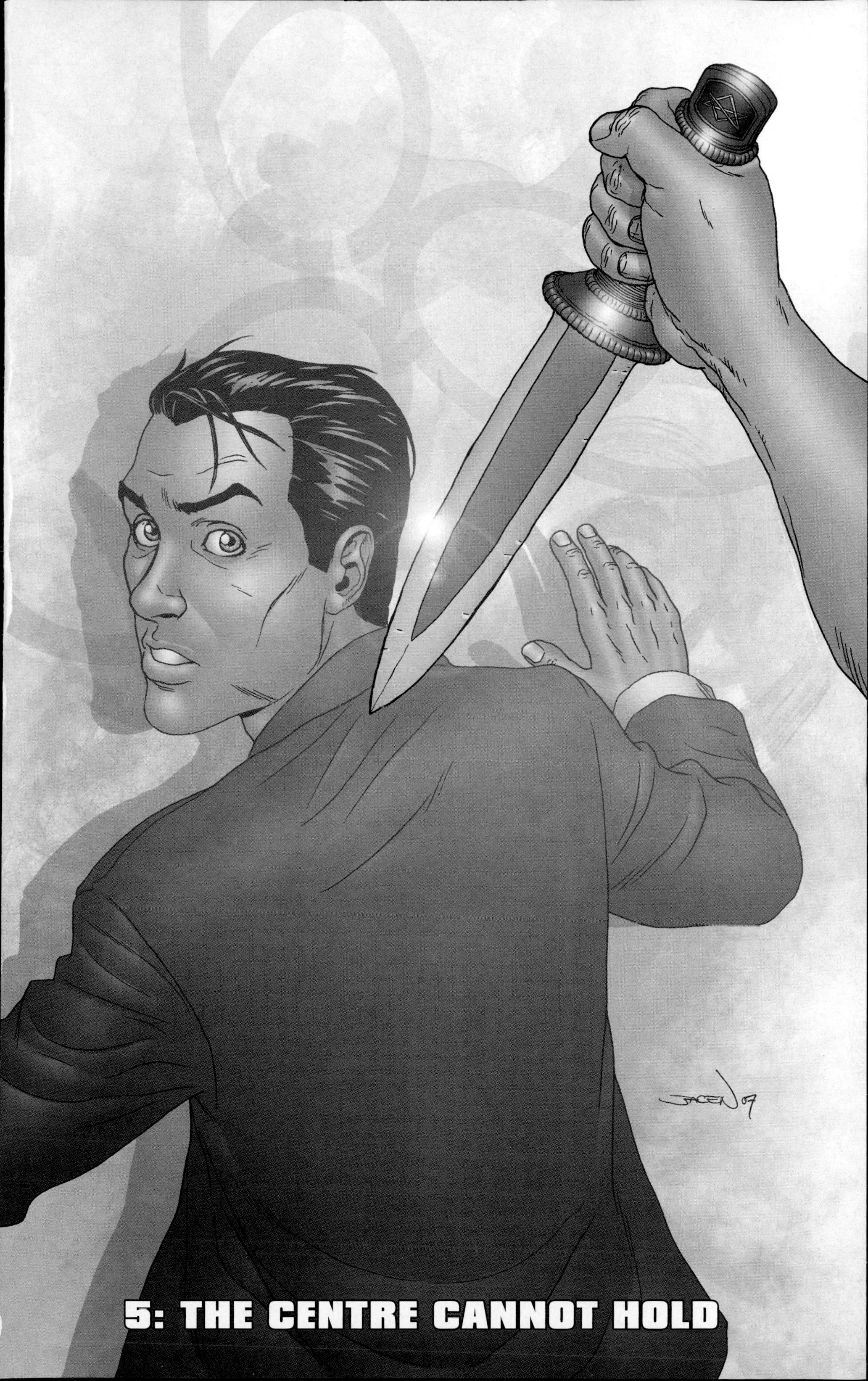
5: THE CENTRE CANNOT HOLD

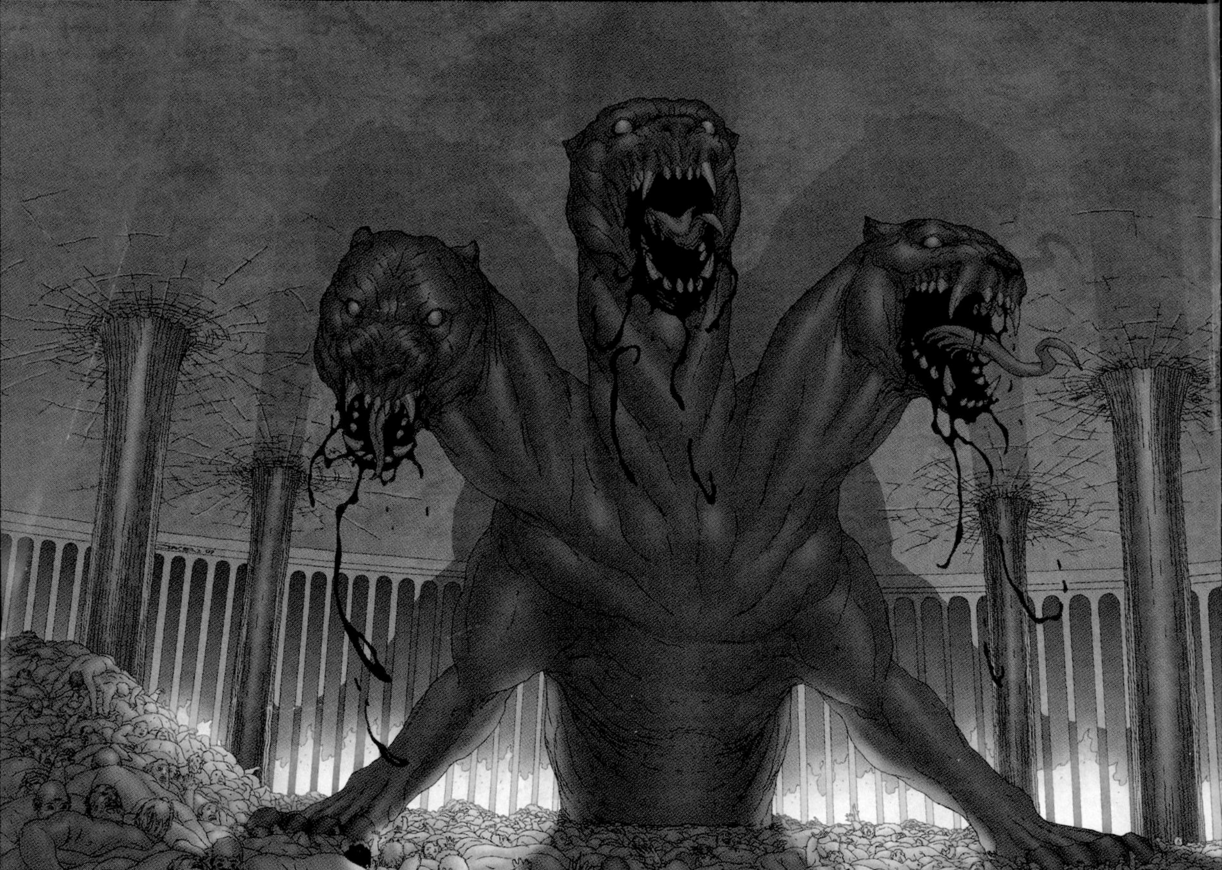

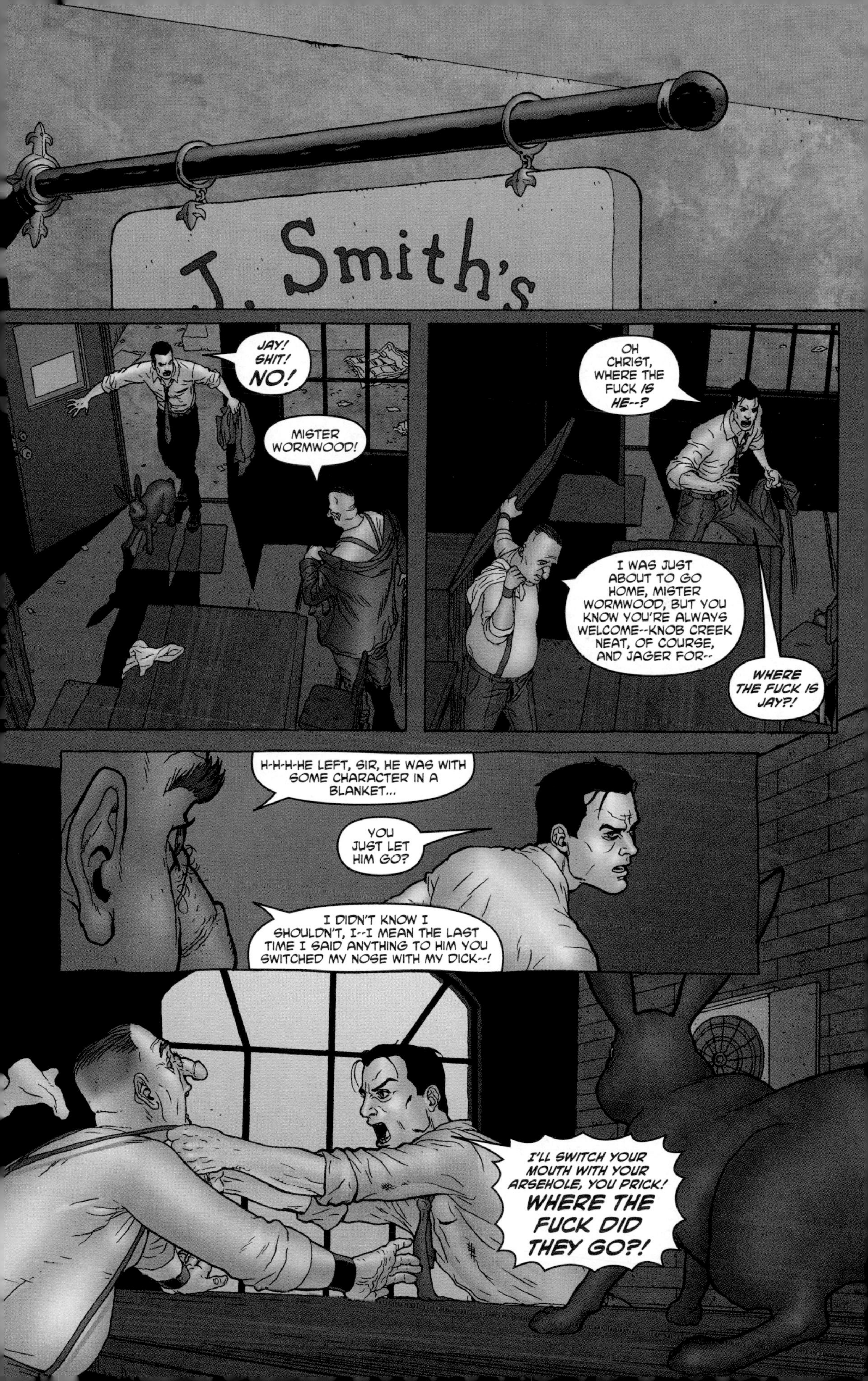
J. Smith's
JAY! SHIT! NO!
MISTER WORMWOOD!
OH CHRIST, WHERE THE FUCK *IS* HE--?
I WAS JUST ABOUT TO GO HOME, MISTER WORMWOOD, BUT YOU KNOW YOU'RE ALWAYS WELCOME--KNOB CREEK NEAT, OF COURSE, AND JAGER FOR--
WHERE THE FUCK IS JAY?!
H-H-H-HE LEFT, SIR, HE WAS WITH SOME CHARACTER IN A BLANKET...
YOU JUST LET HIM GO?
I DIDN'T KNOW I SHOULDN'T, I--I MEAN THE LAST TIME I SAID ANYTHING TO HIM YOU SWITCHED MY NOSE WITH MY DICK--!
I'LL SWITCH YOUR MOUTH WITH YOUR ARSEHOLE, YOU PRICK! WHERE THE FUCK DID THEY GO?!

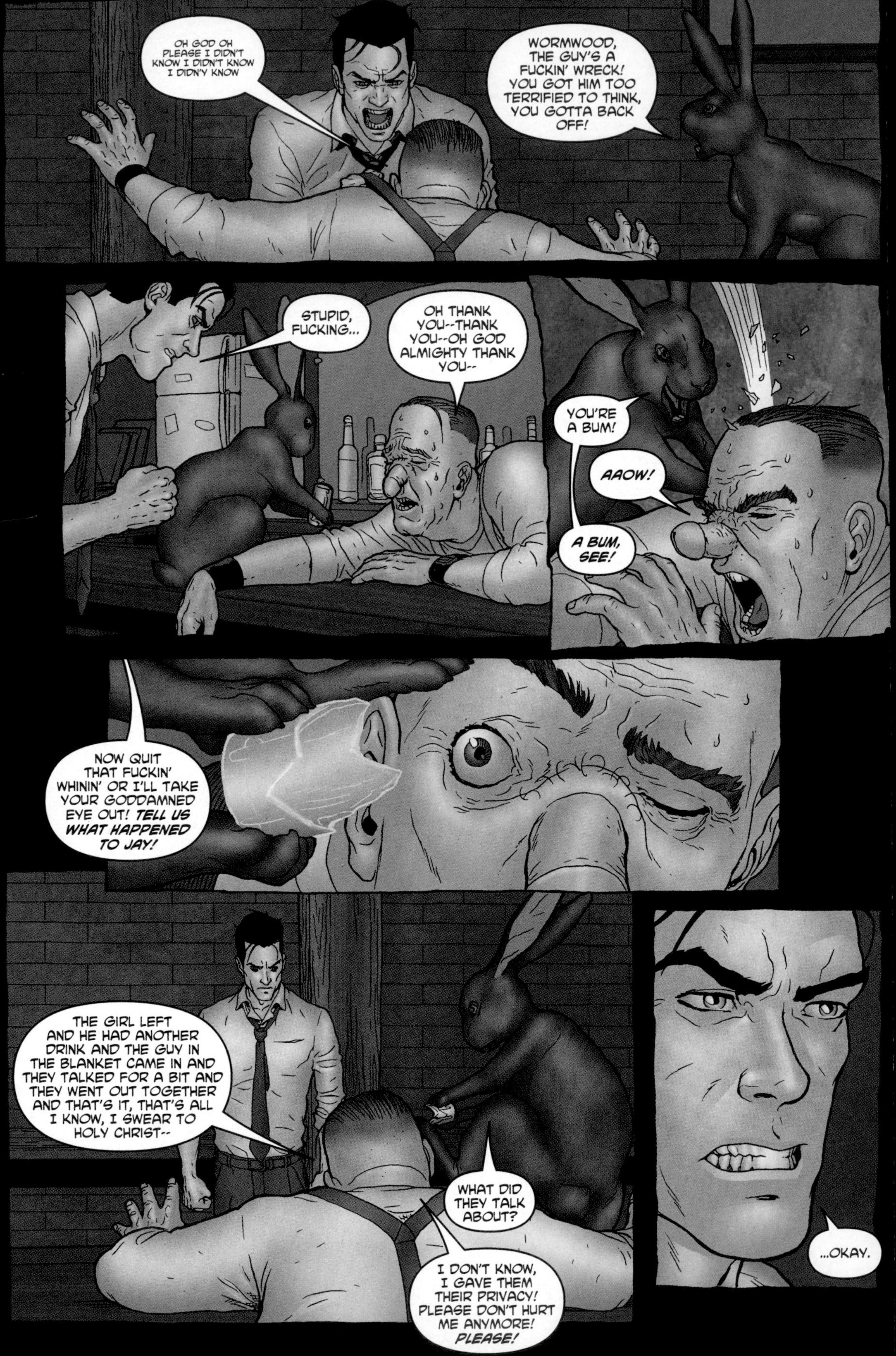
OH GOD OH PLEASE I DIDN'T KNOW I DIDN'T KNOW I DIDN'Y KNOW
WORMWOOD, THE GUY'S A FUCKIN' WRECK! YOU GOT HIM TOO TERRIFIED TO THINK, YOU GOTTA BACK OFF!
STUPID, FUCKING...
OH THANK YOU--THANK YOU--OH GOD ALMIGHTY THANK YOU--
YOU'RE A BUM!
AAOW!
A BUM, SEE!
NOW QUIT THAT FUCKIN' WHININ' OR I'LL TAKE YOUR GODDAMNED EYE OUT! TELL US WHAT HAPPENED TO JAY!
THE GIRL LEFT AND HE HAD ANOTHER DRINK AND THE GUY IN THE BLANKET CAME IN AND THEY TALKED FOR A BIT AND THEY WENT OUT TOGETHER AND THAT'S IT, THAT'S ALL I KNOW, I SWEAR TO HOLY CHRIST--
WHAT DID THEY TALK ABOUT?
I DON'T KNOW, I GAVE THEM THEIR PRIVACY! PLEASE DON'T HURT ME ANYMORE! PLEASE!
...OKAY.

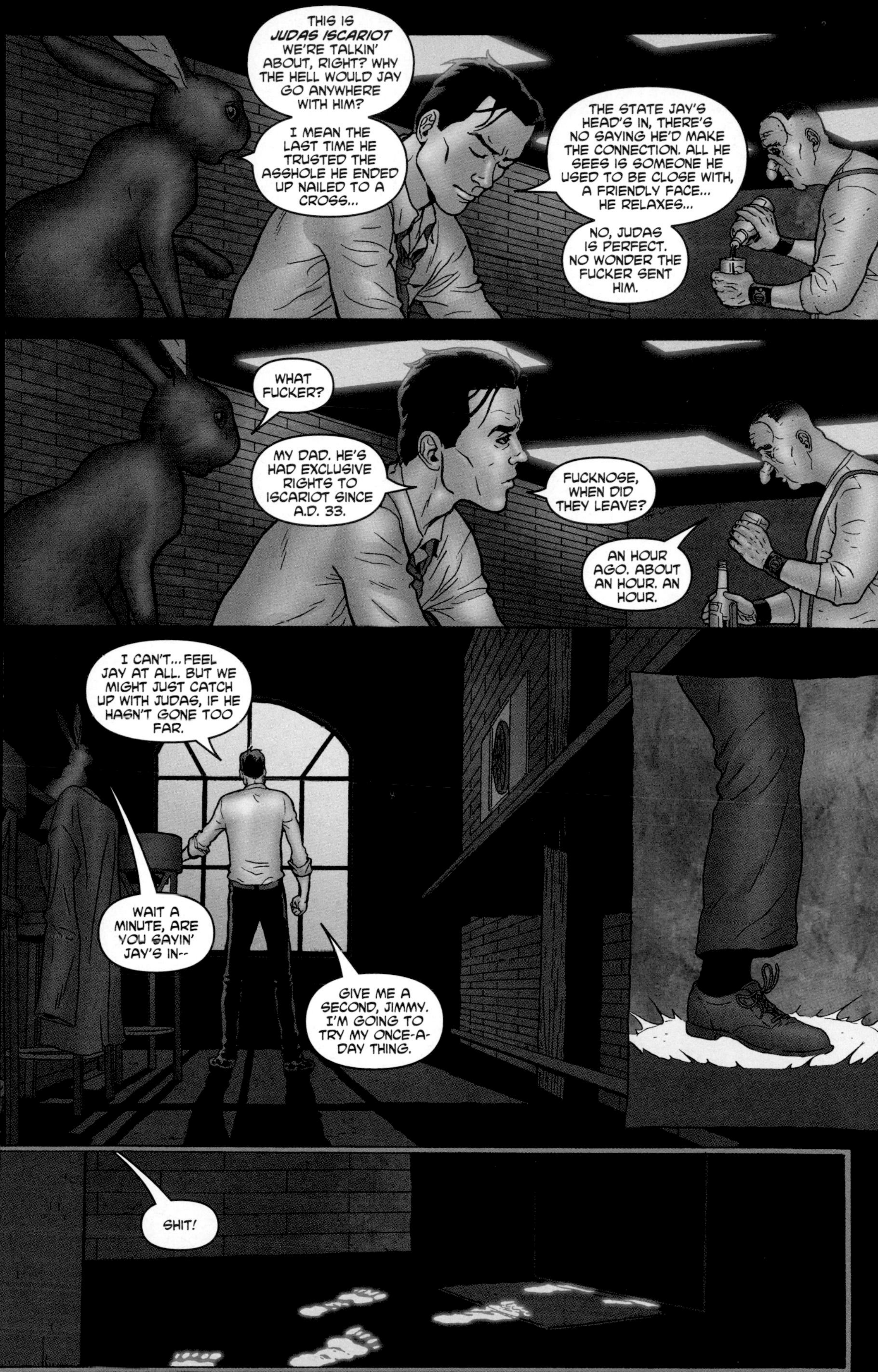
THIS IS *JUDAS ISCARIOT* WE'RE TALKIN' ABOUT, RIGHT? WHY THE HELL WOULD JAY GO ANYWHERE WITH HIM?
I MEAN THE LAST TIME HE TRUSTED THE ASSHOLE HE ENDED UP NAILED TO A CROSS...
THE STATE JAY'S HEAD'S IN, THERE'S NO SAYING HE'D MAKE THE CONNECTION. ALL HE SEES IS SOMEONE HE USED TO BE CLOSE WITH, A FRIENDLY FACE... HE RELAXES...
NO, JUDAS IS PERFECT. NO WONDER THE FUCKER SENT HIM.
WHAT FUCKER?
MY DAD. HE'S HAD EXCLUSIVE RIGHTS TO ISCARIOT SINCE A.D. 33.
FUCKNOSE, WHEN DID THEY LEAVE?
AN HOUR AGO. ABOUT AN HOUR. AN HOUR.
I CAN'T... FEEL JAY AT ALL. BUT WE MIGHT JUST CATCH UP WITH JUDAS, IF HE HASN'T GONE TOO FAR.
WAIT A MINUTE, ARE YOU SAYIN' JAY'S IN--
GIVE ME A SECOND, JIMMY. I'M GOING TO TRY MY ONCE-A-DAY THING.
SHIT!

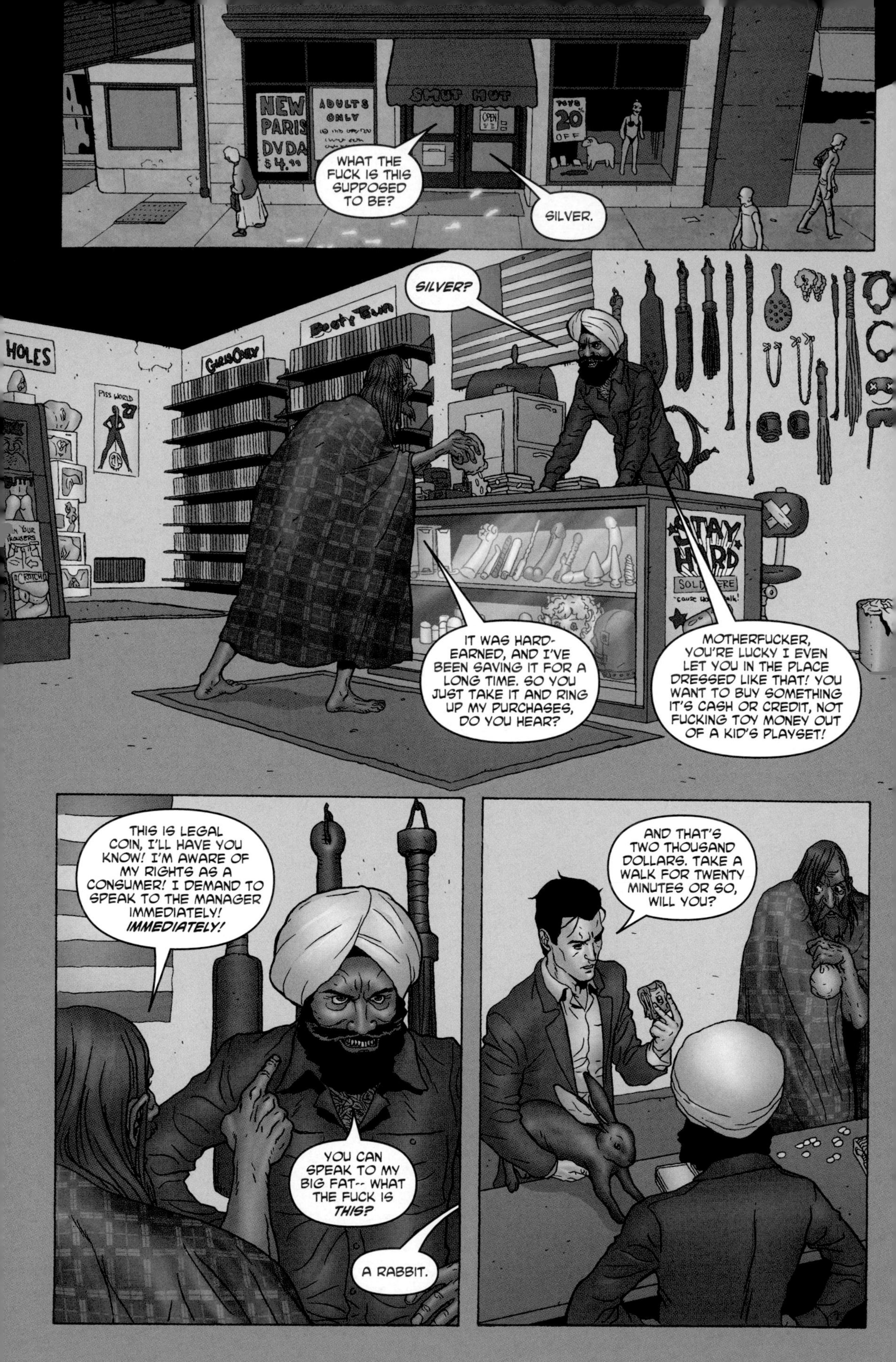
SMUT HUT
ADULTS ONLY
OPEN
WHAT THE FUCK IS THIS SUPPOSED TO BE?
SILVER.
HOLES
GIRLS ONLY
SILVER?
STAY HARD
IT WAS HARD-EARNED, AND I'VE BEEN SAVING IT FOR A LONG TIME. SO YOU JUST TAKE IT AND RING UP MY PURCHASES, DO YOU HEAR?
MOTHERFUCKER, YOU'RE LUCKY I EVEN LET YOU IN THE PLACE DRESSED LIKE THAT! YOU WANT TO BUY SOMETHING IT'S CASH OR CREDIT, NOT FUCKING TOY MONEY OUT OF A KID'S PLAYSET!
THIS IS LEGAL COIN, I'LL HAVE YOU KNOW! I'M AWARE OF MY RIGHTS AS A CONSUMER! I DEMAND TO SPEAK TO THE MANAGER IMMEDIATELY! *IMMEDIATELY!*
YOU CAN SPEAK TO MY BIG FAT-- WHAT THE FUCK IS *THIS?*
A RABBIT.
AND THAT'S TWO THOUSAND DOLLARS. TAKE A WALK FOR TWENTY MINUTES OR SO, WILL YOU?

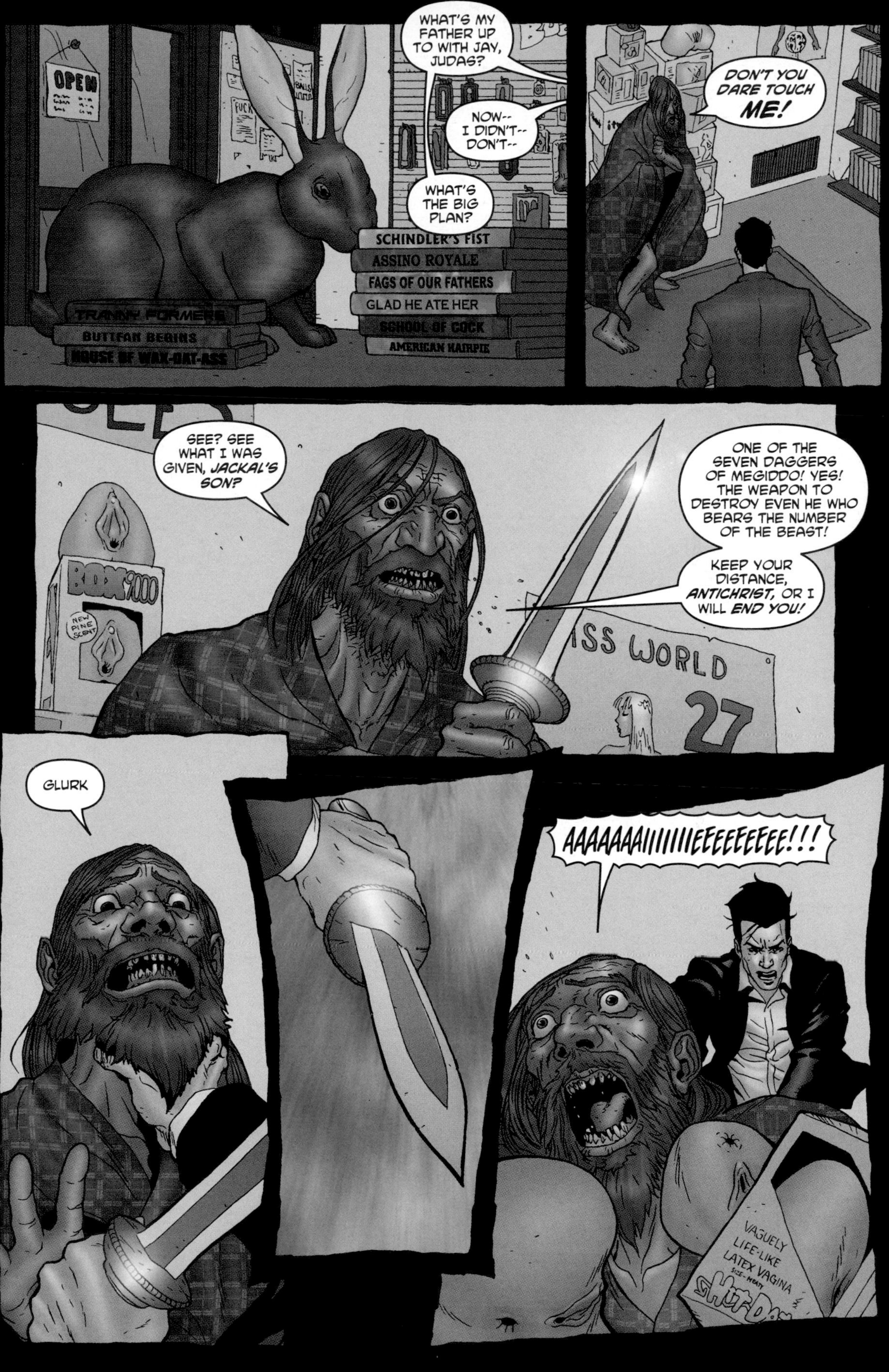
OPEN
WHAT'S MY FATHER UP TO WITH JAY, JUDAS?
NOW-- I DIDN'T-- DON'T--
WHAT'S THE BIG PLAN?
SCHINDLER'S FIST
ASSINO ROYALE
FAGS OF OUR FATHERS
GLAD HE ATE HER
SCHOOL OF COCK
AMERICAN HAIRPIE
TRANNY FORMERS
BUTTFAN BEGINS
HOUSE OF WAX-DAT-ASS
DON'T YOU *DARE* TOUCH ***ME!***
SEE? SEE WHAT I WAS GIVEN, *JACKAL'S SON?*
ONE OF THE SEVEN DAGGERS OF MEGIDDO! YES! THE WEAPON TO DESTROY EVEN HE WHO BEARS THE NUMBER OF THE BEAST!
KEEP YOUR DISTANCE, *ANTICHRIST,* OR I WILL *END YOU!*
NEW PINE SCENT
ISS WORLD
27
GLURK
AAAAAAAIIIIIIIEEEEEEEEE!!!
VAGUELY LIFE-LIKE LATEX VAGINA

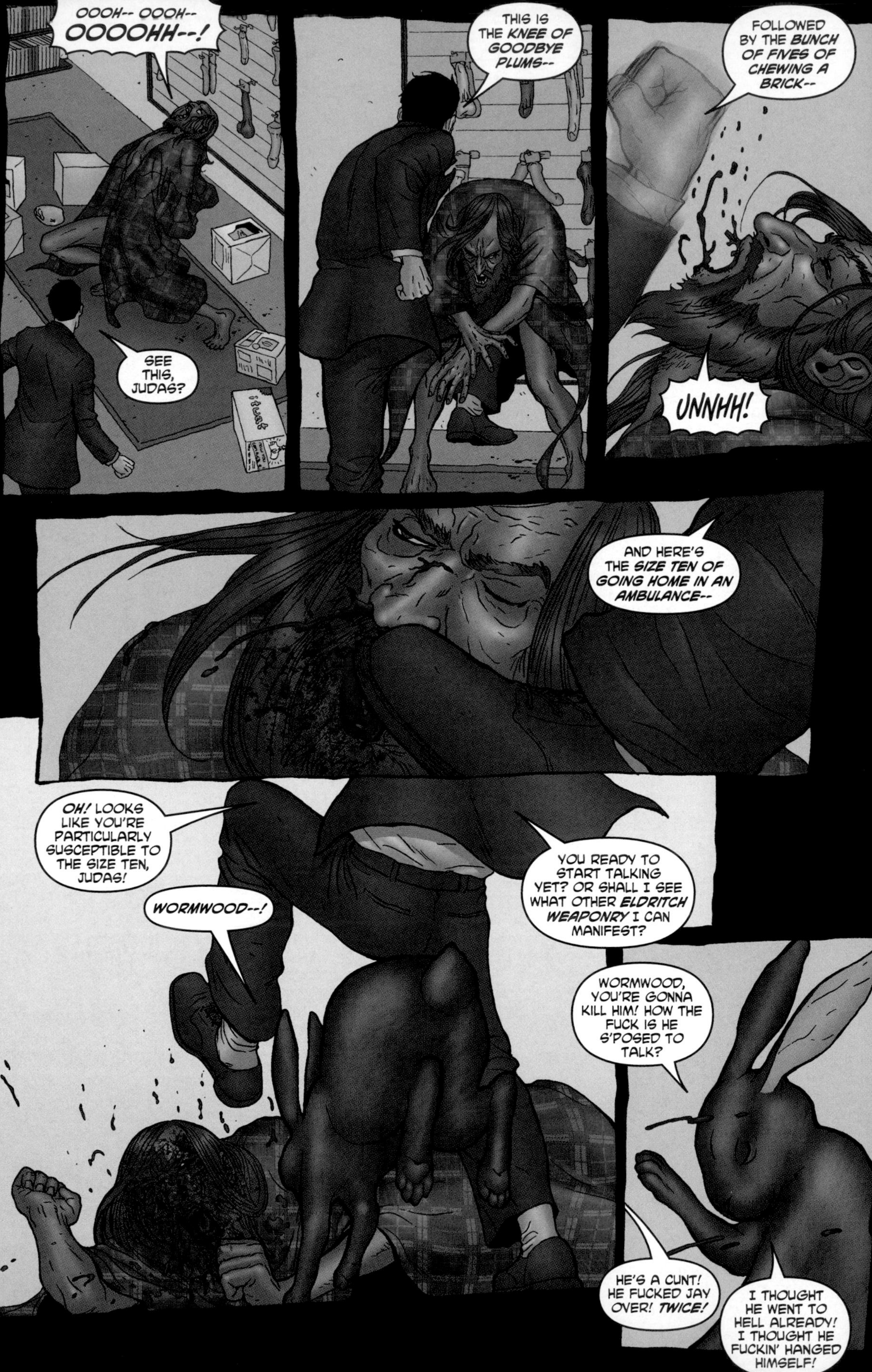
OOOH-- OOOH-- OOOOHH--!
SEE THIS, JUDAS?
THIS IS THE KNEE OF GOODBYE PLUMS--
FOLLOWED BY THE BUNCH OF FIVES OF CHEWING A BRICK--
UNNHH!
AND HERE'S THE SIZE TEN OF GOING HOME IN AN AMBULANCE--
OH! LOOKS LIKE YOU'RE PARTICULARLY SUSCEPTIBLE TO THE SIZE TEN, JUDAS!
WORMWOOD--!
YOU READY TO START TALKING YET? OR SHALL I SEE WHAT OTHER ELDRITCH WEAPONRY I CAN MANIFEST?
WORMWOOD, YOU'RE GONNA KILL HIM! HOW THE FUCK IS HE S'POSED TO TALK?
HE'S A CUNT! HE FUCKED JAY OVER! TWICE!
I THOUGHT HE WENT TO HELL ALREADY! I THOUGHT HE FUCKIN' HANGED HIMSELF!

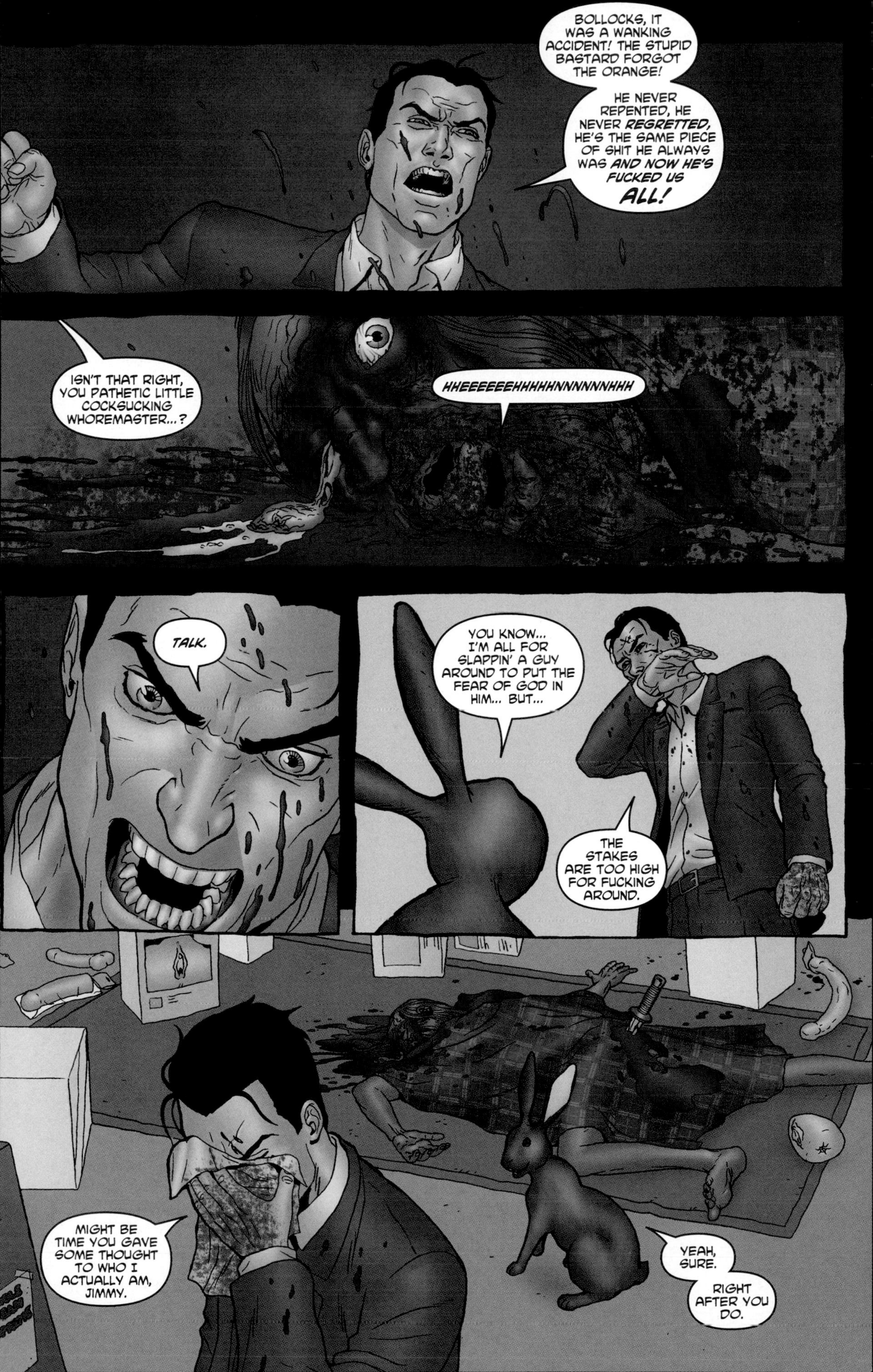
BOLLOCKS, IT WAS A WANKING ACCIDENT! THE STUPID BASTARD FORGOT THE ORANGE!
HE NEVER REPENTED, HE NEVER REGRETTED, HE'S THE SAME PIECE OF SHIT HE ALWAYS WAS AND NOW HE'S FUCKED US ALL!
ISN'T THAT RIGHT, YOU PATHETIC LITTLE COCKSUCKING WHOREMASTER...?
HHEEEEEEHHHHHHNNNNNNHHH
TALK.
YOU KNOW... I'M ALL FOR SLAPPIN' A GUY AROUND TO PUT THE FEAR OF GOD IN HIM... BUT...
THE STAKES ARE TOO HIGH FOR FUCKING AROUND.
MIGHT BE TIME YOU GAVE SOME THOUGHT TO WHO I ACTUALLY AM, JIMMY.
YEAH, SURE.
RIGHT AFTER YOU DO.

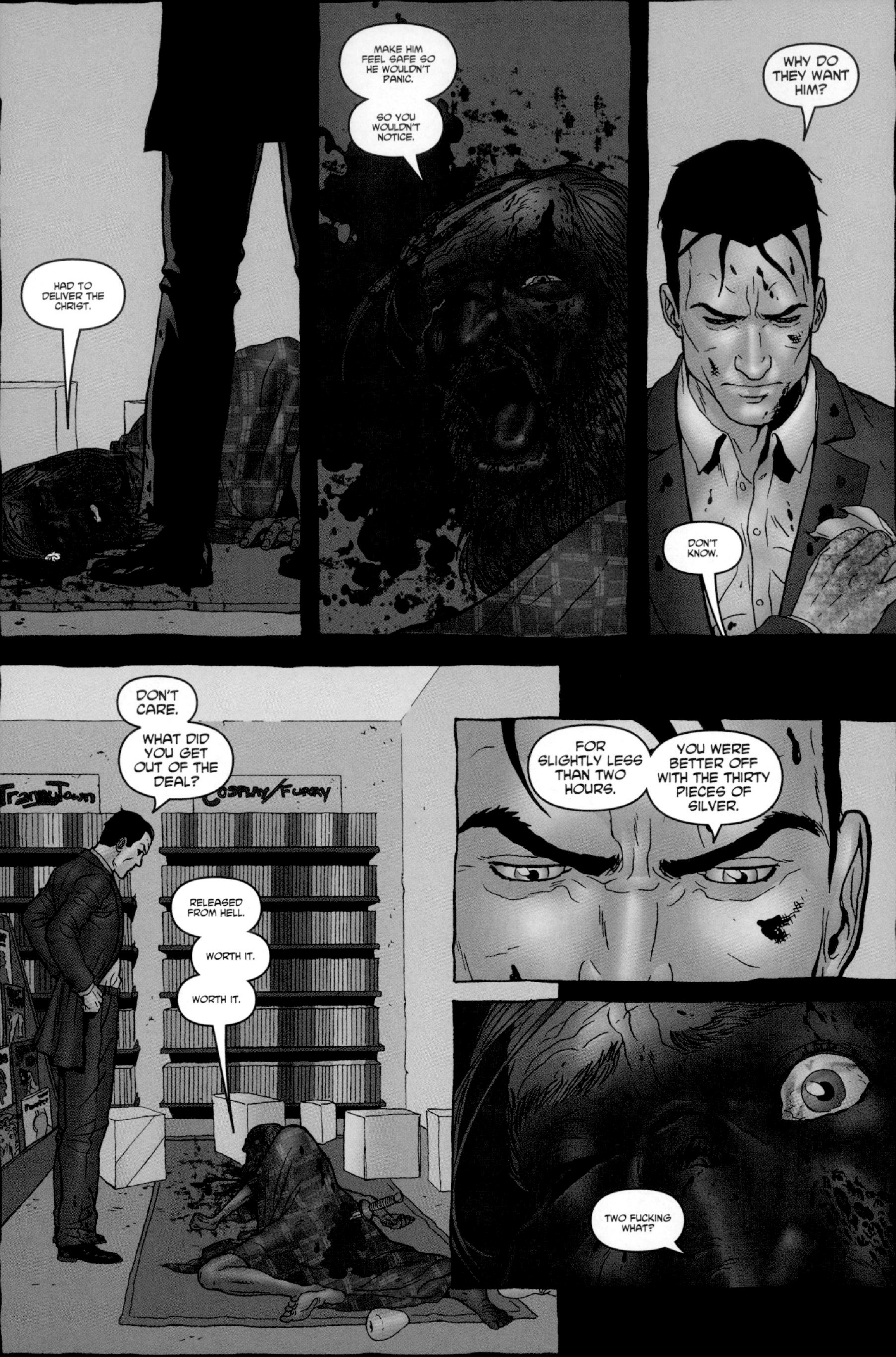
HAD TO DELIVER THE CHRIST.
MAKE HIM FEEL SAFE SO HE WOULDN'T PANIC.
SO YOU WOULDN'T NOTICE.
WHY DO THEY WANT HIM?
DON'T KNOW.
DON'T CARE.
WHAT DID YOU GET OUT OF THE DEAL?
TrannyTown
COSPLAY/FURRY
RELEASED FROM HELL.
WORTH IT.
WORTH IT.
FOR SLIGHTLY LESS THAN TWO HOURS.
YOU WERE BETTER OFF WITH THE THIRTY PIECES OF SILVER.
TWO FUCKING WHAT?

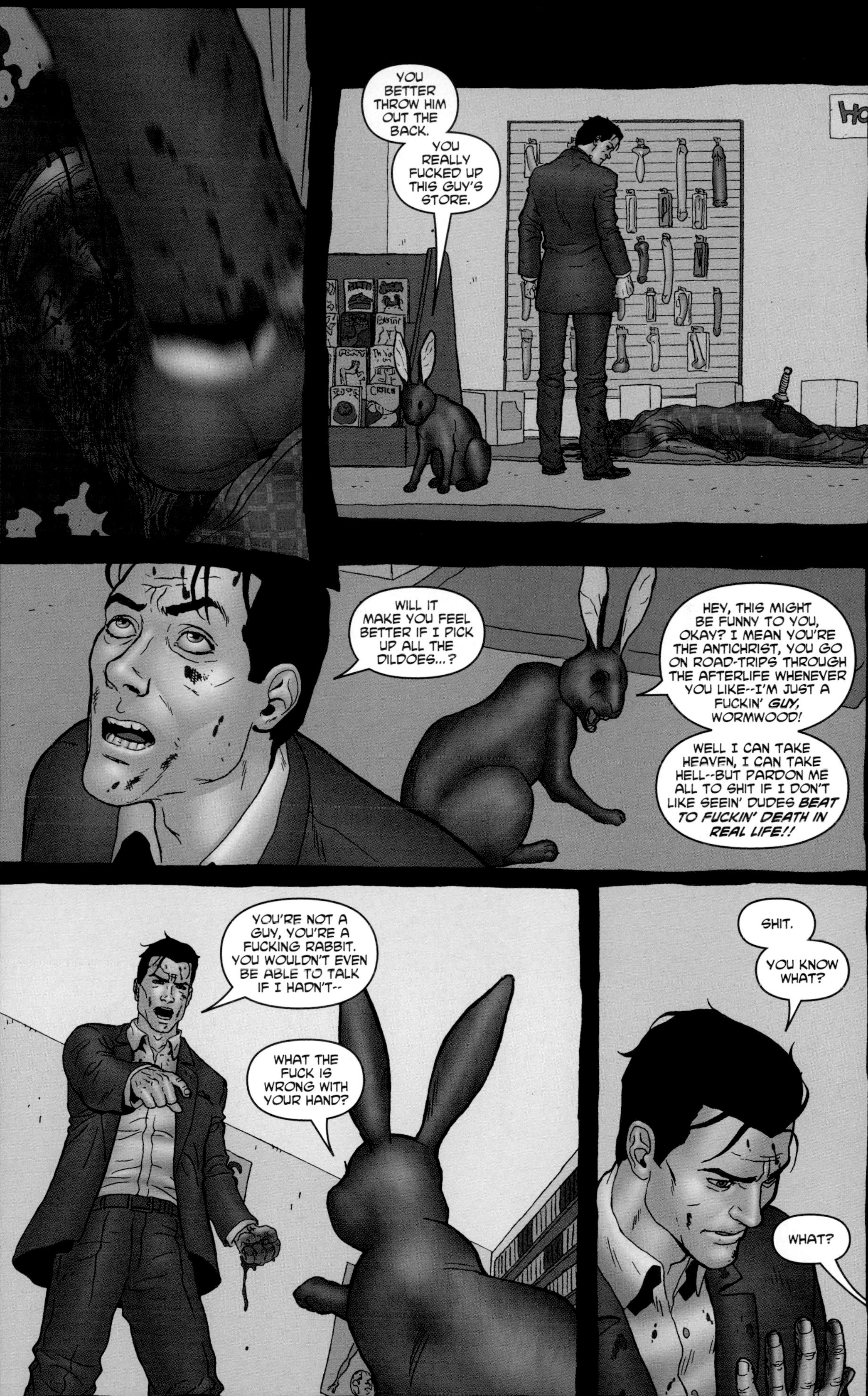

YOU BETTER THROW HIM OUT THE BACK.
YOU REALLY FUCKED UP THIS GUY'S STORE.
WILL IT MAKE YOU FEEL BETTER IF I PICK UP ALL THE DILDOES...?
HEY, THIS MIGHT BE FUNNY TO YOU, OKAY? I MEAN YOU'RE THE ANTICHRIST, YOU GO ON ROAD-TRIPS THROUGH THE AFTERLIFE WHENEVER YOU LIKE--I'M JUST A FUCKIN' GUY, WORMWOOD!
WELL I CAN TAKE HEAVEN, I CAN TAKE HELL--BUT PARDON ME ALL TO SHIT IF I DON'T LIKE SEEIN' DUDES BEAT TO FUCKIN' DEATH IN REAL LIFE!!
YOU'RE NOT A GUY, YOU'RE A FUCKING RABBIT. YOU WOULDN'T EVEN BE ABLE TO TALK IF I HADN'T--
WHAT THE FUCK IS WRONG WITH YOUR HAND?
SHIT.
YOU KNOW WHAT?
WHAT?

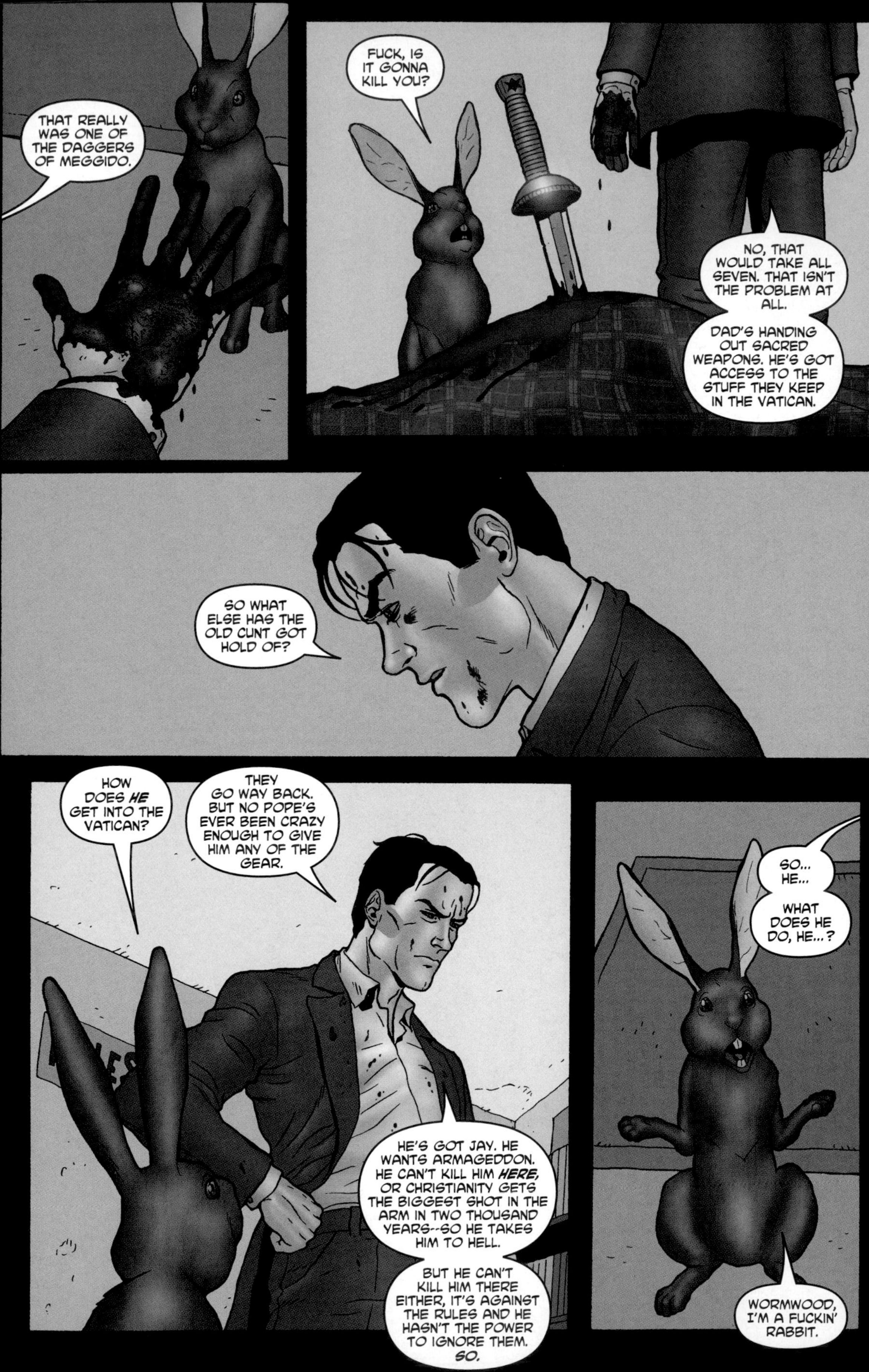
THAT REALLY WAS ONE OF THE DAGGERS OF MEGGIDO.
FUCK, IS IT GONNA KILL YOU?
NO, THAT WOULD TAKE ALL SEVEN. THAT ISN'T THE PROBLEM AT ALL.
DAD'S HANDING OUT SACRED WEAPONS. HE'S GOT ACCESS TO THE STUFF THEY KEEP IN THE VATICAN.
SO WHAT ELSE HAS THE OLD CUNT GOT HOLD OF?
HOW DOES *HE* GET INTO THE VATICAN?
THEY GO WAY BACK. BUT NO POPE'S EVER BEEN CRAZY ENOUGH TO GIVE HIM ANY OF THE GEAR.
HE'S GOT JAY. HE WANTS ARMAGEDDON. HE CAN'T KILL HIM *HERE,* OR CHRISTIANITY GETS THE BIGGEST SHOT IN THE ARM IN TWO THOUSAND YEARS--SO HE TAKES HIM TO HELL.
BUT HE CAN'T KILL HIM THERE EITHER, IT'S AGAINST THE RULES AND HE HASN'T THE POWER TO IGNORE THEM. *SO.*
SO... HE...
WHAT DOES HE DO, HE...?
WORMWOOD, I'M A FUCKIN' RABBIT.

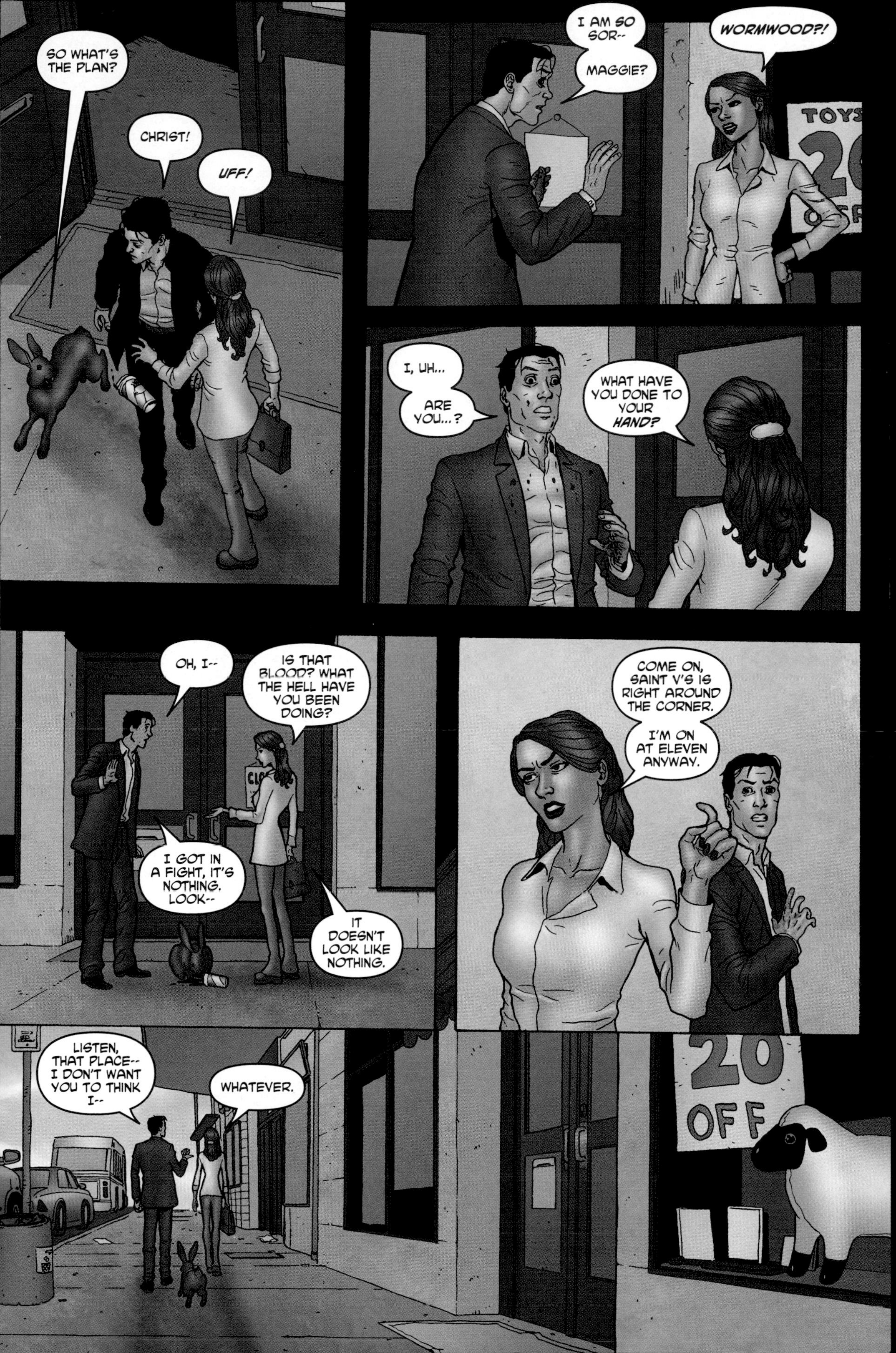
SO WHAT'S THE PLAN?
CHRIST!
UFF!
I AM SO SOR--
MAGGIE?
WORMWOOD?!
TOYS
20
I, UH...
ARE YOU...?
WHAT HAVE YOU DONE TO YOUR HAND?
OH, I--
IS THAT BLOOD? WHAT THE HELL HAVE YOU BEEN DOING?
I GOT IN A FIGHT, IT'S NOTHING. LOOK--
IT DOESN'T LOOK LIKE NOTHING.
COME ON, SAINT V'S IS RIGHT AROUND THE CORNER.
I'M ON AT ELEVEN ANYWAY.
LISTEN, THAT PLACE-- I DON'T WANT YOU TO THINK I--
WHATEVER.
20
OFF

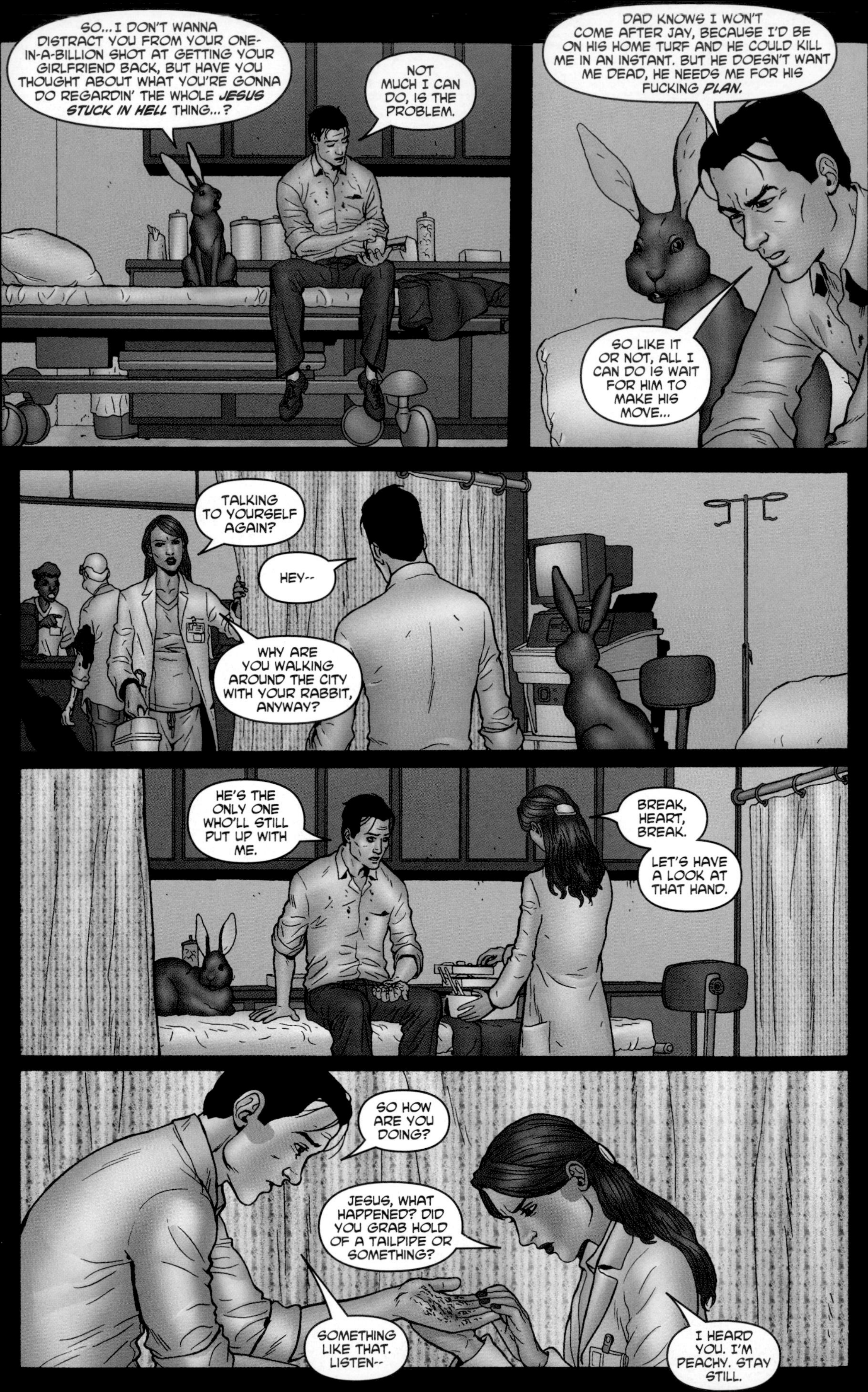
SO...I DON'T WANNA DISTRACT YOU FROM YOUR ONE-IN-A-BILLION SHOT AT GETTING YOUR GIRLFRIEND BACK, BUT HAVE YOU THOUGHT ABOUT WHAT YOU'RE GONNA DO REGARDIN' THE WHOLE *JESUS STUCK IN HELL* THING...?
NOT MUCH I CAN DO, IS THE PROBLEM.
DAD KNOWS I WON'T COME AFTER JAY, BECAUSE I'D BE ON HIS HOME TURF AND HE COULD KILL ME IN AN INSTANT. BUT HE DOESN'T WANT ME DEAD, HE NEEDS ME FOR HIS FUCKING *PLAN.*
SO LIKE IT OR NOT, ALL I CAN DO IS WAIT FOR HIM TO MAKE HIS MOVE...
TALKING TO YOURSELF AGAIN?
HEY--
WHY ARE YOU WALKING AROUND THE CITY WITH YOUR RABBIT, ANYWAY?
HE'S THE ONLY ONE WHO'LL STILL PUT UP WITH ME.
BREAK, HEART, BREAK.
LET'S HAVE A LOOK AT THAT HAND.
SO HOW ARE YOU DOING?
JESUS, WHAT HAPPENED? DID YOU GRAB HOLD OF A TAILPIPE OR SOMETHING?
SOMETHING LIKE THAT. LISTEN--
I HEARD YOU. I'M PEACHY. STAY STILL.

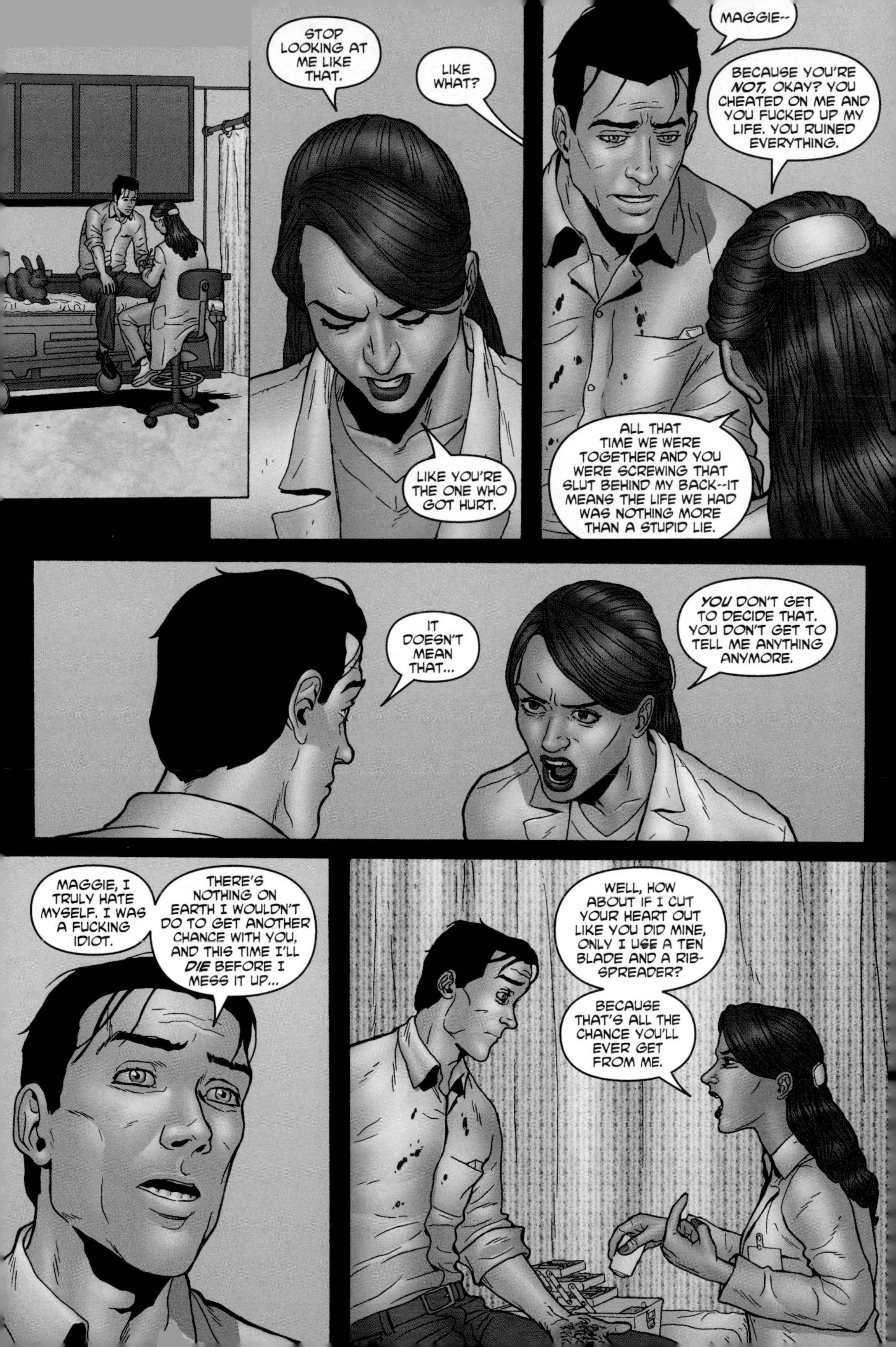
STOP LOOKING AT ME LIKE THAT.
LIKE WHAT?
LIKE YOU'RE THE ONE WHO GOT HURT.
MAGGIE--
BECAUSE YOU'RE NOT, OKAY? YOU CHEATED ON ME AND YOU FUCKED UP MY LIFE. YOU RUINED EVERYTHING.
ALL THAT TIME WE WERE TOGETHER AND YOU WERE SCREWING THAT SLUT BEHIND MY BACK--IT MEANS THE LIFE WE HAD WAS NOTHING MORE THAN A STUPID LIE.
IT DOESN'T MEAN THAT...
YOU DON'T GET TO DECIDE THAT. YOU DON'T GET TO TELL ME ANYTHING ANYMORE.
MAGGIE, I TRULY HATE MYSELF. I WAS A FUCKING IDIOT.
THERE'S NOTHING ON EARTH I WOULDN'T DO TO GET ANOTHER CHANCE WITH YOU, AND THIS TIME I'LL DIE BEFORE I MESS IT UP...
WELL, HOW ABOUT IF I CUT YOUR HEART OUT LIKE YOU DID MINE, ONLY I USE A TEN BLADE AND A RIB-SPREADER?
BECAUSE THAT'S ALL THE CHANCE YOU'LL EVER GET FROM ME.

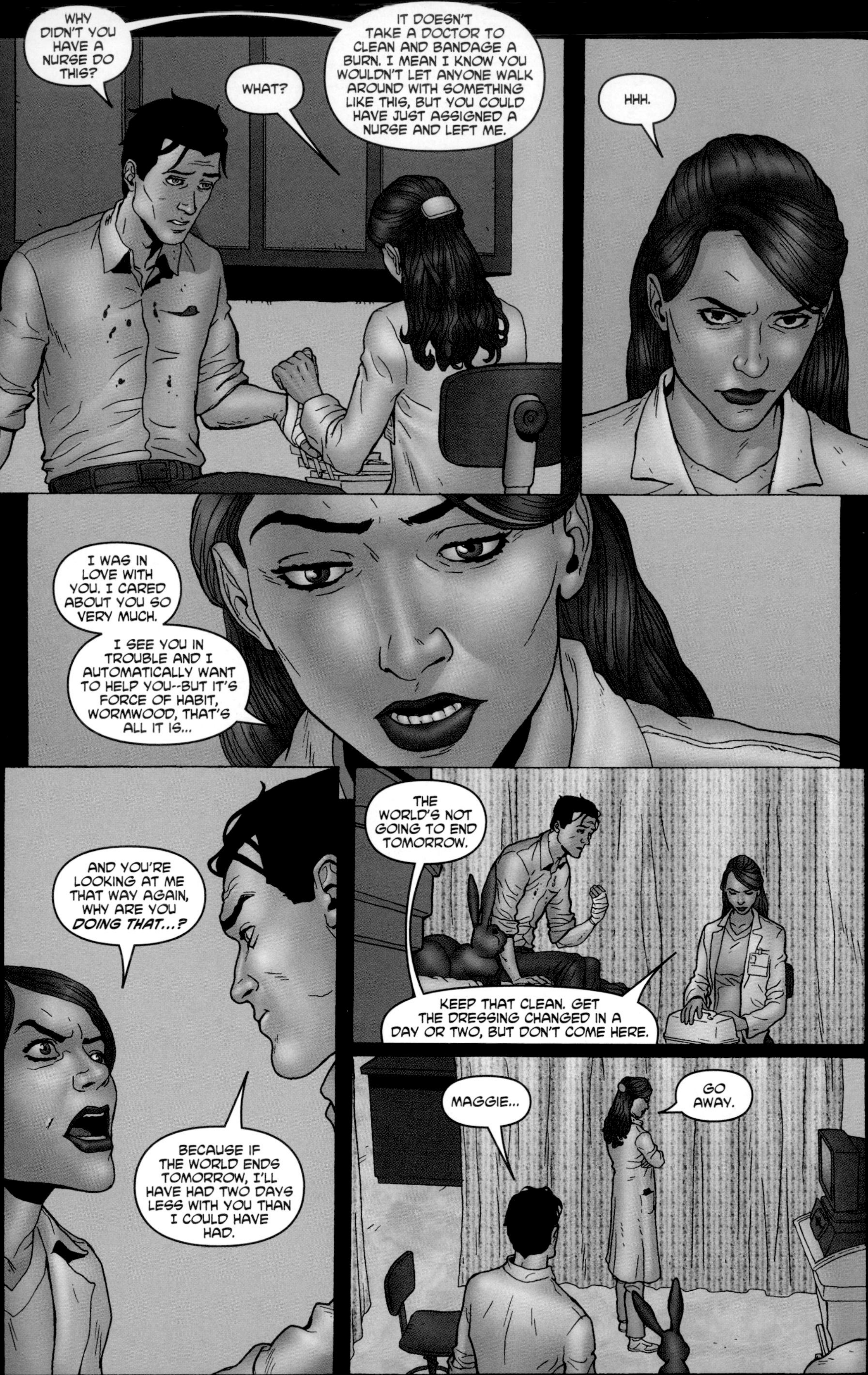
WHY DIDN'T YOU HAVE A NURSE DO THIS?
WHAT?
IT DOESN'T TAKE A DOCTOR TO CLEAN AND BANDAGE A BURN. I MEAN I KNOW YOU WOULDN'T LET ANYONE WALK AROUND WITH SOMETHING LIKE THIS, BUT YOU COULD HAVE JUST ASSIGNED A NURSE AND LEFT ME.
HHH.
I WAS IN LOVE WITH YOU. I CARED ABOUT YOU SO VERY MUCH.
I SEE YOU IN TROUBLE AND I AUTOMATICALLY WANT TO HELP YOU--BUT IT'S FORCE OF HABIT, WORMWOOD, THAT'S ALL IT IS...
AND YOU'RE LOOKING AT ME THAT WAY AGAIN, WHY ARE YOU *DOING THAT...?*
BECAUSE IF THE WORLD ENDS TOMORROW, I'LL HAVE HAD TWO DAYS LESS WITH YOU THAN I COULD HAVE HAD.
THE WORLD'S NOT GOING TO END TOMORROW.
KEEP THAT CLEAN. GET THE DRESSING CHANGED IN A DAY OR TWO, BUT DON'T COME HERE.
MAGGIE...
GO AWAY.

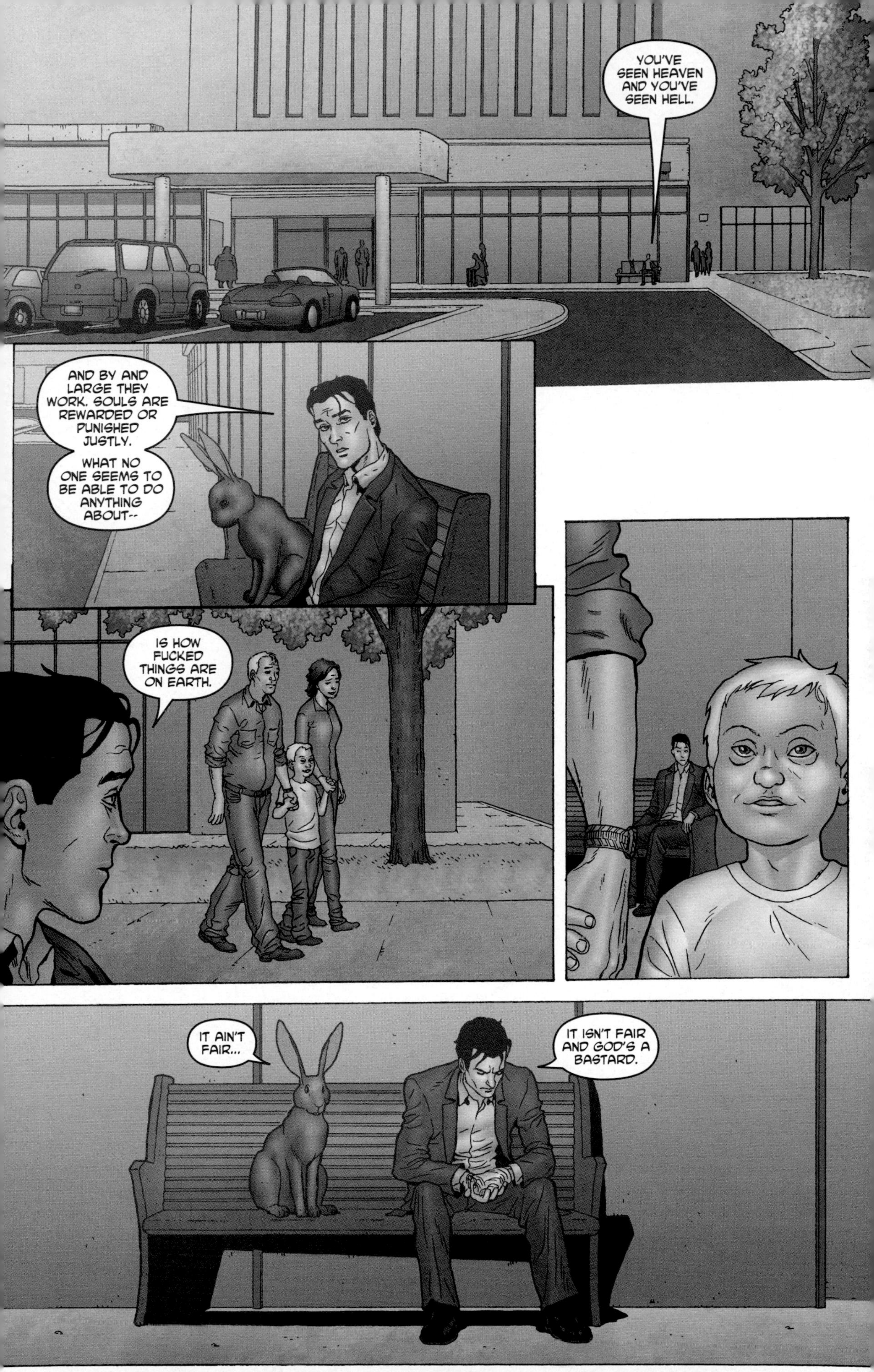
YOU'VE SEEN HEAVEN AND YOU'VE SEEN HELL.
AND BY AND LARGE THEY WORK. SOULS ARE REWARDED OR PUNISHED JUSTLY.
WHAT NO ONE SEEMS TO BE ABLE TO DO ANYTHING ABOUT--
IS HOW FUCKED THINGS ARE ON EARTH.
IT AIN'T FAIR...
IT ISN'T FAIR AND GOD'S A BASTARD.

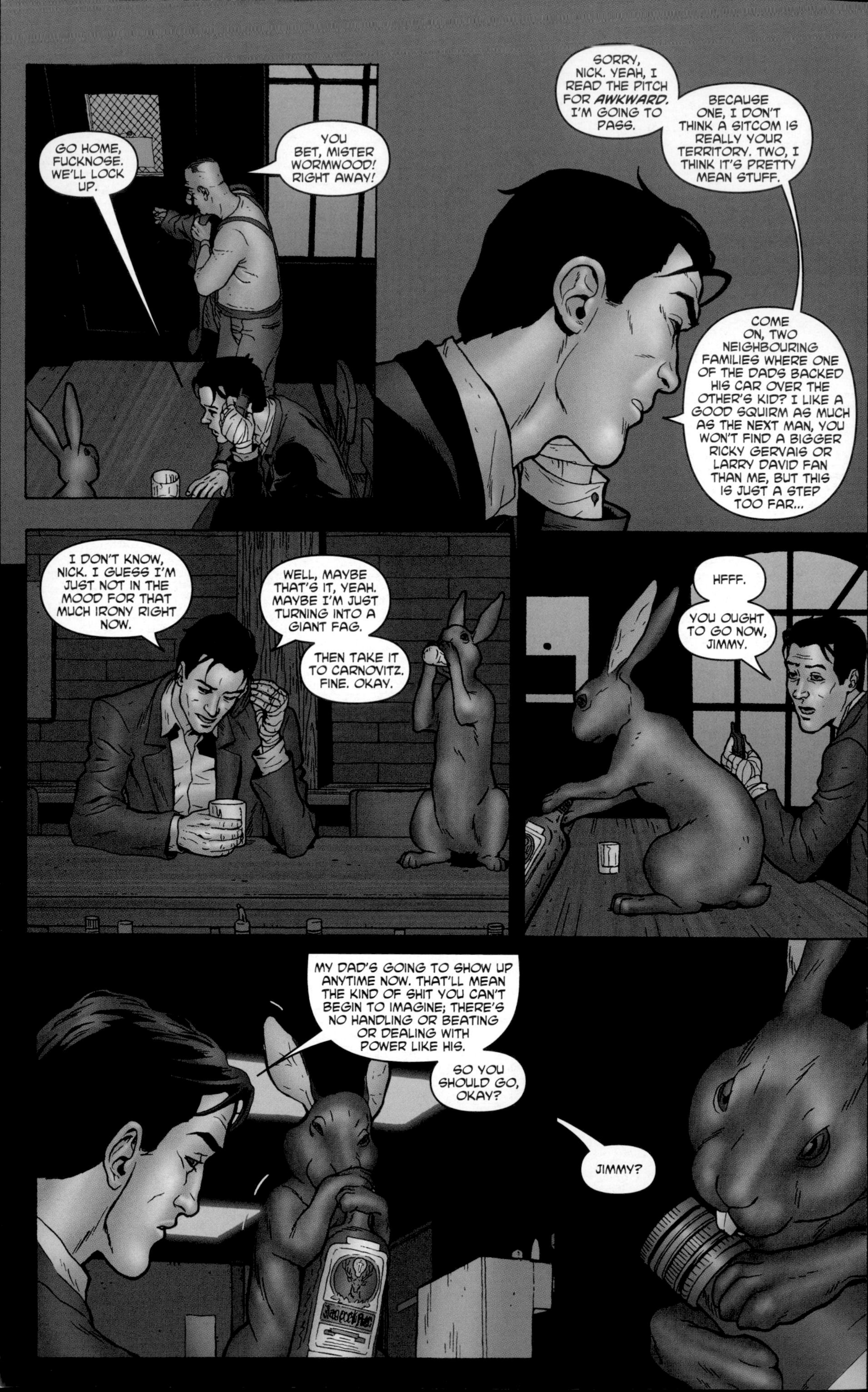
GO HOME, FUCKNOSE. WE'LL LOCK UP.
YOU BET, MISTER WORMWOOD! RIGHT AWAY!
SORRY, NICK. YEAH, I READ THE PITCH FOR AWKWARD. I'M GOING TO PASS.
BECAUSE ONE, I DON'T THINK A SITCOM IS REALLY YOUR TERRITORY. TWO, I THINK IT'S PRETTY MEAN STUFF.
COME ON, TWO NEIGHBOURING FAMILIES WHERE ONE OF THE DADS BACKED HIS CAR OVER THE OTHER'S KID? I LIKE A GOOD SQUIRM AS MUCH AS THE NEXT MAN, YOU WON'T FIND A BIGGER RICKY GERVAIS OR LARRY DAVID FAN THAN ME, BUT THIS IS JUST A STEP TOO FAR...
I DON'T KNOW, NICK. I GUESS I'M JUST NOT IN THE MOOD FOR THAT MUCH IRONY RIGHT NOW.
WELL, MAYBE THAT'S IT, YEAH. MAYBE I'M JUST TURNING INTO A GIANT FAG.
THEN TAKE IT TO CARNOVITZ. FINE. OKAY.
HFFF.
YOU OUGHT TO GO NOW, JIMMY.
MY DAD'S GOING TO SHOW UP ANYTIME NOW. THAT'LL MEAN THE KIND OF SHIT YOU CAN'T BEGIN TO IMAGINE; THERE'S NO HANDLING OR BEATING OR DEALING WITH POWER LIKE HIS.
SO YOU SHOULD GO, OKAY?
JIMMY?

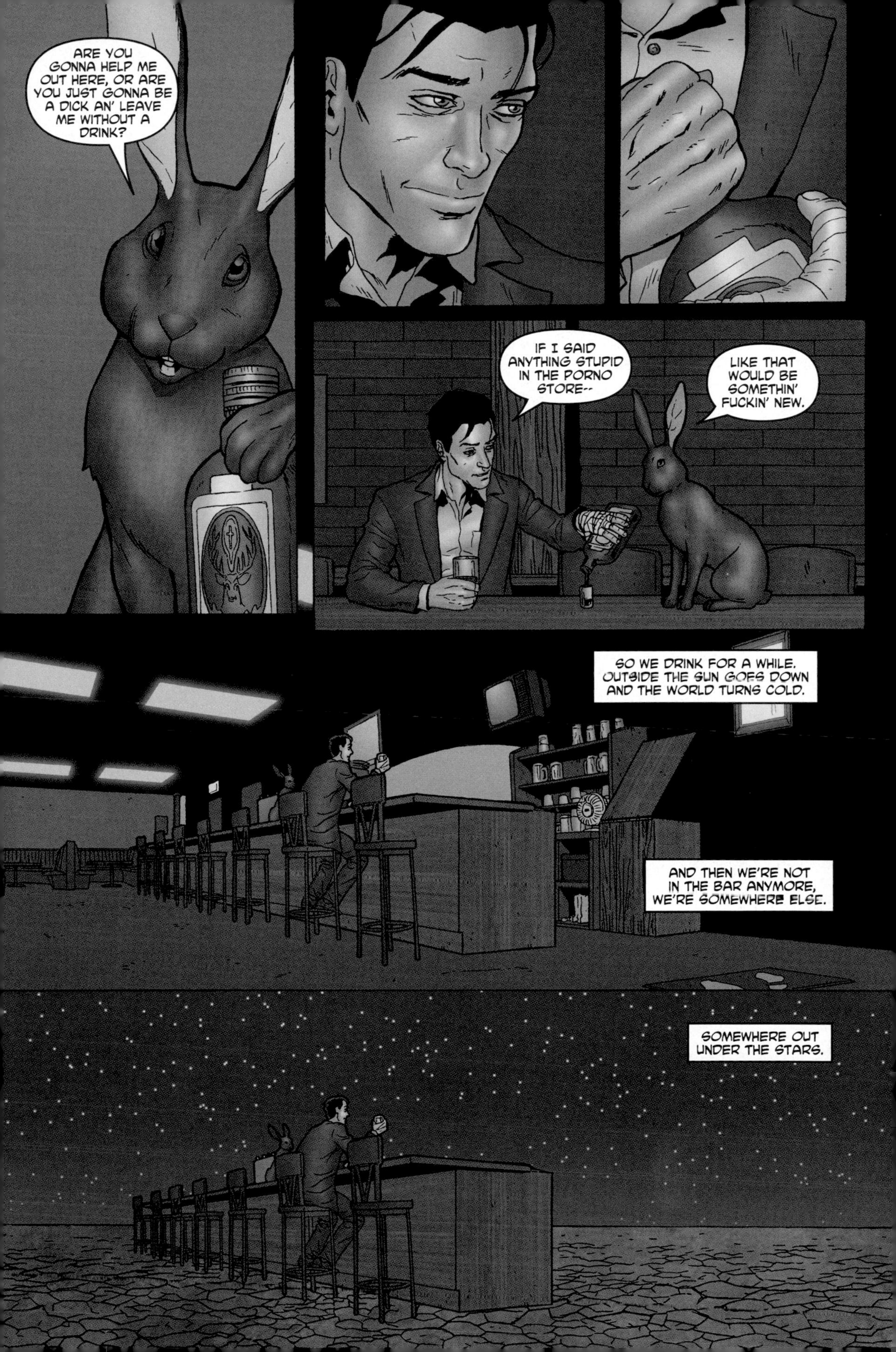
ARE YOU GONNA HELP ME OUT HERE, OR ARE YOU JUST GONNA BE A DICK AN' LEAVE ME WITHOUT A DRINK?
IF I SAID ANYTHING STUPID IN THE PORNO STORE--
LIKE THAT WOULD BE SOMETHIN' FUCKIN' NEW.
SO WE DRINK FOR A WHILE. OUTSIDE THE SUN GOES DOWN AND THE WORLD TURNS COLD.
AND THEN WE'RE NOT IN THE BAR ANYMORE, WE'RE SOMEWHERE ELSE.
SOMEWHERE OUT UNDER THE STARS.

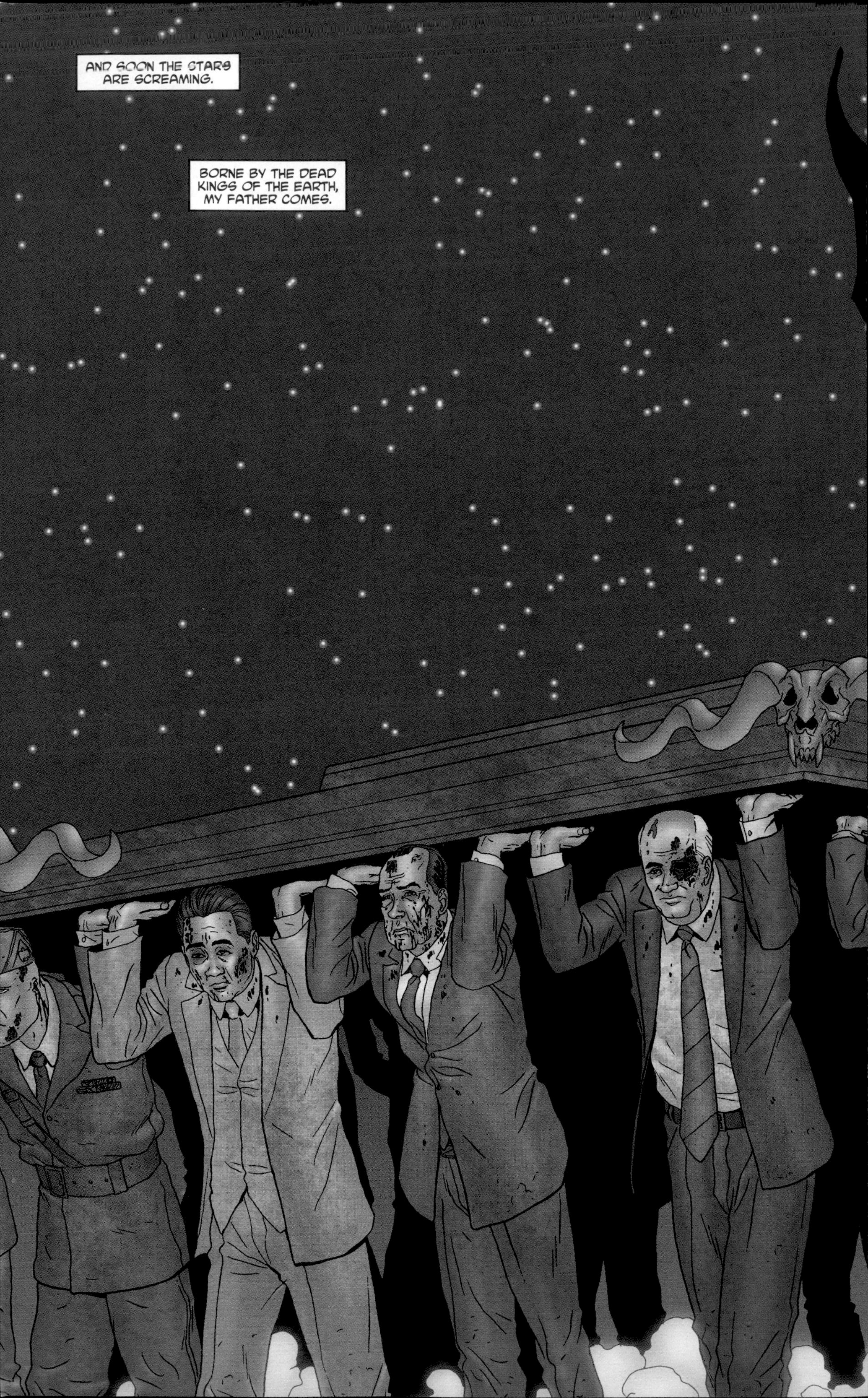
AND SOON THE STARS ARE SCREAMING.
BORNE BY THE DEAD KINGS OF THE EARTH, MY FATHER COMES.

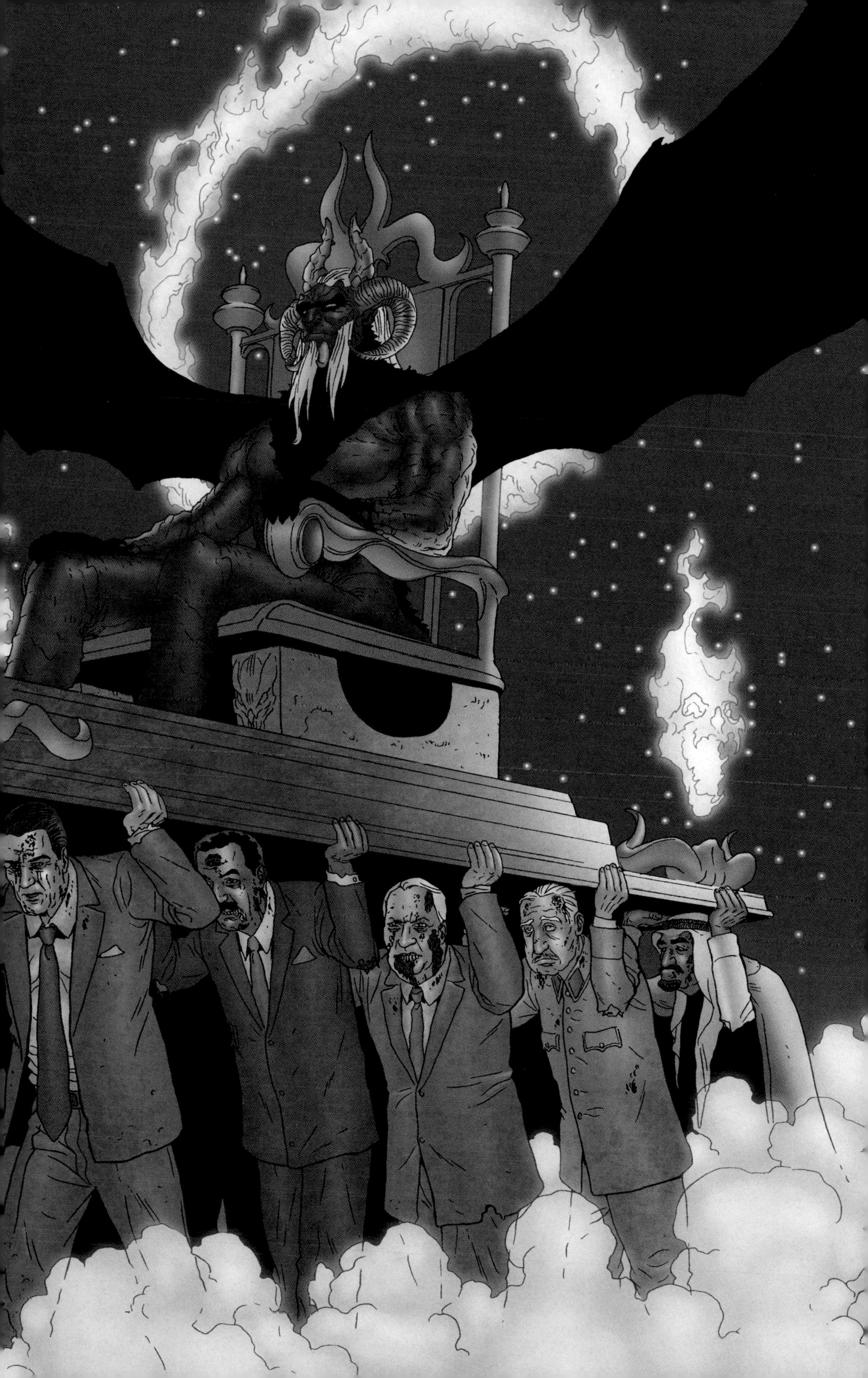

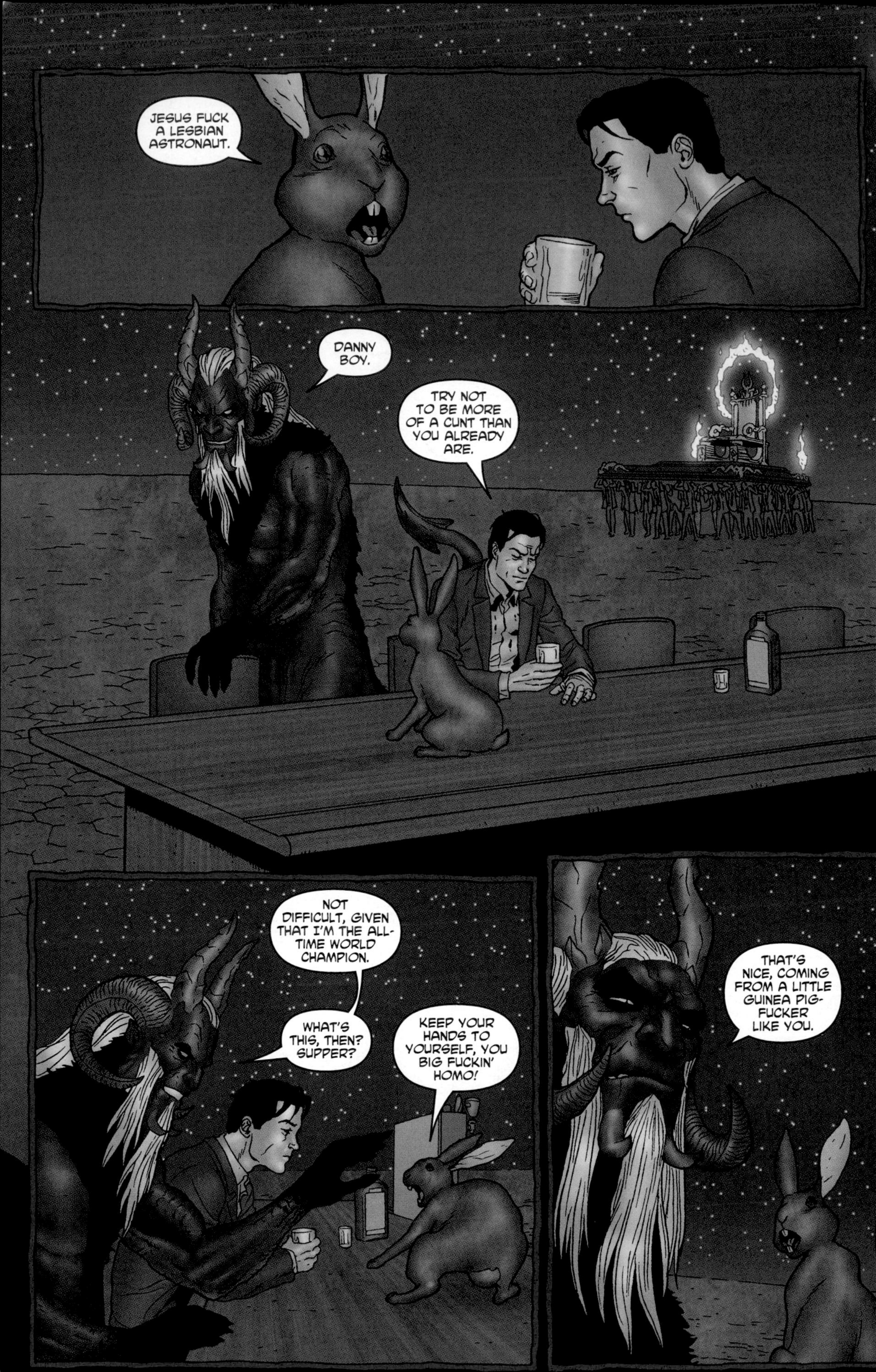
JESUS FUCK A LESBIAN ASTRONAUT.
DANNY BOY.
TRY NOT TO BE MORE OF A CUNT THAN YOU ALREADY ARE.
NOT DIFFICULT, GIVEN THAT I'M THE ALL-TIME WORLD CHAMPION.
WHAT'S THIS, THEN? SUPPER?
KEEP YOUR HANDS TO YOURSELF, YOU BIG FUCKIN' HOMO!
THAT'S NICE, COMING FROM A LITTLE GUINEA PIG-FUCKER LIKE YOU.

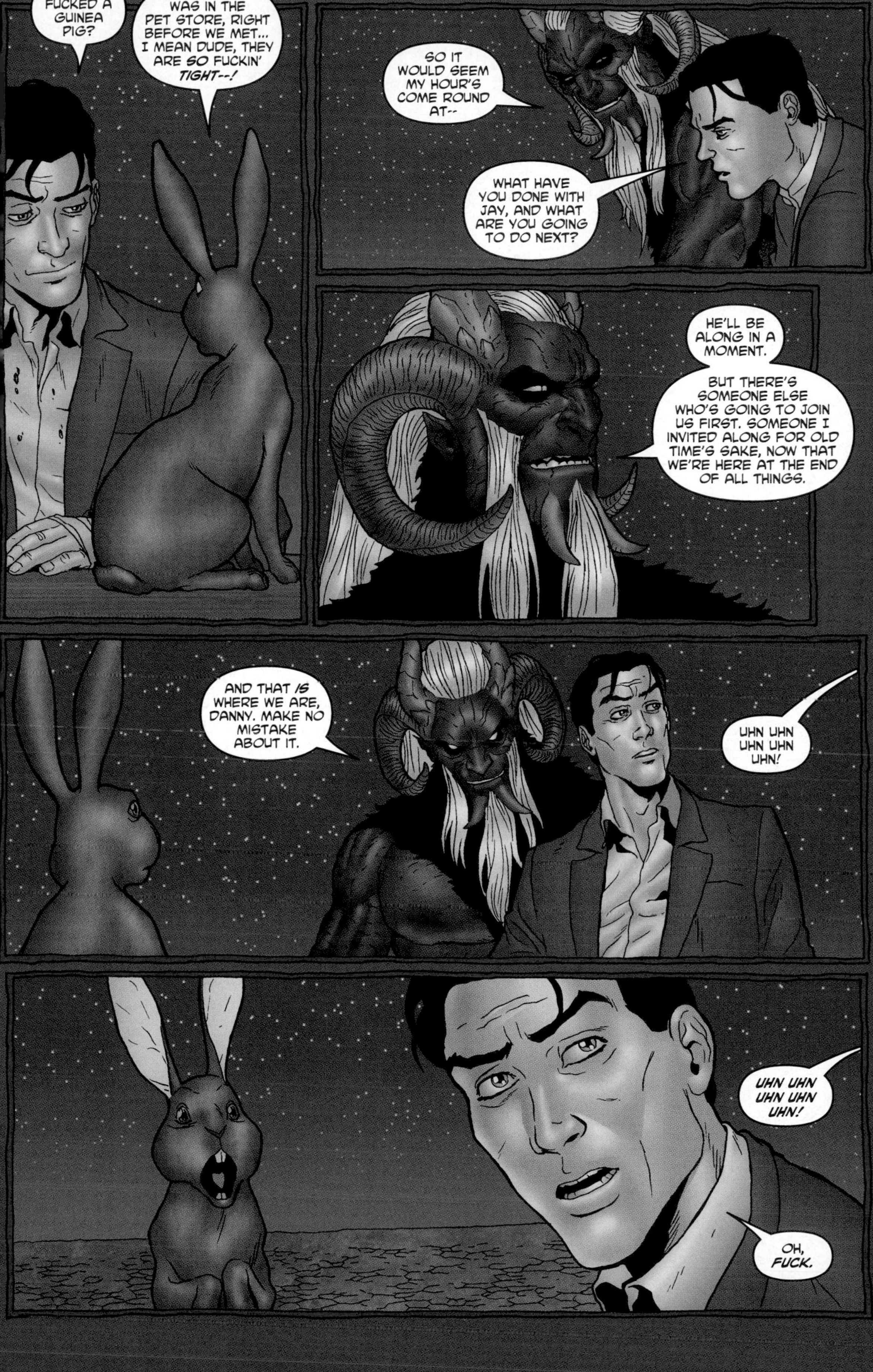
YOU FUCKED A GUINEA PIG?
IT WAS IN THE PET STORE, RIGHT BEFORE WE MET... I MEAN DUDE, THEY ARE *SO* FUCKIN' *TIGHT*--!
SO IT WOULD SEEM MY HOUR'S COME ROUND AT--
WHAT HAVE YOU DONE WITH JAY, AND WHAT ARE YOU GOING TO DO NEXT?
HE'LL BE ALONG IN A MOMENT.
BUT THERE'S SOMEONE ELSE WHO'S GOING TO JOIN US FIRST. SOMEONE I INVITED ALONG FOR OLD TIME'S SAKE, NOW THAT WE'RE HERE AT THE END OF ALL THINGS.
AND THAT *IS* WHERE WE ARE, DANNY. MAKE NO MISTAKE ABOUT IT.
UHN UHN UHN UHN UHN!
UHN UHN UHN UHN UHN!
OH, *FUCK.*

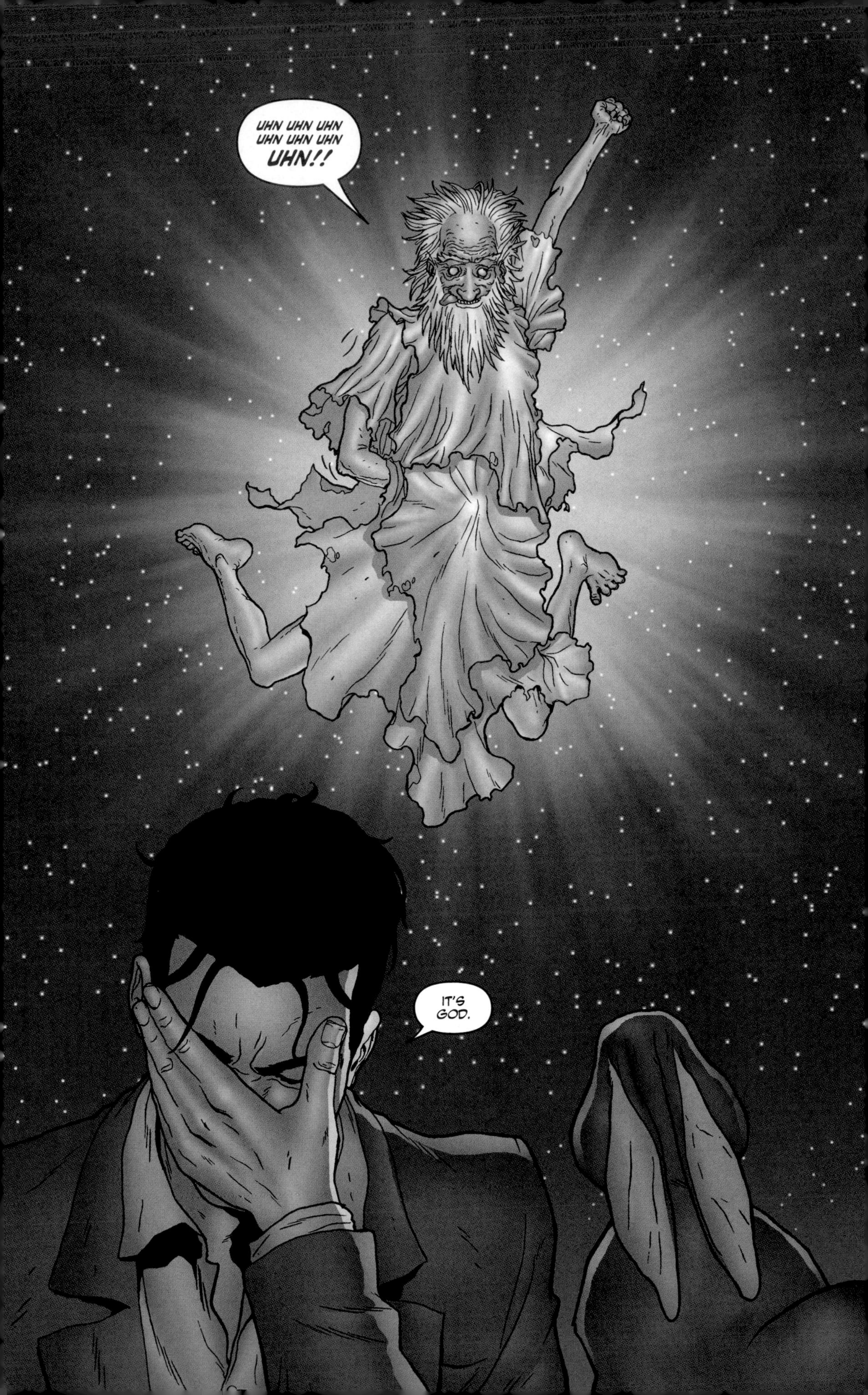
UHN UHN UHN UHN UHN UHN UHN!!
IT'S GOD.

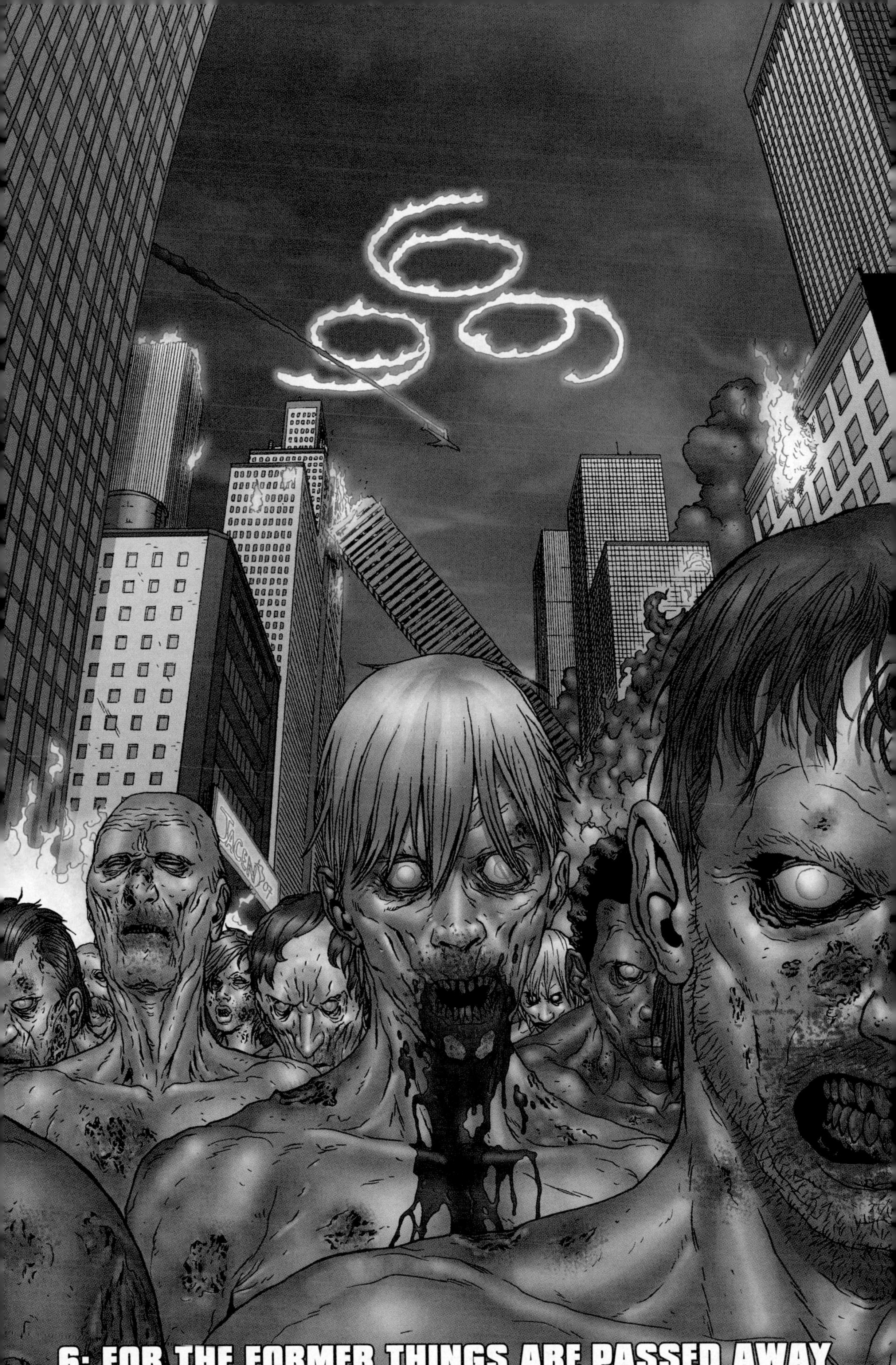

6: FOR THE FORMER THINGS ARE PASSED AWAY

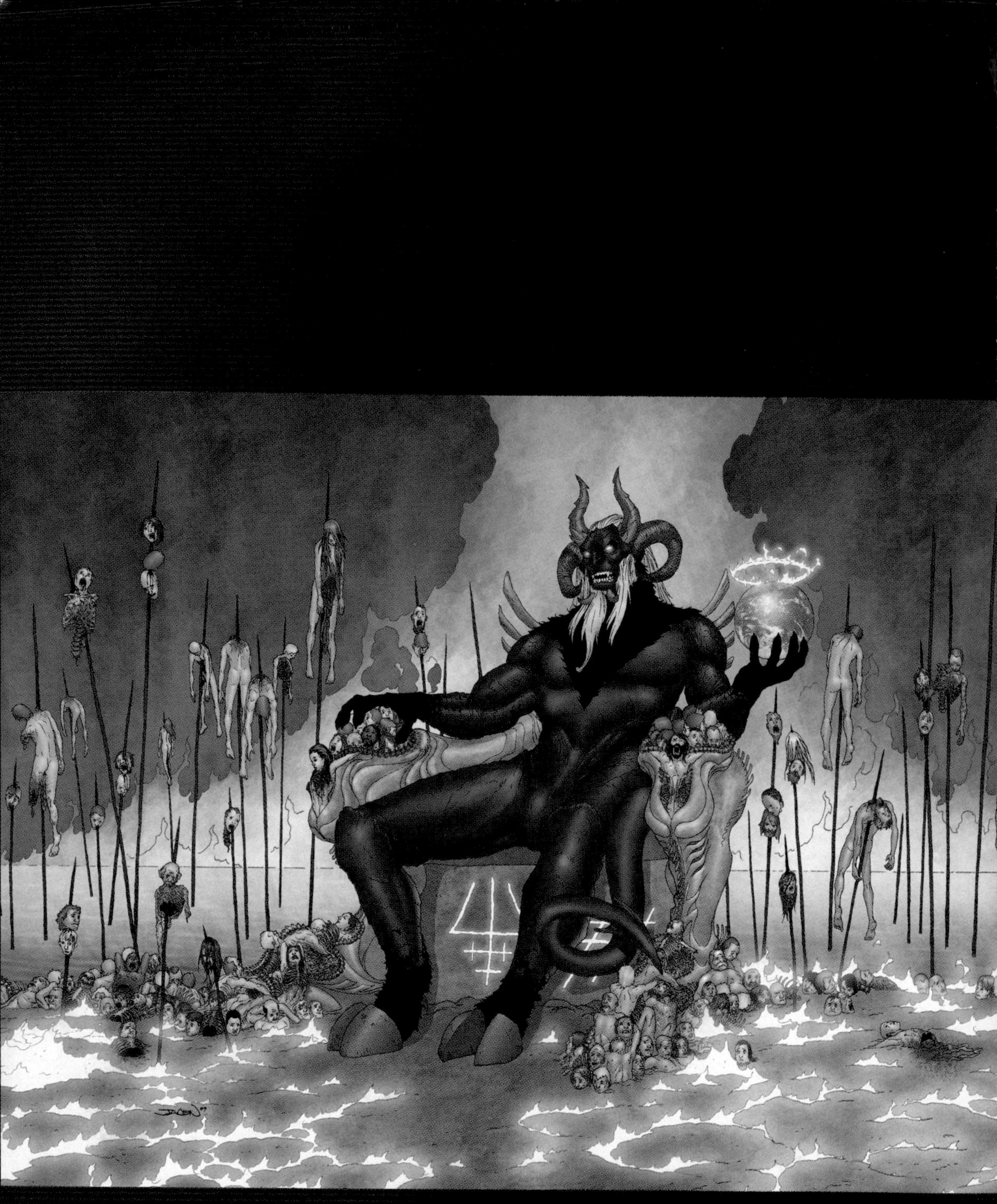

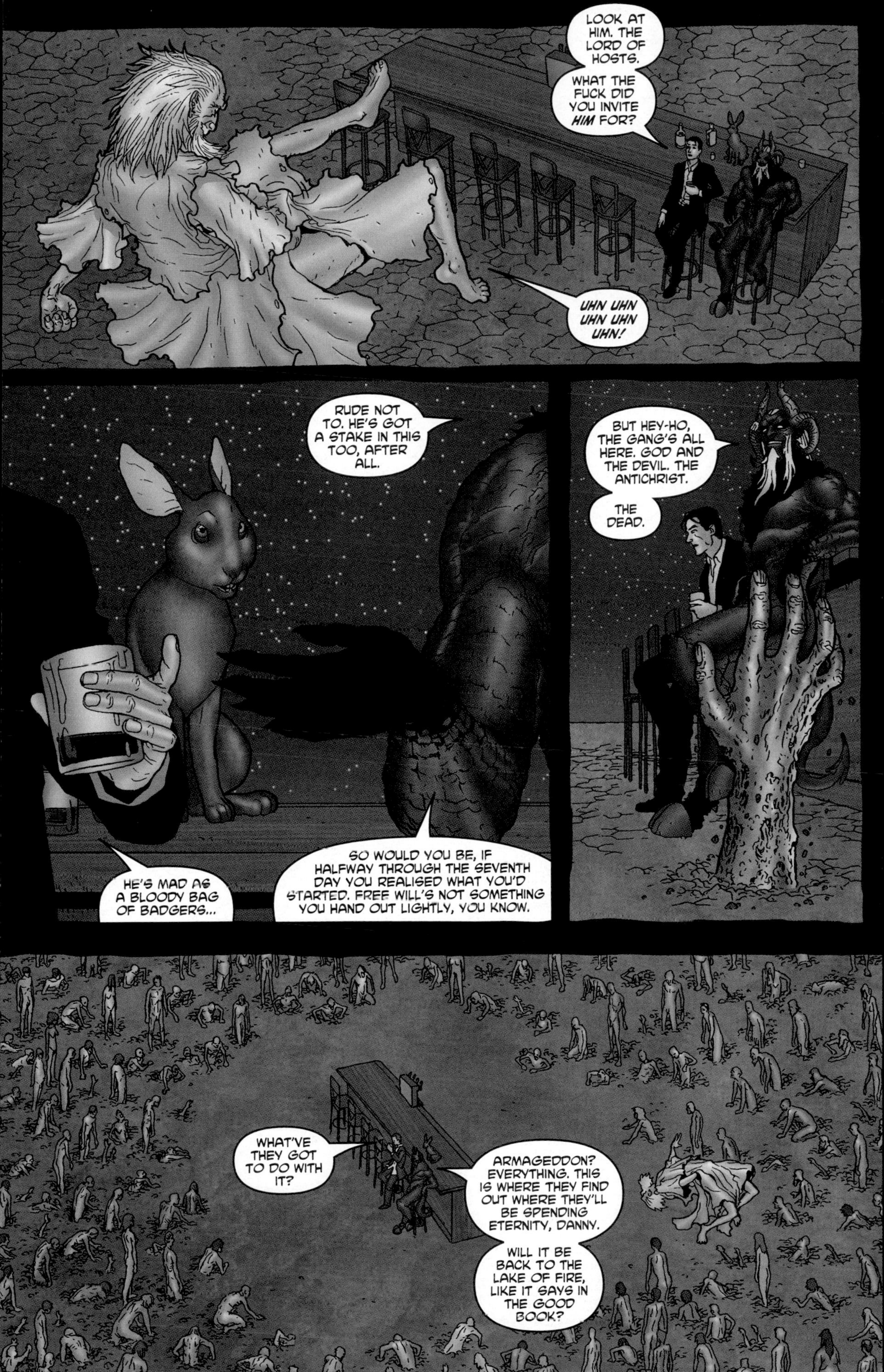
LOOK AT HIM. THE LORD OF HOSTS.
WHAT THE FUCK DID YOU INVITE *HIM* FOR?
UHN UHN UHN UHN UHN!
RUDE NOT TO. HE'S GOT A STAKE IN THIS TOO, AFTER ALL.
HE'S MAD AS A BLOODY BAG OF BADGERS...
SO WOULD YOU BE, IF HALFWAY THROUGH THE SEVENTH DAY YOU REALISED WHAT YOU'D STARTED. FREE WILL'S NOT SOMETHING YOU HAND OUT LIGHTLY, YOU KNOW.
BUT HEY-HO, THE GANG'S ALL HERE. GOD AND THE DEVIL. THE ANTICHRIST.
THE DEAD.
WHAT'VE THEY GOT TO DO WITH IT?
ARMAGEDDON? EVERYTHING. THIS IS WHERE THEY FIND OUT WHERE THEY'LL BE SPENDING ETERNITY, DANNY.
WILL IT BE BACK TO THE LAKE OF FIRE, LIKE IT SAYS IN THE GOOD BOOK?

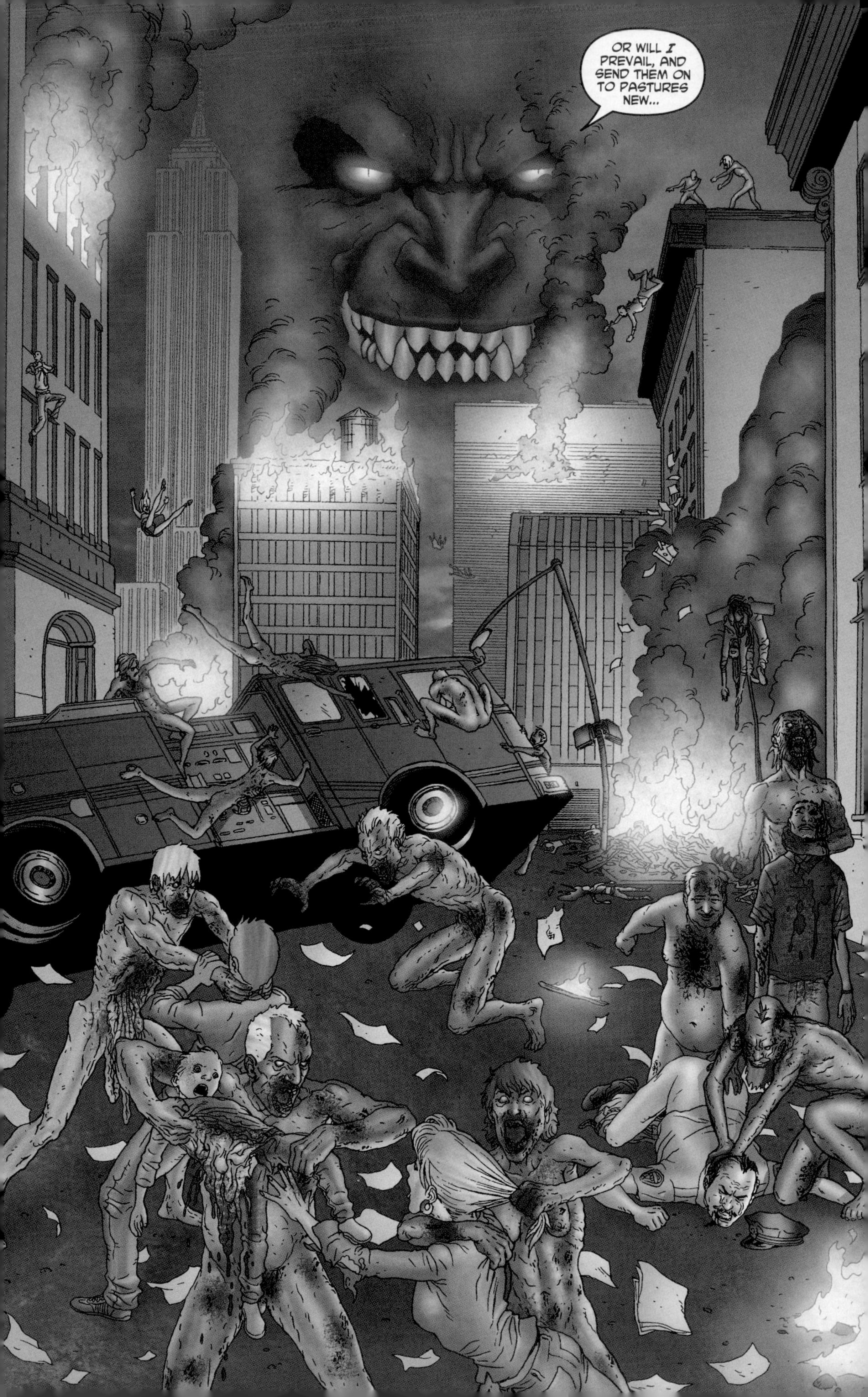
OR WILL I PREVAIL, AND SEND THEM ON TO PASTURES NEW...

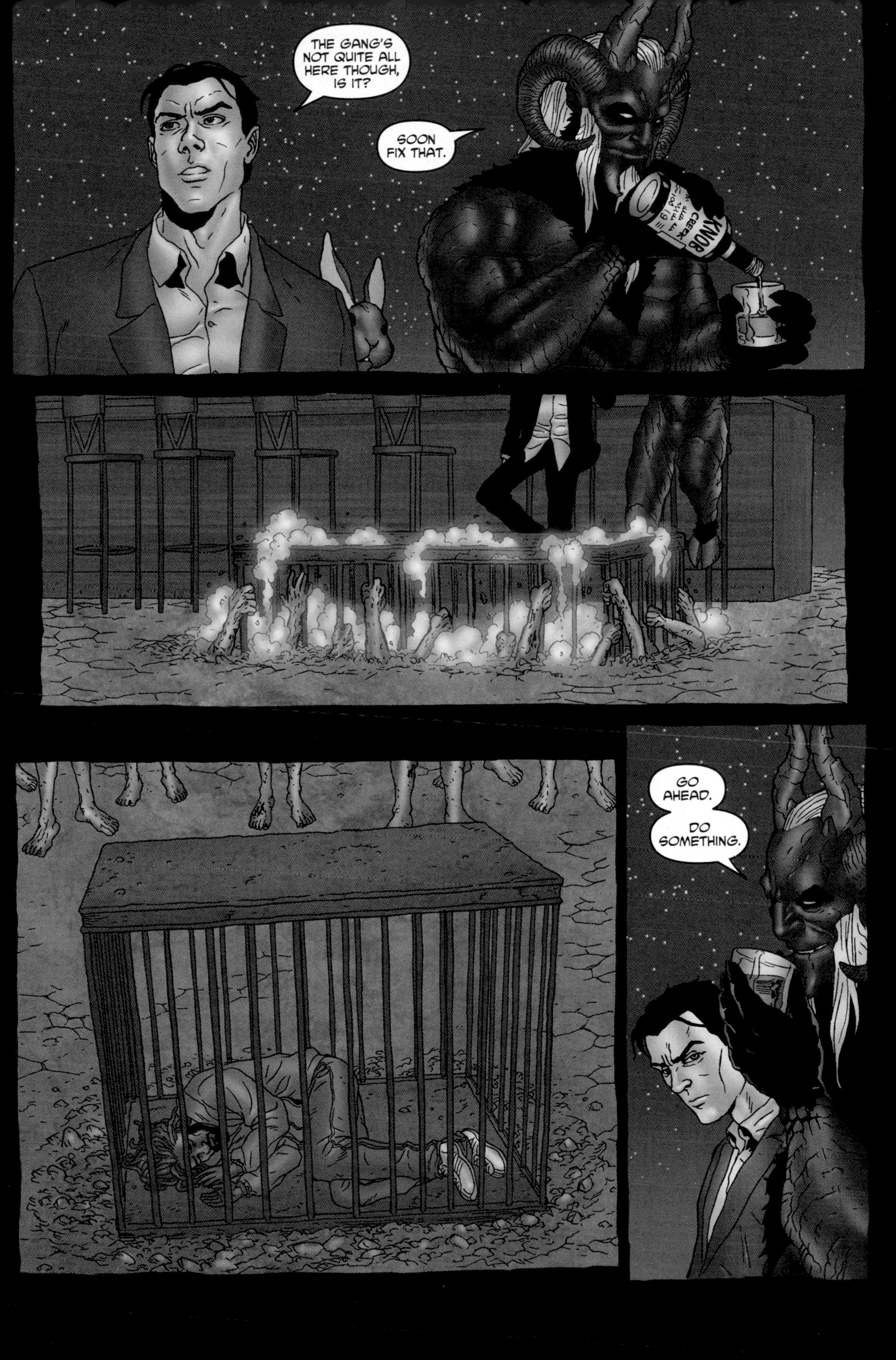
THE GANG'S NOT QUITE ALL HERE THOUGH, IS IT?
SOON FIX THAT.
KNOB CREEK
GO AHEAD.
DO SOMETHING.

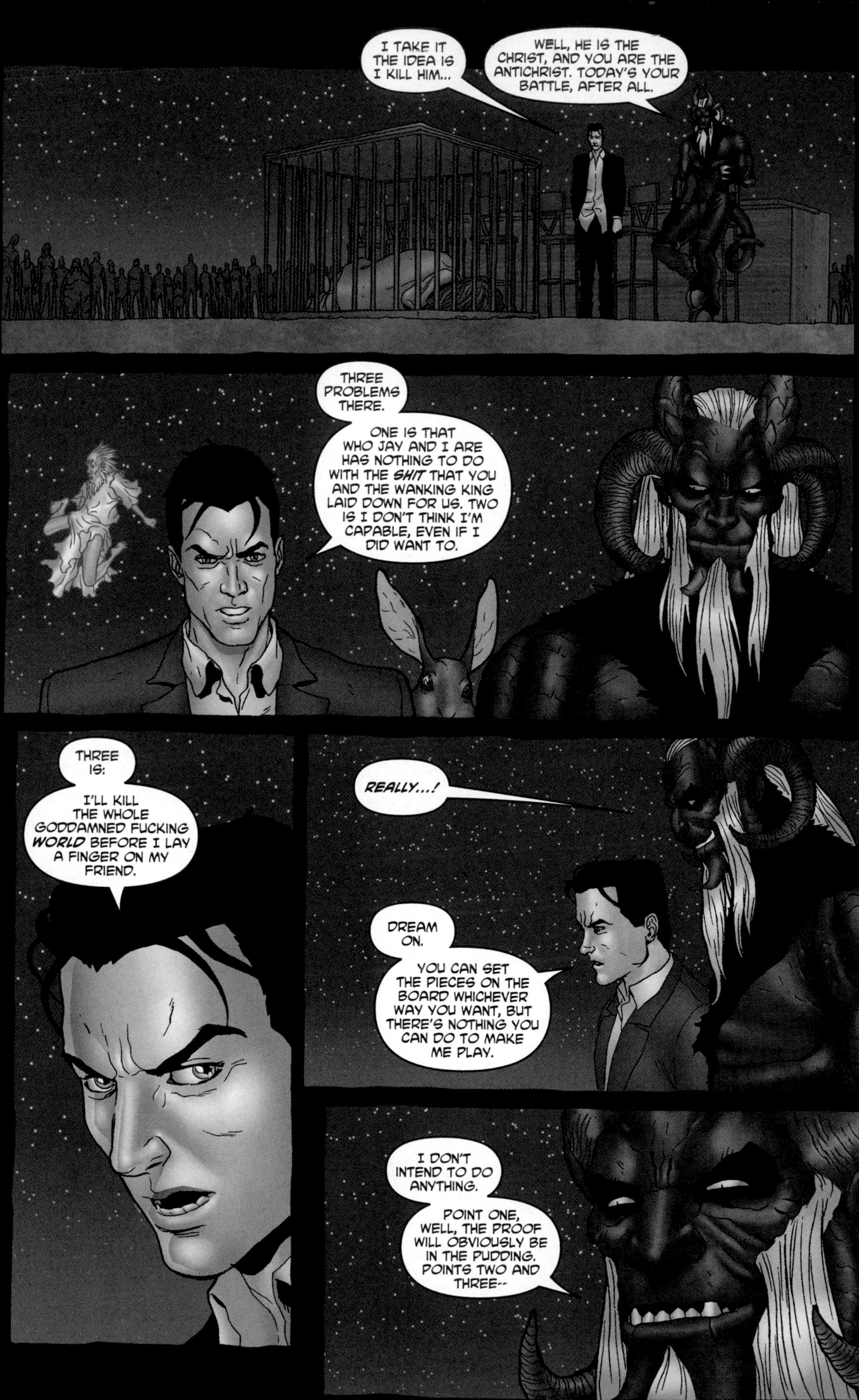
I TAKE IT THE IDEA IS I KILL HIM...
WELL, HE IS THE CHRIST, AND YOU ARE THE ANTICHRIST. TODAY'S YOUR BATTLE, AFTER ALL.
THREE PROBLEMS THERE.
ONE IS THAT WHO JAY AND I ARE HAS NOTHING TO DO WITH THE *SHIT* THAT YOU AND THE WANKING KING LAID DOWN FOR US. TWO IS I DON'T THINK I'M CAPABLE, EVEN IF I DID WANT TO.
THREE IS:
I'LL KILL THE WHOLE GODDAMNED FUCKING *WORLD* BEFORE I LAY A FINGER ON MY FRIEND.
REALLY...!
DREAM ON.
YOU CAN SET THE PIECES ON THE BOARD WHICHEVER WAY YOU WANT, BUT THERE'S NOTHING YOU CAN DO TO MAKE ME PLAY.
I DON'T INTEND TO DO ANYTHING.
POINT ONE, WELL, THE PROOF WILL OBVIOUSLY BE IN THE PUDDING. POINTS TWO AND THREE--

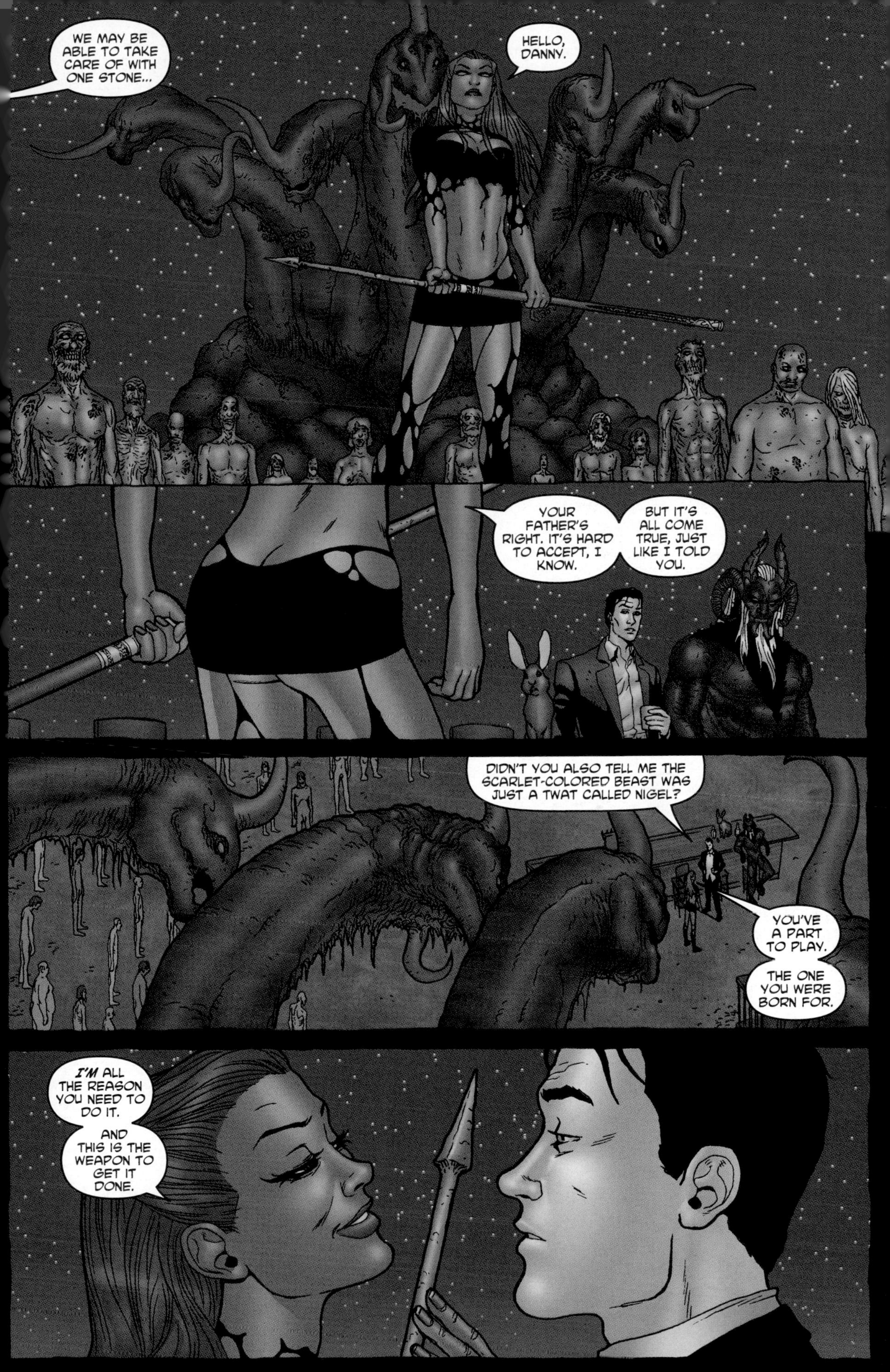
WE MAY BE ABLE TO TAKE CARE OF WITH ONE STONE...
HELLO, DANNY.
YOUR FATHER'S RIGHT. IT'S HARD TO ACCEPT, I KNOW.
BUT IT'S ALL COME TRUE, JUST LIKE I TOLD YOU.
DIDN'T YOU ALSO TELL ME THE SCARLET-COLORED BEAST WAS JUST A TWAT CALLED NIGEL?
YOU'VE A PART TO PLAY.
THE ONE YOU WERE BORN FOR.
I'M ALL THE REASON YOU NEED TO DO IT.
AND THIS IS THE WEAPON TO GET IT DONE.

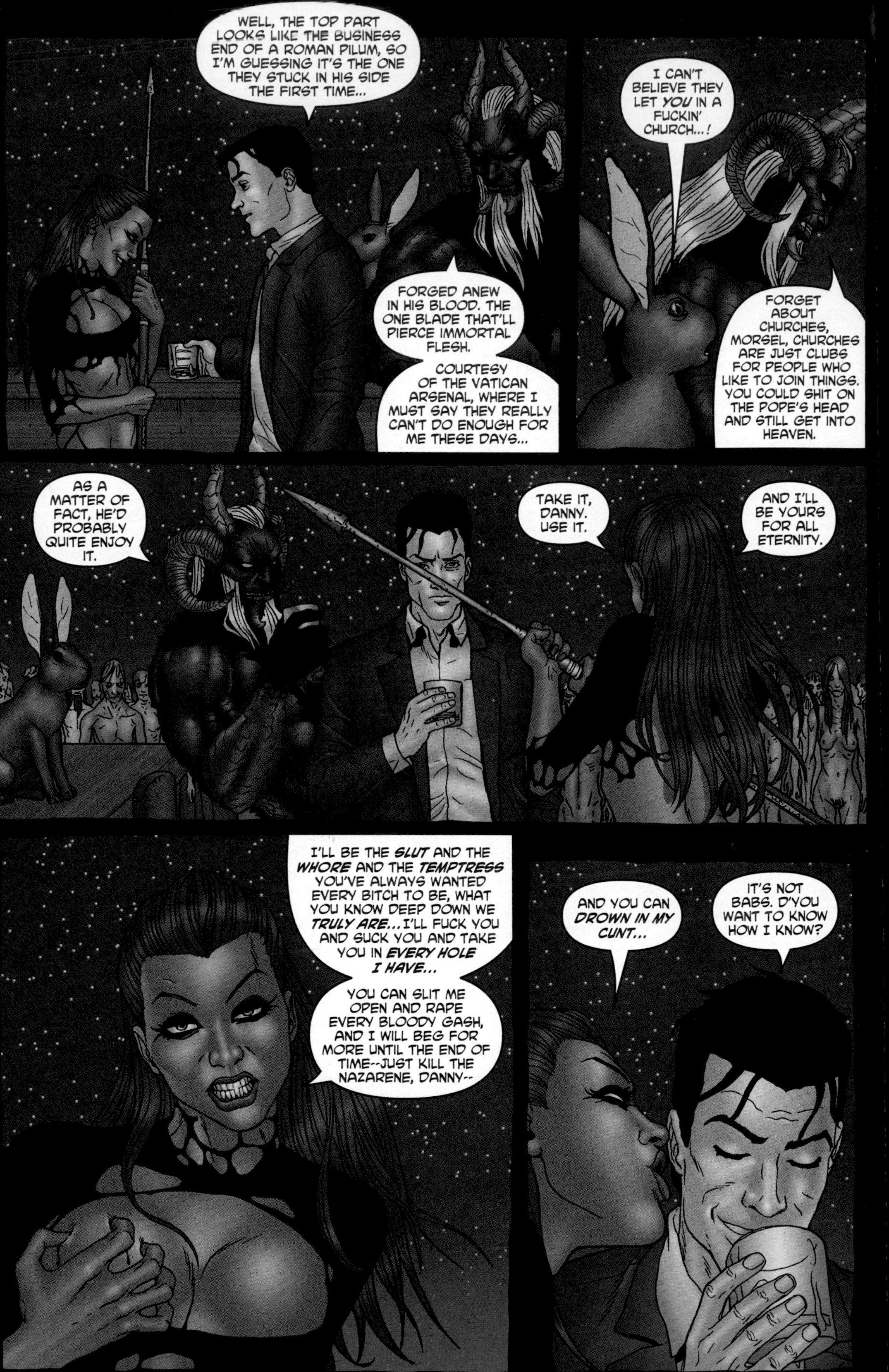
WELL, THE TOP PART LOOKS LIKE THE BUSINESS END OF A ROMAN PILUM, SO I'M GUESSING IT'S THE ONE THEY STUCK IN HIS SIDE THE FIRST TIME...
FORGED ANEW IN HIS BLOOD. THE ONE BLADE THAT'LL PIERCE IMMORTAL FLESH.
COURTESY OF THE VATICAN ARSENAL, WHERE I MUST SAY THEY REALLY CAN'T DO ENOUGH FOR ME THESE DAYS...
I CAN'T BELIEVE THEY LET YOU IN A FUCKIN' CHURCH...!
FORGET ABOUT CHURCHES, MORSEL, CHURCHES ARE JUST CLUBS FOR PEOPLE WHO LIKE TO JOIN THINGS. YOU COULD SHIT ON THE POPE'S HEAD AND STILL GET INTO HEAVEN.
AS A MATTER OF FACT, HE'D PROBABLY QUITE ENJOY IT.
TAKE IT, DANNY. USE IT.
AND I'LL BE YOURS FOR ALL ETERNITY.
I'LL BE THE SLUT AND THE WHORE AND THE TEMPTRESS YOU'VE ALWAYS WANTED EVERY BITCH TO BE, WHAT YOU KNOW DEEP DOWN WE TRULY ARE... I'LL FUCK YOU AND SUCK YOU AND TAKE YOU IN EVERY HOLE I HAVE...
YOU CAN SLIT ME OPEN AND RAPE EVERY BLOODY GASH, AND I WILL BEG FOR MORE UNTIL THE END OF TIME--JUST KILL THE NAZARENE, DANNY--
AND YOU CAN DROWN IN MY CUNT...
IT'S NOT BABS. D'YOU WANT TO KNOW HOW I KNOW?

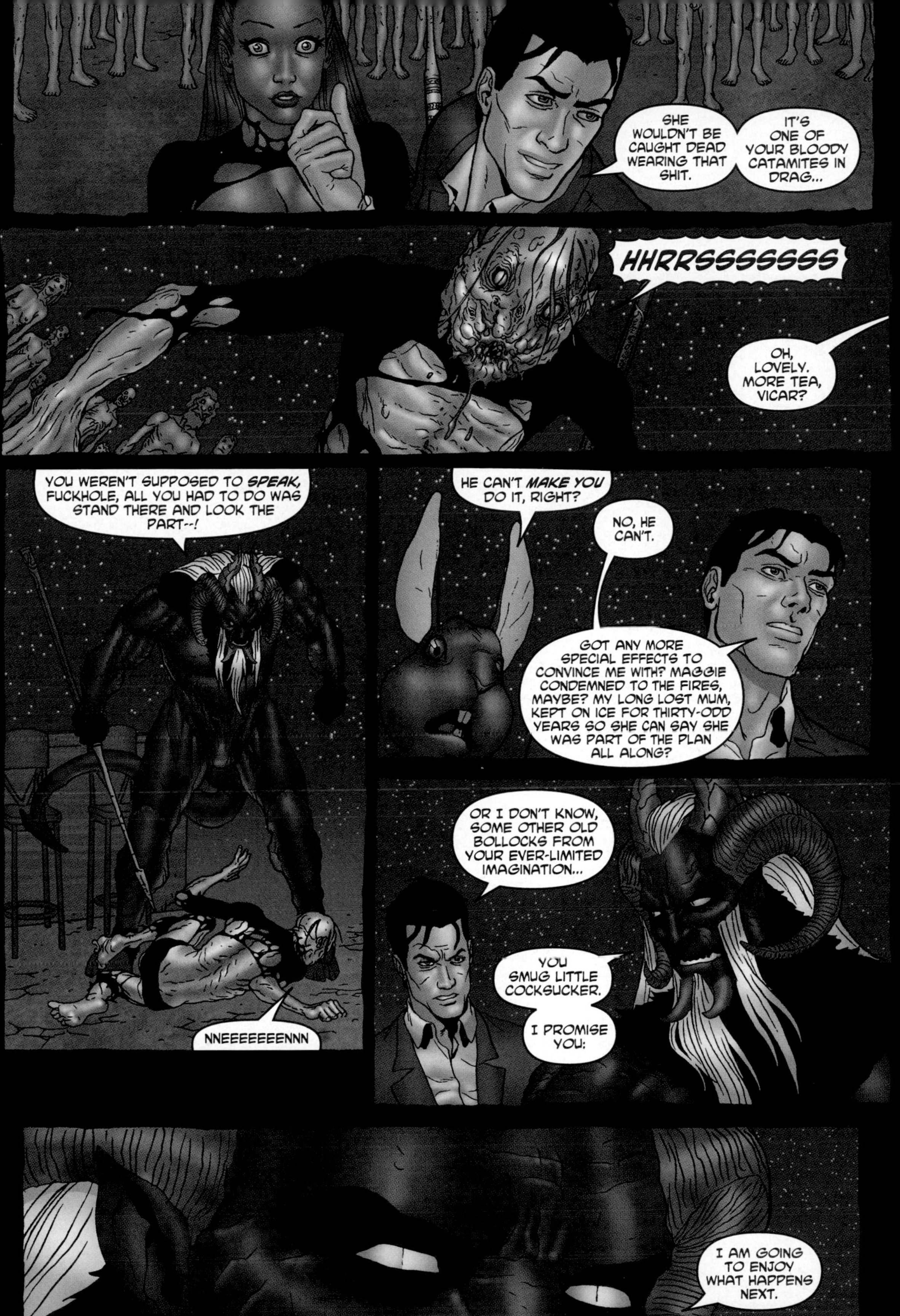
SHE WOULDN'T BE CAUGHT DEAD WEARING THAT SHIT.
IT'S ONE OF YOUR BLOODY CATAMITES IN DRAG...
HHRRSSSSSSS
OH, LOVELY. MORE TEA, VICAR?
YOU WEREN'T SUPPOSED TO *SPEAK*, FUCKHOLE, ALL YOU HAD TO DO WAS STAND THERE AND LOOK THE PART--!
NNEEEEEEEENNN
HE CAN'T *MAKE YOU* DO IT, RIGHT?
NO, HE CAN'T.
GOT ANY MORE SPECIAL EFFECTS TO CONVINCE ME WITH? MAGGIE CONDEMNED TO THE FIRES, MAYBE? MY LONG LOST MUM, KEPT ON ICE FOR THIRTY-ODD YEARS SO SHE CAN SAY SHE WAS PART OF THE PLAN ALL ALONG?
OR I DON'T KNOW, SOME OTHER OLD BOLLOCKS FROM YOUR EVER-LIMITED IMAGINATION...
YOU SMUG LITTLE COCKSUCKER.
I PROMISE YOU:
I AM GOING TO ENJOY WHAT HAPPENS NEXT.

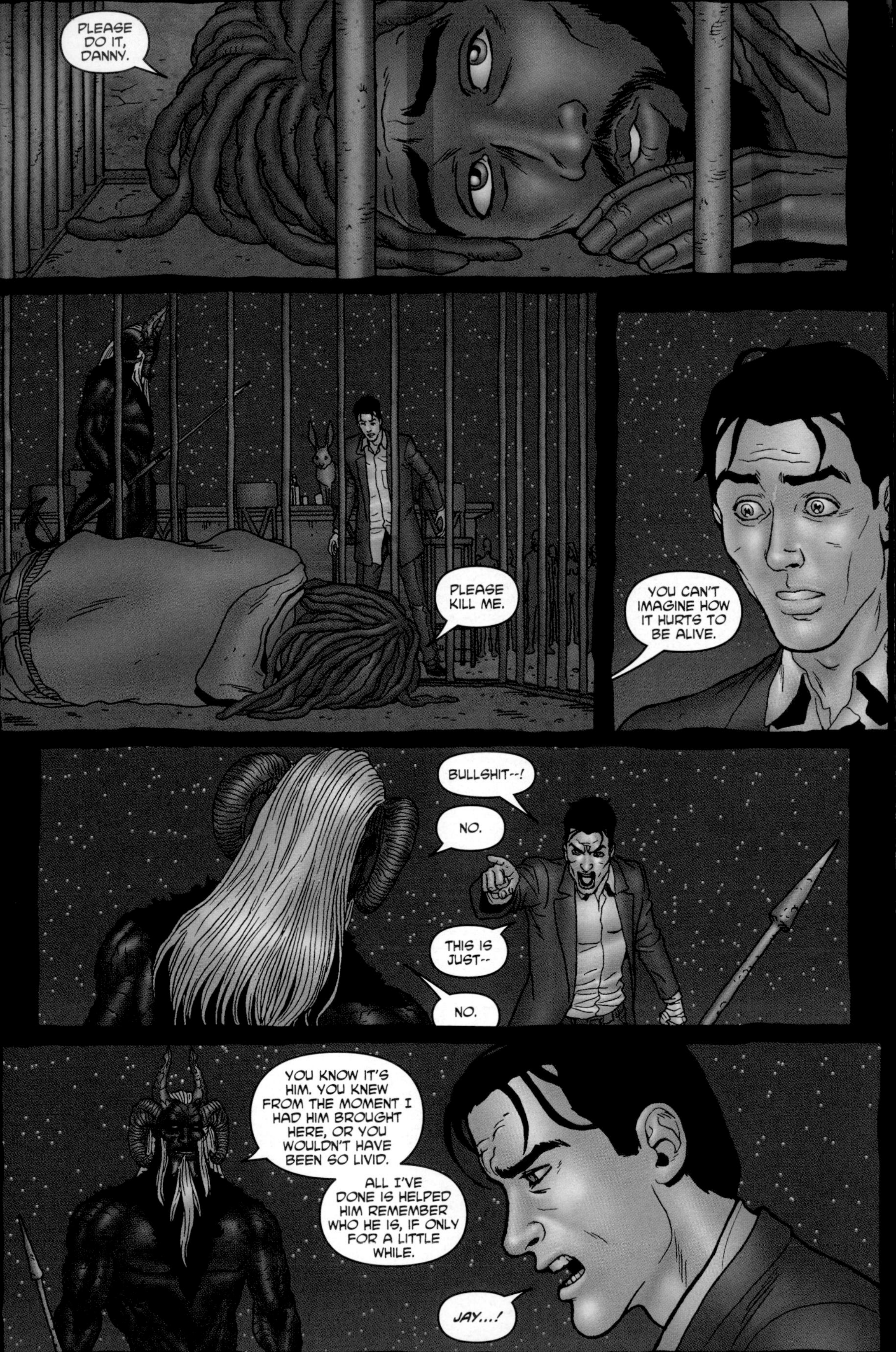
PLEASE DO IT, DANNY.
PLEASE KILL ME.
YOU CAN'T IMAGINE HOW IT HURTS TO BE ALIVE.
BULLSHIT--!
NO.
THIS IS JUST--
NO.
YOU KNOW IT'S HIM. YOU KNEW FROM THE MOMENT I HAD HIM BROUGHT HERE, OR YOU WOULDN'T HAVE BEEN SO LIVID.
ALL I'VE DONE IS HELPED HIM REMEMBER WHO HE IS, IF ONLY FOR A LITTLE WHILE.
JAY...!

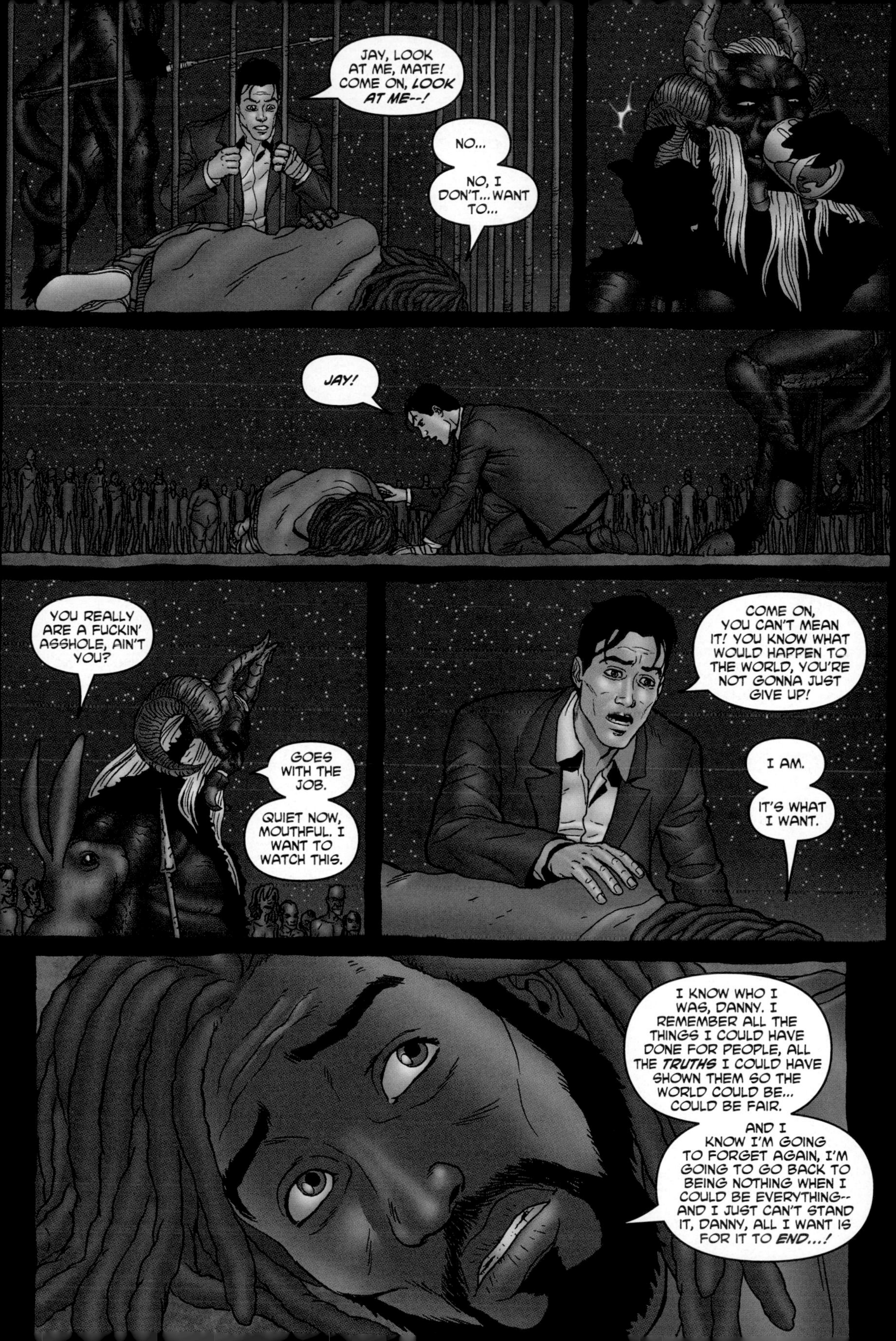
JAY, LOOK AT ME, MATE! COME ON, *LOOK AT ME--!*
NO...
NO, I DON'T... WANT TO...
JAY!
YOU REALLY ARE A FUCKIN' ASSHOLE, AIN'T YOU?
GOES WITH THE JOB.
QUIET NOW, MOUTHFUL. I WANT TO WATCH THIS.
COME ON, YOU CAN'T MEAN IT! YOU KNOW WHAT WOULD HAPPEN TO THE WORLD, YOU'RE NOT GONNA JUST GIVE UP!
I AM.
IT'S WHAT I WANT.
I KNOW WHO I WAS, DANNY. I REMEMBER ALL THE THINGS I COULD HAVE DONE FOR PEOPLE, ALL THE *TRUTHS* I COULD HAVE SHOWN THEM SO THE WORLD COULD BE... COULD BE FAIR.
AND I KNOW I'M GOING TO FORGET AGAIN, I'M GOING TO GO BACK TO BEING NOTHING WHEN I COULD BE EVERYTHING-- AND I JUST CAN'T STAND IT, DANNY, ALL I WANT IS FOR IT TO *END...!*

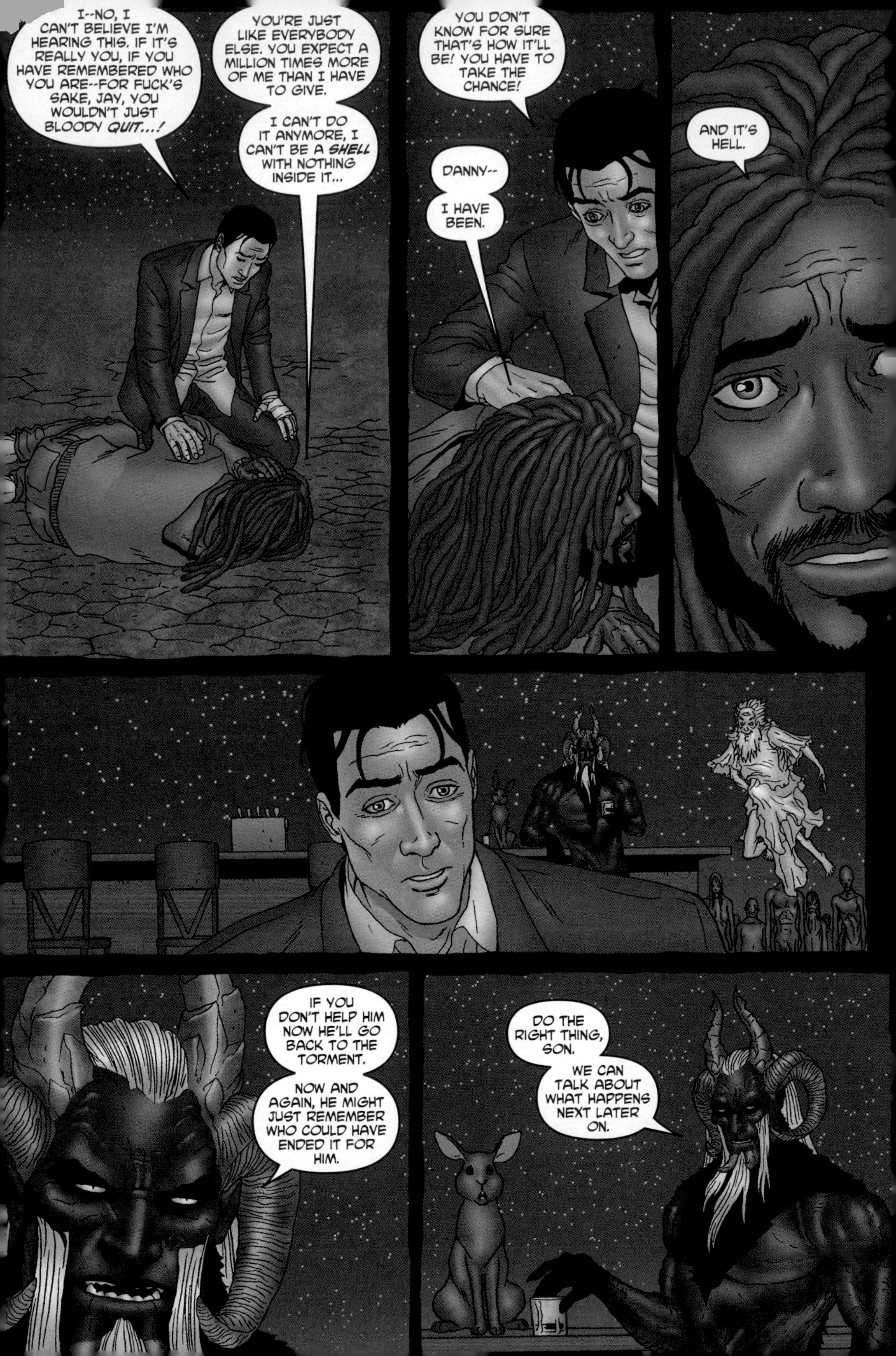
I--NO, I CAN'T BELIEVE I'M HEARING THIS. IF IT'S REALLY YOU, IF YOU HAVE REMEMBERED WHO YOU ARE--FOR FUCK'S SAKE, JAY, YOU WOULDN'T JUST BLOODY *QUIT...!*
YOU'RE JUST LIKE EVERYBODY ELSE. YOU EXPECT A MILLION TIMES MORE OF ME THAN I HAVE TO GIVE.
I CAN'T DO IT ANYMORE, I CAN'T BE A *SHELL* WITH NOTHING INSIDE IT...
YOU DON'T KNOW FOR SURE THAT'S HOW IT'LL BE! YOU HAVE TO TAKE THE CHANCE!
DANNY--
I HAVE BEEN.
AND IT'S HELL.
IF YOU DON'T HELP HIM NOW HE'LL GO BACK TO THE TORMENT.
NOW AND AGAIN, HE MIGHT JUST REMEMBER WHO COULD HAVE ENDED IT FOR HIM.
DO THE RIGHT THING, SON.
WE CAN TALK ABOUT WHAT HAPPENS NEXT LATER ON.

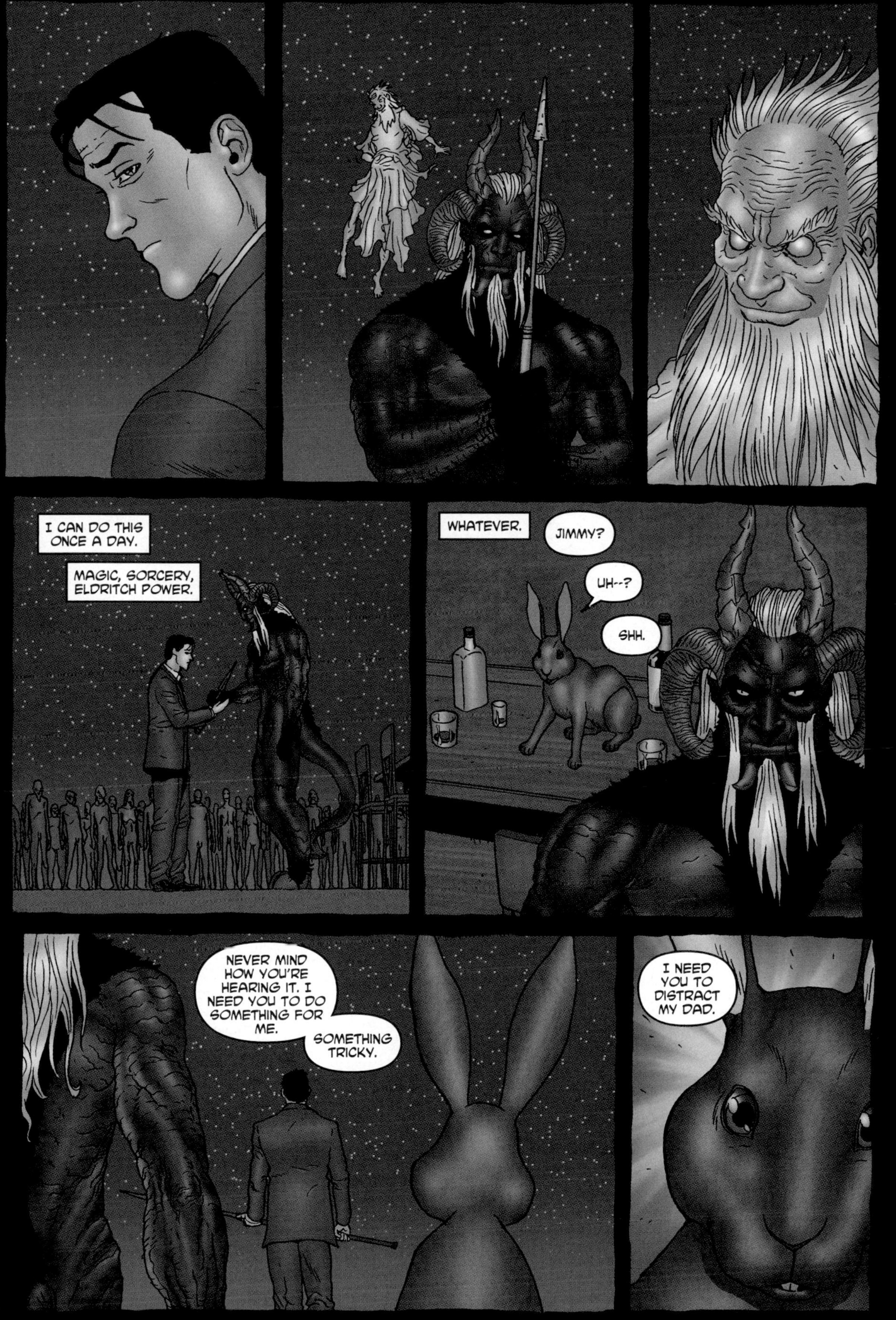
I CAN DO THIS ONCE A DAY.
MAGIC, SORCERY, ELDRITCH POWER.
WHATEVER.
JIMMY?
UH--?
SHH.
NEVER MIND HOW YOU'RE HEARING IT. I NEED YOU TO DO SOMETHING FOR ME.
SOMETHING TRICKY.
I NEED YOU TO DISTRACT MY DAD.

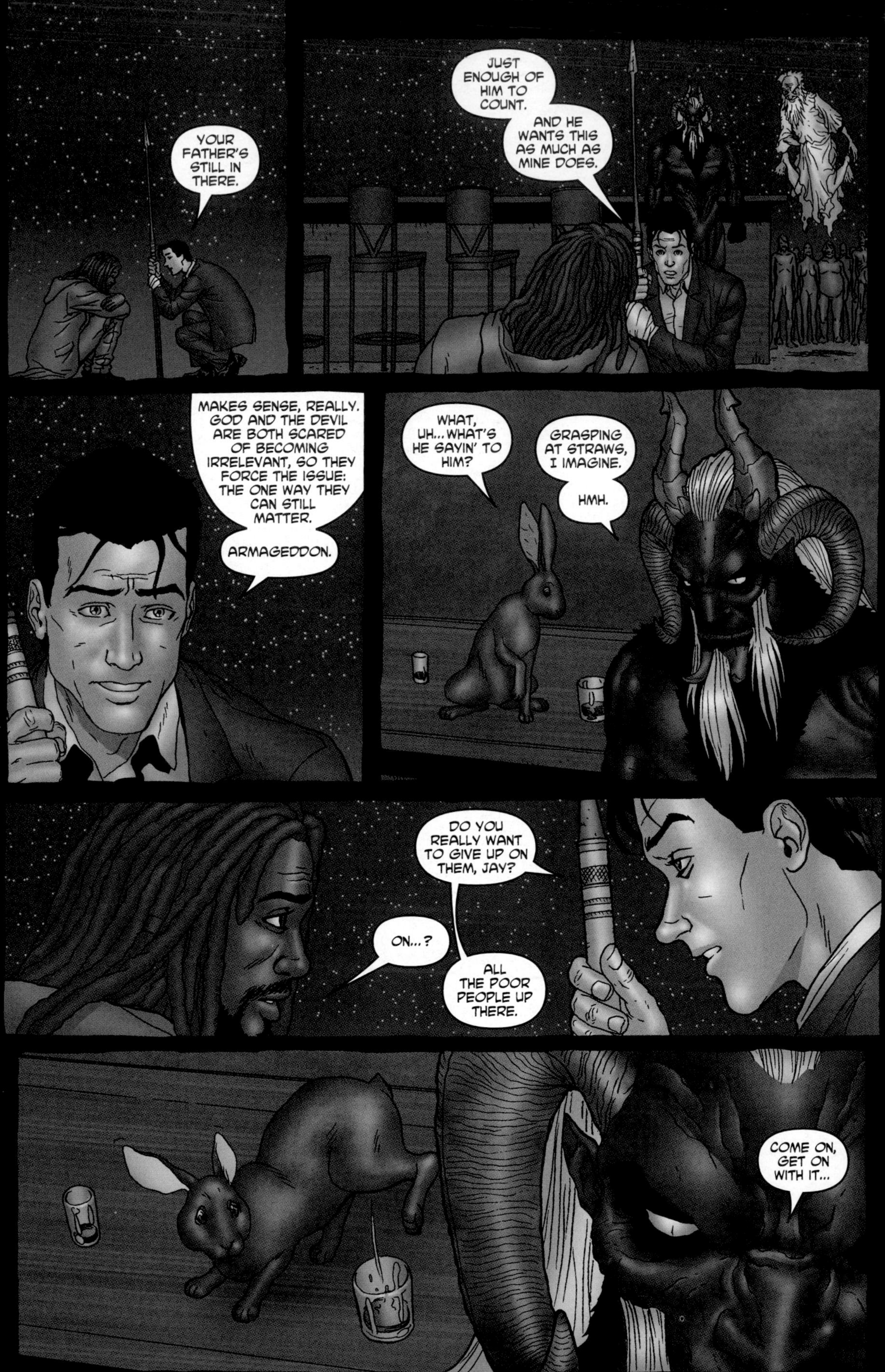
YOUR FATHER'S STILL IN THERE.
JUST ENOUGH OF HIM TO COUNT.
AND HE WANTS THIS AS MUCH AS MINE DOES.
MAKES SENSE, REALLY. GOD AND THE DEVIL ARE BOTH SCARED OF BECOMING IRRELEVANT, SO THEY FORCE THE ISSUE: THE ONE WAY THEY CAN STILL MATTER.
ARMAGEDDON.
WHAT, UH... WHAT'S HE SAYIN' TO HIM?
GRASPING AT STRAWS, I IMAGINE.
HMH.
DO YOU REALLY WANT TO GIVE UP ON THEM, JAY?
ON...?
ALL THE POOR PEOPLE UP THERE.
COME ON, GET ON WITH IT...

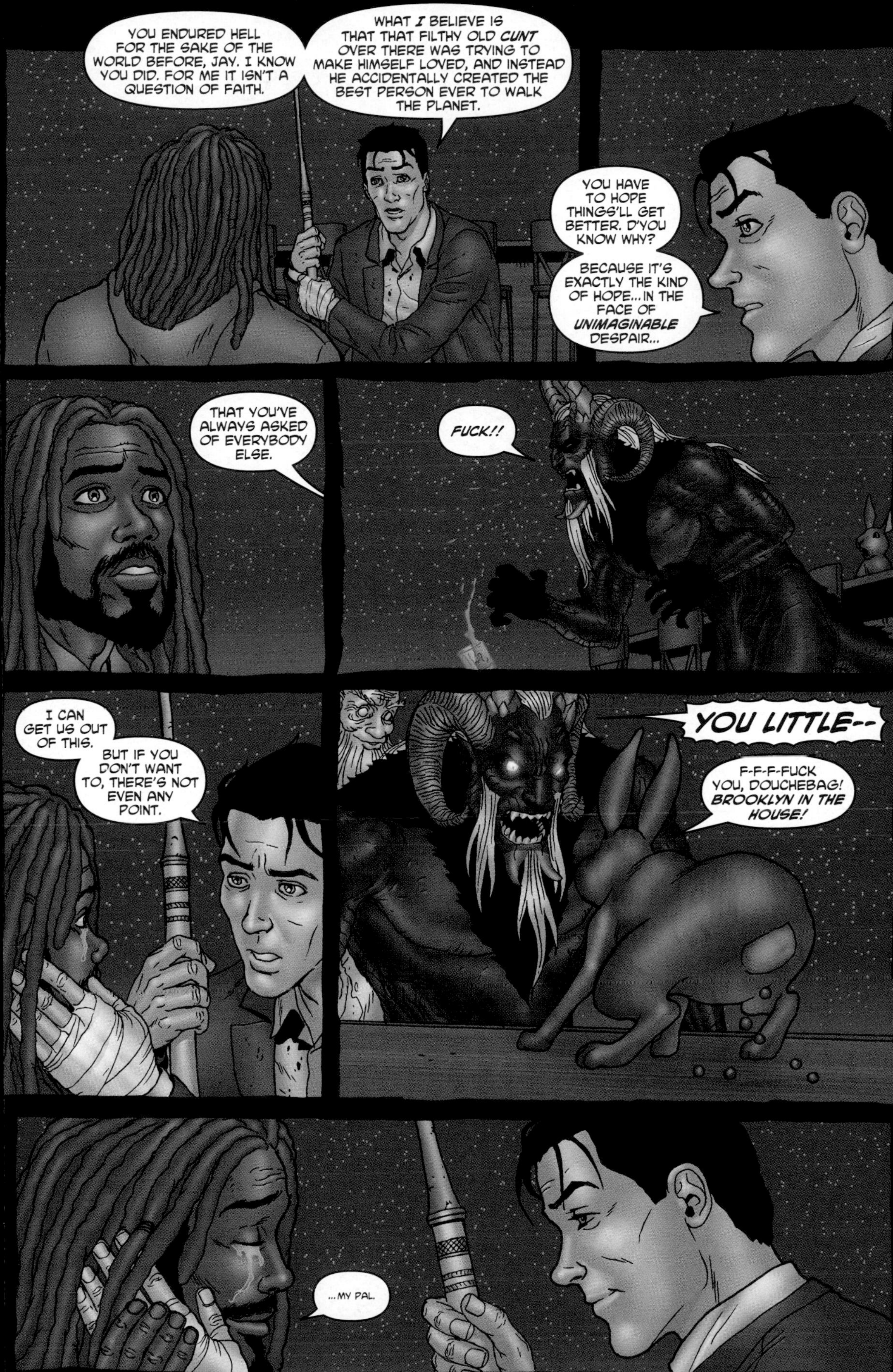
YOU ENDURED HELL FOR THE SAKE OF THE WORLD BEFORE, JAY. I KNOW YOU DID. FOR ME IT ISN'T A QUESTION OF FAITH.
WHAT *I* BELIEVE IS THAT THAT FILTHY OLD *CUNT* OVER THERE WAS TRYING TO MAKE HIMSELF LOVED, AND INSTEAD HE ACCIDENTALLY CREATED THE BEST PERSON EVER TO WALK THE PLANET.
YOU HAVE TO HOPE THINGS'LL GET BETTER. D'YOU KNOW WHY?
BECAUSE IT'S EXACTLY THE KIND OF HOPE... IN THE FACE OF *UNIMAGINABLE* DESPAIR...
THAT YOU'VE ALWAYS ASKED OF EVERYBODY ELSE.
FUCK!!
I CAN GET US OUT OF THIS.
BUT IF YOU DON'T WANT TO, THERE'S NOT EVEN ANY POINT.
YOU LITTLE--
F-F-F-FUCK YOU, DOUCHEBAG! *BROOKLYN IN THE HOUSE!*
...MY PAL.

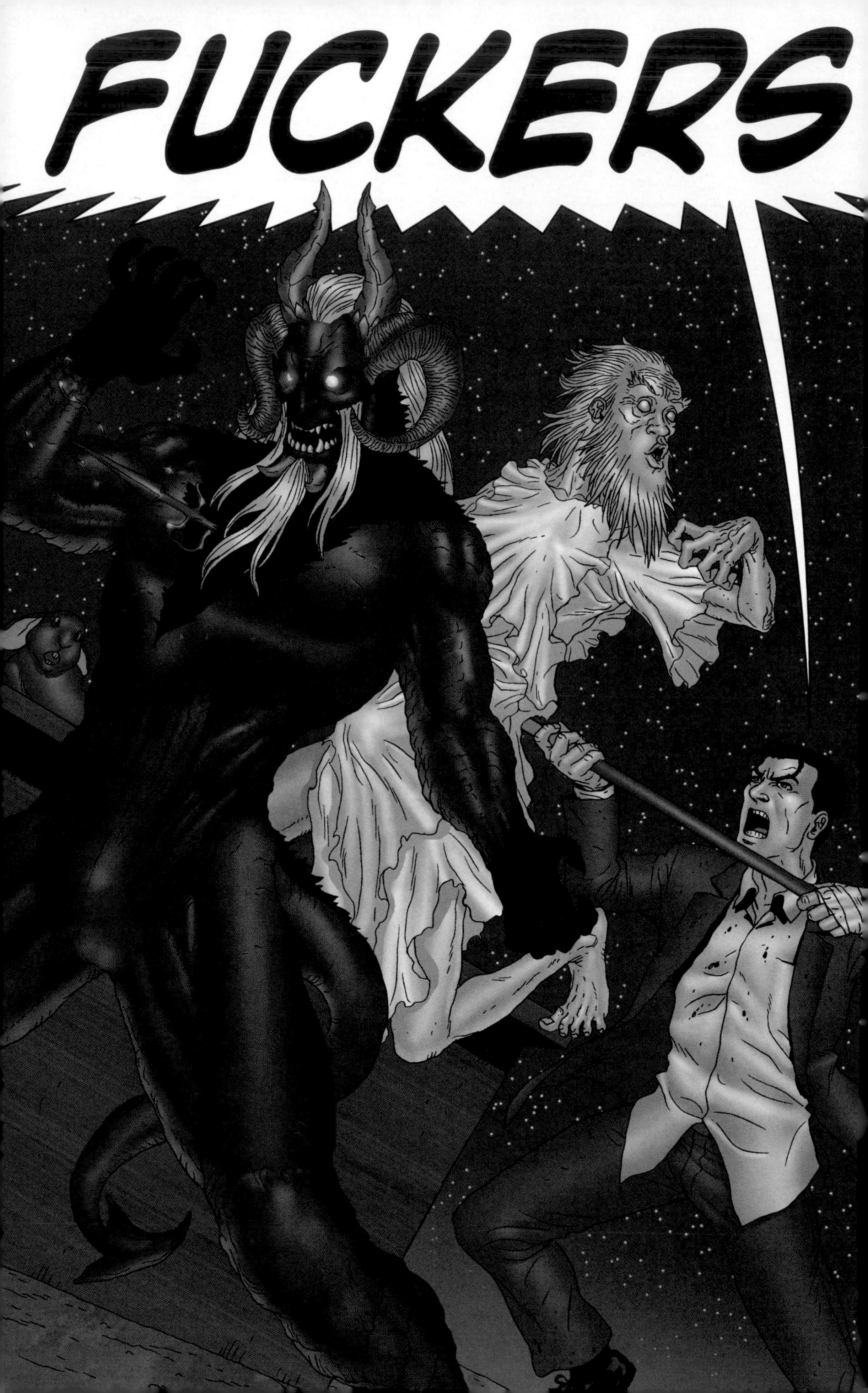
FUCKERS

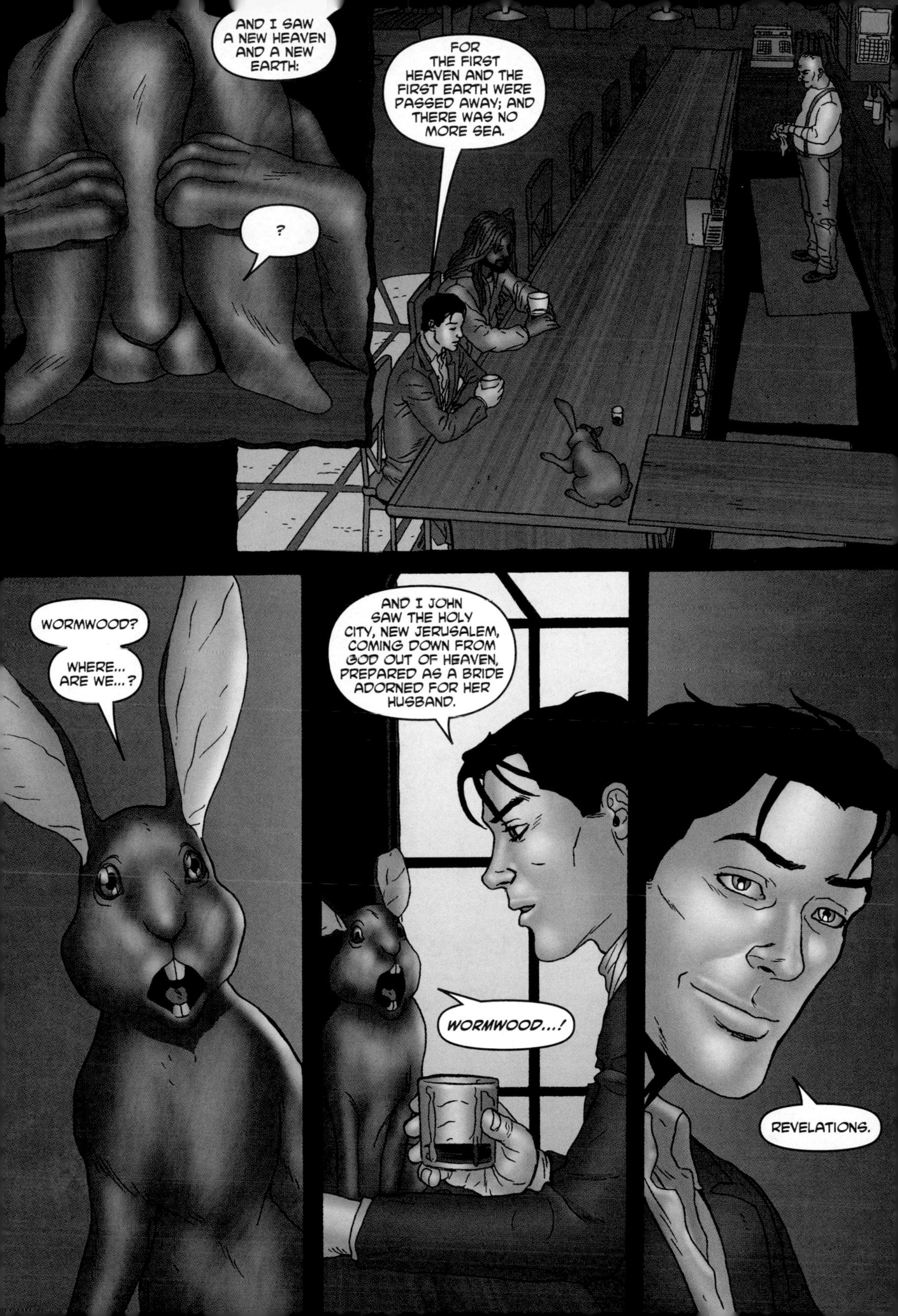
AND I SAW A NEW HEAVEN AND A NEW EARTH:
?
FOR THE FIRST HEAVEN AND THE FIRST EARTH WERE PASSED AWAY; AND THERE WAS NO MORE SEA.
WORMWOOD?
WHERE... ARE WE...?
AND I JOHN SAW THE HOLY CITY, NEW JERUSALEM, COMING DOWN FROM GOD OUT OF HEAVEN, PREPARED AS A BRIDE ADORNED FOR HER HUSBAND.
WORMWOOD...!
REVELATIONS.

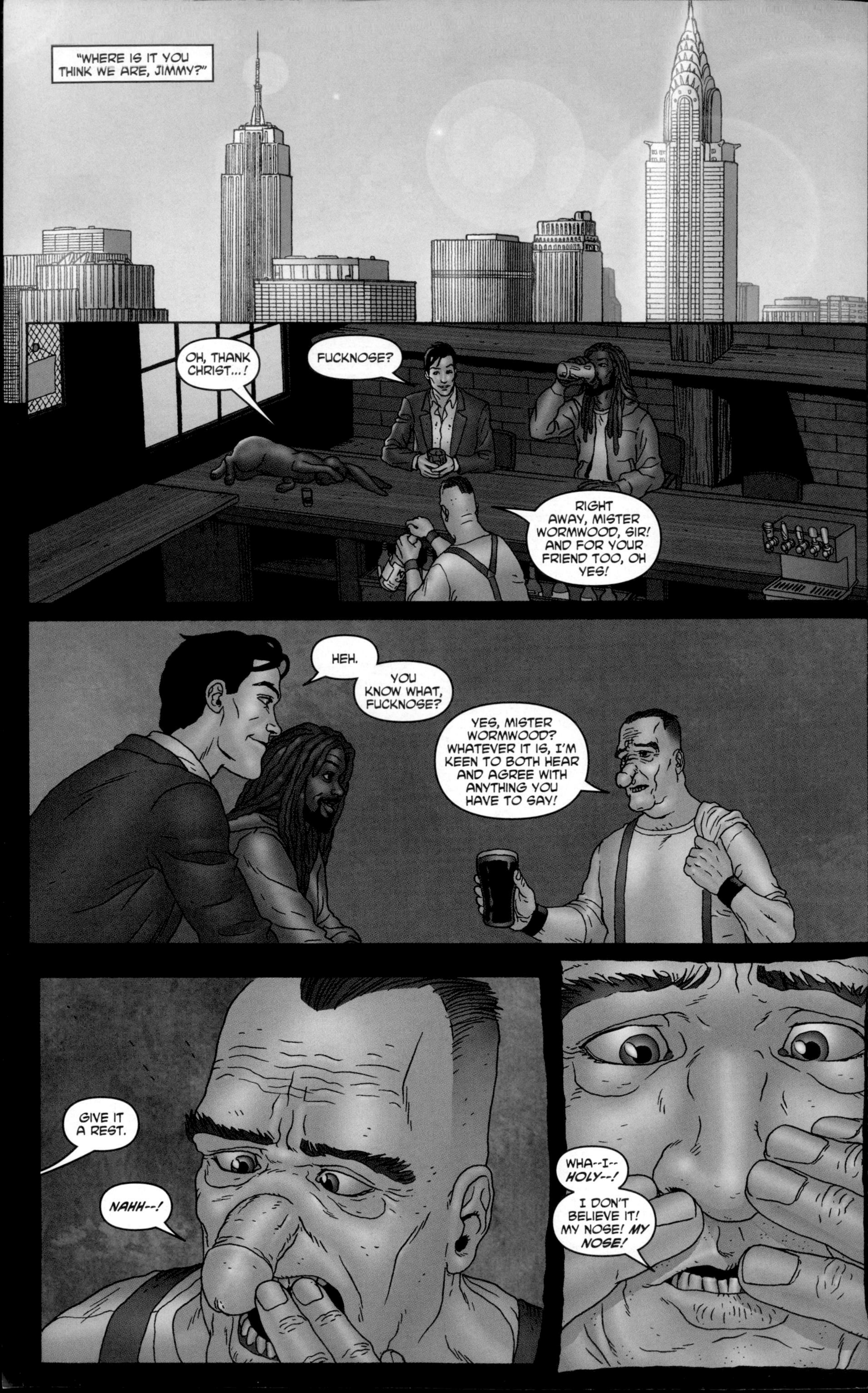
"WHERE IS IT YOU THINK WE ARE, JIMMY?"
OH, THANK CHRIST...!
FUCKNOSE?
RIGHT AWAY, MISTER WORMWOOD, SIR! AND FOR YOUR FRIEND TOO, OH YES!
HEH.
YOU KNOW WHAT, FUCKNOSE?
YES, MISTER WORMWOOD? WHATEVER IT IS, I'M KEEN TO BOTH HEAR AND AGREE WITH ANYTHING YOU HAVE TO SAY!
GIVE IT A REST.
NAHH--!
WHA--I-- HOLY--!
I DON'T BELIEVE IT! MY NOSE! MY NOSE!

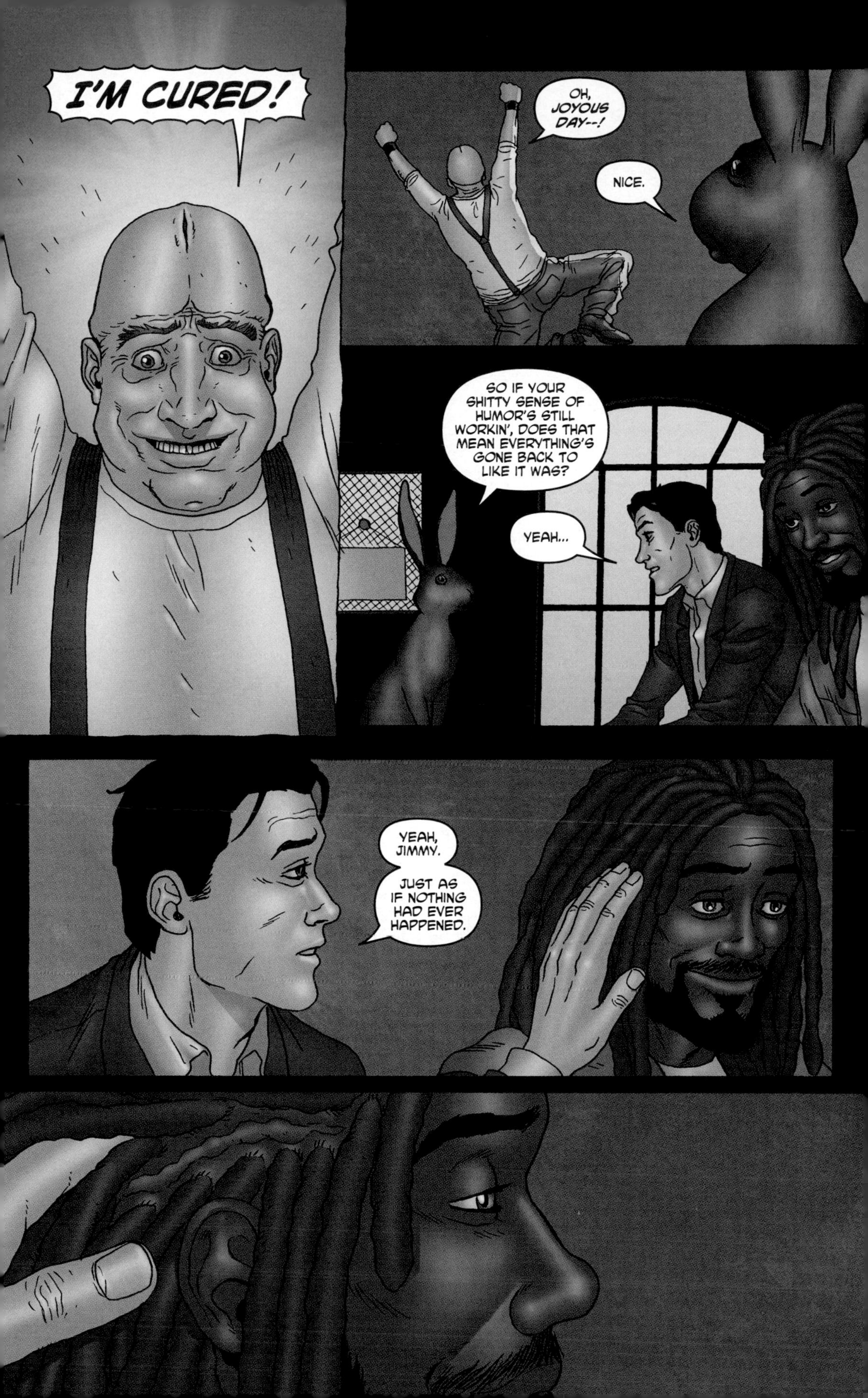

I'M CURED!
OH, JOYOUS DAY--!
NICE.
SO IF YOUR SHITTY SENSE OF HUMOR'S STILL WORKIN', DOES THAT MEAN EVERYTHING'S GONE BACK TO LIKE IT WAS?
YEAH...
YEAH, JIMMY.
JUST AS IF NOTHING HAD EVER HAPPENED.

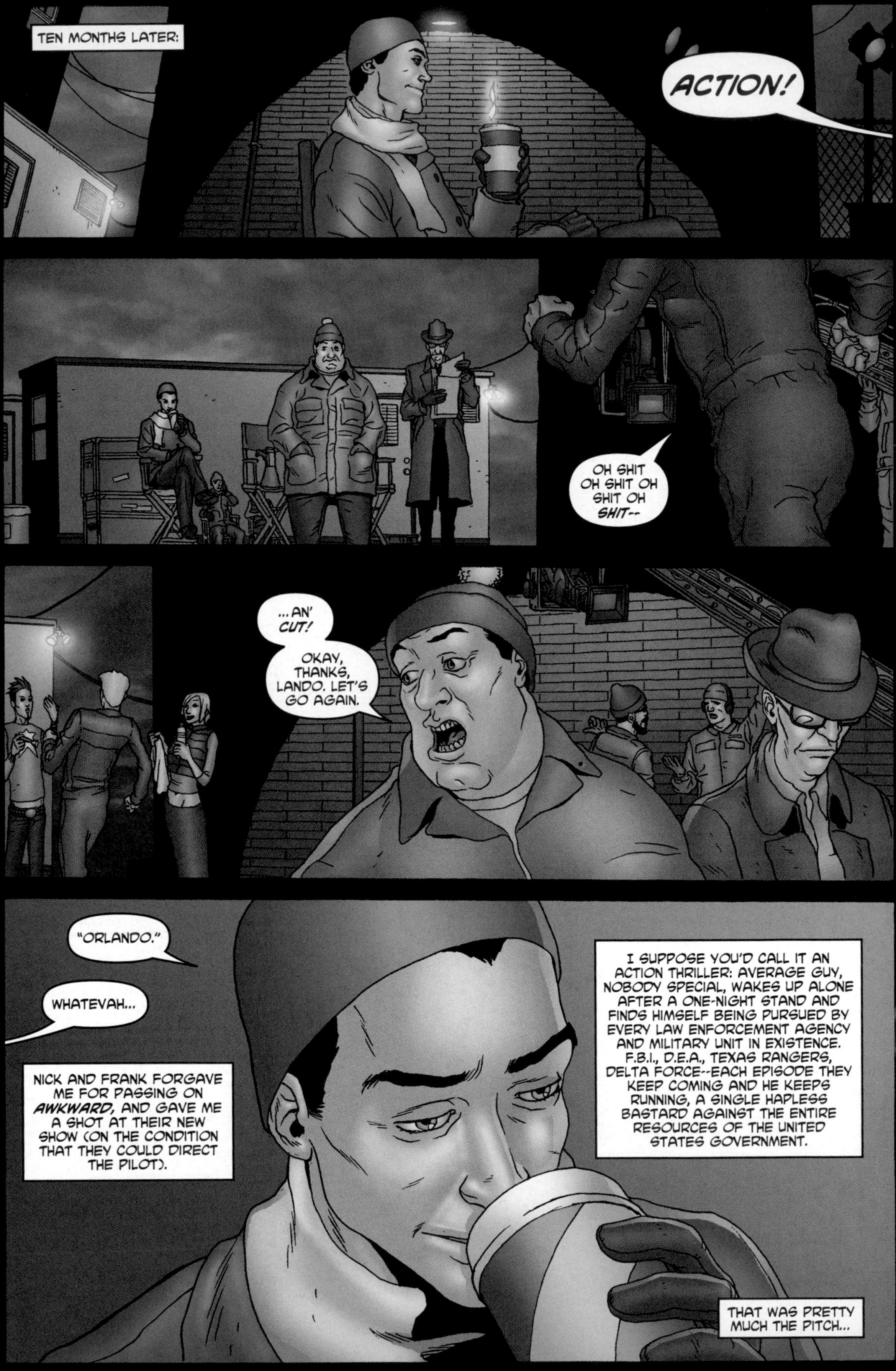
TEN MONTHS LATER:
ACTION!
OH SHIT OH SHIT OH SHIT OH SHIT--
...AN' CUT!
OKAY, THANKS, LANDO. LET'S GO AGAIN.
"ORLANDO."
WHATEVAH...
NICK AND FRANK FORGAVE ME FOR PASSING ON AWKWARD, AND GAVE ME A SHOT AT THEIR NEW SHOW (ON THE CONDITION THAT THEY COULD DIRECT THE PILOT).
I SUPPOSE YOU'D CALL IT AN ACTION THRILLER: AVERAGE GUY, NOBODY SPECIAL, WAKES UP ALONE AFTER A ONE-NIGHT STAND AND FINDS HIMSELF BEING PURSUED BY EVERY LAW ENFORCEMENT AGENCY AND MILITARY UNIT IN EXISTENCE. F.B.I., D.E.A., TEXAS RANGERS, DELTA FORCE--EACH EPISODE THEY KEEP COMING AND HE KEEPS RUNNING, A SINGLE HAPLESS BASTARD AGAINST THE ENTIRE RESOURCES OF THE UNITED STATES GOVERNMENT.
THAT WAS PRETTY MUCH THE PITCH...

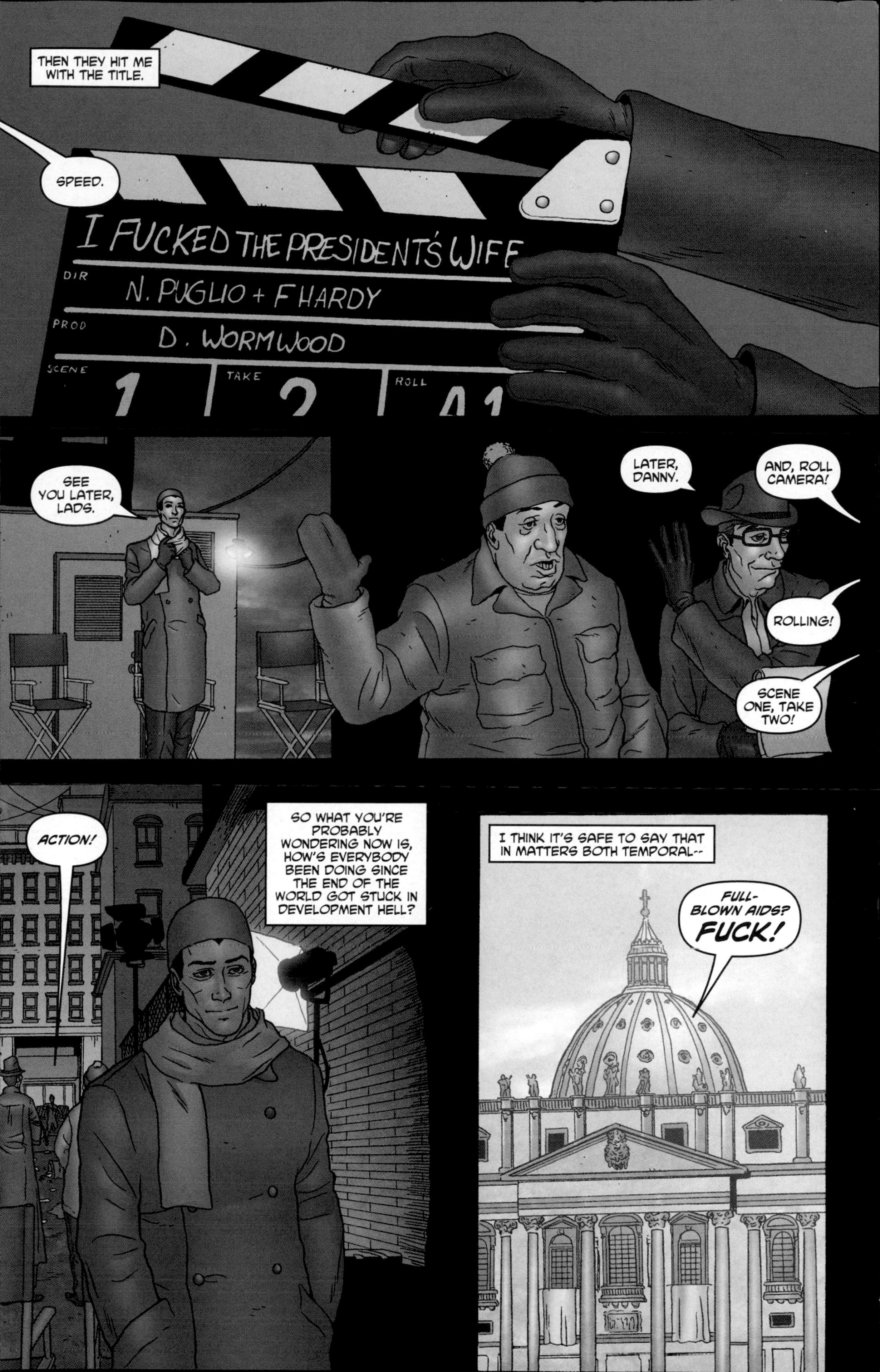

THEN THEY HIT ME WITH THE TITLE.
SPEED.
I FUCKED THE PRESIDENT'S WIFE
DIR
N. PUGLIO + F HARDY
PROD
D. WORMWOOD
SCENE
1
TAKE
2
ROLL
41
SEE YOU LATER, LADS.
LATER, DANNY.
AND, ROLL CAMERA!
ROLLING!
SCENE ONE, TAKE TWO!
ACTION!
SO WHAT YOU'RE PROBABLY WONDERING NOW IS, HOW'S EVERYBODY BEEN DOING SINCE THE END OF THE WORLD GOT STUCK IN DEVELOPMENT HELL?
I THINK IT'S SAFE TO SAY THAT IN MATTERS BOTH TEMPORAL--
FULL-BLOWN AIDS? FUCK!

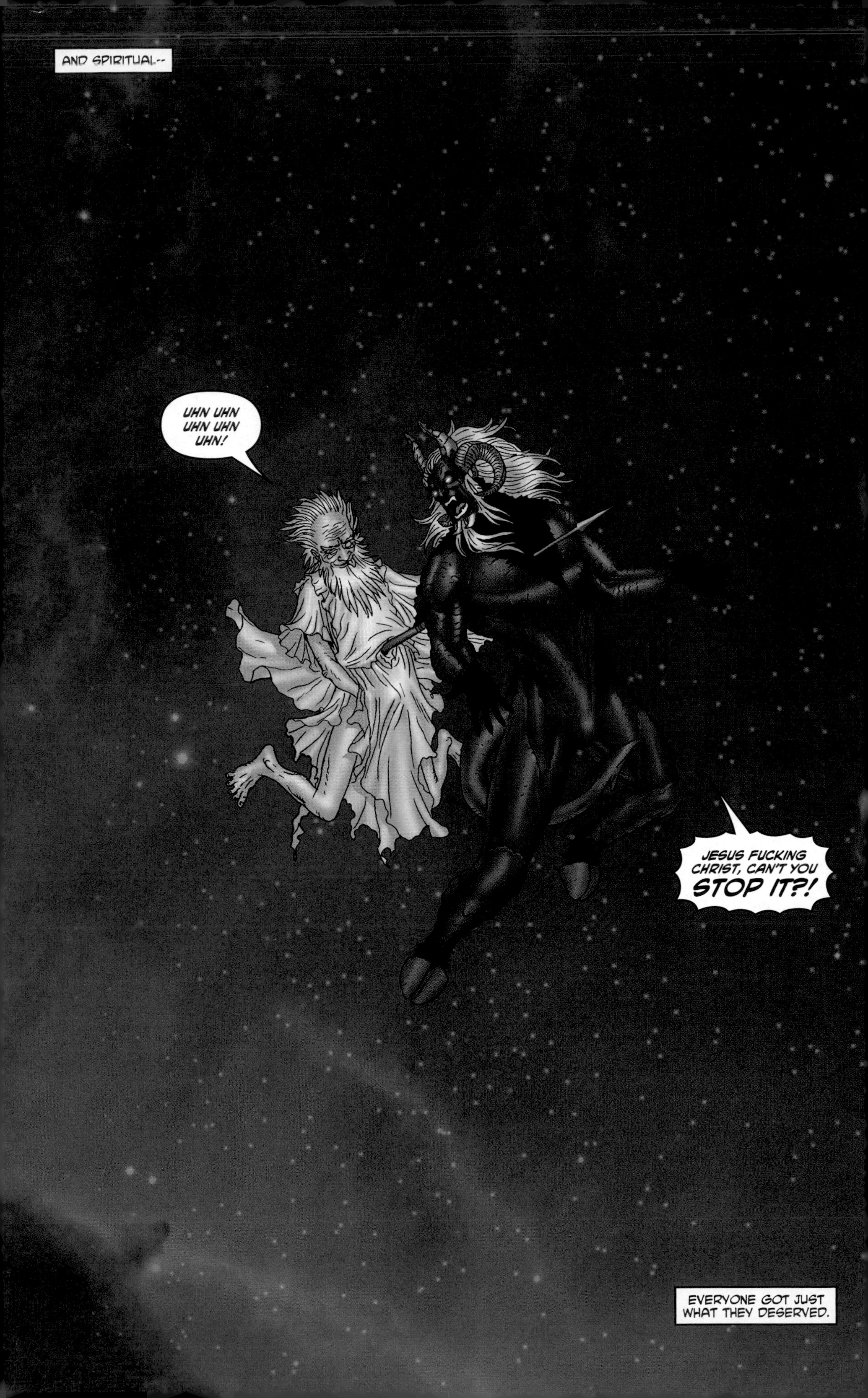
AND SPIRITUAL--
UHN UHN UHN UHN UHN!
JESUS FUCKING CHRIST, CAN'T YOU STOP IT?!
EVERYONE GOT JUST WHAT THEY DESERVED.

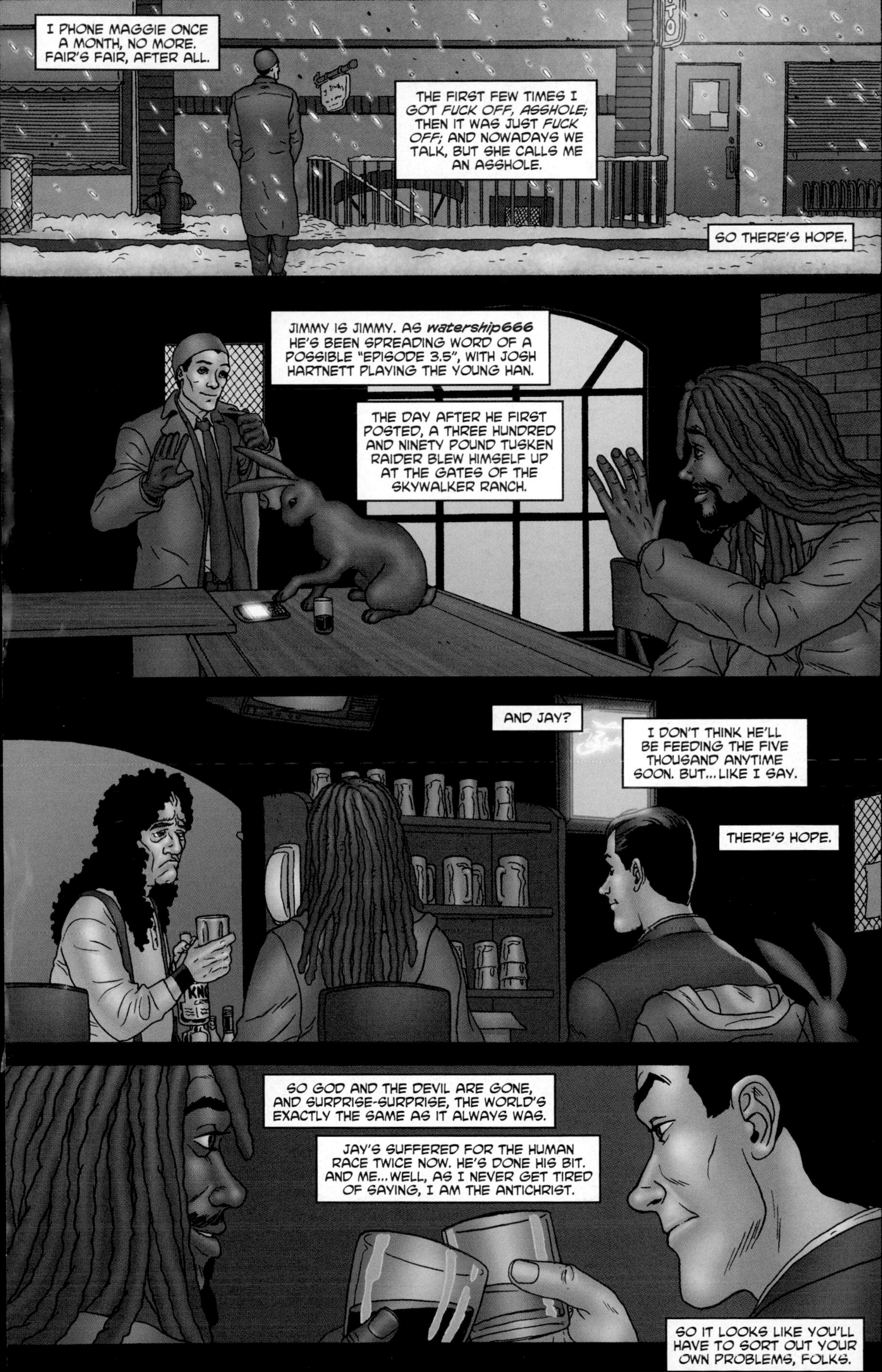

I PHONE MAGGIE ONCE A MONTH, NO MORE. FAIR'S FAIR, AFTER ALL.
THE FIRST FEW TIMES I GOT *FUCK OFF, ASSHOLE;* THEN IT WAS JUST *FUCK OFF;* AND NOWADAYS WE TALK, BUT SHE CALLS ME AN ASSHOLE.
SO THERE'S HOPE.
JIMMY IS JIMMY. AS ***watership666*** HE'S BEEN SPREADING WORD OF A POSSIBLE "EPISODE 3.5", WITH JOSH HARTNETT PLAYING THE YOUNG HAN.
THE DAY AFTER HE FIRST POSTED, A THREE HUNDRED AND NINETY POUND TUSKEN RAIDER BLEW HIMSELF UP AT THE GATES OF THE SKYWALKER RANCH.
AND JAY?
I DON'T THINK HE'LL BE FEEDING THE FIVE THOUSAND ANYTIME SOON. BUT... LIKE I SAY.
THERE'S HOPE.
SO GOD AND THE DEVIL ARE GONE, AND SURPRISE-SURPRISE, THE WORLD'S EXACTLY THE SAME AS IT ALWAYS WAS.
JAY'S SUFFERED FOR THE HUMAN RACE TWICE NOW. HE'S DONE HIS BIT. AND ME... WELL, AS I NEVER GET TIRED OF SAYING, I AM THE ANTICHRIST.
SO IT LOOKS LIKE YOU'LL HAVE TO SORT OUT YOUR OWN PROBLEMS, FOLKS.

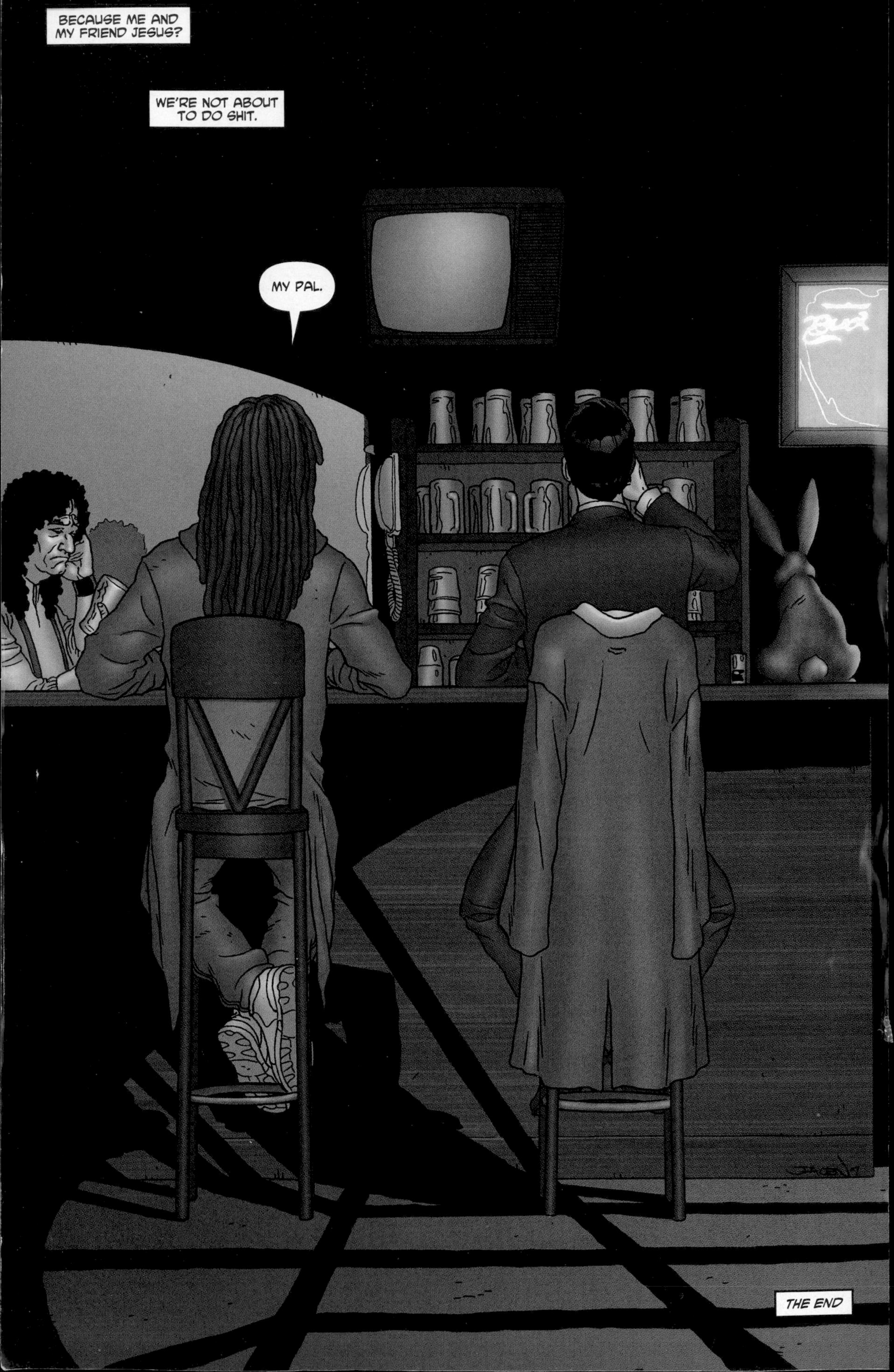
BECAUSE ME AND MY FRIEND JESUS?
WE'RE NOT ABOUT TO DO SHIT.
MY PAL.
THE END